D0533644

The Penguin Book of

BRITISH COMIC WRITING

Compiled and with an Introduction by
PATRICIA CRAIG

BCA
LONDON · NEW YORK · SYDNEY · TORONTO

This edition published 1992 by BCA by arrangement with Penguin Books Ltd

CN 8647

Set in $10\frac{1}{2}$/$12\frac{1}{2}$ pt Lasercomp Plantin by Selwood Systems, Midsomer Norton, Avon
Printed in Great Britain by Butler & Tanner Ltd, Frome and London

A CIP catalogue record for this book is available from the British Library

ISBN 0–670–83658–3

Contents

Contents

Contents

Introduction

Once I had made the final selection for *The Penguin Book of British Comic Stories* (1990), I became aware that one or two things had crept into it that weren't, strictly speaking, stories at all. How, for instance, should one classify Michael Frayn's enjoyable 'Through the Wilderness'? A work of the imagination, certainly, but originally written for the author's *Observer* column and therefore disqualified as fiction pure and simple? (Not as far as I was concerned.) And E. M. Delafield: looked at in one light, the 'Provincial Lady' is an invented character – but at the same time it's a portrait of the author herself, with all her daily doings magnified into a comedy of tribulations. Then, it is hard to decide whether a parodist such as Max Beerbohm is writing fiction or non-fiction: to the extent that he is making a comment on an author's style, the work in question may be placed in the second category (though I put the Henry James parody from *A Christmas Garland* in the first). And so on, and so on. I wasn't prepared to relinquish any of the above, as they all made me laugh, and I hoped they would pass muster as short stories.

Now I have put together a collection of humorous non-fiction articles, and what do I find? I have had to allow myself some leeway here as well, to accommodate such borderline pieces as the extract from *Through Darkest Pondelayo* by Serena Livingstone-Stanley (the dauntless English woman traveller, medical cabinet and all, held up to the most amiable ridicule), Mary Dunn's *Mipsie* (the incorrigible antics of an upper-crust *femme fatale*) and Julian Maclaren-Ross's Wodehouse imitation, which postulates the satisfying ennoblement of Jeeves. No matter: these simply add to the different kinds of humour on offer to the reader of *The Penguin Book of British Comic Writing*, in which a large number of categories are represented. I have searched out episodes, anecdotes and assessments with a decided comic slant, whether these come under the heading of autobiography, social comment, random observation, idiosyncratic meditation or whatever. As with the previous volume, I have confined my selections to the twentieth century to keep the book in a manageable state and to preserve at least a minimal consistency of approach. Although the forms of humour remain essentially the same at all periods, its expression varies with different epochs; and I think it's true to say that as far as most of us are concerned, the more accessible kinds of entertainment belong to the present century (a pretty wide time-span, I know), and all the comic angles and devices with which we are familiar. The available material is so rich and multifarious, indeed, that it is clearly not necessary to rifle the past to eke it out. (It would be interesting and instructive to compile an anthology of English humour, going back to the Middle Ages, in which continuity, and not immediacy, was the touchstone, but that is something else altogether.) Literary criticism, for instance, is an especially fruitful field, and when it comes to light literature the critic often has a field day, as we see in Arthur Marshall's diverting appraisals of books for girls (to take that example). Unabashed frivolity is Arthur Marshall's trait – but the whole 'silly novels by lady novelists' syndrome goes back a long way, and has engendered innumerable modes of repudiation. The authors of these 'silly novels' were not always female, of course; as far as the young Rebecca West was concerned (and quite right too), nothing could be sillier than Mr Hubert Wales or Mr Hall Caine.

P. G. Wodehouse is in topping form while considering the fatal ingenuity peculiar to the villains of thrillers ('I have known a villain to sit the heroine on a keg of gunpowder and expect it to be struck by lightning. You can't run a business that way'). One of the unrestrained entertainers he had in mind was Edgar Wallace, a writer responsible for leading another humorist – Robert Lynd – to a tongue-in-cheek appreciation of the English peer in 'Noblesse Oblige'. The author of popular literature, indeed, is fair game for the satirist, and soon they are all at it; Hugh Kingsmill having a go at Ouida; D. B. Wyndham Lewis approaching a work of Amanda McKittrick Ros's very gingerly ('I am going to be extremely careful about this superb book'), but not evading the author's ire for all his effort; even Malcolm Muggeridge looking askance at Beverley Nichols and the dog he just wanted to be its own woolly self. Muggeridge, in *The Thirties*, keeps up a spirited commentary on the peculiarities of English life, letting a kind of bemused amusement set the tone.

The particulars of social requirements make another outstanding topic for ridicule – and thus we have the infant Elizabeth Bowen 'not rising to the occasion', recalling, in a mood of self-deprecation, 'the awful number of marks that I overshot'. Comic self-assurance – *pace* A. J. P. Taylor and his diaries for the *London Review of Books* – can be equally engaging ('Recently my reputation has been vindicated'; 'I found I was the only historian in this compendium and quite right too'). It is all a matter of tone, whether the effect is aggravating or invigorating.

It seems to me that the scope of this anthology is really quite extensive, what with George Orwell on boys' weeklies, Arthur Marshall on schoolgirls' goings-on, Germaine Greer on women's romances and Harold Nicolson on men's clothes ... The last contains a memorable impression of Herbert Spencer in the suit he wore to announce ill-humour; and when we come to Denton Welch's account of an afternoon with Sickert, we find the famous painter in an outfit apparently designed to put the wind up visitors – a rough-looking jacket and thigh-length sewer-boots. And the whole idea of correct dress provokes Beachcomber (J. B. Morton) to one of his most inspired *jeux d'esprit*, 'Trousers Over Africa', in which the unfortunate Carstairs is driven to dine in a bath towel.

It is one thing, and a jolly good thing, to take a balanced view of the oddities of social life – what gets Brigid Brophy going, though, is an oddity of literary judgement: the overestimation of Henry Miller. By the time she has finished with him, the egregious American has really had the stuffing knocked out of him, and not without cause. Disbelief at what readers will swallow: this determines the mood in which Germaine Greer approaches magazine fiction of the less exacting sort, and also – with disapproval added – the spirit of George Orwell's confrontation with those exasperating boys' weeklies in which horse-play abounds, and class-consciousness is not undermined. (The same social phenomenon – that is, the popularity of such papers – is treated rather more genially by Dylan Thomas, in 'How to Begin a Story'.) If it's urbanity we're after, we should perhaps turn first of all to Claud Cockburn on the vogue for gentlemanly tramps in low-grade literature, and all the conse-quent vicissitudes envisaged by over-imaginative authors.

What else? E. M. Delafield provides a sparkling 'woman's page' parody ('Femina's Supplement'), while Cyril Connolly, in 'Where Engels Fears to Tread', parodies not just an aspect of literary or social practice, but a whole blasé, recherché mood peculiar to the 1920s. Bernard Levin makes a spirited objection to his programme notes at a Festival Hall concert, and Peter Fleming ponders on the possible effect of Mrs Dale's death on radio-serial addicts. From Patrick Campbell comes a fearsome situation, disarmingly presented. Evelyn Waugh first exhibits annoyance at an unsolicited visit from a journalist and a noble-man, and then lets us in on a few of the hazards of being interviewed. James Stephens has trouble in finding his way around London. Fiona Pitt-Kethley goes in for naughtiness abroad. Anthony Carson's rather off-hand memoirs yield a good account of a scrape or two. The headlong arrival of the Durrells in Crete, *c.* 1935, is re-created some time later by the youngest son of the family, while his brother turns out a series of anecdotes concerning mishaps in diplomatic circles. Kingsley Amis pre-sides over a beauty contest in Wales, and Louis MacNeice experiences an updated Bloomsday.

These jottings, I hope, give some indication of the riches to come (and I haven't even touched on such pleasures as John Mortimer's priceless account of his prep-school days, or P. Y. Betts and her robust attitude to the reported death of an acquaintance, a Belgian refugee). What unites all the authors in this collection, I think, is a relish for the untoward or the ludi-crous, whether the resulting narration is drolly over-the-top, or more in the dry and sardonic mould. (We might think of Graham Greene lighting on a curiosity from the past, a hoax perpetrated on an eighteenth-century London printseller, and gleefully passing on the story to his readers; or Alan Bennett taking his eye for absurdities on a trip to Russia.) In making this selection, I have tried to strike a balance between the inescapable and the unexpected. Certain obvious names simply cannot be kept out of an anthology such as this, even if one wanted to omit them; on the other hand, an endless assembly of out-and-out comedians would, I feel, be lowering to the spirits, rather than otherwise. So you will find quite a few contributors whose names do not immediately spring to mind whenever humour is mooted (for instance, V. S. Pritchett, Louis MacNeice, A. J. P. Taylor, P. Y. Betts and Denton Welch), and some of them are among the funniest. But it is, indeed, impossible to predict what is going to raise the loudest laughs, and foolhardy to attempt any definition of humour itself. Those who've done it have generally been flattened for their pains. 'This is utter balderdash and offensive balderdash into the bargain,' says George Mikes about a pronouncement of Bergson's in his book *Laughter* (a book the critic liked, on the whole). And as for Harold Nicolson, his entire work on English humour 'tells us very little'. So I will merely say that, while reading for this anthology, I have kept two comments in mind: one is Brigid Brophy's assertion that humour is 'a twist in the aesthetic faculty'; the other, which comes from Hugh Kingsmill, holds up humour as an illumination of reality and never an evasion of it. I hope that, between them, they have kept me on the right lines.

Thanks are due to a number of people: above all to Jeffrey Morgan, Nigel May and Gerry Keenan, for constant advice and interest in the project; to Nora T. Craig, John Christopherson, Bill McCulloch, Bernard Hills, Emily Mallaby and Val Warner for help of various kinds; to Tony Lacey of Viking Penguin and to my agent, Araminta Whitley.

Patricia Craig
London 1992

Max Beerbohm

Then and Now

By Vera Lady Elderton

Yes, I shall be a hundred years old tomorrow morning – at 4.15, to be exact. And I think it was a very good idea of the Editor's to invite me to write a few words about the many changes that I must have seen in the course of a long life. Long, but not nearly long enough for *me*! I am not (but, thank Heaven, I feel as though I were) as young as ever I was; and to all intents and purposes, I *am*.

My earliest memory is of a summer's day when I was still an infant in arms. Mamma was dandling me up and down in the air, when in came Papa. I can see him now, flushed and with shining eyes, wearing his Garter star and riband, and can hear the exact tone in which he cried out, 'By God, she has the prettiest little voice I ever heard!' Who 'she' was I did not know till I was older. Papa had just come back from Kensington Palace, after hearing the speech delivered to her Privy Council by the young Queen Victoria.

Our town house was in Grosvenor Square, which I remember as being in those days a rather dismal place. I thank Heaven that I am and shall always be abreast of the times. The great tall buildings are a great improvement, in my humble but animated opinion. Indeed, the whole of Mayfair has changed for the better. In my young days there was still a turnpike at each end of every street there, as a protection against the highwaymen who still abounded. These ramshackle old barriers did not, however, keep the bears away in wintry weather (and weather in those days could be far wintrier than it can now). The bears used to come down, maddened with hunger, from Hampstead and from

Campden Hill, seeking whom they might devour. All doors had to be bolted at sunset. I remember how night after night in 'the hungry 'forties' Papa would sit, loaded for bear, at the open window of the dining-room and account for many of these marauders. He left me his London gamebook in his will, and I always wish I hadn't mislaid it. For he was one of the crack shots of his day.

Public executions must already, I think, have been abolished; for I certainly never saw one. But the famous Tyburn gibbet still reared its great height just where the eastern end of Connaught Place is now; and I remember that I once dared my twin-brother Henry to climb it – which he did, for he was a plucky and agile little rascal. One morning soon after that exploit, he dared me, *en revanche*, to sweep the main chimney of our house. I was rather daunted at first, but, to cut a long story short, I did in due course triumphantly wave my broom from the chimney-pot and scramble down again, black but proud. It so happened that Mr Charles Lamb, now famous as 'the gentle Elia', dined at our house that evening (for Papa and Mamma, though they had not, I think, much in common, were both of them very fond of hearing puns made). Having recently written an article about chimneysweeps, Mr Lamb was much excited at hearing of my deed, and when I came down to dessert he said, 'You ought to be a good card-player, for you follow *soot*', and I remember wondering rather, until the joke was explained to me, why every one laughed so much at what had been said by this gentleman. I can see him now – a short, thick-set man with a humorous twinkle.

Children in those days were, I think, more at liberty to go their own way than they are now. I don't know whether this was a good thing. I am inclined to think it must have been a bad one, so firmly do I believe in what is called 'the latest'. But the fact does, I think, remain that we Early-Victorian kiddies (or kids, as we were then less fondly called) enjoyed a larger latitude in climbing, etc, than our successors in the next, the present, the better century. And perhaps the reason was that we were so vastly in the majority. What were a father and mother against twelve children? Families of twelve were *de rigueur* in those days.

My parents' family numbered upwards of twenty, so that many of us knew each other only by sight, as it were. But even so there was, I think, more *camaraderie* among us than there is in the modern family of one or at most two.

On great occasions there would be a full muster of us, young and old. For instance, the whole tribe attended the opening of the Crystal Palace in '51, and I remember that during the ceremony I said in a shrill voice, 'I'd like to smash all this glass!' But Papa, who was a friend of Sir Joseph Paxton, said '*Sh!*' and I quieted down – which was unlike me. If there had been some stones handy, things might have been different. I am always proud of the part I played in the Suffragette disturbances that occurred not so very long ago. But to return to earlier days. The funeral of the Duke of Wellington was a great event in our lives. The victor of Waterloo – 'the Iron Duke', as he was called because of the iron shutters that he had put up at Apsley House when the mob broke his windows at the time of his opposition to the first Franchise Bill – had a great hold on the public imagination, and on ours especially, because as a young man he had made a proposal of marriage to Mamma, and had always remained, I think, rather *épris*. He often used to call on her, always with a bouquet of pink and white roses. I can see him now – a tall man with a cocked hat and rather a Jewish nose. I wish he could have lived long enough to lead the Balaclava Charge with Lord Cardigan, for indeed he was young to the last, and I am old-fashioned enough not to be able to write of him without emotion – at the risk of being (very rightly) sneered at by those gay young 'intellectuals' with whom I get along so well.

Mention of Balaclava reminds me of the great night when news reached us of the fall of Sebastopol. That was 'something like' a night! But it was destined to pale beside the night when we heard of the relief of Mafeking, many years later. My dear husband and I had dined at home that evening, and I remember we were having a violent quarrel about something or other when in rushed our young friend Mr Rudyard Kipling, waving a small Union Jack. He sank down, breathless, on to a chair, and then, 'Mafeking,' he said, 'is relieved!' A few minutes later the three of us were dancing arm in arm up and down Piccadilly, and round and round Trafalgar Square, three among many millions of revellers like ourselves, but next morning Kipling wrote his well-known poem 'Recessional'. This was considered rather a sudden volte-face by some of his friends. But genius cannot be judged by ordinary standards. 'Rudkip', as we all called him, was certainly a man of genius. I often regret that he never went into the House of Commons, for I think he would have had a success there, being so interested in politics.

Of the older school of politicians, I think the famous 'Dizzy' was the one whose company I liked best. He had a wonderful way of coining phrases. I was once privileged to hear from his lips a pronouncement that became historic. This was at one of Lord Houghton's famous breakfast parties in Charles Street. The aged Premier had arrived in London late on the previous night from the Congress of Berlin. Lord H, as we sat down to table, inquired, 'What was the upshot of it all?' After a pause, Dizzy replied in his deep, hollow voice, 'I have brought back Peace, Retrenchment and Reform.' The effect was electrical; and there ensued a long silence, in which one could have heard a pin drop, before the conversation became general. Mr Whistler, that very clever American painter and wit, was among the guests, and so was his rival Oscar Wilde, and I think the following anecdote has never found its way into print. Whistler said something more than usually witty. 'Good heavens,' said Wilde, 'I wish I had said that!' Whistler, quick as lightning, replied, 'Well, Oscar, I have noticed in the course of years that you do not always avoid the vice of plagiarism, and I think it not unlikely that sooner or later you will repeat what I have just said, leaving your hearers to suppose that you, not I, originated it!' After the roars of laughter had subsided, Mr Alec Yorke (who was a Groom-in-Waiting) said, 'I must tell that to the Queen.' A few weeks later he told me that he had done so, and that the Queen had said that she was not amused; but it must be remembered that she was still in deep mourning for the Prince Consort, whom, by the way, I never met, for he 'went out' very little, except in the circles frequented by 'Candle' Faraday, 'Evolution' Huxley, and others of the scientific persuasion. Not that I have anything to say against science. I regard it as an immense blessing and improvement in every way.

And now I must break off, for I have so much to do at the Cabaret-Canteen that I am running. But what I have written is not all that I shall write. I see no reason why I should not in the course of nature live to be two hundred, and I shall then offer to generations yet unborn many spicy memorials of the years to come.

Robert Lynd

'Noblesse Oblige'

Hearing that I had never read Edgar Wallace's novel *The Flying Fifty-five*, a friend sent it to me with warm commendations. My test of a moderately good book is whether it tempts me to neglect my work. My test of a really good book is whether it tempts me to neglect all my other pleasures. *The Flying Fifty-five* came through the second test with flying colours. I would not have laid it down to go out and see a hitherto unknown species of woodpecker. I could not have been lured from it by any cross-word puzzle, wireless programme, football match, poet, or invitation to a walk in the pleasantest company this side of Paradise. Lovers of measure in speech sometimes complain of the way in which reviewers call book after book 'fascinating'. It seems to me, however, that 'fascinating' is an exact, cold-blooded description of the effect certain books produce on the reader. Did not a critic once write of a novel that, while he was reading it, his eyes were 'literally glued to the page'? That may have been a slight exaggeration, but I doubt whether the word 'literally' was ever misused in a better cause.

I am not suggesting that the books that fascinate us are necessarily the greatest books. There used to be a fascination about penny dreadfuls such as Dante never exercises on his most devoted readers. The penny novelette of the nineteenth century fascinated millions more women and girls than the novels of Balzac. While not comparing *The Flying Fifty-five* with penny dreadfuls and novelettes, I can see that it would be equally misleading to compare it with the best pages of Dante or Balzac. At the same time, I am, I believe, about the millionth person to have found it fascinating.

Having finished it, I could not help reflecting on the immensity of the debt that English fiction owes to the peerage – for the hero, Lord Fontwell, is one of the finest peers in or out of fiction. Disguised as a tramp, he is offered a job as stable-lad by Stella Barrington, impoverished owner of race-horses, who is moved to pity by his condition. He performs miracles with her horses at Ascot, Goodwood, and elsewhere, and in races in which he or his friends have horses that might beat Stella's he arranges for these horses to be withdrawn. The crisis comes when her chief hope for the Derby proves to be unqualified to run. She has also Fifty-five in the race, believed to be only a sprinter, but her jockey is kidnapped at the last moment by the agent of her enemy, Sir Jacques Godfrey, who has also bought up all the other spare jockeys. What is the disguised Lord Fontwell to do? He is a man of nine stone seven – half a stone more than Derby horses carry – but he decides, none the less, to take out apprenticeship papers as a jockey, and to ride Fifty-five in the race. Does he win? He does. And not only this, but he beats his own horse, Meyrick, by a short head. ' "Bill, why did you do it?" He took her unresisting hand in his. "Because I love you," he said in a low voice.' That is what I call something like fiction.

Now, in the nineteenth century, popular fiction was full of peers like that. Not quite so near perfection as Bill Fontwell, perhaps, but near enough to convince hundreds of thousands of readers that the House of Lords was a veritable home of romance. In the nursery, no doubt, little girls dreamed of fairy princes and believed stories like those of Cinderella and of King Cophetua and the Beggar-maid. As they came to years of discretion, however, they acquired common sense; they became realistic. They saw that the events reported in stories like 'Cinderella' simply could not happen in the modern world – that they were inventions intended for consumption by children. The notion that a coal-heaver's daughter might suddenly find that her lover was a member of the royal house they dismissed as romantic rubbish. In this hard-headed mood, they turned from royalty to the peerage, working it out mathematically that it was about a hundred times more likely that a lover would turn out to be a disguised peer than a disguised prince. And,

7

unquestionably, the writers of novelettes made such a situation sound extremely probable.

I have often wondered why the peerage never played up to the novel-reader's conception of it – why peers in real life allow themselves to be surpassed to such a degree by peers in fiction. Has there ever been a peer in real life who has ridden as a jockey in the Derby at half a stone overweight and beaten his own horse for love of a beautiful girl, as Lord Fontwell did? I glanced through the Duke of Portland's entertaining book of racing reminiscences the other day, and, though there is a peer on nearly every page, I could find none of them who was not an 'also ran' in comparison with Lord Fontwell. There is an old motto, *noblesse oblige*. Were British peers not a little forgetful of it in the last century? Did even one per cent of them attempt to live up to the picture of the ordinary decent, self-sacrificing, disguised peer painted by the novelists? If they had, I fancy the general election on the abolition of the Lords veto would have taken a different turn. The Liberal Party, if it had attempted to abolish the veto of a House of Lords composed of men like Lord Fontwell, would have had a rude awakening. It would have been swept out of existence by infuriated novel-readers, and it is probable that to-day one of the Lord Fontwells would be prime minister of a nation united in its love of fiction and of horses.

Even in the decadent pre-war world, indeed, I think the House of Lords would have been worth saving for the sake of the libraries. Yet, during the debates on the veto, not a single Diehard, so far as I can remember, ever raised the point that, while peers might be a political nuisance, they were a literary necessity. Even the Society of Authors, usually vigilant in the cause of literature, seems to have overlooked the fact that fiction, deprived of a really effective peerage, was likely more and more to wallow in Zolaism and so ultimately to lose its popularity. If this had been understood at the time, we should have seen British authors lined up to a man behind Lord Willoughby de Broke when he declared that blood would flow under London Bridge before the veto of the House of Lords was abolished.

There is no denying that since the all but disfranchisement of the peerage gloom has spread to an alarming extent over literature. Cinderella now remains miserable in her kitchen for ever. There is no rescue for the progeny either of a moss-gatherer or of a tallow chandler. What you are born you remain – only worse. It might be thought that there are plenty of millionaires to take the place of the debilitated peers. But millionaires are not the same thing. A millionaire is only an ordinary man grown rich, and sometimes all the more vulgar for having done so. He is not a being belonging to a superior world – the world of robes and coronets that has ennobled literature since the days of Shakespeare. I was reading the new edition of Mrs Amanda M. Ros's famous novel, *Delina Delaney*, recently, and I was struck by the thought that it would have lost half its dignity if the hero, instead of being a peer, had been merely a millionaire. I doubt whether Delina herself, the humble fisherman's orphan daughter, would have been swept off her feet so rapidly if her lover had come to her with the offer of anything less than a title. After all, no millionaire could talk like Lord Gifford. It is only a peer – and a novelist's peer at that – who could have shown such a command of language as Lord Gifford shows in telling Delina of Lady Mattie, the 'high-toned society-mover' whom his mother wishes him to marry. 'I must tell you, my idol of innocence,' he declares, 'that every day of my life I hate her more and more, while her feelings for me are quite the reverse. O Lord, I simply can't bear her.' Continuing, he says:

Lady Mattie (Heaven knows who died, and if any, died and legacied her the title) is one of those willowy-washy figures who keeps rushing into this room or the other room, wherever by chance she finds a mirror to throw her image back to her in flattered fashion. She stands almost a six-footer, with her treadles thrust into shoes you'd swear that once long ago belonged to a Chinese madman; her long, thin wallopy legs enveloped in silken hose, with birds, fish, fowl, cabbage-leaves, ay, by Jove, with every species of animal, vegetable and mineral rainbowed in coloured fashioned over their flimsy fronts.

Go into any commoner's house in England – even into the house of the richest commoner – and you will hear no such high-toned aristocratic utterance as that. Scorn of unwanted brides is expressed differently in baronial halls and suburban villas.

What commoner, for example, could emulate Lord Gifford's derisive description to Delina of Lady Mattie's garter:

Then her garters! Ah, ha!

How I remember one fine day finding a lost one that had fastened itself, I presume, above or below her knee, and, thirsting, probably for a dash of fresh air, broke loose and there it lay. That garter! Composed of every colour, resembling the amethyst, opal, emerald, jasper, garnet, onyx, pearl, and sapphire, terminating in a cat's face studded with diamonds. I remember perfectly examining the article, at first wondering under Heaven what it was. I concluded it must be a necklet, and proceeded to carefully roll it up. As I coiled it, I couldn't fail seeing the word 'garter' worked in emeralds about its centre . . .

No, whatever you may say about politics, the House of Lords has amply justified its existence in fiction. Lady Mattie's garter, Lord Fontwell's victory in the Derby – how much more exciting it all sounds than life even on the best collective farm! If more peers rode horses like Lord Fontwell, and talked like Lord Gifford, the aristocratic régime might yet be saved for Europe.

E. M. Forster

Mrs Grundy at the Parkers'

When Mrs Grundy called recently at the Nosey Parkers', she was informed by the maid that they were 'Not at home.'

'Do you mean that your mistress is out or is not out?' she asked. Doris collapsed, and said that Mrs Parker was in, but had rather a headache, and so was resting.

'Then have the goodness to tell her I am here, without further prevarication,' said Mrs Grundy, and seated herself in the austere drawing-room – such a contrast to her own cosy parlour. The Parkers enjoyed making themselves as well as other people uncomfortable, which she had never been able to understand.

'Ah, Amelia,' said her friend, coming in. 'Quite a voice from the past!'

'Edith, I called about something or other, but Doris's untruthfulness has put it clean out of my head. Why did she say you were not at home when you are?'

'Well, it is only a form of words; a modern convention. One has to keep pace with the times if one is to guide them and they sorely need our guidance.'

'And have you the headache or have you not?' Mrs Grundy persisted.

'I have. Still I am glad you forced your way in, for I want to talk about our methods of work. You don't interfere with people in quite the right way, you know. You are too desultory and impetuous. That was all right in the nineteenth century, when life was slow, and one could point to one impropriety after another with one's umbrella as they crossed the street – but today! Why, you'll get knocked down. You'll be run over by a motor bicycle, and before you can see whether it was a girl on the pillion she will have disappeared. Today one must select and one must plan; civilization is so complicated. Think of our triumph the other month – that man who was arrested for bathing at Worthing.'

'Ah, don't talk to me about bathing. I often wish there was no such place in these islands as the sea-shore.'

'That is shallow of you. If there was no sea-shore, how could we catch people on it? Besides, I approve of bathing, provided it is so regulated that no one can enjoy it. We are working toward that. You were a great pioneer, but you made the mistake of trying to suppress people's pleasure. I try to spoil their pleasure. It's much more effective. I don't say, "You shan't bathe." I say, "You shall bathe in an atmosphere of self-consciousness and fear", and I think I am succeeding. I certainly have at Worthing.'

'I expect I read about Worthing, but where everything is so shameless one gets bewildered.'

'Why, the case of the visitor who bathed, properly clad, and then returned to his bathing machine to dry. Thinking no one could see him, since the machine faced the ocean, he left its door open. He had reckoned without my foresight. I had arranged that a policewoman should be swimming out at sea. As soon as she observed him, she signalled to a policeman on shore, who went to the machine and arrested him. Now, Amelia, would you have ever thought of that?'

'I certainly shouldn't have. I don't like the idea of women policemen at all. A woman's proper place is in her home.'

'But surely there can't be too many women anywhere.'

'I don't know. Anyhow, I am glad the visitor was arrested. It will stop him and others going to English seaside resorts, which is a step in the right direction, and I hope the magistrate convicted.'

'Oh, yes. Magistrates nearly always convict. They are afraid of being thought to condone immorality. As my husband points out, that is one of our strong cards. In his private capacity the magistrate was probably not shocked. The average man simply doesn't mind, you see. He doesn't mind about bathing costumes or their absence, or bad language, or indecent literature, or even about sex.' At this point she rang the bell. 'Doris, bring the smelling salts,' she said, for Mrs Grundy had fainted. When consciousness had been restored, she continued: 'No, nor even about sex, and we social workers of the twentieth century cannot ignore sex; what we can do is to make it a burden. And we are faced with the difficulty that the average man, if left to himself, does not brood, and forgets to persecute. He has habits instead of ideals. Isn't that too dreadful! He says in effect, "I go my way about sex or whatever it is, and I let others go theirs, even if I think it queer. It isn't my funeral." But it is going to be his funeral – at least I hope so.'

'And what of the average woman?'

'She is a little more satisfactory, a little more apt to be scared. Though I have known sad cases of women saying, "Pore thing, we don't take no notice although she did 'ave a little Unwanted, we treats her like one of ourselves." You see what we are up against – tolerance, good temper, and unsuspiciousness. It has been no easy matter to cover England with regulations from end to end.'

Mrs Grundy sighed. 'I admit you manage to interfere more than I did,' she said. 'I expect it is as you say, and I was too impulsive. I hurried too much from vice to vice when I was young. I stood outside the music halls, to stop people going in, and then I heard profanity in the cab-shelter, and went to silence that, and while I was doing so the music hall filled up. I went to Africa to make the cannibals monogamous and during my absence the Deceased Wife's Sister's Bill became law in England. When it's daylight I can see people, which is scandalous, and at night-time I can't see them, which is worse. I simply don't know where to turn, and while I am insisting on ulsters for sunbathing the Deceased Husband's Brother's Bill will probably become law, too. You have a sounder method, Edith. You have brought in education, of which I never dreamt, and I am not surprised that your wonderful work gives you the headache.'

'My headache, to which you now refer, has nothing to do with my work,' replied her hostess. 'It has been caused by a piece of bad news which has just arrived from the Continent. Even my husband is upset by it.'

'If I had my way there never would have been any Continent,' cried Mrs Grundy, and proceeded to ask a series of agitated questions, such as had the bad news to do with chocolates being allowed in theatres, were sweepstakes to be legalized, was Sunday cricket spreading, had the King been seen patting a race-horse, and so on.

'No, you are quite off the lines. It has to do with something inside us.'

'And pray, what can the Continent have to do with my inside?'

'Amelia, you must make an effort to understand. It concerns you as much as myself. It is a sort of discovery that has been made by a kind of doctor. Just as our work was prospering and we were making people stodgy and self-conscious under the pretence of building better citizens, just as we had bullied the lay authorities and coaxed the clerical into supporting us, just as interference was about to be launched on a colossal scale –. But I despair of explaining what it is. Perhaps my husband will be able to.' And she called out, 'Nosey!'

Mr Nosey Parker, who now joined the ladies, was scarcely their equal as a field worker. Where he excelled was on committees. Without being obtrusive, he managed to generate that official uneasiness upon which all their work depended. Let me explain. Each member of any committee has, of course, broken the law at some time or other, and desires to prove to his colleagues that he hasn't; he can do this best by being timid in discussion, and by voting for any measure that deprives the public of enjoyment. Furthermore, each member either has a daughter or feels that he ought to have one, and dares not oppose any censorship of art or literature in consequence. Mr Parker realized all this. He had only to say 'We must think of our daughters' and everyone thought of their skins. He had only to say 'I am not narrow-minded, but . . .' and broadness became impossible. He raised the banner of respectability and called it idealism. *Sauve qui peut* was embroidered in brown on its folds. And under it the municipal councillors or the board of magistrates or the jurymen gathered, all afraid of being found out, and when their duties concluded they had not done at all what they intended (which was, generally speaking, to let their fellow creatures alone), but had stopped one man from doing this and another from doing that, and had sent a third man to prison.

'Nosey, do explain what has happened,' his wife said.

'Nothing has happened. It is only an idea.'

'Ideas have never troubled me, especially from abroad,' said Mrs Grundy.

'You are fortunate. I own myself worried by this one. The idea is that we, who have helped others, ought now to be helped, and it is proposed to help us by pulling us to pieces.' He shuddered. 'To you that means little. But I have always had doubts of my own solidity. How can I bring it home to you? They desire to examine your intimate fabric, Mrs Grundy: they suspect it of being diseased. My wife's and my own they assert to be even fouler than yours. They believe that we all three try to improve people because we envy their happiness and had bad luck ourselves when we were young. What so alarms me is that there is no bitterness in the new attack. We are actually objects of pity.'

'And, pray, is that all?' said Mrs Grundy, with her dry little laugh. 'You may have given Edith a headache over this, but you have no such effect on me. I am quite accustomed to pity. I got a lot as a girl. It is merely a term of abuse, and I shall castigate it in due season. Good-bye, my dear sir, and take an old woman's advice: keep away from foreign newspapers in the future.' And, gathering up her skirts, she left their house – perhaps for her doom.

'Poor thing, she doesn't know the danger,' said Mrs Parker, looking after their friend anxiously, and observing how she first scowled at Doris and then lectured some navvies for using a word which had been devitalized twenty years previously by Mr Bernard Shaw. 'She is brave because she is out of date. But we – oh Nosey, Nosey! Fancy, if it gets known that interference is a disease which ought to be interfered with. Men and women will live as they like, they will be natural and decent about one another, and we shall boss and nag at them no more.'

'Too true, too true,' said her husband, 'and yet I see a ray of hope. Our enemies cannot interfere with us unless they organize. As individuals they are helpless. They will have to form Freedom Leagues, or Anti-Fuss Societies or sign Beach Pyjama Covenants, and they cannot do so without constituting themselves into committees. And as soon as they meet on committees ... yes, I think we shall survive after all.'

Will they survive? Only Doris, who is the future, can tell.

P. G. Wodehouse

Thrillers

It is an odd fact, frequently commented upon by thoughtful observers, that most of the great plagues in history have crept upon the world insidiously and without warning. Nobody notices that anything in particular is happening until one day the populace wakes up to find the trouble full-blown in its midst.

In the Middle Ages, for instance, everything was perfectly peaceful and normal – knights jousting, swineherds herding swine, landowners busy with soc and seisin and all that sort of thing – when one morning – on a Tuesday it was, six weeks come Lammas Eve – a varlet, strolling along the road between Southampton and Winchester (where the filling-station is now), encountered a malapert knave and fell into conversation with him after the sociable habit of those days.

'How now?' quoth the varlet.

'Ye same to you,' said the knave, courteously.

After which, as usually happens when two sons of the soil get together for a chat, there was a pause of about twenty minutes. At the end of this period the varlet spoke.

'In my village there has chanced a happening,' he said, 'which hath caused much marvel. Rummy, is ye general verdict. Old Bill of ye Mill suddenly turned black yesterday.'

'Black?' said the knave, wondering.

'Black is right.'

'Well, by St James of Compostella, if that doth not beat ye band!' exclaimed the knave. 'Down where I live, George ye Cowherd hath turned black, too.'

'Thou dost not say!'

'Of a verity I do say.'

'What can have caused this?' cried the varlet.

'I could not tell thee,' said the knave. 'I am a stranger in these parts myself.'

And a week later the Black Death was all over the country, and a man who did not look like Al Jolson singing 'Sonny Boy' could scarcely be found anywhere.

In much the same way, quietly and, as it were, surreptitiously, the present flood of Mystery Thrillers has engulfed the British Isles. Only a short while ago the evil appeared merely sporadic. Now we are up to our necks in the things, and more coming all the time. There seems to be some virus in the human system just now which causes the best of writers to turn out thrillers. This would not matter so much, only, unfortunately, it causes the worst of writers to turn them out, too.

The result is that this royal throne of kings, this sceptred isle, this earth of majesty, this seat of Mars, this other Eden, demi-Paradise, this fortress built by Nature for herself against infection and the hand of war, this happy breed of men, this little world, this precious stone set in the silver sea, which serves it in the office of a wall or as the moat defensive of a house ... well, to cut a long story short, England ... has degenerated into an asylum full of patients reading each other's mystery stories. And ninety-nine out of every hundred a dud.

A disquieting thought.

And the worst of it is that ninety-six out of every hundred contain a heroine and a love-story.

Who ever first got the idea that any one wants a beastly girl messing about and getting in the way when the automatics are popping I am at a loss to imagine. Nobody has a greater respect than myself for girls in their proper place – in the paddock at Ascot, fine: at Lord's during the luncheon interval of the Eton and Harrow match, capital: if I went to a night-club and found no girls there, I should be the first to complain: but what I do say is that they have no business in Lascar Joe's Underground Den at Limehouse on a busy evening. Apart from anything else, Woman seems to me to lose her queenly dignity when she is being shoved into cupboards with a bag over her head. And, if there is one thing certain, it is that sooner or later something of that sort will be happening to the heroine of a thriller.

For, though beautiful, with large grey eyes and hair the colour of ripe corn, the heroine of the thriller is almost never a very intelligent girl. Indeed, it would scarcely be overstating it to say that her mentality is that of a cockroach – and not an ordinary cockroach, at that, but one which has been dropped on its head as a baby. She may have escaped death a dozen times. She may know perfectly well that the notorious Blackbird Gang is after her to secure the papers. The police may have warned her on no account to stir outside her house. But when a messenger calls at half-past two in the morning with an unsigned note saying 'Come at once', she just snatches at her hat and goes. The messenger is a one-eyed Chinaman with a pock-marked face and an evil grin, so she trusts him immediately and, having accompanied him to the closed car with steel shutters over the windows, bowls off in it to the ruined cottage in the swamp. And when the hero, at great risk and inconvenience to himself, comes to rescue her, she will have nothing to do with him because she has been told by a mulatto with half a nose that it was he who murdered her brother Jim.

This girl must go. We readers demand it. We know the publishers want a female in the story so that they can put her on the jacket with her hands clasped and a wild look of agony in her eyes, but nevertheless we stick to it that she must go. Better a jacket with only a masked man pushing a paper-knife into a millionaire in his library than this continued poisoning of sensational fiction with imbeciles like Myrtle or Gladys or Elaine or whatever her name may be.

What we all liked so much about Sherlock Holmes was his correct attitude in this matter of girls in mystery stories. True, he would sometimes permit them to call at Baker Street and tell him about the odd behaviour of their uncles or step-fathers ... in a pinch he might even allow them to marry Watson ... but once the story was under way they had to retire into the background and stay there. That was the spirit, and we want a little more of it nowadays.

The obvious person, of course, to rid us of these pests is the villain, and in fairness to a willing worker it cannot be denied that he does his best. He has the zeal, the enthusiasm – every quality, you would say, which is required for the task. And yet, for one reason or another, he always fails. Even when he has got the girl chained up in the cellar under the wharf with the water pouring through the grating we never in our hearts really expect the happy ending. Experience has taught us that we cannot rely on this man. He has let us down too often, and forfeited our confidence. We know him for what he is, a broken reed.

Broadly speaking, the trouble with every villain of a thriller is that he suffers from a fatal excess of ingenuity. When he was a boy, his parents must thoughtlessly have told him that he was clever, and it has absolutely spoiled him for effective work.

The ordinary man, when circumstances compel him to murder a female acquaintance, borrows a revolver and a few cartridges and does the thing in some odd five minutes of the day when he is not at the office or the pictures. He does not bother about art or technique or scientific methods. He just goes and does it.

But the villain cannot understand simplicity. A hundred times he manoeuvres the girl into a position where one good dig with a knife or a carefully directed pistol-shot would produce the happiest results, and then, poor ass, he goes and ruins it all by being too clever. It never occurs to him just to point a pistol at the heroine and fire it. If you told him the thing could be done that way, he would suspect you of pulling his leg. The only method he can imagine is to tie her in a chair, erect a tripod, place the revolver on it, tie a string to the trigger, pass the string along the walls till it rests on a hook, attach another string to it, pass this over a hook, tie a brick to the end of the second string and light a candle under it. He has got the thing reasoned out. The candle will burn the second string, the brick will fall, the weight will tighten the first string, thus pulling the trigger, and there you are.

Then somebody comes along and blows the candle out, and all the weary work to do over again.

Still, I suppose it is no use being angry with the poor fellows. They are doing their best according to their lights. It is simply that they are trying to tackle a highly specialized job without the requisite training. What the villain needs is to forget all he thinks he knows and go right back to the beginning and start learning the business from the bottom up. He requires careful schooling. And this is what he ought to be given at once if thrillers are to be purged of heroines.

The keynote of the curriculum of this School for Villains would be the inculcation of simplicity and directness. The pupil would receive at first what one might call a kindergarten education. For the greater part of his opening term he would confine himself to swatting flies. From this he would work up through the animal kingdom in easy stages till eventually he arrived at heroines. By the time he had taken his degree, the Myrtles and Gladyses would be climbing trees and pulling them up after them to avoid the man, for by then he would be really dangerous.

The great difficulty, of course, would be to restrain and hold in check that infernal ingenuity of his. The average villain's natural impulse, if called upon to kill a fly, would be to saw away the supports of the floor, tie a string across the doorway, and then send the fly an anonymous letter urging it to come at once in order to hear of something to its advantage. The idea being that it would hurry to the room, trip over the string, fall on the floor, tumble into the depths, and break its neck.

That, to the villain's mind, is not merely the simplest, it is the only way of killing flies. And the hardest task facing his form-master would be to persuade him that excellent results may be obtained through the medium of a rolled-up *Daily Mail* gripped by the Football Coupon.

The maddening thing is that it is only when dealing with the heroine that he is so beastly clever. With anybody of his own sex he can be as straightforward as a medieval headsman. Give him a baronet and he will stick a knife in his back without a second thought. But the moment he finds himself up against a heroine he seems to go all to pieces, and we get all this stuff of suspending snakes from the chandelier and fooling about with bombs which can only be exploded by means of a gramophone record with an A in alt on it.

I have known a villain to sit the heroine on a keg of gunpowder and expect it to be struck by lightning. You can't run a business that way.

What these men have got to learn is that the best way of disposing of a girl with hair the colour of ripe corn is to hit that hair as hard as possible with a bit of gas-pipe. Buying tarantulas to put in her vanity-bag or little-known Asiatic poisons with which to smear her lipstick do no good whatever and only add to the overhead.

Let them master this fundamental truth, and then we shall see what we shall see.

But even supposing that one day we succeed in ridding mystery fiction of the heroine, can we say sincerely that the Millennium will have arrived? I think not. Even without a feminine interest your average thriller-writer can turn out a pretty painful product.

Of course, there are exceptions. Dorothy Sayers is good. So is Anthony Berkeley. So is Philip Macdonald. So are H. C. Bailey and Agatha Christie. Oppenheim is still the Old Reliable. And nine hundred of every thousand of Edgar Wallace's are worth the seven-and-sixpence every time. But the others . . .

It does not seem to occur to the ordinary man how hard it is to do this sort of thing well, nor does he appear to realize that unless it is done well the result is ghastly. If I had a son who was thinking of writing thrillers – and if I had a son of penholding age that is certainly what he would be doing nowadays – I should take him aside and try to point out some of the drawbacks to this form of authorship.

'James(or John),' I should say, 'think well! There is still time to turn aside and write about unhappy marriages and the pro-miscuous amours of the Intelligentsia. But you have thought it all out, you say? You are resolved to try a mystery story? Then, Edward, the moment has come when you must learn the facts of life. I must tell you that there is a snag in this mystery-story business, and a bad snag. Over every mystery story there broods the shadow of a yawning reader saying "What of it?" You inform this reader that Sir Gregory Bulstrode has been murdered in his library. "Oh, yes?" is his reply, and his manner is indifferent and even bored. He has known so many libraries, you see – such hundreds and hundreds of libraries, and all with corpses in them ... thin corpses, stout corpses, medium-sized corpses. He has grown to expect corpses in libraries.

'A little discouraged, you add that all the doors and windows were locked.

' "They always are," he says.

' "And suspicion points to at least half a dozen people."

' "Oh, well," he mumbles, dozing off, "it turns out in the end that one of them did it, I suppose?" '

That is the trouble. For the mystery-novel Suspicion Handicap, the field is so limited. The reader knows it wasn't the hero or heroine who did the murder. He is practically sure it couldn't have been Reggie Banks, because he is a comic character and any vestige of humour in any character in a mystery story automatically rules him out as a potential criminal. It can't have been Uncle Joe, because he is explicitly stated to be kind to dogs. And he naturally rules out all hysterical governesses and brooding butlers, because their behaviour throughout has been so suspicious as to clear them from the start.

So he assumes it must have been some totally uninteresting minor character who hardly ever appears and who is disclosed in the last chapter as the son of the inventor whom the murdered man swindled forty years ago. At any rate, he knows quite well it's one of them.

If I were writing a mystery story, I would go boldly out for the big sensation. I would not have the crime committed by anybody in the book at all. Here are the last few paragraphs of a little thing I have been turning over in my mind against the time when I myself fall a victim to the epidemic.

'You say, Jerningham,' I gasped, 'that you have solved this inscrutable problem? You really know who it was that put the puncture in Sir Ralph?'

Travers Jerningham nodded curtly. I was astonished to see that he displayed none of the satisfaction which one would naturally have expected. There was a cloud on his forehead and his thin mouth had drawn itself into a tight line.

'I do,' he said.

'But you seem gloomy, Jerningham – moody, why is this?'

'Because it is impossible to bring the criminals to justice.'

'Criminals? Was there, then, more than one?'

'There were two. Two of the blackest-hearted menaces to Society that ever clutched a knife-handle. One held Sir Ralph down, the other did the stabbing.'

'But if you are so sure of this, how is it that you cannot give the scoundrels their just deserts?'

Travers Jerningham laughed a bitter laugh.

'Because, my dear fellow, they aren't in the book at all. The fiends were too cunning to let themselves get beyond the title page. The murderers of Sir Ralph Rackstraw were Messrs Hodder and Stoughton.'

THE END

That would be something like a punch. But the next thing that would happen would be the usual flood of imitations. Somebody would write a thriller in which the crime was traced to Otis and Googe, Bespoke Printers, London, Harringay and Glasgow: and then somebody else would hit on the author's best friend, J. B. Stokes, without whose never-failing sympathy and encouragement this book would not have been written: and so on and so on. You cannot copyright an idea, and times have become so hard for thriller-writers that they are after any possible new murderer like a pack of wolves.

You see, the supply of murderers is giving out. They have all been used so often. You cannot even be sure of the detective's friend now. Ever since Agatha Christie's *Roger Ackroyd* we keep a very sharp eye on that friend. It is very lucky for Doctor Watson that he belonged to the pre-Christie era.

It will be noted that in the above I have stuck to what I might call the Gents' Ordinary or Stock-size detective. Travers Jerningham will be just one more of those curt, hawk-faced amateur investigators. It is not merely that I cannot be bothered to vary the type; I feel that, if you are going to have an amateur investigator, this even now is still the best sort to employ. Try to deviate from the type, and you only find yourself in trouble.

There are three alternatives:

(*a*) The Dry;

(*b*) The Dull;

(c) The Effervescent;
and I am not very fond of any of them.

The Dry detective is elderly. He wears pince-nez and a funny hat and is apt to cough primly. He is fussy and old-maidish. Of course, get him in a corner and he suddenly produces a punch like a prize-fighter; but out of his corner he is rather a bore.

Not such a bore, of course, as the Dull detective. This is the one who unmasks the criminals by means of his special knowledge of toxics and things and gets on the villain's track owing to the discovery that the latter is definitely brachiocephalic. Avoid this man.

The Effervescent detective is rather a new invention. He is a bright young fellow of independent means whose hobby is the solution of problems. They like him at Scotland Yard, and he chaffs them. Sometimes Inspector Faraday is a little inclined to shake his head at the young man's suggestions, but he is the first to admit that Tony Dalrymple has an uncanny knack of being right.

And the dear chap is so flippant with it all. None of that 'Holmes, who has done this fearful thing?' stuff about him. Violence to the person cannot damp Tony's spirits, provided it is to some other person. Viewing the body brings out all that is gayest and sprightliest in him.

'So this is the jolly old corpse, is it, Inspector? Well, well, well! Bean bashed in and a bit of no-good done to the merry old jugular, what? Tut, tut, mother won't like this at all. You're on to the fact that the merchant who messed this cove up was left-handed and parted his hair in the middle, of course? And a good job he made of it, didn't he?'

Not a frightfully attractive young man. But spreading, I regret to say. You meet him everywhere nowadays.

The best detectives – Edgar Wallace's – are always Scotland Yard men. To a public surfeited with brilliant amateurs there is something very restful about the man from Scotland Yard. He has a background. You can believe in him. If I found it impossible to head my son off from writing mystery stories, I should certainly advise him to give his heroes an official standing. Then he would have the Record and Fingerprint Department at his back, and if he wanted to stop the villain leaving London could tell off three thousand policemen to watch the roads.

It is true that the villain would get through just the same, but you can't say it isn't nice to have the sympathy and moral support of three thousand policemen.

I have got James – or John, as the case may be – pretty clear, then, on the detective end of the job. He has now to face a far more serious problem. What of the villain?

Villains in mystery stories may be divided broadly into three classes – all silly:

(*a*) Sinister men from China or Assam or Java or India or Tibet (or practically anywhere except Ponder's End and Peebles), who are on the track of the jewel stolen from the temple.

(*b*) Men with a grudge which has lasted as fresh as ever for thirty years.

(*c*) Master Criminals.

With regard to (*a*), I should advise James to try almost anything else first. I rather fancy that sinister jewel-trackers have about reached saturation-point. Besides, what I might call the villain-supplying nationalities have grown so absurdly touchy these days. Make your murderer a Chinaman now, and within a week of your story's appearance letters are pouring into the publisher's office, signed Disgusted Coolie and Mother of Five (Hankow), protesting against the unfair libel. Go elsewhere and you run up against Paterfamilias (Java) and Fair-Play (Tibet). It is not worth it.

And yet the idea of falling back on (*b*) is not agreeable. The age in which we live is so practical, so matter-of-fact. We are no longer able to believe as readily as our fathers did in the man who cherishes a grudge for a quarter of a century. It was all very well in the old days, when there were fewer distractions, but what with Golf and Tennis and Cross-word Puzzles and the Flat-Race Season and the Jumping Season, and looking after the car and airing the dog and having to learn how to score at Contract Bridge, it seems simply incredible that a man should be able to keep his mind on some unpleasantness which happened in the early spring of 1904.

Which brings us to the last class, Master Criminals.

The psychology of the Master Criminal is a thing I have never been able to understand. I can follow the reasoning of the man who, wishing to put by something for a rainy day, poisons an uncle, shoots a couple of cousins, and forges a will. That is business. It is based on sound commercial principles. But the Master Criminal is simply a ditherer. He does not need money. He has got the stuff. What with the Delancy Emeralds and the Stuyvesant Pearls and the Montresor Holbein and the bearer bonds he stole from the Bank, he must have salted away well over a million. Then what on earth does he want to go on for? Why not retire?

But do you think you could drive that into a Master Criminal's head? Not in a million years. I have just been reading the latest story about one of these poor half-wits. This one, in order to go on being a Master Criminal, was obliged to live in a broken-down cellar on a smelly wharf on the river, posing as a lodging-house keeper. All he did with his time was chop wood in the backyard. And at a conservative estimate, after paying salaries to his staff of one-eyed Chinamen, pock-marked Mexicans, and knife-throwing deaf-mutes, he must have been worth between two and three million pounds.

He could have had a yacht, a fleet of motor-cars, a house in Grosvenor Square, a nice place in the country, a bit of shooting in Scotland, a few miles of fishing on some good river, a villa on the Riviera, and a racing-stable. He could have run a paper, revived British opera, and put on Shakespeare at popular prices. But no, he preferred to go on living in his riverside cellar, which was flooded every time there was a high tide, simply because he wanted to be a Master Criminal.

One scarcely knows whether to laugh or weep.

I remember one Master Criminal, just as rich as this man, who set his whole organization at work for weeks digging a tunnel into a bank. And what do you think he got out of it? Twelve thousand pounds. Not guineas. Pounds.

Twelve thousand pounds! Can you beat it? Just about what I am paid for writing this article.

★

Perhaps, on the whole, then, James, you had better avoid all three of the types of villain which I have mentioned and stick to the Fiend in Human Shape. This variety has the enormous advantage that he has not got to be made plausible. He is a homicidal lunatic, and as such can get away with anything. To the man with the thirty-year-old grudge we say, 'But, my dear fellow, consider. If you stick that knife into Sir George, what of the future? What will you do in the long winter evenings with no dream of vengeance to nurse?' To the Master Criminal we point out that he is giving himself a lot of trouble to add to an income which is already absurdly large. He cannot *like* having to put on false whiskers and stand outside the hero's bedroom on a chilly night, pumping poison-gas through it, or enjoy climbing up a slippery roof to drop cobras down the chimney. But the Fiend in Human Shape we merely pat encouragingly on the back and speed on his way with a cheery 'Good luck, Fiend, old man! Go as far as you like!'

And he gnashes his teeth amiably and snaps into it with an animal snarl.

James Stephens

Trying to Find the Strand

For a long time I knew London as an Underground system whereby one got from Euston to Victoria, and thus to Paris, and I diligently sought to perfect myself in the English language as it was spoken by Undergrounders.

I noticed that my native land had endowed me with many small errors of pronunciation. For example, I said 'twopence' when I should have said 'tuppence', and when I overheard a man saying 'thrippence' I began to distrust the numerals I was born to, and even to surmise that I might have to learn arithmetic all over again. A taxi-driver to whom I said Maison Lyons in a way that I thought creditable assured me that not only was there no such place in London, but that there couldn't be any such sounding place in the world.

Later on I had to remain in London for a week. I then discovered that, where before I had imagined London to be entirely composed of Undergrounds, it could be exceedingly difficult to find an Underground at all when one was urgently needed.

ONE PLACE I KNEW

I took a ride on a bus. All places were alike to me. Every place was virgin soil. I got something of the sense of London, the mighty city. I had a sense of throng and solidity, of intensity, of wealth and imperturbability which I did not get from Paris, and which I did not get afterwards even from New York.

New York is wonderful indeed. No city in the world is more wonderful, but London is beautiful. The wonder of New York is instantly revealed to its visitor, and is, in an extraordinarily short time, accepted and even forgotten; but the sense of the beauty of London is slow-growing, and abides.

So, going peacefully on my bus I came to a place which I recognized from having seen it on picture postcards and in many newspapers. It was Trafalgar Square. I dismounted. I felt almost at home.

There is a curious superstition in Dublin that if one has not been in the Strand one has not been in London; that, in fact, the Strand is London; and, consequently, the majority of Irish visitors search for the Strand with the same precipitancy that all lunatics at home are supposed to head for Glen-na-Gelt.

While I was admiring Trafalgar Square this curious superstition occurred to me. I at once removed a pigeon from my left shoulder and banished its brother from my hat, and I cogitated within me as to how I might get to the famous Strand.

A policeman was standing close to an Underground station, and I asked him my simple question. He looked at me with some of the interest that one might bestow upon an uneatable whelk, and he told me rapidly and concisely how to get there.

My ear was accustomed to the rather slow speech and the low-pitched voices of Ireland; but this policeman's voice was on another pitch altogether; and the tune of his sentence also was different from that to which I was accustomed: his pace of utterance was far more rapid than my ear could allow for – and, as a consequence of all these facts, I had not understood a single word that he had uttered.

I still did not know how to get to the Strand from Trafalgar Square.

MY NINE BUSES

When a sufficiency of traffic had swirled between the policeman and me I got on to another bus, for an idea had struck me. This idea was that a really energetic man can find any place that he is looking for, given the indispensable condition that he is in the town to which that place belongs, and that he has some faith in the law of averages.

Given these, the method of finding a thus unknown place is simplicity itself – one takes a bus and watches the names of the streets it passes through. At the end of five minutes one should leave that bus and take another one that is going in a different or contrary or oblique direction, again watching the streets, and only remaining in the new bus for five minutes; and one should continue to change his bus and his direction every five minutes until the street he is in need of reveals itself.

This result should normally be achieved inside of twelve buses. If not, the search should be discontinued in that area of the town and taken up on another day in another quarter.

Leaving Trafalgar Square, I reached the Strand in nine buses, and I was as delighted to get there as Columbus must have been when he raised the Woolworth Building on his port and felt that now he might go home again.

I went home by the Underground station at the end of the Strand, and as I passed down the steps I fancied that the policeman who was on duty there regarded me with interest and affection. I also thought that he looked like the very twin brother of the officer from whom I had sought advice an hour and a half before that.

I thought further that, if I were ever to become a good writer of English, I should live in London and learn the language properly. At the beginning one is apt to exaggerate the difficulty of any study, but I am inclined to believe now that, on the whole, English is not really as difficult as French.

Harold Nicolson

Men's Clothes

It is related of Mr Herbert Spencer that he possessed a suit which had been specially made for him. He only wore this suit when he was feeling irritable, but he sometimes wore it for weeks at a time. It was made all in one piece and of a soft soothing Jaeger sort of texture. He entered the suit from the middle, huddling his angry legs into the lower part, as if he were putting on bed-socks; working his impatient head into the upper part, as if entering a bathing-dress. Then down the front was an arrangement for lacing the thing together. Today that arrangement would run on a ratchet on what I believe is called the Zip method. In one would get, and then Zip ... one would be dressed with no greater effort than is required to close a tobacco pouch. In the evening one would reverse this process and tumble quickly into bed as a banana released from its sheath.

Clearly such a system would be soothing to the nerves. But it was not aesthetic. The members of Mr Herbert Spencer's household, seeing him descend to breakfast in what had come to be known as 'his angry suit', would quail, would bend apprehensive ringlets over their bacon and their eggs. And then these ringlets would begin to shake with what (although nervous laughter) was still laughter. Mr Spencer, it must be confessed, looked very odd in his combination suit. Those fierce and prominent eyes would glare out above the Jaeger wrappings, too proud to ask why all those bent ringlets should be shaking (with suppressed merriment, but still with merriment) above their bacon and their eggs.

Mr Spencer was an obstinate as well as an egoistic man. Still dressed in his angry suit, he would take his daily drive down Bond Street, and so round the Green and then St James's Park.

Angrier and still angrier would he become as people stared at this odd old man enveloped like Dr Peary or Doctor Cook upon a June morning. The angry suit ceased to soothe; it irritated gratuitously; it became a shirt of Nessus excruciating to its wearer. Mr Spencer would stop the carriage and feel his pulse, holding a large gold watch in his veined and bony hand. His pulse would be fast that morning, and the carriage would thus lumber back up Bond Street, flop, flop, flop from the single horse, and an indignant philosopher would be returned to Park Terrace, or to Hanover Row. (For I forget at this moment what was Mr Spencer's address.) He would sit upstairs in his angry overalls, too angry to come down to luncheon. And next morning he would dress in a neat suit of grey tweed, and be again his bright and petulant self.

These facts are historical, but, as with so much of history, they have not been digested. Why was it that the Jaeger combinations invented by Mr Herbert Spencer failed, when put to it, to soothe his nerves? Why was it that 'his angry suit' made him angrier still? Carlyle, who wrote much turgid nonsense upon the philosophy of clothes, makes no contribution to this problem. Carlyle, poor ignoramus, knew nothing of Mr Spencer's suit. But the problem, as a problem, existed before Mr Spencer, and persists after his death. It is the problem of how to reconcile comfort with decency. It is the problem of how to steer between the rocks of discomfort and the sandbanks of looking a joke. It is the problem of how to be individual without being funny.

Other people in their time have worn odd clothes. Lord Byron, when he proceeded to liberate Greece, designed for himself a little Hussar uniform of green cloth with white frogs and tags. On the top of his fussy little jacket he had meant to wear a huge helmet with a horsehair plume, such as one sees in heroic representations of the siege of Troy. But people laughed at this hat, and he put it back again in its pink bandbox. It can be seen today in his bedroom at Newstead.

Leigh Hunt for his part dressed, when over sixty, like little Lord Fauntleroy. But then Leigh Hunt, in later life, became very odd indeed. And Lord Salisbury, and Lord Beaconsfield, and the late Lord Astor – these each in his own way were either dirty or strange. And yet they all took trouble about their clothes. There must have been moments, let us say in January and June, when Lord Salisbury stood in his shirt sleeves in Arlington Street, while deferential tailors stretched measuring tapes around his frame. There must have been moments when similar tailors were summoned to Cliveden or to Hever and pinned upon Lord Astor the scaffoldings of those smart alpaca jackets in which, together with a boiled shirt and tie, he would walk majestically among his Italian gardens. Even Mussolini must sometimes be tried on.

It is a little painful to picture our heroes at such moments. Not merely is it disgraceful to visualize such vital and important beings submitting to the fingering and fussing of persons who, if they will forgive my saying so, evoke no very romantic image; not merely is it unpleasant to envisage them as standing there, turning round when told to, raising their arms like zanies ('A little higher, My Lord, *if* you please. 49.3, Mr Burkinshaw!' '49.3,' repeats the subservient Mr Burkinshaw, scribbling in his note-book); not merely is it humiliating to conceive of a mere tailor making chalk-marks upon the backs of statesmen rounded with the weight of half the world; nay, the impression created is more profound than any pain evoked by the picture of the magnificent in humiliation, it is an impression which derives its deep poignancy from the realization that even the most majestic among us wear two buttons on the back of a tail coat. Why do we do this thing? Both these particular buttons are otiose. And yet even the most liberated among us would miss these buttons if they failed to appear.

It is well enough for the fashionable and the slim. Their bodies fall naturally into the shape of their clothes, their waistcoats sit lightly, concavely, upon their adolescent frames. Couth and gainly they rise in the morning, couth and gainly they don their silken pyjamas for the night. Buttons for them are mere finishing touches to a lineal design, mere points of break in the monotony of what might otherwise appear too rigidly perpendicular. A button more, a button less, what matters it to those whose bodies are encased *in* but not *by* their clothes? It is only for those whose buttons are things which are apt to bulge and burst that this clothes question assumes the proportions of a deep human drama. It is for such people that I write these words of encouragement. I write for men. I do not write for boys and maidens. I write for men who, though still young in conscience, are yet not slim in shape. I do not write for women. It is not necessary, it would in fact be a mistake, to give women any gratuitous encouragement about their clothes.

It is thus for convex males that I write, and above all for those among them who are not exuberantly young. There comes a time, there comes, alas, a moment, when men of this type are apt to feel a sudden self-consciousness in regard to their pockets. A day in their life arrives when they hesitate, as never before, to cram that passport, that book of railway tickets, that diary and that letter-case into their breast pocket. They find themselves dividing so bulky a bundle, distributing its contents among pockets that hang at the sides of one, placing the lot in some separate bag. That is the first stage.

The second stage centres round the strap which sustains, maintains, and retains the waistcoat at the back. With the slim and the adolescent, this strap is a static object; it is just a strap; it is just there. But after the age, let us say, of twenty-seven, there are times when that strap, by a deft backward movement of the hands, is released or loosened. It is a terrible moment for any man when he catches himself loosening his strap. It marks the second stage in the grim progress from elegance to comfort.

The third stage is reached (it would be idle to defend it) when the top, and in extreme cases the two top, button or buttons of the trousers are, after a heavy meal, undone. By insensible degrees this third stage melts into one in which Swedish exercises figure, and Turkish baths, and a doubt whether waistcoats after all are a very sensible form of wear. Better a pullover. Better, in summer at least, nothing at all.

Then, Americans, so I am told, do not wear braces. They call them 'suspenders', a word applied, in our grey and pitiful island, only to socks. Americans, so I am assured, wear belts. I am sorry for them in this respect, since belts are a cruel register of girth; one can count the holes. That dark and glossy bar upon the leather which marked the limit of 1937, is not by any means the bar on which, in 1938, the buckle comes to its readiest repose. In 1939, maybe, that bar may move a further fraction of an inch along the leather scale of roundness. Very human will be the expedients by which a man will try to hide from himself the slow shifting of that mark upon the belt. But shift it does. He will suddenly catch sight of himself one evening at some night club: he may be laughing at the moment, he may be smiling brightly, he may be feeling at his best. Then suddenly, from some mirror opposite will leer at him a stout though not wholly unfamiliar face and form. His uncle in Texas? Not a bit of it. *Himself.* The laughter, at that, will die in his throat, that bright smile will fade upon his lips.

It will be then and not till then that the problem of clothes will loom for him in its true significance: not as the daily indulgence of the spring-time; but as some dour and compelling necessity of the autumn months. It will be then that he will think, with that exquisite sensibility which I have above displayed, of Lords Salisbury and Astor. It will be then, unless he be very wise or very lacking in all forms of sensuousness, that he will decide that his style of clothing must, and at once, be subjected to some radical change.

He does not confess, of course, that this metamorphosis is dictated by any desire to conceal the fading flower of his youth. He discovers, as I have already indicated, that waistcoats are but ungainly objects, devoid of real backing. He begins, unless he be indeed the late Lord Astor, to manifest an objection to stiff shirts, which indeed are apt to pop away from all but the slimmest frame, and to bulge outwards, away from all restraining bands. Stiff collars, also, are intolerable, intolerable to the fattening neck. A certain Bohemianism thereafter descends upon his vesture, and his clothes take on a tendency to slop and flop. A velvet smoking-jacket is not recommendable, but it will be tried. It is always tried. Then the hats grow wider, the hair longer, the ties daily more large and strange. Boots, during this Bohemian phase, remain the same: it is only in the succeeding phase that they also become challenging. For the succeeding phase is frequently very fierce indeed.

It comes upon vain and virile people who wish to hide their middle-age by an appearance of violence. It is a butcher phase. Essentially, if subconsciously, the impression which this phase is intended to convey is that although there *has* been an increase, it has been an increase of muscle rather than of flesh. Rough grey shirts are much affected during such periods, and heavy odorous tweed. Shoes, as I have stated, become arrogant, assuming a St Moritz appearance, as if about to be employed on winter sports. Fishing-hooks are worn in the hat, and in the breast pockets (which button outwards on a flap), silk handkerchiefs are carried, or any other object which occupies less space than would appear. This particular phase is both tiring and expensive. It leads rich people to take grouse-moors in Scotland, and poor people to go on walking tours in the Adirondacks. A knapsack, if skilfully slung, can cover a multitude of sins. The phase, however, is not a long one. It is the last flicker of resistance before collapse.

Mr William James, if I recollect aright, has some very penetrating passages upon this collapse. He is speaking of false claims. He speaks of the great joy which comes to a man when he abandons all hope of not becoming fat. This, says Mr William James, is the last release. I am inclined to agree with him. I look forward to my own collapse, let us say (if God will) in 1949. A large and amiable old bumble bee in huge grey flannels. In a huge all-embracing belt. Puffing around. Then, and then only, shall I have solved the problem of clothes.

But meanwhile, some words of advice. (1) Never take any exercise. Exercise develops the muscles, and when once muscles have been developed, they have to be banged to prevent them turning into fat. It is extremely painful to be banged. (2) When young, always have your clothes made a little too large for you. This, as the real estate agents say, will give you a margin of development. (3) Concentrate on colour rather than on shape. Colour can be bought in any shop. (4) Cultivate an impression of vitality rather than of Bohemianism. This can be done by frequently slapping the thighs. It is curious how vital a man becomes if he frequently slaps his thighs. (5) Be very successful in your public life. Fame, more than anything else, enables one to wear comfortable and even becoming clothes. (6) Avoid elegance in any form after the age of twenty-five.

And yet, and yet ... It is all very difficult. You see, I have said very little about clothes really because they do not interest me. What does interest me is the inevitable approach of the sit-and-grunt period of later middle-age. Can clothes retard its approach, or disguise its advent? They can do nothing of the kind. The worst thing, I fear, about being no longer young is that one is no longer young.

Hugh Kingsmill

High Life in Victorian Fiction

If it did nothing else for burdened mankind, the French Revolution did at any rate enrich and deepen the appeal of the upper classes to the novel-reading public. In the eighteenth century aristocrats were 'the Great', which was impressive rather than romantic. The guillotine brought the Olympians down to earth, and while not really impairing their divinity won for them the sympathy due to human suffering. Royal though ruined, victim yet victor – that, more or less, was the formula with which, when the aristocrat emerged on the other side of the French Revolution, Byron in *Childe Harold* launched him on his dazzling pilgrimage through the popular literature of the nineteenth century.

In *Novels of High Society from the Victorian Age*, a massive tome of nine hundred closely printed pages, Mr Anthony Powell has culled three of the most luxuriant blooms from the hothouse of Victorian romanticism. His first choice is Benjamin Disraeli's *Henrietta Temple*, which appeared in the year of Queen Victoria's accession. Disraeli, who had already published seven books, was now thirty-three, he had just entered Parliament, and, as he had recently told Lord Melbourne, was resolved one day to become Prime Minister. That day, except to Disraeli, seemed unlikely ever to dawn, for though his novels and his dandyism had attracted a good deal of attention, it was not of a kind to further his political ambitions. Even in the eighteen-thirties green velvet trousers and a black satin shirt were considered excessive, and although in later years Disraeli wrote to the papers to say that he had never worn green trousers the impression that he had lingered on. Nor did his novels help him. After he had held high office he was taken seriously as a writer, after his first premiership his wit and wisdom were universally applauded, and after his second premiership and death his literary genius was no longer in dispute. But in his early years these collateral aids to appreciation were lacking, and, judged bleakly on their actual contents, the novels of his first period seemed designed solely to add to their author's bank balance by purveying a diluted Byronism to a generation nicely balanced between the licence of the Regency and the domestic ideals of the Victorians. Ferdinand Armine, the hero of *Henrietta Temple*, starts off with the full Byronic equipment. He is of ancient lineage, and has a fiery imagination, violent passions and a daring soul. He glitters in brilliant circles, he is followed by the report of strange and flattering adventures, he breaks into profuse expenditure, and seems, in short, to be storing up endless difficulties both for himself and for the wealthy cousin whom he has decided to marry so that he may be in a position to disencumber the family estate of its mortgages and, incidentally, settle his personal debts (feelingly described by himself as 'private cares of my own of no slight nature'). Then he meets Henrietta Temple, a beautiful girl, of ancient lineage of course, but relatively penniless. From that moment he is a changed man. No more strange and flattering adventures, nothing but an unalterable, an at times even monomaniacal, fidelity to Henrietta. There are complications; Henrietta, on a false, though in all the circumstances plausible, report of his unfaithfulness, becomes engaged to a wealthy peer, and Ferdinand's creditors get him into a sponging-house. But all ends happily on the emotional plane, and satisfactorily on the economic, for Henrietta unexpectedly becomes one of the greatest heiresses in the country. To say that there is no reality at all in the book would be to pay even Disraeli's intelligence and self-command too high a compliment. The sponging-house is real enough, there is an astute moneylender with social ambitions who might have struck Mr Gladstone as like someone or other, and there is a very genuine ring in Ferdinand's cry of agony when he hears that Henrietta, now betrothed to another, has come into a vast fortune.

The second book chosen by Mr Powell, *Guy Livingstone*, was published in 1857 and enjoyed a huge success. In the twenty years since the Queen's accession the middle classes had expanded enormously in wealth and importance, but half-way through the 'fifties the Crimean War stimulated a latent distaste for their prudential outlook and sober domestic routine. Kingsley's *Westward Ho!* was one sign of the growing restlessness; Tennyson's *Maud*, with its denunciation of trade and dithyrambic approval of 'loud war by land and sea', was another; *Guy Livingstone* was a third. Not much is known of its author, George Lawrence, but one may reasonably assume that he put a good deal of himself into Frank Hammond, the faithful friend and chronicler of Guy Livingstone. Hammond says of himself that he is weak in body and nerve, and one can deduce from his narrative that he is not particularly strong in the head. So he is well equipped to picture in loving detail and with meek adoration an embodiment of pagan force and arrogance. Guy Livingstone is the bearer of an ancient name, heir to a large estate, and free from money cares, handing a blank cheque to a friend for his honeymoon expenses and showing a faintly disdainful surprise when the cheque is filled in for a meagre thousand pounds. After trampling his way through school and Oxford, where he batters a prize-fighter into 'a heap of blind, senseless, bleeding humanity', Livingstone takes a commission in the Life Guards. Even as a boy there was a set sternness about his lips and lower jaw, and this effect, Hammond noticed, was increased after he joined the Life Guards by a heavy moustache which 'fell over his lips in a black cascade'. A very different person, one would say, from Dean Farrar's Eric, whose history appeared in the year after Livingstone's. Yet no one in a popular novel can escape the spirit of his age. A deadly duellist, an intrepid rider to hounds, a heavy player, an irresistible lover, with never fewer than two affairs in hand, Livingstone nevertheless becomes, like Eric, a prize for which the powers of good and evil contend. As Russell, Eric's good angel, and Brigson, 'a fore-front fighter in the Devil's battles', struggle for Eric's soul, so Constance Brandon and the seductive enchantress Flora Bellasys struggle for Livingstone's. The odds seem against Constance, in spite of her rare loveliness, for she is an ardent ritualist, and to go to church with a beautiful woman is foreign to Livingstone's temperament. The reader senses his increasing restlessness, and is less taken aback than Constance when Guy and Flora, withdrawing into a conservatory heavy with tropical scents, are surprised in a long embrace. But the last round goes to Constance, who, as is usual with virtuous characters in Victorian fiction, lacks physical stamina. Sinking into a rapid decline, she sends for Guy on her death-bed, and makes him promise to break with Flora and to become gentler and more unselfish. Having broken with Flora in an interview marked by even more than his usual ferocity, Livingstone goes for a Mediterranean cruise with Hammond, who takes it as a sign of his friend's growing gentleness when Livingstone, instead of smashing in a recalcitrant Italian's face, lifts the man up by his throat, holds him suspended against a wall, and eventually lets him drop, green with terror, but unhurt. The further efflorescence of Livingstone's kindlier side is delayed by an episode in which a man who has killed one of Guy's friends collapses into idiocy under the menace of his pitiless thirst for vengeance. But all ends well. Livingstone, fatally injured in the hunting-field, expresses himself in such penitent and affectionate terms on his death-bed that Hammond breaks down, and when all is over leans his forehead against the corpse's cheek, sobbing like a helpless child. Guy's grave, even in the depth of winter, is strewn with the choicest of exotic flowers. The hand that strews them is Flora's.

Ouida's *Moths*, the third novel in this volume, appeared in 1889, the year when Zola published *Nana* and Ibsen was writing *Ghosts*. The sun of Byron was setting at last. Ouida (Louise Ramé, as Mr Powell accurately but rather unkindly calls her, Louise de la Ramée as she preferred to call herself) did not belong to high society by birth, and, though her novels brought her into contact with it, her unattractive appearance, rasping voice and bad manners debarred, or saved, her from the vicious and hollow triumphs enjoyed by the corrupt and cankered beauties whom she flays in all her writings with such unflagging zest. To balance matters, she was accustomed, by the exercise of a powerful imagination, to identify herself with her proudly innocent and peerlessly beautiful heroines. When *Moths* came out, Mr Powell tells us, Ouida wore the white gown of its martyred heroine, Vera Herbert, who, to save her mother's honour, marries Prince Zouroff, a vile profligate of immense wealth and a lineage more ancient than the Romanoffs. Vera's innocence, the magnet which attracts Prince Zouroff, casts a spell no less potent, though incomparably more elevated, on Corrèze, the great opera-singer, whose father, son of a marquis beggared in the Terror, had tended goats on the pastures fronting the Pennine Alps across the valley of the Rhone. An unspoken love springs up between Corrèze, weary of countless conquests, and Vera, surrounded by flatterers, destitute of friends. Now here, now there, by a rushing river in the Austrian Alps, in a lonely church on the bleak Polish plains, the divine voice of Corrèze rises unexpectedly to comfort her sad heart. People begin to talk, there is a duel, and Prince Zouroff shoots Corrèze in the throat.

High above the Rhone valley, in an old house, simple yet noble and filled with the gifts of kings and emperors and cities, Corrèze and Vera live alone. Some hundreds of miles to the north-west Zola is poring over the latest statistics of infanticide. Up there in Norway Ibsen is collating his notes on general paralysis of the insane. No matter. Corrèze is leaning over the stone balustrade of his terrace, some pages of written music, the score of an opera, on a marble table near by. Beside him stands Vera, a serious sweet luminance in her eyes. The air is pure and clear as crystal, strong as wine. A cattle maiden sings on the high grass slopes, a freshwater fisherman answers the song from his boat on the lake below.

A. P. Herbert

Topsy and the Fresh Mind

Trix darling I've made the *most* voluminous error I've *alienated* the Editor of *Undies* and now I don't believe I'll *ever* be a dramatic critic, well my dear you shall hear what happened and judge for yourself, well I told you he's been giving me *little* commissions to test a girl's mettle didn't I, and the other night he rang up in a *great* state my dear *two* minutes to cocktail-time and said *could* I fly *straight* off to Hammersmith (*Hammersmith!* darling) and go to the first night of a play called Othello, well my dear I'd *just* dressed as it happened but not for Hammersmith which it seems is half-way to *Bath* darling and *quite* insanitary, however that's the sort of horror an economic girl has got to face, well when I tell you that I had *no* dinner and the taxi took me *right* across England, my dear at Hammersmith they talk *pure* Somerset, well of course I was *madly* late and I merely *wriggled* over *nine* pairs of the largest knees, all in the dark, my dear *too* unpopular, and I had no programme and no dinner and no cigarettes so I merely *swooned* into my seat and prepared to enjoy the new play.

Well after all this *agony* what was my horror, well when I tell you that it was the most *old-fashioned* mellodrama and *rather* poor taste I thought, my dear all about a *black* man who marries a white girl, my dear *too* American, and what was so *perfectly* pusillanimous so as to make the thing a *little* less incompatible the man who acted the black man was only *brown*, the merest *beige* darling, pale sheik-colour, but the *whole* time they were talking about how *black* he was, my dear *too* English. Well of course the *plot* was *quite* defective and really my dear if they put it on in the West End not a *soul* would go to it except the police possibly because my dear there were the *rudest* remarks, well this *inane* black man gets *inanely* jealous about his *anaemic* wife the *moment* they're married, and my dear she's a *complete* cow of a woman, my dear *too* clinging, only there's an *obstruse* villain called Yahgo or something who *never* stops lying and my dear for *no* reason at all that I could discover, my dear it was *so* unreasonable that every now and then he had to have the *hugest* soliloquies, is that right, to explain what he's going to do next, well he keeps telling the old black man that the white girl has a fancy-friend, well my dear they've only been *married* about ten days but the black man merely *laps* it up, one moment he's *Nature's* honeymooner and the next he's knocking her down, and what I thought was so *perfectly* heterodox he was supposed to be the *world's* successful *general* but my dear I've always understood the *sole* point of a real he-soldier is that they're the *most* elaborate judges of *character* and *always* know when you're *lying*, and if this black man couldn't see through Yahgo it's *too* unsatisfying to think of him winning a *single* battle against the *Turks*. Well for that matter this Yahgo was the *sole* person in the play who had the *embryo* of a brain and *whatever* he said they *all* swallowed it, but my dear I *do* think that a really professional liar like that must have had *years* of practice and you'd think anyhow Yahgo's *wife* would have known something about it, but *oh* no my dear she went on like the others as if Yahgo was *George* Washington, well so it went on and at last the black man smothers the girl, my dear *too* physical, but of course if *any* of them had had the *sense* of a Socialist it would *never* have happened, because my dear simply *all* the black man had to do was to say to the subaltern Look here they say you've been taking my wife out, is there anything in it, and he would have said Not likely General, I've a girl of my own, which he had though my dear the young man was *Nature's* fish and only a half-wit would have suspected him of an anti-conjugal *thought*, well then the black man would have said Well Yahgo says you have, and then there would have been explanations and everything, but of course it never *occurs* to the black man to talk to the subaltern, he *merely* goes and bullies his wife, who *merely* crumples up, poor cattle, but if only she'd said Look here less of it what's your evidence, oh yes and I forgot there's the *most* adolescent business with an *embroidered* handkerchief, my dear the wife drops her *favourite* handkerchief which the black man gave her and Yahgo's wife who adores her and looks after her clothes *picks* it up, but my dear *instead* of giving it back to the wife she gives it to Yahgo who puts it in the young man's room, and my dear the young man *must* have known it was the wife's because she *always* wore it, but *instead* of taking steps he *merely* gives it to his own girl and asks her to *take out* the embroidery, my dear *too* likely, well she gives it back to him in the *public* street while the black man is watching, and when the black man sees *another* girl giving the young man his wife's handkerchief *instead* of saying Hi that's my wife's property how did you get it he *merely* goes off and murders his wife, my dear *too* uncalled-for.

Well my dear when a play is *perfectly* hypothetical from beginning to end I do think a play is a little *redundant* don't you, even if it's very well written, but my dear *this* was written in the *most* amateur style, my dear never using one word if it was possible to use three, and my dear the *oldest* quotations and the *floppiest* puns, my dear *cashier* and *Cassio*, *too* infantile, and my dear the *crudest* pantomime couplets at the end of the scene, and immense *floods* of the *longest* words which *sounded* rather marvellous I must admit but my dear meant *simply* nothing, but everyone else seemed to think it was *too* ecstatic so perhaps they'd had dinner, well at the end there was the *most* unnecessary slaughter and the *entire* stage was *sanded* with bodies, because the black man having killed his wife Yahgo killed *his* too because she argued, my dear *too* Harrovian, and really my dear I thought the whole thing was a fraction unhealthy and *saditious*, don't you?

Well at the end there were the *most* reluctant speeches and dahlias and everything, and I stayed for a bit in case the author appeared, because I thought it might be one of those *primitive* women, and then I *rushed* home and wrote down *just* what I thought about it and really I was *rather* proud of it, but my dear this morning the Editor of *Undies* rang up, my dear it's *too* wounding it seems the *whole* thing was written by *Shakespeare* and it's *quite* well-known, well of course my dear I've scarcely *looked* at the man, so I said to the Editor Well you said you wanted a *fresh mind* didn't you, and he said Yes of course but you mustn't have a fresh mind about *Shakespeare*, because it

A. P. Herbert

isn't done and so there we are, well I rang up Mr Haddock and asked him to buy me a Shakespeare because I want to see if it's true, well he's been in and he gave me *rather* a lecture because he said it's a bad sign if a girl can't appreciate great tragedy because he said Aristotel or some *sedimentary* Greek said that tragedy was better than comedy because tragedy was about fine people and comedy was about mean people, well I said tragedy must have changed since Aristotel then because this play was about one absolute cad and one absolute half-wit and one absolute *cow*, and then suddenly my dear I had emotional trouble and merely *burst* into tears, my dear what *is* the matter with me I'm *always* liquidating these days, however Mr Haddock comforted me, my dear *too* understanding, and after a bit he sat down and read some Shakespeare to me, which was *rather* flower-like I thought, and really my dear on a comfy sofa in front of a good fire with Mr Haddock and some hot-buttered toast a great deal of Shakespeare sounds *quite* meritricious, so try it Trix, your *cultured* little Topsy.

E. M. Delafield

Femina's Supplement

THE EDITOR WHISPERS TO WOMEN

What a week it has been for us women! Our men-folk have been more than a little preoccupied with the big Ministerial crisis, those terrible air-disasters, and the imminent threat of a European conflagration on no mean scale. But to us it has meant the ever-present anxiety of keeping our husbands good-tempered, and of knowing just the right moment to bring up the question of that little bill from the Stores! Who was it, I wonder, who said that *Life is made up of little things*?

This week you will find Femina's Supplement just brimming over with Features. There is the Guiding Star column, in which our astrological expert tells you how to face life in the coming week. Then your friend, Ann Applecart, has, as usual, answered all questions dealing with those intimate heart-problems peculiar to women. Ann Applecart's mail-bag, I can assure you, is by no means the lightest one in the office.

For mothers there is a very simple, very homely, page of advice in which questions of diet, health, psychology, eurhythmics, religious instruction, summer-weight clothing, table-manners, parties, and sex-lore are reverently and yet competently dealt with by a trained expert. And the not-so-young, as well as the not-so-old, will surely revel in the article on Loveliness, that will help you to look different. It's that differentness, as we all know in our heart of hearts, that makes a girl or woman feel, as well as look, different, so that men realize she's somehow different, and look at her in quite a different way.

Don't fail, either, to dip into Hints Corner. Your men-friends will come in to Sunday supper ever so readily when you serve the delightful, yet thoroughly economical, dishes of which you will read in Hints Corner.

Then, for the very thoughtful, there is Miss Vera Hopchalk's provocative, authoritative, and profoundly moving article: 'How Shall I Tell Baby the Truth?' specially written for Femina's Supplement. You are invited to send in *your* views on this very vital and urgent question of the day. (Postcards only.)

Nor must you overlook the Philosopher's Corner, where there may be just that quiet word in season that is going to help you through the week. So many of our readers write us gratefully to say that the Poet-Philosopher has put into words just what they themselves had been thinking. Who knows but that *you* may be the next one to write in? And speaking of writing, the Correspondence Column has never been more popular. Read it, and learn what the world is thinking today.

In lighter vein madame and mademoiselle alike will enjoy the sparkling account, written by a titled Marchioness, of recent social functions, a very intimate glimpse into some of Society's loveliest bathroom-decoration schemes, and, last but not least, our very unique 'Pot-pourrie'd Paragraphs', in which the world-news of the day is offered to women in convenient tabloid form. As was said in the days of Merrie England – but the words are none the less true in this so-called twentieth century of ours – 'a feast of reason and a flow of soul'. THE EDITOR.

GUIDING STAR FOR THE WEEK

This is a week when you must not expect too much from husbands, fathers, or boy-friends. Mars being in the ascendant will cause many moments of irritability and these will be specially noticeable amongst those who are staying with relations. Mothers-in-law, beware! It will be better not to give advice unasked, borrow money, or arrive uninvited for a long stay just at present.

The stars are not too propitious for affairs of the heart. It will be difficult to get men to come to the point, and almost impossible to keep them there. At the same time, lovers need not despair, provided they keep their tempers, eschew jealousy, suspicion and mutual nagging, and avoid anything like a tête-à-tête.

In business, fortunes will be made and lost. Journeys will be taken, and letters both read and written.

To those whose birthday occurs this month: The coming year will bring you a certain number of worries. These, however, if taken in the right way, will help to develop your character. They will also, if taken in the wrong way, help to develop your character. The transit of Venus should cause you to remember that each birthday leaves you a year older than did the previous one. Try not to let this discourage you.

The week's colour-vibration is eau-de-nil, nude or oyster.

FOR MOTHER
By Nurse Katherine

Today I want to say something about *carefulness*. So many mothers today seem to neglect this homely, simple, somewhat old-fashioned virtue. Only the other day I heard of two dear kiddies being dropped from a fourth-storey window from sheer carelessness. A really careful mother, giving her mind to what is after all a woman's foremost job, would probably never have let this happen. '*There is more evil wrought by want of thought than want of heart.*'

Keep the little ones from eating toadstools, playing with red-hot pokers, paddling in dangerously deep waters, and the like – even though it *does* mean that little extra ounce of carefulness on mother's part.

Nail-biting, too, is a bad habit and should be guarded against. And one word, finally, about winter-woollies. These must not be put on, or left off, either too late or too early.

Now goodbye until next week, when I shall have something to tell mothers about that fascinating hobby for child-lovers: psycho-analysis.

E. M. Delafield

PHILOSOPHER'S CORNER

We are none of us ever too old to learn. Dame Nature's teaching I, for one, never spurn. Today, in a wood, I saw trees and trees. What, I thought, can I learn from these? Then, clinging tenderly, climbing high, a twining ivy caught my eye. It clung to the oak through wind and rain, tempests had tugged at its fronds in vain. And the oak, with sheltering boughs above, seemed to look down with protective love. Call me fanciful, sentimental an' you will, the vision is one I cling to still. And as I bent my steps workward again, I knew that the ivy had not clung in vain. It had brought a vision of Love to cheer a tired man through the coming year. THE POET-PHILOSOPHER.

LOVELINESS
An Outspoken Whisper

Are you as lovely as you ought to be at fifty-eight? Do men run after you, call you glamorous and Garbo-like – or do they take one look and then ask your granddaughter to dance?

Many a woman has turned away from the ballroom stamping and shrieking because she has caught the whisper: *Too old to romp.* And how unnecessary it all is! No one need be too old to romp. What does it matter if your birth certificate says sixty-one so long as your face screams eighteen?

The newest discovery of science, brought from the mystic East by a titled beauty of Mayfair, and put up in artistic alabaster jars in our own salons at moderate prices, will turn you into a Marlene Dietrich or a Shirley Temple.

And one word more: A two-guinea jar contains exactly *twice* the amount that a one-guinea one does. You will therefore effect a veritable economy in purchasing the larger size at once.

And oh, the difference!

ANN APPLECART'S ADVICE

Last week I wrote frankly about the type of man who will dance with a girl but will not propose. This time I want to tell you just what I think of those girls who take away other girls' boy-friends. This is, literally, a very unfair thing to do. The competition nowadays is so keen that the motto of each of we girls must be: 'Don't interfere with me and I won't interfere with you.' Of course, if a man breaks away from a girl because he is sick and tired of her, the position is somewhat different. In that case anyone is free to have a try for him and very often the best friend of the girl he has thrown over gets him on the rebound, by showing him a sweet, womanly sympathy in his disappointment.

But so long as a girl is actually still going with a man it ought to be a matter of honour amongst other girls to keep off the grass. Anything else is not only unsporting, unladylike, and un-English, but it is even bad policy, because a girl who tells damaging stories about another, or steams open her love-letters, or deliberately makes mischief, is unlikely to make a really good wife, and men instinctively realize this, although they may not say so. So remember, hands off *fiancés* and near-*fiancés*. It will pay you in the end.

Now for some of my readers' love-problems.

Annoyed and Heart-broken:

Yours is a very difficult position. To be told in so many words by the man who is taking you out that ninepence is more than he is willing to spend on chocolates seems to indicate that he does not think you worth a very great deal. If the same thing happens again you might try a little raillery, saying that you suppose he is saving up for the dining-room suite, or something of the kind. This may bring matters to a head.

He Married my Sister:

Time is a great healer.

E. M. Delafield

Inferiority Complex:

Frankly, dear girl, this is your own fault. You cannot hope to be a success with men if you never meet any. Look up some of the girls with whom you were at school, especially those with brothers, and say how much you would like to meet them again and talk over those jolly days in the Fourth Form. If nothing comes of that make friends with any girl in the office who has a widowed father or a bachelor uncle.

Engaged but Doubtful:

You must remember that in a country where there are not enough men to go round almost any boy is better than none. Try and point out lovingly to your *fiancé* that his behaviour is unmanly, cruel, treacherous, despicable, ungentlemanly and liable to get him sent to prison. Do not, however, break off the engagement.

Jilted:

There is no reason why you should not keep the diamond ring, and he cannot force you to return it. If it is, as you say, a really *good* stone, it will be of some comfort to your wounded affection in the dreary years ahead.

Next week I want to discuss quite openly the reason why some men seem to prefer their typists to their great-grandmothers.

SOME SOCIETY BATHROOMS
By a Special Correspondent

The party of the week, needless to say, was the one given at Lady Pinto-Thistleby-Wagge's new town house on Thursday last. We all ended up in the bathroom, admiring the new scheme of decoration – cork walls, a cork floor, cork ceiling, and, with just that touch of originality that makes all the difference, no bath of any kind.

Pretty sub-deb. 'Winkie' de Blue has designed her own bathroom – talking of these so necessary adjuncts to our modern craze for beauty culture. 'Winkie' has very definite views about the importance of *colour*, and her choice is *escargot*-grey and the new plum-pudding shade.

Lord Egglime – better known to us all as 'Eggie' – gave me a wonderful tip *à propos de* bathrooms. (Like so many of our ex-public school boys, he has gone to work in earnest, and is a fully qualified plumber.) He tells me that it is *never* advisable to let the bath overflow, as it leads to so many things getting wet. Thanks a lot, Eggie.

Next week I hope to tell you just what Society is doing in the way of good works, which I hear are being taken up with enthusiasm this season by some of our smartest young unmarrieds.

HOW SHALL I TELL BABY THE TRUTH?
By Vera Hopchalk

(Miss Hopchalk, who lives in Surrey and is devoted to Siberian crabs, has written this article especially for Femina's Supplement. In it she discusses frankly and fully the difficult question of WHAT to tell your baby, HOW, WHEN and WHY.

What are YOUR views? Read what Miss Hopchalk has to say, and you will find that you will either agree with her or disagree with her.)

It is never too early to tell Baby the truth. The old-fashioned mother did not always realize this and left the eager little six-months-old mind to work out for itself the meaning of the Facts of Life. And oh! how soon Baby realizes that the truth is being kept from him! Once let him find out that he is not being told the *whole* truth about *everything in the world* by his mother, and his faith in her is shattered for ever. As a wise old friend of mine once said to me in the *Bois de Boulogne*:

'The truth is the truth, my dear.'

And that's so true, isn't it?

In my own case – though I'm not 'mummy', alas, to any little chicks, but only 'auntie' – I find that it is always best to answer questions when they are asked. Never before, never afterwards. Just *at the time*.

I cannot lay down any hard-and-fast rule as to when that time will be. Instinct must guide you. Some little ones ask questions before they can talk, others never ask at all. But that does not mean that they do not want to know.

There is only one Golden Rule: whether Baby wants to know or not, it is up to you to tell him everything.

POT-POURRIE'D PARAGRAPHS
(World-news presented to Women Readers)

Politics

The Foreign Secretary's favourite colour is blue, his lucky stone the peridot, and his white Persian cat is named Artaxerxes.

Sport

A Scottish lassie playing cricket in Australia has made twenty-three runs *not out*. Well done, Caledonia!

At Wimbledon, shorts will be worn.

The World of Science

Professor Tod Mangleby, speaking at Popville, Texas, said recently that a safe and speedy method of slimming is to eat no starches, fats, protein, alkali or vitamins for eleven months in each year.

Art

Film-star Colleen Clifford is seeking a divorce from her fourth husband, Gum Breeches, on the grounds of cruelty, incompatibility, and false pretences. Colleen is now featuring in the name part of the new big production: 'Uncomplaining Angel'.

America's newest craze, shortly to be heard over here, is a hot swing-number entitled: 'I'm Standing on my Head about You'.

Literature

A new serial, with a strong love-appeal, starts in this paper next week. It deals with the daring, but age-old, problem: What does a woman want from Life?

Our readers will find the answer next week in Femina's Supplement.

D. B. Wyndham Lewis

Meet Irene

One has to be careful about this fine book. Some years ago, when the first edition was published in Belfast, Mr Barry Pain allowed his joy to get the better of his discretion, and retribution was swift. '*This so-called Barry Pain*,' wrote the indignant authoress, beginning a commination of the most fearful description ...

The admirable Nonesuch Press, which prints such beautiful editions of the classics, has just issued 'Irene Iddesleigh' in a charming *format*, with three of the original wood engravings by Mr W. M. R. Quick. I am going to be extremely careful about this superb book. I am going to begin by warmly but judiciously praising the picture on page 49, which is a portrait of Sir John Dunfern, a Baronet accustomed to peruse the evening papers with 'his accustomed grace'. We see Sir John at the moment when he is exclaiming to his bride:

'Speak! Irene! Wife! Woman! Do not sit in silence and allow the blood that now boils in my veins to ooze through cavities of unrestrained passion and trickle down to drench me with its crimson hue!

'Speak, I implore you, for my sake, and act no more the deceitful Duchess of Nanté, who, when taken to task by the great Napoleon for refusing to dance with him at a State ball, replied "You honoured me too highly" – acting the hypocrite to his very face. Are you doing likewise?'

Here, I observe from the text, Sir John, whose flushed face, swollen temples and fiery looks were the image of indignation, restlessly awaited her reply. I see from the illustration that in his agony Sir John has allowed his trousers to sag. One hand is clutching his whiskers, the other grasps the back of a plush armchair. I presume that he has been tearing wildly at his braces.

In the year 1897, recollect, Baronets wore their trousers baggy. Sir John's are simply incredible.

Reflection. Perhaps his wife grew cold to him on this account.

We may glance briefly at another illustration. It shows Sir John extracting from his Davenport (a kind of bureau) a letter concerning the wicked tutor, Oscar Otwell, who has robbed him of his bride. Sir John's trousers are still dastardly. In his anguish he has forgotten to pull them up at the knees. His moustache is drooping a great deal. A little Macassar Oil would have improved it. His –. But you are no doubt waiting for a précis of the plot. We should most fittingly begin, perhaps, with the opening words of the authoress herself:

'Sympathize with me, indeed! Ah, no! Cast your sympathy on the chill waves of troubled waters; fling it on the oases of futurity; dash it against the rock of gossip; or, better still, allow it to remain within the false and faithless bosom of buried scorn!'

Such were a few remarks of Irene as she paced the beach of limited freedom, alone and unprotected.

Now we can get on. The characters are:

SIR JOHN DUNFERN, of Dunfern Mansion; a man of 'forty summers, he never yet had entertained the thought of yielding up his bacheloric ideas to supplace them with others which eventually should coincide with those of a different sex.' Marries –

IRENE IDDESLEIGH, 'another beam of life's bright rays'. An able and beautiful girl. She runs away with –

OSCAR OTWELL, 'her noble and well-learned tutor', and emigrates with him to America, leaving behind her little son –

HUGH, whose bright nature 'chased away all gloomy cavities from the mind of Sir John'.

I need not say that the Baronet is well avenged. After his wife's flight with the tutor – she was one of the women who like tutors – Sir John sent for his solicitors, and, ordering his will to be produced,

Demanded then and there that the pen of persuasion be dipped into the ink of revenge and spread thickly along the paragraph of blood-related charity to blank the intolerable words that referred to the woman he was now convinced, beyond doubt, had braved the bridge of bigamy.

Observe in passing that in 1897 bigamy among smart people was considered a sign of ill-breeding. But wait! Irene's Oscar turns out a dirty dog. He gets a post in a public school in America, but is soon compelled to resign 'through courting too great love for the all-powerful monster of mangled might – Intemperance'. What follows is inevitable:

With beastly force did Oscar Otwell enter Shandon Cottage on the night of his open dismissal from Waketown Public School, and rousing from sleep his wife, with monster oaths inflicted upon her strokes of abuse which time could never efface.

Oscar then drowns himself and Irene sails for England, to be discovered at Sir John's tomb by her son. 'False woman! Wicked wife! Detested mother! Bereft widow!' exclaims the young Sir Hugh. 'How darest thou set foot on the premises your chastity should have protected and secured! What wind of transparent touch must have blown its blasts of boldest bravery around your poisoned person and guided you within miles of the mansion I proudly own?'

We leave Irene in the grounds of Dilworth Castle, 'cold, stiff, and lifeless as Nero', with the Marquis of Dilworth casting stinging looks of shame on her body. Sir Hugh, I am pleased to say, 'being strongly prejudiced by a father of faultless bearing, resolved that the sharers of beauty, youth, and false love should never have the slightest catch on his affections'. And so the story ends.

Well (to resume), it is difficult to realize the existence of trousers like that. Lovers of the illustrations to the novels of Miss Charlotte M. Yonge will remember that the Heir of Redclyffe's trousers closely resemble Sir John Dunfern's. I forget what happened to the Heir. 'Love, alas,' says Mrs Amanda McKittrick Ros, discussing the affair of the tutor, 'when smitten with the sword of indifference, dieth soon, but once struck on the tunnelled cheek of secrecy with the hand of pity there leaves a scar of indelible intolerance, until wiped out for ever with the curative balsam of battled freedom.'

My personal feeling is that Oscar, though a drunkard and a wife-beater, *pressed his trousers under the bed*, and was for that reason irresistible to every woman who beheld him. It is curious that Carlyle, who wrote such a lot of rugged and incoherent Germanic jargon about clothes, never discovered what must have been a deciding factor in the home and foreign policy of the Victorians: their trousers. Take Gladst –. No. Take Disraeli, who had the Old English love for green velvet waistcoats, perfumed hair-oil, jewellery, and fal-lals. His canary trousers (though not the kind I should care to be seen about town in myself) were undoubtedly smooth and flowing: and everybody knows what influence he had over the Queen. The pair now preserved at Hughenden, which are venerated by the Primrose League, once a year, are proof of this. It is patent to me that Oscar Otwell's trousers insensibly gained him the ascendancy over the heart of Lady Dunfern. Her eyes rested on them with a pang of pleasure; and then, turning and seeing Sir John in the old concertinas, she felt nothing but scorn. She then committed bigamy.

Another reason why 'Irene Iddesleigh' is a better book than 'Lord Raingo' – I am still praising this book, observe – is that it has far more exclamation marks. It is also a better book than 'The Outline of History', 'May Fair', 'Some Reactions of Colloidal Protozoids', and 'The Chartered Accountants' Year Book for 1926'. I first read it very lovingly in 1914, and almost immediately afterwards was called upon to fight. It will live. In a few years scholars will quarrel over its text, collating, comparing, indexing, and being generally tiresome. In the year 1936 Mr Tipplegrape will write a long authoritative critical study of it for the *London Apollo*; but till then, I say, it will undoubtedly live.

Rebecca West

from *The Young Rebecca*

SPINSTERS AND ART
The Considine Luck by H. A. Hinkson
The Spinster by H. Wales

The baldness and badness of popular novels is as touching as
the ugliness of a cherished rag-doll. What overflowing tenderness
must be in the heart of the child who loves this monstrosity, we
think. And so with the people who read these novels – what
tireless imaginations they must have, to perceive joy in these bare
chronicles! We superior persons are too feeble to go searching for
beauty on our own like that. We wait idly until Thomas Hardy
comes back from witnessing fierce wars between the flesh and
the spirit, and Conrad sails home from the strangest and most
distant tropic. But the common man picks up some artless work
such as *The Considine Luck* by H. A. Hinkson, and creates his
own beauty. He takes the puppet heroine, Grace Smith, and
paints her wooden cheeks with the flush of his sensuous dreams;
he lights her eyes with the radiance he has seen in unattainable
women in pictures or at theatres, till Grace Smith is more fair
than his first love. In a sense he writes his own books.

I fancy that *The Considine Luck* is the sort of book that the
Bishop of Bristol referred to as 'wholesome literature', in his
recent address to the pupils of Colston Girls' School, advising
the young ladies not to adopt as a profession the writing of
objectionable fiction. (Surely his Lordship is mistaken in regard-
ing this as an important opening for women. Nobody ever tried
to bribe me to write objectionable fiction. And the people who
tell you that they came to London five years ago with three
shillings and are now worth half a million, did it by inventing

new kinds of sausages and things like that, not by writing objectionable fiction.) The only thing that distresses me about the work is the startling promiscuity of the second heroine, Flo Dallas. A simple child of nature, reared on the Irish hills, she nourishes in her young bosom a pure passion for Sir Jasper, the hero, until one day her cousin, Hugh Venables, breaks the news to her.

'I suppose you have heard the news?'
    'What news?' she inquired, with a throb of anxiety.
    'That Sir Jasper is going to marry Grace Smith.'
    'Marry her,' echoed Flo blankly.
    'Yes, no doubt about it ...' But Flo was not listening. She had sat down at the foot of the tree and, after making several brave attempts to control her emotion, she suddenly burst into tears.

I regret to say that when she got up again she was engaged to Hugh Venables. This is a form of treachery that constantly takes place in novels. For a lesser thing than this Winston Churchill was called a turncoat. And there is still some scandal talked about St Peter. The hero who suffers from unrequited love is allowed to go away and shoot big game in decent despair. But the heroine may transfer her allegiance with horrid facility.

Another lady of trying habits is Mr Hubert Wales' *The Spinster*. We have all of us had experience of the terribly confidential old lady in the crowded railway-carriage who will tell us about the operation her son has just undergone, and how it runs in the family. The Spinster was troubled with a similar unbridled candour. Although close on forty, and gifted with that training in deceit which an unattractive appearance imposes on women, she goes about confessing (with imbecile quiet dignity) the secret of her life to her sisters, her cousins and her aunts, the butcher, the baker and the candlestick-maker, and – finally – a coroner's jury. I abstain from revealing what the Spinster's secret really was, in view of the fact that Mrs Humphry Ward is a reader of *The Freewoman*.

All the same, *The Spinster* is a great work. This is the first production by Mr Hubert Wales that I have ever read. I was held from the very first page, whereon I read: 'There were reservoirs of love in her – of wife-love and of mother-love – accumulating reservoirs, which had never been tapped.' This is luscious imagery. 'The Tapping of the Spinster' would be an exquisite title for a poetical play. And the conception of fate as a Metropolitan Water Board regulating the flow of spiritual liquids is immense. I find Mr Wales difficult to place as an artist. Undoubtedly his style derives largely from Mr Frederick Harrison, though the breezy incident of the Spinster's mother throwing the new potatoes at the housemaid obviously shows the influence of Strindberg. In philosophy it would not be too much to say that Mr Wales stands shoulder to shoulder with Ella Wheeler Wilcox.

THE FOOL AND THE WISE MAN
The Woman Thou Gavest Me by Hall Caine

A Manchester bookseller, provoked to articulateness by the Press on the subject of banned books, said surprisingly: 'People in Manchester are very particular about what they read. Hall Caine, H. G. Wells and Corelli are not a bit more read than Arnold Bennett, Galsworthy and Hichens.' Only by marrying that bookseller and by living with him for years could one come to the roots of this marvellous classification. He may have divined the common fate which undoubtedly lies before Mr Caine and Mr Wells. Their books get longer and longer. Some day the parlourmaid, pushing back the study door against the rising tide of manuscript, will discover the distinguished author suffocated by the proof sheets of his new novel. And there is a tie between their latest productions. Both take the position of woman with an extreme seriousness which we must find very flattering.

To us intellectuals *The Woman Thou Gavest Me* has a personal appeal which *The Passionate Friends* has not, for the heroine, Mary O'Neill, is undoubtedly drawn from Mrs Beatrice Hastings of *The New Age*. Her incapacity for forming friendships with her own sex and her extraordinarily rich emotional life constantly remind us of *Pages From an Unpublished Novel*. She was naturally pure, blind-pure, and this quality was fostered by early upbringing in a convent, the atmosphere of which was perhaps all that could be expected of an institution whose Mother Superior had first been found on the doorstep at six o'clock in the morning dressed as Bacchante with a cluster of grapes in her hair and an extremely unconvincing story on her lips. That had, of course, an effect on the discipline. For instance Mary's favourite novice eloped with the father confessor and maintained him in London in a way that would now be interfered with by the Criminal Law Amendment Act (1912). From this stimulating atmosphere Mary was torn by her father and forced into a loveless marriage with Lord Raa. On their wedding-night she rebuffed his advances in a scene that would look well on the cinematograph, and henceforth they lived a celibate life. Unfortunately poor Lord Raa fell in with one of Mary's schoolfellows from that phallic convent and naturally ceased to be a celibate. About the same time Mary fell in love with an Antarctic explorer. It was the kind of chaste love which one stucco angel perched above a sausage-maker in Kensal Green Cemetery might feel for the angel perched above the draper across the path; but the convent breeding would out. 'I did not knock at Martin's door. I took hold of the handle as one who had a right. It turned of itself and the door opened. My mind was in a whirl, black rings were circling round my eyes, but I heard my trembling, quivering, throbbing voice, as if it had been the voice of somebody else, saying: "Martin, I am coming in." '

The Antarctic explorer, ignorant of Mr Caine's artistic economy of material, left the next day: but of course there was a baby. For the rest of the story Mr Caine suffers from a perpetual cold in the emotions: there is an extraordinary indecency about catarrh. As soon as Mary finds out that she is going to have a child she runs away from the Isle of Man to London, wishing that she had never left the sympathetic atmosphere of the convent. She had no money but was at first succoured by the one respectable schoolfellow of whom we hear, who had taken up rescue work; probably to keep in touch with things. However, this aid fails her and she has fallen into dreadful poverty when she receives the last blow: it is rumoured that the explorer has been lost in the Southern snows. Thereafter her story, apart from its general bearing on the segregation of the feeble-minded, has the same moral as Tennyson's 'Maud': always keep a half-penny for the *Star*. The young man in 'Maud' languished on the Breton strand because he had not the sense to read the papers to see if he had really winged his man. Mary never had the curiosity to buy a paper to see whether the rumour about her lover was ever verified. So, lonely and penniless, she is about to sell herself on the streets to get money for her starving child when the explorer embraces her in Piccadilly Circus. That catarrh of the emotions impels Mr Caine to shatter the obvious happy ending and to kill her off by a catastrophe unparalleled in English literature: she dies of cold caused by drying her baby's more intimate garments – I have not the happy domestic touch that enables Mr Caine to be more explicit – on her own body when she was too poor to afford a fire. By the time one reaches this tragedy one is soggy with viscous emotion, like the toast under a poached egg.

The immense significance of this work lies in its binding. It is rich and restrained. It is the red of the suburban dining-room and has a loathsome granulated surface that sets the fingertips in a frenzy. To pamper the eye still further it is adorned with deep black lines, heavy gold lettering and two unconvincing designs of the dandelion rampant and couchant. One envisages the hundreds of thousands of quite repulsive people who will buy this book: people who live in unspacious houses and perform tedious duties and slake their voluptuousness on caraway seeds and the sermons of Mr R. J. Campbell and such mean pleasures. So now they are going to listen to Mr Caine on the wrongs of woman as they have listened to Mr Lloyd George on the wrongs of the poor. It will probably have the same effect on them. Just as this squalid mass that makes the damned compact Liberal majority has given doles like Old Age Pensions and the Insurance Act to the working class and kept them all the more the expro-priated classes, so it will give women a few little liberties and grind them down into the profounder slavery. The vote and economic independence must be used to subserve the insti-tutions that break the teeth of the hungry who bite into the earth to find their souls' appropriate food; the old Christian ideals of self-sacrifice will shackle them like irons. Though the monkey may have its chain taken off it will have to go on grinding the barrel-organ.

Beachcomber

Trousers Over Africa

Big White Carstairs has been spending a few days at the Residency in Jaboola. Imagine, then, his chagrin on discovering that his fool of a native servant has not packed his dress clothes. Being too humiliated to admit this, and too decent by far to pollute the dinner table by appearing in day clothes, he stayed in his room last night, pleading a headache. His hostess herself brought him up some dirtibeeste soup, but he had locked his door, and dared not open it, lest she should note the absence of the ritual uniform. He pleaded giddiness. Whereupon the Resident sent Dr Gilmartin up a ladder to break into the room. Poor Carstairs, half-starved and mortified with shame, unlatched the window, and confessed the whole truth to the kindly physician, who promised to keep the secret, and later brought him a cupful of cold curry. But what, oh what, will tomorrow bring forth? The native tailor, perhaps, may come to the rescue.

Meanwhile the hostess tried once more to bring Carstairs some comfort, this time with light literature. The Resident found her, at 10 p.m., whispering outside his door, 'Let me in. I have a *Life of Livingstone* for you.' 'My dear,' said the Resident, 'don't you think? I mean to say – the natives – this time of night – better come away.' Amazed at the scurviness of her husband's mind, she flounced away from the door, leaving Carstairs to his martyrdom.

Poor Carstairs! Having feigned illness rather than admit that he had no dress clothes with him, he has had to keep up the pretence, and cannot even appear during the day. His hostess, with diabolical persistence, sends him dull books by the ton. Yesterday he determined to confess the truth, and when the Resident called from the veranda, 'How are you today?' Carstairs began, 'The fact is I –' But he got no further. The words stuck in his throat like shark-bones. How could a fellow admit that he hadn't got any dress clothes with him? He would be the laughing-stock of Africa. So he kept his guilty secret, and remained in his room until – oh joy – a trader who happened to look in for a drink brought word of a dress suit left in his hut long ago by a political officer. Carstairs confessed his predicament, and the Resident at once sent a native to fetch the suit. But Carstairs, fuming in his room, said to himself, 'It'll be years out of date. Wrong pockets. Stripe down trousers too narrow. What a pos-ition to be in!'

A pretty kettle of fish! A beautiful cauldron of mackerel! A fine saucepan of turbot! The dress suit arrived at the Residency yesterday, and Carstairs unpacked it with feverish fingers. Ha! No trousers!

A fellow in the middle of Africa without dress trousers! A tiny cog in the great machine of Empire! A ball-bearing in the skates of the Raj! And no dress trousers!

Poor Carstairs! When the Resident banged on his door and asked if he was dressed, he had to pretend he had had a relapse, and couldn't appear at dinner. The Resident then informed him that on the next night there was a large party, and that it was most important for him to meet a new political officer and various high officials.

On rejoining his wife, the Resident said, 'He may be big, he may be white, and his name may be Carstairs, but he's a queer bird. Seems to be always ill.'

In his room Carstairs paced to and fro, almost tempted to envy those backward and superstitious foreigners who dine in ordinary clothes. And that foul thought, against which so many Englishmen have battled successfully, remained with him until he fell asleep.

Once more, last night, Carstairs had his evening meal alone in his bedroom. The Resident, having been once more informed of the truth, feels that the whole situation is becoming rather absurd, and is hinting that the visit has lasted long enough. After dinner both he and his wife talked to their guest through the half-open door of his room, for, of course, he could not appear in day clothes, even after dinner was over. The conversation was stilted and dull, and all three were soon yawning.

'I suppose,' said the Resident's wife, loudly enough for Carstairs to hear, 'I suppose, my dear, he couldn't just wear his dinner jacket and stiff shirt and so on, with ordinary lounge suit or flannel trousers.'

'Impossible!' snapped the Resident. 'Nor would he consent to do so.'

'Not for a moment!' said Carstairs indignantly.

For decent men always stick together in a crisis.

So it is stalemate still. All day long Carstairs takes part in the normal life of the Residency, but the moment it is time to dress for dinner he retires and is seen no more.

The Resident sat at his desk writing a confidential report to the Colonial Secretary on the subject of a grant for a local fire brigade in Jamalawoo. A faint hum in the air made him raise his head. Far above the Residency a single air machine was circling. It came lower and lower. Carstairs, sunning himself on the veranda, shaded his eyes to watch it. The machine descended to about 200 feet above the ground, and the pilot, leaning out, threw a small object overboard. This object floated down until it got caught on the flagstaff. The Resident dashed out. 'Saved!' cried Carstairs excitedly, as he waved to the departing machine.

'What do you mean – "saved"?' asked the Resident peevishly.

Carstairs pointed to the flagstaff. 'My dress trousers,' he said simply, and he added: 'I hope you will include in your next report to the Colonial Office, sir, a strong recommendation for the fellow who brought them.'

'That's a personal matter,' said the Resident touchily. 'Your trousers are not a State affair. And, damn it, we can't have dress trousers up there when the flag is hoisted at sundown. We must get 'em down.'

They got the trousers down from the flagstaff, and everybody was happy. Even the natives whistled at their work. The Resident said, 'Now we can dine together like civilized people.' Old Umtifooti grinned broadly as he sounded the dressing gong. The household was at peace.

But what is this, dirty reader? In his room Carstairs almost weeps with rage. For the dress trousers are not his own, and are apparently intended for a man the size of a house. He tries them on. They are monstrous. And at that moment the cheery voice of the Resident cries, 'Are you ready, old boy? Get a move on.' Desperately the empire-builder tries expedients. The trousers are so big round the waist that he has to wear four shirts, one on top of the other. They are so long that when he has finished tightening his braces the trouser-top shows above the bulging waistcoat. They are bell-bottomed, like a sailor's, and still so long that his dress shoes are muffled in them. And the Resident is shouting impatiently. With beads of perspiration twinkling on his forehead like fairy lights, the miserable Carstairs stumbles and shuffles towards the drawing-room. His paunch of shirt is so fat that he cannot see the trailing trousers. But he sets his teeth and enters the room with as jaunty an air as he can manage.

The appearance of Carstairs in the doorway of the drawing-room was followed by a ghastly hush. The Resident's eyes grew round with horror. His wife wanted to laugh. For Carstairs looked like a circus clown in his enormous billowing trousers and with his padded stomach bulging. He himself, as though conscious of all this, paused on the threshold in some anxiety.

'What – on – earth –?' gasped the Resident. 'Look here, old man, I don't want to be personal, but why don't you wear braces?'

'I am wearing braces, sir,' said Carstairs, flushing angrily.

'Well, what the devil is the matter with your trousers? And why have you padded yourself out? This is not a circus, after all.'

The Resident's wife, shaking with mirth, moved away to a window.

'I must apologize, sir,' said Carstairs with ridiculous dignity. 'These trousers aren't mine. They don't fit.'

'So I observe,' remarked the Resident, with an angry glance at the floor, where several inches of trouser obscured each of the empire-builder's feet.

Shrugging his shoulders, the Resident called to his wife to lead the way into dinner.

Stumbling and shuffling, and with one of his four shirts over-flowing outside his waistcoat, Carstairs followed.

Dinner was a dreadful meal. Carstairs, owing to the four shirts which he wore to make the enormous trousers fit round his waist, had to sit back from the table, and as he leaned forward to his food the trouser-tops appeared above the straining waistcoat. The Resident affecting not to notice these things, clicked his teeth impatiently. When finally the waistcoat burst with a report like a small airgun, one button hit him on the cheek, another fell into his wife's glass, and a third rebounded from the ceiling on to the head of the native waiter, who fled screaming from the room. 'I'm really most terribly sorry,' said Carstairs.

'Deuced awkward,' said the Resident. And then, very loudly, 'Of course, we can't go on like this. We must get you some proper dress clothes somehow, damn it. Look here, can't you, I mean, tighten up your confounded braces?'

'They're as tight as they'll go,' said Carstairs. 'If they burst –'

'If *they* burst,' roared the Resident, 'the whole show will come tumbling down, and a nice pack of savages we'll all look. Why four shirts should be necessary to hold your trousers up is beyond me. However, things have changed since my young days.'

'I think I'll leave you men to your fun,' said the Resident's wife with a tolerant smile.

The manly conduct of Carstairs at the Residency, while enhancing his popularity, has done nothing to solve the immediate problem. *He has no dress trousers.* The Resident's wife, a kindly lady, said yesterday to her lord and master, 'Look here, old divot, tonight there'll be only a few at dinner. No guests. Couldn't we kind of stretch a point for Carstairs?' 'You mean,' thundered the Resident, 'you mean, *let him dine in day clothes?*'

'Why not?' said the châtelaine.

For a moment the Resident seemed to be about to burst in pieces. His neck swelled. His face turned magenta under its chemical sunburn. Then he shouted:

'Have you gone mad? *What on earth would the natives think?*'

'Ah, I had not thought of that,' said she.

'One must never cease to think of that,' roared the Resident. 'Better he should starve than give a lot of agitators in England a chance to say that Greater England is represented by fellows who can't even dress decently.'

'Yes, dear,' said his wife soothingly.

'Time to dress.'

The voice of the Resident broke in on the despair of our hero. Hot African twilight, guests about to arrive, and he trouserless. Suddenly he shot to his feet. He had thought of a way out. 'Oh, sir,' he shouted, 'I wonder if you'd mind if I wore my kilt tonight. It's the gathering of our clan, back in Busby, tonight, and the old customs, you know . . .' 'Delighted, old boy,' said the Resident.

In his bedroom he said to his wife, 'That fellow Carstairs is an odd customer. Wants to wear a kilt. Some damned local Scottish nonsense or other.'

Carstairs, meanwhile, was rigging up a bath towel with safety-pins.

The guests were arriving – traders, political officers, agents, *dibris*, a doctor, a missionary, and so on. The entry of Carstairs, in evening dress, save for what looked like a bath towel, caused a stir. 'His clan,' explained the Resident. 'What clan?' queried one of the ladies. 'The Clan Lochjaugh,' said the Resident, on the spur of the moment. 'They have the right to wear a white kilt.' Carstairs hung his head in shame, and when the Resident's wife said loudly, 'The white kilt of the Lochjaughs looks very like the white bath towel of the Resident,' the empire-builder flushed and stammered. There was a ghastly silence.

All were silent at the dining-table, while Carstairs, with rare courage, explained what had occurred.

'My kilt,' he said, 'is a bath towel. I am not a Lochjaugh. I deceived you all. But what was the alternative? I had no dress trousers.'

A murmur of admiration greeted this manly confession, made so simply and quietly.

'Anybody,' said the doctor, rather churlishly, 'could have lent you a spare pair.'

Carstairs lowered his eyes. 'I didn't dare to admit I needed them,' he said.

Here the Resident came to his aid. 'Knew a chap down-country, at Papawatta, who came to dinner in ordinary togs. Sheer ignorance, I suppose. Or damned Bolshevism. He was sent home. Damned good cricketer. Outsider, though. Grammar school or something. Knew another chap, up-country, at Wappapoopa. All right. Top drawer. But *made-up* tie. Tied by some infernal machine. Came off at dance. Picked up by his poor wife. She tried to hide it. No good. Sent home. Plucky little woman. Met 'em last year after Henley. Tie still made-up. Hopeless.'

'A man like that would murder his own grandmother,' said a young political agent.

'Probably did,' said the Resident.

'Look here, sir,' said Carstairs, 'we must settle this. Either I must come in to dinner tonight in ordinary clothes, or else we must go through this farce again, with four shirts and those awful trousers.'

The Resident looked at him icily.

'Are you suggesting,' he asked, 'that I should encourage you not to dress for dinner?'

'Certainly not, sir,' said Carstairs. 'You know what my choice would be. I'm only thinking of you and your wife.'

'Then don't,' said the Resident with a bark. 'Think only of the Raj.'

Carstairs was about to leave the room when the Resident added, 'But, damn it, try to be presentable. Can't you *cut* off the ends of the trousers?'

'By Jove, sir,' said Carstairs, his eyes alight. 'That's the idea.'

That night, happily and carelessly, the scissors were wielded – too carelessly. The trousers became shorts. There was nothing for it but to go in to dinner. The Resident hated unpunctuality. In the doorway appeared Carstairs, still with four shirts to fill up the waistline, and with dress trousers which ended at the knee. The Resident's wife went into screaming hysterics. The Resident said in his parade voice, 'Major Carstairs, are you a political officer or a – a – some damned kind of fat Boy Scout in mourning?'

And then – oh, joy! a parcel arrived from up-country, addressed to Carstairs. His dress clothes. At last everything was going to be all right again. The Resident, when he heard the news, smiled broadly. 'Now,' he said, 'we can get back to normal decent living.' An American lady explorer was asked to dinner, and Carstairs regained his self-confidence. During the day he inspected the native cricket team, and gave a short lecture on the team spirit. When he went to his room to dress for dinner, he found the dear, well-remembered clothes laid out on the bed. He could have hugged them. He fingered the coat, the waistcoat – and then horror caught him by the throat. There were no trousers! Feverishly he examined every corner of the room. He summoned the native servants. No. No trousers. In a rage he paced his room, ignoring the dressing gong. And when the Resident knocked on the door and shouted cheerfully, 'Get a move on, old man!' he gritted his teeth.

The dinner gong went. The Resident knocked and shouted again. 'What's keeping you?' he cried. 'That parcel,' answered Carstairs in a voice of despair, 'contained everything but my trousers.' Outside the door there was a short, sharp gasp, and then the bellow of a creature mortally wounded. 'Damnation!' shouted the Resident, 'this is more than I can stand!'

It cannot be said that any tears were shed when Carstairs left the Residency at the end of his visit. It had been a nerve-racking time for everybody. The Resident, with bluff good humour, said, 'Next time you come, old boy, I suggest you bring your dress clothes.'

Hardly had he left when the post arrived. Bale after bale of parcels addressed to Carstairs, and all marked, 'Dress Clothes. Handle With Care.' They were offerings from well-wishers all over the Empire, but, alas, they arrived too late.

'One more day,' said the Resident, 'and he'd have had enough trousers to make a sleeping-bag for an elephant.'

'One more day,' said his wife, 'and I should have forgotten my

Position and begged him to dine in day clothes.' The Resident glared at her as though she had plunged a dagger into his chest. 'I know you don't mean that, little woman,' he said uncomfortably.

To the Editor,
The Daily Express

Dear Sir,

I am sure many of your readers will fail to see anything excruciatingly funny in the idea of a gentleman habitually dressing for dinner. 'Beachcomber', like all subversive snobs, probably has no notion of the meaning of self-respect and prestige. I consider the whole Carstairs episode as not only bad manners, but disgracefully bad taste. And it is not the Empire-builders who are made to look absurd, but 'Beachcomber' himself. Of course, the idea of a man without trousers will always raise a cheap laugh from certain types of people, but I am sure it is not on the taste of such as these that your great newspaper has built up its popularity.

Yours faithfully,
'Not Amused.'

I enclose my card.

Serena Livingstone-Stanley

from *Through Darkest Pondelayo*

July 29th. Tikki Bahaar ... Well here I am in my first Pondelayan village encamped on what I suppose would be called the Village Green though practically nothing but sand. A few so-called houses scattered about like beehives built of palm leaves mostly containing copper coloured babies and old men with shells in their hair and things like bicycle pumps in their noses. Only two women so far with soupplates in their ears but Wogga Wogga says mostly away picking spinnach.

Well already Tikki Bahaar has made me quite homesick for Little Waghornet, – I mean the sanitary arrangements are so much like home with almost total absence of drains in the village street, though Placket says like their impertinence to call it a village at all having tried to buy some garter elastic this morning but not a sign of a shop. So Placket has come back very disgusted with Tikki Bahaar because all she could find to buy was an old woman cooking up something in a pot like black eels and seemed to be offering to sell her some but as Placket says 'What is the use of wasting good English money on a heathen mess like that when what you really want is a yard of white elastic!' Which almost seems as if Foreign Travel was teaching Placket a little commonsense at last.

Well I suppose I really ought to be trying to describe my first Pondelayan village while sitting here waiting for tiffin but somehow scenery seems quite the hardest thing to write down correctly in my Diary. I mean even though the forest is all very quaint and artistic with wild apes in the trees etc. somehow when describing scenery I always seem to run out of adjectives. I mean in England all the scenery is perfectly straightforward and historical like Queen Elizabeth's Beds and Ruins which everyone knows to admire but here in Tikki Bahaar there are no Beds and nothing historical except the Chief of the Village who is a hundred and seventy years old with a long beard but hardly counts as scenery.

So already I have begun admiring all the wrong things to admire in Tikki Bahaar like a young man sitting under a tree beating a camel's ear drum and anyone would think v. respectable and I have just taken his photograph with all his teeth showing, but Wogga Wogga tells me not respectable at all in fact a celebrated murderer and the Government offering half a crown for his skull dead or alive and quite out of place in my album. So if Alice Snaggers asks who he is when pasted in I shall merely say 'a friend' which is after all only a white lie though black. Also photographed a girl waddling past our tent with a ring in her nose exactly like Ork's bull at home and equally fat and in need of corsets, thinking it would be nice to have a good laugh with Alice and Mrs Whitecorn over the fire some wet afternoon with the album but Wogga Wogga says she is the Village Beauty and all the bachelors madly in love with her in spite of those hips and far from a joke. So evidently Ork's bull would be quite a roaring success with the bachelors of Tikki Bahaar – or perhaps I should say Ork's cow if they could see him – I mean her – but most unlikely.

Well to get back to the village even the Chief lives in one of the beehive houses at the end of the row and not even a doormat otherwise a very pleasant spoken old man with his hair in curl papers – at all events three wives and a couple of donkeys tethered to what I suppose the poor old gentleman calls his front door when we called with Mr Garble this morning. However, he welcomed us with great civility and presented us with the freedom of Tikki Bahaar, even Placket, who instantly sat down to write to her mother. Mr Garble presented the Chief with a nickel plated toast rack and a pair of braces in return. The Chief said he would wear the toast rack in his hair forever in memory of our visit and the braces as bangles having no trousers to keep up, although Francis and I hardly seem to notice nowadays who has trousers and who has not – except of course Mr G.

Tomorrow Griselda is to go and see the witch doctor who

practises in a cave a few miles out of Tikki Bahaar. Wogga Wogga says he knows the doctor personally and can highly recommend him, having cured his cousin of warts in a night so evidently something of a Beauty Specialist as well. Mr Garble is seriously thinking of seeing the Doctor about his bunion and has asked Wogga Wogga to find out about the fee.

July 30th... Lay awake all night tormented by wild apes scampering about on the polished top of our table tent who had come to visit Griselda. Mr G. took the precaution of chaining Griselda to the pole of her tent who kept up a hideous screaming till sunrise when F. and I fell asleep. When we woke up the wretched little creature had gone away with Wogga Wogga to her appointment with the Witch Doctor. All hoping that housemaid's knee takes a long time to cure so we can leave Griselda behind.

Wogga Wogga returned at lunch time looking very solemn without poor little Griselda which is very very sad. Because as soon as they got into the consulting room Wogga Wogga says she had a dreadful fit and fell down on the floor breaking both her legs and died of heart disease before the Doctor had begun to examine her. Everyone agreed how the poor little thing was almost human and Mr Garble said he felt the least he could do for Mr Marchmont's sake was to knock up a nice little memorial to Griselda here in the heart of the jungle she loved so well.

... Mr G. busy all afternoon knocking up a simple monument out of butter having no clay like an artist he knows called Michael Angelo who was too poor to buy any clay but we think not in such a hot climate as Pondelayo. Because in the end Mr G. had to put a saucer for the butter to run into on top of the pedestal instead of a portrait bust of Griselda but he thinks Mr Marchmont will be just as pleased with the kind thought which is after all what counts in Heaven just as much as a proper equestrian memorial. Because I have often noticed how all really famous people seem to be put on horseback once they are dead. F. says she is glad she is not famous enough to be set up on a marble horse for all her friends to have a good laugh at after she is dead and gone ...

Wogga Wogga reports the Witch Doctor agrees to cure Mr G's bunion for twenty bags of rice and one tin of asparagus. Very awkward, as we have only two bags of rice and no asparagus at all! Asked Mr G. why he does not write the Doctor a cheque instead? Mr G. explained there are no cheques in Pondelayo but only barter which he says is a very oldfashioned method of doing business and seems to be exchanging something you don't want for something else such as a crocodile's egg for a cocoanut though personally would not care about carrying a crocodile's egg round all day in my purse but then I should not want the cocoanut either. So Mr G. is thinking it over about the bunion.

Spent a pleasant hour with F. and Mr G. after dinner discussing a variety of subjects round the campfire such as the action of spinnach on the gastric juices and if Napoleon was really such a fine soldier which Mr G. thinks greatly exaggerated by the French, and Nature. Remarked what an ideal life one could lead in the jungle with no shops or post offices but close to the Great Heart of Nature. F. said 'Great Heart of your Grandmother! How about a bath now again and what happens when your hair brush wears out?' Afraid F. is apt to miss the poetical side of things like Nature, who said the pritzi flies were biting her ankles and went early to bed. Mr Garble and I stayed up a little longer to admire the moon. Somehow the moon made us talk about Romance and Money and all that sort of thing. Agreed how people can be ever so happy with ever so little so long as it is Debentures and not Love at First Sight. I said 'Look at Judge Wiggin he seems quite contented and he has hardly any.' Mr G. said 'Don't worry, little woman – the Judge has more than enough for what he likes to spend it on.' On the tip of my tongue to let the cat out of the bag on to thin ice about Judge W. being so hard up and my lending him five pounds but remembered my promise in time and said nothing. A pity Mr G. does not seem to properly appreciate Judge W's finer qualities! For instance how impressed he would be if only I could tell him about Judge W's wonderful kindness in looking after our money all this time ...

(Letter to Mrs Marchmont,
Mission House,
Bogtuk,
Pondelayo.)

TIKKI BAHAAR
July 31st

MY DEAR MRS MARCHMONT,

At last comes an opportunity to write to you my dear kind hostess. We miss you more than words can say! Spending a quiet day in camp alone with Nature and our fancywork as Mr Garble has gone off to visit the Witch Doctor, some five miles from here as the fly crows.

Well dear Mrs Marchmont How is the Tatting Class? Has that very dark girl finished her tray cloth yet – the one with the protruding stomach – Francis and I both thought it very bold in design. Have seen some pretty bead work here amongst the women but cannot buy any as there is only Barter, and the only thing these women seem to like is red flannel by the yard – very awkward – or concertinas – equally so. F. tried to tempt some of the women with an old lefthand kid glove but no success. Placket on the other hand managed to barter a set of muslin collar and cuffs for a rhinocheros horn from a blind man who instantly put them all on top of his head at once tied under the chin with a bit of grass and probably thinks he has bought a bowler hat at least poor fellow! – but how Placket is to get that horn home as big as herself is a mystery ...

Poor Mr G. has had a lot of trouble arranging to pay the witch Doctor's fee especially the tin of asparagus because the only tin in the village belongs to the Chief who got it from a missionary forty years ago and has used it to ward off evil spirits ever since. But you know what a way Mr G. has with the natives, somehow he has managed to persuade the old man to part with the tin – I think an electric torch without a battery.

Well dear Mrs Marchmont I must now close as Francis is waiting to borrow the ink. With all kind regards to your husband, Judge Wiggin and any other friends in Bogtuk and much love to yourself.

Yours sincerely,
SERENA LIVINGSTONE-STANLEY

P.S. We have not yet seen Professor Tronson though we hear he is somewhere in the district. Am looking forward to making his acquaintance. S. L-S.

... Mr Garble returned from the Doctor's in great spirits saying the Doctor has made a wonderful job of the bunion. At least he says it will be a wonderful job when Mr G. has taken all the jaguar's blood pills and recited all the poetry up to his waist in running water. Mr G. says the Doctor was so impressed with the size of his bunion he was obliged to give him twice as much poetry as usual which always comes expensive the Witch Doctor says and has told him to call back in a month's time on his way back from the Cataract.

August 1st ... As soon as he had told us the good news about the bunion yesterday Our Leader seemed on tentacles to be off and ordered the camels to be uncobbled for an immediate start intending to reach a place called the Lake of a Million Fishes in time for a late dinner but it was not to be. As bad luck would have it the medical cabinet had broken down for the twentieth time since leaving Bogtuk and Wogga Wogga and the boys had to go back to the nearest cocoanut plantation for some new sets of wheels some five miles away on the opposite side of Tikki Bahaar. Mr Garble obviously upset at the delay. Would have gladly suggested leaving without the cabinet but did not like to break our promise to the dear Colonel, never to travel without it, even though the skeleton key was left behind at the Cove but as F. says it is the Principle.

At all events while we were waiting for the cocoanut wheels Placket laid the table for afternoon tea with Mr G's watch leaning against the teapot counting the minutes and I had just begun on my first ham sandwich when something moved in the bushes behind the tea table and Placket though handing cream at the time called out 'Coo! Look at all them War Lords excuse me, Miss', and dropped the tray. Well if anyone had told me six months ago I should be attacked by armed warriors stark naked while half way through a ham sandwich! I would have laughed them to scorn but such was now the case! With bloodcurdling yells and shrieks they came leaping from the bushes in all directions waving their spears, and on every spear a paperbag marked Rice in black letters which is a sight I shall never forget to my dying day nor Mr Garble's face, white and drawn though half from *Through Darkest Pondelayo*

full of plum cake. Nor the Leader – a sort of devil painted bright red all over his body with little dabs of white paint on top and a great contraption on his head rather like Placket's rhinocheros horn but red too and huge goggling eyes. When this frightful apparition planted himself in front of poor Mr Garble actually knocking over the sugar basin with his club I thought my last hour had come, the other savages meanwhile falling on the sandwiches while F. and I slipped past them under the table and crawled under a cactus bush. It seemed a lifetime that we lay under that cactus bush listening to Mr G's heart-rending cries of 'Hoki Poki!' (It is a Lie! in Pondelayan). When the warriors had eaten every crumb of the sandwiches and all the jam the Leader gave orders for poor Mr G. to be bound hand and foot and after licking the jam off their fingers the warriors tied the unfortunate man up in a bundle in Francis' best table-cloth with the Maltese lace edging, and put a paper bag over his head marked rice and another over his two feet tied together and carried him off still shouting 'Hoki Poki' from underneath the bag. As soon as the warriors had disappeared into the jungle Placket crawled out of another cactus bush with her face covered in cream and Googli out of another the only one of the boys not away looking for cocoanut. Francis said to Googli 'If crawling under a cactus bush is all you can do in an emergency you are about as much use as a hardboiled egg – go and save your Master at once' just as the wretched Googli pointed with trembling fingers towards the Jungle and there were some more warriors crashing through the undergrowth, if anything fiercer than before! So three of the strongest warriors picked up Francis and Placket and me like three brown paper parcels and trotted away through the jungle but leaving Googli behind.

Well even the most respectable Englishwoman cannot go on screaming for an hour on end, even when being carried upside down by a naked savage through the heart of a tropical forest as I can prove by experience. I mean after the first hundred yards or so I managed to twist myself round a little, enough to get a look at my warrior, and he had quite a pleasant smile and I should think by the way he carried me quite a family man. I mean I must say in fairness to my warrior he did all he could to

81

make the journey as comfortable as possible and Placket and Francis say the same of theirs. So as it was very exhausting screaming all the way we agreed to stop, only starting again from self respect as soon as we felt ourselves put down on the grass in a sort of grove leading to a cave at one end and poor Mr Garble still wrapped in the table-cloth lying in front of the cave beside us with the Red Devil glaring down at us with his arms folded and rings of white paint round his eyes and his warriors behind him with raised spears blood red in the setting sun. Then the warriors came crowding round to look at Francis and Placket and me but the Red Devil seemed to be telling them not to touch so only poked us a little with their spears. Meanwhile Mr Garble managed to mumble through the maltese lace covering his mouth that this appaling Devil person was the Witch Doctor himself – though anyone less like a professional man without even a stethoscope and that dreadful colour I cannot imagine. So the whole trouble was over a trifling mistake in the settlement of Mr G's account that morning, which the Witch Doctor had discovered a few hours after Mr G. had left his consulting rooms. Because it seems that when the Witch Doctor opened the twenty bags of rice and found they were full of white river sand (which even an ignorant savage knows is no good at all for milk puddings) he lost his temper and started off in hot pursuit of poor Mr G. who of course knew nothing whatever about the sand, having filled up every bag with best quality rice with his own hands but the obstinate old brute of a doctor would not believe a word of it. In fact just as Francis and I were put down in the grove the Doctor was actually demanding from Mr G. not only rice but female hostages as well before he would let him free, but luckily the warriors were not very enthusiastic about the hostage idea, because Mr Garble told us afterwards they asked if there were no young girls in our party and Mr G. said 'Only this young lady here' meaning Placket. But all the warriors shouted out 'No thank you' so loudly the cocoanuts fell off the trees in shoals which is not a very nice thing for Placket to have to write home to her mother. So the warriors said if it was all the same to the Witch Doctor they would rather have something out of a tin instead of hostages and Mr G. told us what they were saying and so we all agreed to give them anything they wanted from our stores if only they would let us go free and get home before dark. Mr G's bunion all this time giving him Fits on account of the damp air. Upon hearing this the Witch Doctor untied Mr Garble out of the cloth and removed the bonds and we all walked back to the camp, the warriors walking in front and behind. P. said 'Coo! it feels like the Salvation Army walking along with all them drums.'

Reached our camp long after dark and still no sign of Wogga Wogga and the boys but only Googli asleep under the Pack Yam with plum pudding all over his mouth having opened the last tin, who I am afraid is a regular glutton. Well as soon as the Witch Doctor and his men saw the store chest full of tins etc. they got wildly excited and lit their torches and set the grass alight and threw the tins at each other and broke down the medical cabinet and smashed open the bottles and ate and drank everything in it even the Beechams Pills which I have always thought a strange hobby for such a great conductor to go in for making pills to that extent – but they say Sara Bernhardt was devoted to pingpong so you never can tell with celebrities – and Francis even saw one of the warriors spreading a packet of Epsom salts on a mangrove and eating that.

So they took the tinned peaches and all the jam and all the rice and sugar and flour and the sweet biscuits and all the sardines and ginger beer and the curried prawns from Fortnum and Masons and Francis says she only hopes they will cook them all up together and have a bilious attack, because to make a long story short the Witch Doctor and his men have really taken everything eatable in the whole camp including a pair of grey cotton gloves belonging to Placket drying on a bush which Francis says she hopes the Witch Doctor will eat himself pearl buttons and all as a punishment for treating a patient in such a disgraceful manner. So about midnight after they had taken everything they could find they went away and Mr Garble found a tin of boiled sweets in his tent and a bottle of Kvassa which is all we had for dinner, and still Wogga Wogga and the boys had not returned with the cocoanut wheels. So after dinner poor Mr G. whose nerves were in a shocking state with being tied up in a table-cloth for four hours felt rather better and had another drink of Kvassa and said he would certainly Air It in the Press so Francis said 'My table-cloth? I did not know we had a Linen Press' but Mr G. said 'No. "The Times"', meaning a gross breech of professional etiquette on the part of the Witch Doctor and the British Medical Association should be told. Presently Mr Garble cheered up a little more and he said it was a warning to him never to consult anyone but a Harley Street man again and if he had known what an old humbug the Witch Doctor was, and suspicious, he would not have paid him anything at all – not even sand.

C. A. Lejeune

Toujours Lamour

QUESTION. Who was She and what was her Jungle Love?

ANSWER. She was a lovely Malayan with plucked eyebrows, geranium lipstick, and two sarongs, one red and one blue, and Baab was her jungle love.

QUESTION. Baab who?

ANSWER. Bob Mitchell, pan-American pilot.

QUESTION. How did they meet?

ANSWER. Quite simply. He was looking for a lost flyer named Atkins, and his 'plane crashed in the Malay Archipelago.

QUESTION. Why did it crash?

ANSWER. Because his *fiancée* rang him up in a storm to ask him if he was thinking about her.

QUESTION. Was the Malayan his *fiancée*?

ANSWER. Of course not. The blonde, Eleanor Martin, was his *fiancée*.

QUESTION. You didn't mention her.

ANSWER. No, I assumed you had seen some jungle pictures.

QUESTION. What did Bob do after the crash?

ANSWER. He bled first, because the film is in Technicolor. Then he saw a chimpanzee and the brunette, Tura.

QUESTION. What did he say to her?

ANSWER. He said she looked like a squirrel in Hyde Park. He was an English actor, you see, and they had to account for his accent somehow.

QUESTION. And did she look like a squirrel in Hyde Park?

ANSWER. She looked to me just like Dorothy Lamour the heroine of *The Hurricane*.

QUESTION. But you said she was a Malayan?

ANSWER. Oh, no, she was English really. She had been brought to the island eighteen years before by a University graduate called Kuaka.

QUESTION. Why?

ANSWER. Because he was rich and cultured, wore sapphires and emeralds alternately according to the day's Technicolor schedule, and wanted his revenge on the white devils.

QUESTION. Rather thankless revenge, wasn't it?

ANSWER. Not at all. Tura was a great asset to the Archipelago. She played the guitar, served fruit dinners, threw a pretty knife, and sewed her sarongs beautifully. Besides, that wasn't all his revenge. He sacrificed one white man per annum to the sacred crocodiles.

QUESTION. Why crocodiles?

ANSWER. Because this is a Paramount picture, and Paramount have always been strong on crocodiles.

QUESTION. Where did Kuaka find the white men?

ANSWER. Oh, they just happened.

QUESTION. But if one year they didn't happen?

ANSWER. Don't be tiresome. With five script-writers on the story one was bound to happen. Besides, he had a white man in hand already – Atkins, the missing flyer.

QUESTION. Did Tura know about this crocodile business?

ANSWER. Certainly. Under hypnosis from Kuaka she beat the drum that summoned the crocodiles to dinner. She tried to warn Bob about it, but her English was hardly serviceable for detailed narrative.

QUESTION. Didn't she learn from Bob?

ANSWER. Oh, very quickly. In a couple of days she was singing 'There's lovelight in the starlight with you' with only the faintest trace of a Malayan accent.

QUESTION. What was Eleanor doing all this time?

ANSWER. Eleanor? Oh Miss Martin, the blonde. She was lying back in a *chaise longue* in a pink negligée.

QUESTION. Not exactly helpful, was she?

ANSWER. Give the girl a chance. Once she got over her first grief and registered a pastel triumph for Technicolor, she called out the U.S. navy and air force and went off to look for Bob herself in a neat yachting costume.

QUESTION. Did she find him?

ANSWER. Not for a long time. He was down in a subterranean temple watching Atkins being fed to the crocodiles.

QUESTION. Didn't he interfere?

ANSWER. He did all that a hero should. He said between clenched teeth, 'I don't like the look of this.' He registered manly horror. And then he embraced Tura.

QUESTION. Wasn't that rather unfair to Eleanor?

ANSWER. Oh, no. He said the two girls would be sure to like each other.

QUESTION. And did they?

ANSWER. Don't anticipate. Bob and Tura had to be thrown to the crocodiles first.

QUESTION. Why?

ANSWER. So that the publicity department should say that this picture *moves*. Against the lush background of the steaming jungle there is an increasing parade of *action*, in which hundreds of gaily-costumed natives and beasts, birds and reptiles of the jungle play their part. The climax is sensational, breathtaking, and realistic. The film is thrill-packed. The jungle is shown in all its colourful glory. There is also a big romantic appeal and much delightful comedy. Besides, what else were the crocodiles for?

QUESTION. Did they eat Bob and Tura?

ANSWER. You're so optimistic. Of course they didn't. The poor beasts never had a chance. There was a volcanic eruption; and the whole temple crashed down on top of them.

QUESTION. How did Bob and Tura escape?

ANSWER. Through a crack in the rock, apparently running on ball-bearings, and beautifully contrived by the script-writers. The earthquake wiped out Kuaka and half the natives, and the surviving crocodiles advanced in mass formation and finished off the others.

QUESTION. And then what happened?

ANSWER. Eleanor came running up the beach in her nice blue yachting costume.

QUESTION. What did she say when she saw Bob?

ANSWER. You're very anxious about Eleanor, aren't you? She's only a *fiancée* really, just a nobody. No jungle glamour, no sarong style, merely the other woman. She said, if you must know, 'Look there! It's Baab!' And then, 'Hullo, Baab, what an attractive native girl.'

QUESTION. And what did he say?

ANSWER. He said, 'Tura, this is Eleanor Martin, and this is her father, Mr Martin.'

QUESTION. Oh, was her father there, too?

ANSWER. Of course, it was his yacht. It was a very nice yacht. They all went back on board for dinner, and Eleanor changed into a black tulle evening gown.

QUESTION. Why had she brought an evening gown to look for a lost *fiancée* in the Malay Archipelago?

ANSWER. Stupid, she had seen jungle pictures, even if you haven't. She knew there would be an attractive native girl. Besides, black tulle is always good for a renunciation scene.

QUESTION. So she renounced him?

ANSWER. Of course. Her heart told her to. So did the five script-writers. So did the art director, who gave her a tropic moon to do it by.

QUESTION. And how did it end?

ANSWER. Tura dived overboard and swam back to the island, heart-broken. She hadn't read the full shooting script. She hadn't seen any jungle pictures. Nobody had told her about the renunciation scene. She crouched by a pool, kissing a crushed camellia, and crooned, 'I fell in love. What else could I do?' without the faintest trace of Malayan. And then she saw Bob's reflection in the water.

QUESTION. And the reflections kissed?

ANSWER. Ah, I see you *have* seen some pictures.

QUESTION. So he married Tura and not Eleanor?

ANSWER. Well, considering the social conditions of the island, that is a theme I would rather not pursue.

Note: 'I think the cinema is the very greatest art, with the possibilities of becoming the greatest art form that has ever existed.' – Mr H. G. WELLS, November 23rd, 1935.

Elizabeth Bowen

On Not Rising to the Occasion

Rising to the occasion: I do not remember that it was ever *called* that. No, I am sure it was not. There was no name for what one was asked to do – in a way, this made it all the more ominous. A name, the grown-ups may have thought, would have made too much of it – pandered too much to juvenile self-importance. Children, in my Edwardian childhood, were decidedly played down rather than played up. 'Just be natural' – they used to say, before the occasion; 'nobody wants you to show off.' What a blow to ambition – what a slap in the face! 'Be natural'; really, what a demand!

PLEASURE, GRATITUDE AND SYMPATHY

I could scent an occasion coming, a mile away. Everybody was going to be implicated in something tricky. Socially, 'they' were about to turn on the heat. It could be some primitive embarrassment was coming a shade nearer the surface than the grown-ups liked. This could have left me cold – *had* they left me out. But no, on what is known as an 'Occasion', children are useful. One was to be on tap. One would be on view. One would be required, and tensely watched. One would have to express, to register, something *extra*. Pleasure: 'Aunt Emmeline is coming, you know, today: do show her how happy you are to see her.' Gratitude, for a present or a party: 'And don't just mumble "Thank you": do smile, too!' Sympathy, with a grief: 'Look, here's poor Mrs X coming down the street: you need not *say* anything, just let her *see* you're sorry!' Interest, in anything that a senior chose to explain to one, tell one or point out to one.

Enthusiasm, for anything one was caused to see – scenery, famous or noble persons, some dreary, intricate curio from the East.

React, child! Demonstrate! That was all they wanted. It was not unreasonable, really – a child like a stuck pig *is* a dreadful sight. I do not want, at all, to give the impression that my childhood was an emotional forcing-house, or, still more, an unduly social one. It was not such a bad preparation for after life. People are always going to expect one to react, in some way: no harm in learning to be quick off the mark. And reactions must be appropriate, not excessive. This cannot be drilled into the young too soon ... or, can it? The Edwardians considered not. Today, I hear, many differ from them: there are some, aren't there, who go so far as to hold that children should not say 'Thank you' unless they do feel a surge of spontaneous gratitude, or 'Sorry' – when they tread on anyone's toe – unless they are truly stabbed by remorse. I do not think I can go into the rights and wrongs of it. I imagine there must be in each generation some children uneasily conscious of what is wanted, and uneasily certain they must fall short. They either cannot or will not deliver the goods.

Would this be recalcitrance, or plain nervousness? In me, it was a mixture of both – plus a wary dread of 'going too far'. If one crossed the very fine line, if one *went* too far, one's behaviour fell into the 'showing off' class. To celebrate the arrival of a visitor by whooping, prancing, clashing imaginary cymbals together over one's head was considered hysterical and excess- ive – I once tried it. And effusiveness, in the matter of gratitude, was, I was to discover, another error. 'Thank you, Mrs Robinson, so very, very much for the absolutely wonderful LOVELY party!' 'Well, dear,' my hostess would say with a frigid smile, 'I'm afraid it was hardly so wonderful as all *that*.' And, 'Who was that gushing little thing?' I could practically hear her say it, as I left the room. To this day I remember – and still with blushes, mortification – the awful number of marks that I overshot. After each excess, I had periods of stand-offish caution; I had to resort to the stodgy gruffness of manner allowed, I had seen, to little boys.

I connect so many occasions with stage-fright, paralysing self-consciousness, all but impotence. And, let me be clear, this was far from shyness. I was not a retiring child – I should not at all have liked to be banished from the scene of activity. I had dreams of glory in which I behaved conspicuously well, well to the point of evoking comment. But alas, in real life for a child to behave 'well' meant – above all things – never to be conspicuous. An occasion is an orderly grown-up concept, an affair of a thousand-and-one rules. The accustomed actors are old stagers; it is only the child who must walk on without having been rehearsed; though, still, with enough instructions to make it nervous. You see, the poor child is in the picture, but not the centre of it – unless of course, it is at its own birthday party. The child dithers somewhere round the margin.

In my long-ago childhood, it was important what grown-ups thought. They were the censors, the judges. Today, they have less prestige, they have abdicated from power, gone down in status: in some families, they seem like a fallen upper-class. Children, like freedmen going round in gangs, are rather more, today, in each others' power. Well, I say 'more', but honestly, looking back, I see that this gang-formation did go on in my childhood also: as an underworld, blinked at by the eye of authority. We children put one another to drastic tests. There was, for one thing, the dire 'I dare you ...' Tree and roof climbing to the extremest heights, blindfold acrobatics on bicycles, one-leg hopping along the tops of walls, balance on parapets over deep railway cuttings – these were the *sine qua non*. I daresay they are today? All the same, physical ordeals were less scorching than non-stop criticism. At day school, we kept a narrow watch on each other – the glances shot from desk to desk in the classroom, and we trailed each other down the streets when we started home. Forever we were keeping each other up to the mark, without committing ourselves by saying what the mark *was*; and this amounted, I see now, to a continuous rising to an occasion which – unlike others – never came to an end.

Friendships, for instance, were exacting: they involved the almost daily exchange of secrets which had to be of a horrific magnitude, and so did plans for Saturday afternoons. This was

Folkestone: there was the switchback railway, there was the outdoor roller skating rink, but we looked for something more desperate and more original. Keeping tryst with the dearest friend of the moment, it was fatal not to produce a bright idea. The search – for some reason – always devolved on me. I was forever devising, racking my brains and fancy, tying myself into knots, to think something up. The approach of a Saturday afternoon loomed over me far more darkly than school work.

'Well,' the friend would say, 'so what *are* we going to do?' A suspicious pause; 'or haven't you thought?'

'Oh yes, I have!'

'I hope it's not something silly.'

Thus encouraged, I would unfold my plan. 'That does not sound much fun,' she would remark. 'Still, it's too late to think of anything else, so I s'pose we may as well try. Come on.'

An un-thrilling Saturday could cool off a friendship. Folkestone in 1910 was dressy, law-abiding, and well patrolled; the amount of things children could do – bring off without being shouted at – was limited. Bye-laws, prohibiting almost everything, were posted up and down the Leas and along the woodsy paths of the undercliff. Oh, that initiative – why was *I* forced to take it? Yes, it took one's contemporaries, it took other children, to put that particular pressure on one. 'You put yourself out too much about your friends!' my mother would declare as, fagged-out, white in the face, I came tottering back to her through the Folkestone dusk. 'Why not let them amuse you, for a change, sometimes?' And indeed in my own mind I often wondered.

Would the strain become less as I grew older? No: on the contrary. When I was fourteen, fifteen, the dress-problem raised its ugly head. It was necessary to look nice, as well as be nice. Still more, it was necessary to look 'suitable'. But, my heavens, suitable to what? For life was to bristle, from now on, with unforeseeable occasions. In advance, these were daydream occasions: I dressed accordingly. In those days, the teenager was unguided. Fashion, now so kind to that age-group, took no account of us. So, trial-and-error it was, for me. Outcome: errors. The rose-pink parasol with which I all but poked out somebody's eye at a cricket match; the picture hat in which I attended a country lunch-party – only to be taken out ratting by my host; the ornamental muslin, with blue bows, in which I turned up at a grown-up beach picnic – *that* I disposed of by slipping off a rock into the sea. The splash was big, though the sea was shallow. The crisis obliterated my frock. Was my accident quite accidental? I cannot answer.

Yes, I think as a child I did better with my back to the wall – in extreme situations, among strangers. Whatever strangers could do to me, they could not bite, and there was the hope I might never meet them again. It was my near ones, my dear ones, the fond, the anxious, the proud-of-me, who set up the inhibition. I could not endure their hopes; I could not bear to fail under loving eyes. I detested causing a disappointment. Perhaps I exaggerated the disappointment? Perhaps I did less badly than I imagined? You see, it mattered too much. I shall never know. For how does one rise – fully, ever – to an occasion?

V. S. Pritchett

Faits Divers

I have been reading Dostoevski again: *The Possessed*. You know the sensation. You are sitting by the fire reflecting that one of the things which reconciles you to life, even at its most tragic, is the low clear daily monotone of its voice. Suddenly comes a knock at the door, there are cries. A man has been murdered at a house down the street. Dostoevski again. Dostoevski, 'the great sinner', the great literary murderer. You put on your thickest coat and go out. What a fog! What a melodramatic fog. You can see nothing. Such is the impression as one turns to those tortured novels again. But there's obviously a crowd somewhere down the road, you can hear voices, people go rushing by. Who is it this time? Shatov, you hear, the student, the ex-radical, the believer in the Russian Christ. Good heavens! There was no one more serious, more honest, more likeable than Shatov; rather difficult in argument because he had never got over a sort of angry awkwardness about his class. He was tongue-tied and shy one moment, violently angry the next. His anger soon passed, however, and then he smiled repentantly. There was absolutely no malice in Shatov. You hurry down the street, still seeing nothing. Shapes move about. They may be human. You call to them and they gesticulate but you can't hear what they're saying. Presently you make a disconcerting discovery, that you are in something like one of Kafka's nightmares; you are walking and yet making no progress. You begin to wonder which street you're in. People bump into you and don't answer questions. No one in Dostoevski ever answers questions. You just detect a scowling face which shouts at you. This one (he says he's an engineer) shouts that he is going to commit suicide. It is necessary to commit suicide to show that he has overcome fear of pain and the beyond. When he has done this he will be God, the Man-God, the superman. He vanishes. A girl shape stands dumbly in front of you; she desires, you gather, to suffer. Which way to the murder? you ask. No answer. Terrible complications. The air full of the sounds of people talking. A drunken Captain is beating his daughter and quoting poetry. You turn a corner and there is a young nobleman, handsome, cultivated, thoughtful, and what is he doing? He's biting the Governor's ear. And still, as in one of those anxiety dreams, your feet stick to the pavement, you make enormous, concentrated efforts of will, and you move about an inch instead of a yard. The fog chokes. 'Russia, the god-fearing nation,' someone shouts. 'Let us start an illegal printing press,' a girl says. 'Destroy everything,' come other voices, 'and then a new man will be born, a new society, harmonious, communistic, brotherly.' Or 'Russia's mission is to save the world.' And another voice, 'Russia must save Germany first from the catastrophe which is coming inevitably in the West.' And what is the catastrophe? 'Socialism! Socialism is the despotism of materialism, the ally of the Roman Catholic Church in the destruction of the soul.' You struggle towards that voice only to be pulled in the opposite direction by another. 'Christianity, communism, through the People and the purification of the heart.' At this moment you very nearly fall over a man who is on his knees before a woman, abased, weak and weeping; she is pulling his hair out. 'Love-hate,' they are murmuring. 'Who,' you ask, 'are all these people, all these voices?' A moan comes from the man: 'Relations,' he says, 'everyone has brought his relations.'

And then, the tension of the nightmare slackens, the fog clears and along come a middle-aged couple and you laugh for the first time. The humour in Dostoevski always clears the fog. They are quarrelling, of course. The man is talking all the time. 'Chère amie,' he says, as she gives him a violent push to make him shut up. Scholarly, noble-looking, vague and slopping a glass of champagne, Stepan Trofimovitch is straying and tottering along, pouring out epigrams, tag ends of French and cultural chit-chat. He will stop to make a speech about his dangerous political past and is alarmed the moment afterwards lest a spy has heard him or, worse still, in case someone lets on that he has no political past whatever and certainly no political future. And behind him comes Varvara Petrovna, twenty years his protector and his 'amie' but only in the sense that he used to smoke a cigar under the lilac tree with her in the evenings. A female rolling-pin, a torment and manager, dusting him, cleaning him up, mocking his feebleness, rating him about his gambling debts, but paying them, awed by his brains. For the last twenty years he has talked of beginning his great book. But there are the club, his cards, the perpetual apprehension of what Varvara Petrovna will do next. He must leave her; he can't leave her. Varvara Petrovna is another Madame de Staël whacking into her pet, Benjamin Constant. She pushes her tame intellectual and toy liberal along.

Man was born free, but not necessarily born with will or cash. What does man achieve? Nothing, except habits. On top of everything, Stepan has been married so many times. It is years since he has seen his son. How terrible the separation of father and son – and yet, just as well, for Stepan Trofimovitch has never been quite straight about money. So he goes on, speaking French, weeping, evading, making noble gestures, cheating, scenting his handkerchief, making 'final stands' about the intrigues of Varvara Petrovna – though not in her presence – while she, the masterful *intrigante*, frankly tells him he's a fool and that she's going to send a servant round to clean up, and then marry him off.

The nightmare, of course, again intercepts that comic intrigue. The fog comes down once more. But you have been distracted from the suicides, ear-biters, daughter-beaters and ideological murderers. As you grope once more it is the figure of Stepan Trofimovitch you seek, the bold voice of Varvara Petrovna you long to hear. He is in love and hates her, but with *them* the love-hate is nostalgia and comedy. And then the nightmare affects Stepan Trofimovitch, too. He *does*, to his own astonishment, make a 'last stand'. He walks out of the house. He is like that. He will take to the road. They said he had not the will to do anything for an idea! That his idealism was a fraud! He goes forth as exalted as Don Quixote (though far more rattled), follows a cow which is following some peasants, flabbergasts them by talking French, picks up with a Bible-seller, and rambles away, tragically, comically, but far from ignobly, to his death. Vanity is a friend to him to the end; it enables him to humbug on the very brink of eternity (this time about the Sacrament) and prevents him from realizing he is dying. It is he who explains the whole nightmare to you, all that fog, talk, intrigue, violence; who all these people are. They are 'The Possessed', 'the devils', and with the detachment of a well-stocked intellect he announces half-nobly, half-cynically, that 'he and everyone else in Russian politics are the Gadarene swine of Russia which must all be cleared out and driven to the sea, so that the wonderful new future may be born'.

The Possessed is a novel which contains one of the great comic characters of all literature; and the first 150 pages contain the best writing in Dostoevski's surprising comic vein. Lytton Strachey was the first to point out the individuality and importance of Dostoevski's humour. It steadies those toppling and seemingly intoxicated monuments. Critics usually refer to this gift as satirical, but as Lytton Strachey said, the humour is not cruel. If it begins cruelly it grows, deepens and broadens into the humour of loving-kindness. But there are other reasons for reading *The Possessed*. It is a political novel which – though many of its premises are derived from inaccurate information – deals prophetically with some of the political issues of our time. Tolstoy, not very sensitive in his old age, once said to Gorky that Dostoevski ought to have been a Buddhist; and Gorky said of Dostoevski that 'you could tell a petit-bourgeois as surely as you could tell a goat'. These are amusing examples of a criticism which seems to be passing out of fashion now that the fanatical Freudians and the narrower kind of Marxist have discovered that they were not really interested in literature. The only proper general political criticism of Dostoevski is, as a recent American critic, Mr Ernest Simmons, has said, that he expresses the confusion in Russian middle-class thought at the time, its ideals, its apprehension, its practice. We see the psychological discoveries of Dostoevski in better perspective when we remember that Constant and many others had written more precisely about the ambivalence of human character. We cool down when we reflect that the Self-Willed Man, the meek and the famous 'doubles of Dostoevski', are the fruits of the romantic movement which came to Russia late.

From the letters, diaries and notes of Dostoevski which have been made available in Russia since the revolution, the curious reader may discover that the fog he had been groping through is nothing to the personal fog in which Dostoevski worked. (I recommend anyone interested in the intimate processes of literary creation to read Ernest Simmons's *Dostoevski: The Making of a Novelist*). The main character types are repeated with growing emphasis from novel to novel, but they emerge from a nightmare of rough drafts and notes. Dostoevski worked in the greatest uncertainty and indecision. He was one of those writers who, having for a long time no clear and fixed idea of his intention, was obliged to lash himself into action by pious ejaculations. He worked, so to speak, on a stage, before an audience, delightfully unaware that there was something comic in his vociferations.

'I am planning' (when was he not 'planning'?) 'a huge novel' (they were always going to be 'huge' and transcendental) 'to be called *Atheism* – for God's sake between ourselves.'

The touch of persecution mania is part of the show. Then: 'the hero falls to the very depths of self-abasement and in the end he returns to find both Christ and the Russian soul. For God's sake do not tell anyone.' Tortured as the reader of the novels may be, lost in the wilderness of a dialogue which has eliminated none of the drooling and rambling of humanity's eternal tongue-wagging, worried by the involutions of the plot and the fact that no character seems to be able to appear without half his family and without at least one family skeleton, he is nevertheless far more certain than Dostoevski himself was as he struggled at his desk. He chops and changes his characters and events. He has constantly to write down the theme of his novel again in order to remind himself of what he is doing; and the theme is always drifting off its course. The change has been noted in *Crime and Punishment*: Raskolnikoff was intended to suicide. Ivan was thought of as the murderer of Karamazov. If Dostoevski's life was a search for God, his novels are a search for a method. The higher synthesis which he laboured after and retreated from in religion, only to labour after it again, plagued him too in the art of writing. The thing that strikes one in Dostoevski's novels is how, both in their ideas and their method of presentation, they convey the struggle, the search for something to be born, the longing to assume a shape. But perhaps it is not a longing for form. Perhaps the profound longing of Dostoevski is to decide nothing for himself, but to be dominated. It is significant that a formal Westernized writer like Turgenev is hated, and that when Dostoevski looks beyond Russia, his eye stops at Germany. That domineering race has attractive wastes of primitive myth behind the façade of its culture; and when the great catastrophe comes Russia, he says, will save Germany from the West and Germany and Russia will save the world. It is curious that the Nazis did not make use of Dostoevski's mysticism, though it goes really far beyond nationalism into mysticism. The race myth is there:

If a great people [Shatov cries in *The Possessed*] does not believe that the truth is to be found in it alone (in itself alone and exclusively in itself), if it does not believe that it alone is fit and destined to raise up and save all by its truth, it at once ceases to be a great nation, and at once turns into ethnographical material and not into a great people. A truly great people can never reconcile itself with a secondary rôle in humanity or even with the first, but without fail must exclusively play the first rôle. A nation which loses this belief ceases to be a nation.

The Russians are, in fact – God-bearing!

It is useless to try and disentangle the confusions from the subtleties of Dostoevski's thought. The great prophets are always playing for both sides. And then Dostoevski is a Victorian journalist. There is always a less exalted strain of compromise running through Dostoevski's life, a sort of left-handed self-interest such as makes the comedy of Stepan Trofimovitch's character. There is frequently something disconcertingly practical if not disingenuous about the mystics. Ideologically, Dostoevski is often in a panic. Yet, there are two perennial kinds of revolutionary thought; there is the political revolutionary who arises to change man by changing society, the religious who arises to change society by changing man. Dostoevski is brought nearer to us also because the catastrophe has come, the problem of suffering has become real; and if we cannot believe in the absolute value of suffering, any more than Dostoevski entirely did, it is arresting when we cry out egotistically against injustice to be reminded, as Zosima reminded Ivan Karamazov, of guilt.

Dostoevski was a spiritual sensationalist, a man of God somewhat stained with the printing ink of the late night final. He lives at first in the upper air as he plans his novels, and gradually comes down to earth, still undetermined until he is pulled up – by what? 'Ordinary' life? No, a newspaper cutting. What a passion he has for the newspapers! What significance things had once they were in headlines! The report of the Nechaev affair clinches *The Possessed*, a *cause célèbre* sets the idea of *The Idiot* in motion. These court cases pinned down his restless mind. Early in *The Possessed* Liza asks Shatov to help her compile an annual collection of newspaper cuttings of all the court cases, trials, speeches, incidents and so on, the child-beatings, thefts, accidents, will-suits, etc., which would serve to give a real picture of the Russian situation year by year. Dostoevski must often have longed for a book like that on his desk. For ordinary people were lost in an anonymity which thwarted the romantic temperament. In the *faits divers* they were transformed; give him the evidence and the process of mystification could begin. The *faits divers* could become the *faits universels*.

Mary Dunn

from *The Memoirs of Mipsie*

COMING OUT

What an auspicious event this was in the good old days, and how different from the present time, when a girl's figure scarcely changes with her début, and young people seem old before their 'teens. 'Do you mind awfully if I cut Lords this afternoon, Grandpapa?' my grandson said to Addle just before the war at the Eton and Harrow. 'There's a new film I want to see.' I was somewhat shocked, I must confess, but Addle said nothing. Indeed, he is inclined to be taciturn during a cricket match, and often his only remark during a whole day is 'Wait till the end of the over, dear.' (I suppose he thinks, in his old-world, courteous way, that the players would have to stop their game if I get up from my seat. He is always so considerate.) I am very fond of watching cricket myself, when with a cushion and a congenial companion one can spend the pleasantest afternoon, chatting of times past and present.

To return to girls' figures in the 'eighties, what miracles of elegance and womanliness they were. The tiny waist, the soft curves above and below, the smart bustle behind. I must admit, though, that the right effect was not achieved without trouble and sometimes tears. Gone were the days my mother knew, when she used to lie on the floor while an exceptionally strong footman (blindfolded of course) used to place one foot in the small of her back and lace her up. But a figure was still sufficiently important, in 1889, for Elsie Rye (Lord Peckham's elder daughter), on the eve of her coming out ball, to get her young sister to hammer in a croquet hoop round her waist while she lay on the lawn. Unfortunately the sister was then called in to bed and poor Elsie lay the whole night pinned to the damp grass and had pneumonia next morning. Another friend, Lady Mary Linsey-Wolsey, who had the misfortune to be very flat-chested, bethought her of wearing an air cushion inside her dress; but in the crush of a reception she unwisely mounted a chair – some one's hatpin punctured the air cushion, and the whole crowd looked on in horror while her corsage collapsed with a long whine.

Another trial was hair. Fashion demanded a hair style which needed great luxuriance of woman's glory, and although of course we Coots all had beautiful hair, others were not so blessed, and were forced to wear false switches or coils pinned on. (I hope my male readers will not be shocked to hear of this deception.) My cousin Clara Twynge was very unlucky in the management of hers. They kept slipping off, once into the offertory plate, and once into a jug of fruit cup at a ball, which added somewhat to her natural shyness. Indeed, between that and the fact that she was distinctly plain (I do not know why, for she was a close cousin of ours), she was scarcely ever asked for a dance, and some unkind girls dubbed her 'Cloakroom Clara' because she used to spend almost every evening in that sad spot. Eventually Mipsie heard of this, and with her usual warm-hearted sympathy soon put things to rights. At the next ball, when Clara entered the ballroom, all eyes were drawn to a card attached to her bustle: 'Still waters run deep.' That evening she was besieged with partners and received three offers of marriage, all of which, in her shyness, she accepted, which was fortunate as two of the suitors threw her over next morning.

Even in that age of beautiful women Mipsie's entrance into Society created something of a sensation. '*Qui est cette demoiselle là?*' asked the French Ambassador, a great connoisseur of beauty. When informed he said simply '*Tiens*' and continued to look at Mipsie. Even his Gallic eloquence was silenced by such loveliness, it seems. The same evening H.R.H. the Prince of Wales – afterwards King Edward VII – was evidently much struck with her. She happened, in the supper-room, to drop her fan almost at his feet. In a flash he had picked it up and handed it to her. A few minutes later she tripped on the staircase (she trips very easily I have often noticed) and his was the hand that came to her rescue. 'You are unfortunate this evening, Lady Millicent,' the Prince said gravely, while Mipsie blushed vividly at the compliment implied. A royal memory for faces is well known of course, but Beauty in Distress had evidently made an indelible impression on her future sovereign.

But, indeed, Mipsie was always the pet of Royalty. Her flashing wit and brilliant repartee often saved some difficult situation and turned a frown from a Royal brow. I remember one party at the Royal Yacht Squadron garden during Cowes week, when the somewhat austere King Crustatian of Iceland was the guest of honour. A sudden thunder shower had turned all the milk sour and H.M. was disposed to be annoyed, when: 'There shouldn't be any shortage of milk at *Cowes*,' said Mipsie audaciously. The Royal displeasure suddenly melted into a smile while every one blessed Mipsie for the quick wit that relieved the tension.

On another occasion she was able to do great service to her country by saving an Eastern potentate from an embarrassing episode. During a house party at the Duc de Tire-Bouchon's lovely château for the Chantilly Races, the vastly rich Great Curd of Bokhara had ordered a beautiful butterfly brooch to be carried out in rubies, amethysts and emeralds, the Duc's racing colours, as a gift for the Duchesse. This lovely jewel was to be placed, as a charming whimsy, in a naturalistic manner amongst the flowers at dinner. But the jeweller had made a mistake and used sapphires instead of amethysts. There was a nervous pause while every one looked at the butterfly and wondered what was wrong, for the Curd's face was like thunder. Then Mipsie, suddenly realizing the situation, took the brooch and swept him a deep curtsey.

'I am honoured, your Highness,' she said, 'both by the gift and by your gracious memory of our armorial colours.' It was a brave, splendid lie (for the Briskett colours are red and silver), told so as to save a foreign power from embarrassment. Relations were distinctly strained between our two countries at the time, so who knows what political strife, or worse, may have been averted by her noble action? But that is not the only time my dear sister, by her tact and brilliance, has helped her country, I am proud to say. At one time she was known as 'The Foreign Office Bag', so many statesmen and State secrets did she hold in the palm of her lovely hand.

ENGAGEMENT

Although my dear father and mother naturally wished to see their daughters married well, they were sufficiently idealistic in their attitude to matrimony to leave us entirely free in our choice, only stipulating that we should marry into the peerage (indeed we scarcely knew any one outside it so this was a needless precaution) and that our future husbands should have not less than £10,000 a year, so that we should be spared the misery of finding out for ourselves that 'Love flies out of the window when Economy comes in at the door' as the old saying goes. 'Ah, my dear,' I recollect an elderly lady saying to me when I was about twenty years of age. 'No one who hasn't experienced it knows the agony of soul that poverty and squalor bring.' She was speaking of the sale of their beautiful steam yacht which had to be effected before her husband could purchase one slightly larger.

My father was perhaps slightly more ambitious for his children than Mama was. I remember his referring to a certain German Prince who sought Mipsie's hand as 'jumped-up eighteenth century Royalty' and on another occasion he nipped in the bud what might have been a serious romance between myself and the very eligible Lord Gordon Dramm, heir to the marquisate of Deoch and Dorris. 'Gor', in spite of his strict Scottish upbringing, had grown up decidedly unconventional, and was rumoured to be friendly with writers and even, some said, *artists*, though it doesn't do to believe all one hears. Apart from this there was nothing serious against him, and he was the jolliest person imaginable, entering into every social function with great gusto and spirit. He had begun to single me out for special attention (giving me once, with lithe impetuosity, a sprig of white heather), and it must be admitted that I was equally taken with him. But one evening, at a dance at my old home, Coots Balder, I was waltzing with another partner and looking out (as girls will!) for my special admirer, when I saw a sight that froze the bones in my marrow. Gor was waltzing with another girl – and *he was reversing*! Immediately the dance finished I fled to my room and flung myself on my bed in floods of tears. Next morning Gor left, after a stinging rebuke from Papa, who afterwards told me never to mention the name of 'that bounder' again. It all shows what can happen to the best people by getting into the wrong company. Now, of course, I bless Gor for that solecism. I am sure my dear Addle has never done anything dishonourable or ungentlemanlike in his life. (Apart from anything else, he has never been sufficiently quick on his feet to manage the waltz at all.)

Perhaps it would be of interest to quote here two letters of my father's and mother's concerning Mipsie's future, which show the infinite and loving care with which parents in those days watched over their children's lives.

House of Lords, October 3rd, 1890.

MY DEAREST ARABELLA,

I have made inquiries about young Harborough. He has 15 thou. it is true, but his estate is heavily encumbered, and his pedigree cattle and his mother cost him too much. They say Ld Skein is a warm man. He is too old for an heir probably, so Mipsie could marry again when he dies, or better still live with us and could enlarge the west wing as I have always planned. On the whole, however, I favour Briskett, even if his money is made in meat. He has the best moor in Scotland and a fine house in town next door to my club.

Yr affectionate husband,
C.

Coots Balder, Oct. 6th.

MY DEAR BOGGLE (my mother's pet name for Papa),

I recd your letter yesterday and hasten to reply. Dearest, do you really think that the Duke of Briskett would make Mipsie happy? Money is not everything, and I cannot bear to think of our dear girl in those stone corridors at Briskett Castle. I know I should never feel anything but shivery there myself. Have you thought about young Ld Bodmin? Such a lovely place, as good as the Sth of France (you know what a shocking sailor I am) and I hear he is a nice young man, though illiterate they say, but of course Mipsie would manage all his affairs for him. I beg you not to decide in a hurry. Mipsie's happiness is all that matters to both of us, I know.

Yr devoted,
NIBBLES.
(My father's pet name for Mama.)

P.S. – I am told the Bodmin fishing is superb.

Eventually, as all the world knows, Papa's wishes for Mipsie's future prevailed over those of my mother, and my sister became engaged to 'Oxo' Briskett. She herself seemed oddly indifferent on the subject. I recollect her saying, with a strange bitterness for one so young, that she was beginning to find out that all men were made on much the same pattern. Yet I think she was happy in those engagement days. We used to have great fun opening the shoals of beautiful presents in the Orangery. Mine was the task of jotting down the shop labels on each present, so that they could be returned later if desired, for Mipsie was far too considerate to return them to the donors direct. Apropos, I cannot resist concluding with an amusing story of Mipsie's only slip in thanking for a gift.

It chanced that two Royal Dukes had both sent her a cake basket, Duke A's being of gold and Duke B's of silver. Mipsie *muddled up the Dukes* (an easy mistake to make) and wrote the following to Duke B.

I shall think of your Royal Highness every time I use your beautiful gift, which will be daily, as I love gold filigree above everything, and although I have been given a silver basket shall never look at it, for it is far inferior in workmanship and material to your Royal Highness's.

A second exquisite gold filigree cake basket arrived by special courier next morning!

MARRIAGE

Of Mipsie's wedding day I can say little, for I myself was in such a whirl that I actually walked up the aisle after her in goloshes with my dainty peacock merino bridesmaid's dress! The service was solemn and beautiful in the extreme, every stone of the lovely old Balder Church, set off to perfection by the cream of Debrett, every flower that Heaven – and our famous hothouses – had created, reflecting the splendour of the occasion. Yet it was all quite simple. Two bishops and one archbishop only performed the ceremony. A humble bandsman from Oxo's regiment played 'Ave Maria' on the bass trombone; while the bridegroom, for all his wealth and many titles, stood alone, save for his best man, at the chancel steps, just like any ordinary wedding. Thus, in that simple country setting, my sister Mipsie gave her hand to a man who never really attempted to understand her, or to appreciate her amazing qualities.

Things really started going wrong, Mipsie tells me, as early as their honeymoon, which was spent at Kings Maunders, the beautiful and romantic home of Lord Dotage, which had been lent for that supposedly happy time. One afternoon, Oxo could not find Mipsie anywhere and after a long search discovered her in a spinney talking to a young man who rented some of the shooting, under the impression that it was her husband. The two men were of much the same height, both fair with small moustaches, and Mipsie had only been married two days. It wasn't such a very serious mistake to make – but Oxo immediately took umbrage, as he always did at the adorable vagueness which was part of her charm.

The next quarrel was about the house. It must be explained that although the dukedom of Briskett was comparatively recent, the family of Loigne,[1] as Earls of Chine,[2] had lived in historic Briskett Castle in Northumberland since the Conquest. Queen Elizabeth had stayed awake all one night in the State bedroom,[3] King Charles II[4] had shot an oak-apple off his brother's head in the park, Perkin Warbeck,[5] as a scullion in the Briskett kitchens,

1 Sometimes spelt Loyne or even Lohoyoillen.
2 The Eighteenth Earl was awarded a dukedom for his brilliant work in remembering the names of all Queen Anne's children.
3 The last person who actually slept there was Oxo's grandmother, who afterwards died of a fractured pelmet.
4 Also dead.
5 See Lambert Simnel.

had served up the meal which caused Henry VII[1] never to smile again. Several well-known ghosts also lived there.

But fine though the castle undoubtedly was, it was an austere and depressing place for a young bride of nineteen, and Mipsie can hardly be blamed for attempting to cheer it up somewhat. Her faultless taste naturally led, after her recent stay in Paris, to French décor, and so she had graceful Louis Quinze legs fitted on to the clumsy oak refectory tables, the fan vaulting of the Great Hall painted in the style of Boucher, and turned one of the dungeons into a *Salle des Glaces* as a compliment to Versailles, besides making a torture chamber into a very cosy little visitors' bathroom. She also gave orders for sprays of orchids to hang from the vizors of the suits of mail – for she just couldn't live without orchids, so great was her love of Nature – and bunches of carnations and roses to be placed daily in the jaws of the various skin rugs which lay all over the castle, for Oxo's father had been a keen big-game hunter. When Oxo seized an armful of these lovely blossoms and threw them into the fire, Mipsie immediately realized, with her delicate feminine intuition, that he was displeased, and essayed to mend matters by taking the best rug in the collection, a magnificent snow leopard, and having it made into a cloak in compliment to the father-in-law she had never seen. Could graceful tact go further? But this only seemed to make Oxo more angry still. He forbade her to alter the castle any more, saying that what was good enough for his ancestors was good enough for him. 'Of course, dear. Too good,' Mipsie said soothingly, but for some unaccountable reason that charming tribute to his forefathers was the last straw. Oxo flung himself out of the room, as he went breaking off the ormulu top which Mipsie had had fixed to a Saxon halberd and hurling it out of the window. It was their first real quarrel.

I have mentioned the Briskett ghosts. These included the headless third Earl, who was said to walk the long gallery every night. For generations a beaker of brandy and a biscuit had been laid out for him each night by the butler. Brandy and biscuit

---

1 Who completed the famous chapel at Westminster, begun by Henry VIII during the Reformation.

were always gone by morning. But Oxo's mother, who was Scottish, thought the custom extravagant and silly and stopped it. The butler immediately gave notice. It is rather touching to think how much family tradition meant to servants in those good old days.

Then there was at one time a white stable cat which was said to have jet-black kittens every time one of the Loigne family died. But there was, I believe, some other explanation of that phenomenon not connected with the supernatural. Lastly, there was the famous Red Sultan, whom Mipsie actually saw.

The sobriquet was given to the seventh Earl for his oriental habits and character, which were known for miles around. He was eventually murdered by an irate farmer who discovered his daughter – a maidservant in the castle – dancing on the dining table before Lord Chine, dressed entirely in strings of coral. The ghost, apparelled in gorgeous Eastern robes and smoking a hookah, is said to haunt a room in the North Tower, which is consequently never used. But one day, both Mipsie and 'Weed' Wastrel (Sir Arthur Wastrel, an old admirer of hers, so nicknamed for his habitual cigar), announced their intention of keeping watch for one night in the haunted room. They tossed – and Mipsie won 'first go'. Next morning she declared that the Red Sultan had indeed appeared, but her description of him was so vague that a sceptic might have thought she had dreamed the whole thing, but for one curious circumstance. A thick, strongly scented ash was found on the carpet afterwards, somewhat reminiscent of cigar ash, but doubtless emanating from the ghostly hookah. So I think there can be no doubt but that my sister really did receive a visitation that night.

PASTURES NEW

Mipsie's Indian tour started off in the most dramatic manner, as things have a way of doing in her vivid and colourful life, I have noticed. She had scarcely reached India's shores when a message arrived from the all powerful Rajah of Badsore, begging her to accept the use of his motor throughout her visit. It was in the early days of motoring when cars were very liable to break down, so the vehicle was accompanied by a huge royal elephant, richly caparisoned and bearing a jewelled howdah, who lumbered behind the car at the then daring pace of fifteen miles an hour. It was a wise precaution. For in going up a steep incline the car suddenly jibbed – then to the horror of the accompanying train of servants, commenced to run back right into the elephant's hairy chest! Mipsie was quite unperturbed. 'An elephant's chest is a welcome change after my husband,' she records in the journal which she kept throughout the tour. A moment later she felt herself being reverently lifted up by the noble beast and deposited in the howdah, none the worse except for the loss of her motor veil, which he ate. 'Evidently,' she adds, 'an elephant never forgets the British aristocracy.'

The Rajah's A.D.C. apologized humbly for the veil's disappearance and promised that his royal master would present her with another. So touched was Mipsie by this that she immediately descended and offered the elephant her gloves and dustcoat. All three articles were subsequently replaced – and the best that money could buy of course – by His Highness.

Soon she arrived at the fabulous saffron palace, which is now well known to tourists. Tier upon tier of bright yellow marble turrets towered high above the town of Badsore, while all the rugs, furniture and curtains were of the same tint, which is the royal colour and therefore cultivated by tradition to such an extent that the women in the Zenana all wear yellow *saris* and tint their eyelids, etc., with saffron. There was a story that an English girl, staying in the neighbourhood, was once stricken with jaundice. The Rajah happened to see her – had her kidnapped and – so great was his admiration – even contemplated marrying her. Time passed, however, and the girl recovered. The Rajah, in disgust, had her thrown off a 500–foot parapet to some starving jackals, after which unhappy incident I believe she died.

Unfortunately, at the time of Mipsie's visit, the Rajah was in failing health from saffron poisoning, so my sister was only able to see him once. He had been a man of vast appetite, but was on a diet of not more than eight chickens and one pea-hen a day. As he ate the yellow flesh – for they were of course cooked in saffron – Mipsie was fascinated to see him throw the bones over his shoulder out of a window. On asking H.H. the reason for this he told her that his people waited below for anything he had touched, which was considered sacred. Fearing that she might suffer the same fate, Mipsie quickly said: 'I should be honoured if your Highness would also present me with a keepsake.' For answer the Rajah held out his hand. 'Take this,' he said. 'Men have died to gain it' – and he handed her a pea-hen's eye. Only Mipsie's ready wit saved her from having to accept the unpleasant object. 'I regret, your Highness,' she said, 'that my religion forbids me certain parts of pea-hens.' The Rajah respected her code and presented her with a magnificent yellow emerald instead.

Mipsie went on to stay – in great contrast to the Rajah of Badsore – with the gentle and cultured Marharaj Rana of Singhit Bunji, who, born of a warrior race in which every prince of the blood had, on attaining his fifteenth birthday, to prove his merit by killing 50 tigers, 50 leopards and either 100 sambur or 200 natives, revolted against this butchery, became a Christian, and a vegetarian and joined the R.S.P.C.A. Subsequently he made a law in his province that no one should take life. This had its disadvantages as, of course, even vermin was preserved, and the fleas wore gold collars and were encouraged to enjoy a good meal from high and low alike. The Marharaj Rana achieved wonders in the taming of beasts of prey and he invited Mipsie to go and see his favourite tiger who he was slowly converting to vegetarianism by placing near its lair exquisite silver dishes containing peaches, asparagus and cream cakes. The only thing that caused the animal to revert to type was, apparently, the sight of another tiger or other creature of prey.

Unfortunately the experiment proved a failure that time, as for some unaccountable reason the moment the tiger set eyes on Mipsie he began to snarl and roar, and so had to be driven away by the servants, leaving untouched a beautiful *omelette aux fines herbes* and a *pêche Melba*.

Space forbids that I should describe the whole of Mipsie's Indian tour. There was the wonderful aviary palace of Hotgong, filled with birds of every species and hue, including the sacred parrots which were trained to screech every time the Newab of Hotgong approached. Mipsie said they made a fearful clamour, especially during the night. Then there was the Rajah of Ahgotodabad, with whom she stayed longest, whose fairy tale jewels extended even to the furniture. Mipsie had a vast bath mat, she says – too big to go into her trunk (she tried) – encrusted round the border with precious stones of the first grade. On another occasion there was an amusing episode when her host had a visitor of equal rank staying with him, and as a matter of etiquette it was impossible to decide with whom an English duchess should go in to dinner. Mipsie solved it by sitting on the shoulders of one with her hands clasping the osprey on the other's turban (the osprey came off in her hands!). A very neat solution I think.

Eventually her tour came to an end. 'I am the richer by some wonderful experiences,' she wrote in her journal, 'but still I feel that the world is an oyster which has not really yielded me up its pearl', and with that ideal in mind she decided to return to England via Arabia and Egypt, of which I shall write in the next chapter.

George Orwell

Boys' Weeklies

You never walk far through any poor quarter in any big town without coming upon a small newsagent's shop. The general appearance of these shops is always very much the same: a few posters for the *Daily Mail* and the *News of the World* outside, a poky little window with sweet-bottles and packets of Players, and a dark interior smelling of liquorice allsorts and festooned from floor to ceiling with vilely printed twopenny papers, most of them with lurid cover-illustrations in three colours.

Except for the daily and evening papers, the stock of these shops hardly overlaps at all with that of the big newsagents. Their main selling line is the twopenny weekly, and the number and variety of these are almost unbelievable. Every hobby and pastime – cage-birds, fretwork, carpentering, bees, carrier-pigeons, home conjuring, philately, chess – has at least one paper devoted to it, and generally several. Gardening and livestock-keeping must have at least a score between them. Then there are the sporting papers, the radio papers, the children's comics, the various snippet papers such as *Tit-bits*, the large range of papers devoted to the movies and all more or less exploiting women's legs, the various trade papers, the women's story-papers (the *Oracle, Secrets, Peg's Paper*, etc. etc.), the needlework papers – these so numerous that a display of them alone will often fill an entire window – and in addition the long series of 'Yank Mags' (*Fight Stories, Action Stories, Western Short Stories,* etc.), which are imported shop-soiled from America and sold at twopence halfpenny or threepence. And the periodical proper shades off into the fourpenny novelette, the *Aldine Boxing Novels*, the *Boys' Friend Library*, the *Schoolgirls' Own Library* and many others.

Probably the contents of these shops is the best available indication of what the mass of the English people really feels and thinks. Certainly nothing half so revealing exists in documentary form. Best-seller novels, for instance, tell one a great deal, but the novel is aimed almost exclusively at people above the £4–a-week level. The movies are probably a very unsafe guide to popular taste, because the film industry is virtually a monopoly, which means that it is not obliged to study its public at all closely. The same applies to some extent to the daily papers, and most of all to the radio. But it does not apply to the weekly paper with a smallish circulation and specialized subject-matter. Papers like the *Exchange and Mart*, for instance, or *Cage-birds*, or the *Oracle*, or the *Prediction*, or the *Matrimonial Times*, only exist because there is a definite demand for them, and they reflect the minds of their readers as a great national daily with a circulation of millions cannot possibly do.

Here I am only dealing with a single series of papers, the boys' twopenny weeklies, often inaccurately described as 'penny dreadfuls'. Falling strictly within this class there are at present ten papers, the *Gem, Magnet, Modern Boy, Triumph* and *Champion*, all owned by the Amalgamated Press, and the *Wizard, Rover, Skipper, Hotspur* and *Adventure*, all owned by D. C. Thomson & Co. What the circulations of these papers are, I do not know. The editors and proprietors refuse to name any figures, and in any case the circulation of a paper carrying serial stories is bound to fluctuate widely. But there is no question that the combined public of the ten papers is a very large one. They are on sale in every town in England, and nearly every boy who reads at all goes through a phase of reading one or more of them. The *Gem* and *Magnet*, which are much the oldest of these papers, are of rather different type from the rest, and they have evidently lost some of their popularity during the past few years. A good many boys now regard them as old fashioned and 'slow'. Nevertheless I want to discuss them first, because they are more interesting psychologically than the others, and also because the mere survival of such papers into the nineteen-thirties is a rather startling phenomenon.

The *Gem* and *Magnet* are sister-papers (characters out of one paper frequently appear in the other), and were both started more than thirty years ago. At that time, together with *Chums* and the old *B.O.P.*, they were the leading papers for boys, and they remained dominant till quite recently. Each of them carries every week a fifteen- or twenty-thousand-word school story, complete in itself, but usually more or less connected with the story of the week before. The *Gem* in addition to its school story carries one or more adventure serial. Otherwise the two papers are so much alike that they can be treated as one, though the *Magnet* has always been the better known of the two, probably because it possesses a really first-rate character in the fat boy, Billy Bunter.

The stories are stories of what purports to be public-school life, and the schools (Greyfriars in the *Magnet* and St Jim's in the *Gem*) are represented as ancient and fashionable foundations of the type of Eton or Winchester. All the leading characters are fourth-form boys aged fourteen or fifteen, older or younger boys only appearing in very minor parts. Like Sexton Blake and Nelson Lee, these boys continue week after week and year after year, never growing any older. Very occasionally a new boy arrives or a minor character drops out, but in at any rate the last twenty-five years the personnel has barely altered. All the principal characters in both papers – Bob Cherry, Tom Merry, Harry Wharton, Johnny Bull, Billy Bunter and the rest of them – were at Greyfriars or St Jim's long before the Great War, exactly the same age as at present, having much the same kind of adventures and talking almost exactly the same dialect. And not only the characters but the whole atmosphere of both *Gem* and *Magnet* has been preserved unchanged, partly by means of very elaborate stylization. The stories in the *Magnet* are signed 'Frank Richards' and those in the *Gem*, 'Martin Clifford', but a series lasting thirty years could hardly be the work of the same person every week.[1] Consequently they have to be written in a style that is easily imitated – an extraordinary, artificial, repetitive style,

1 1945. This is quite incorrect. These stories have been written throughout the whole period by 'Frank Richards' and 'Martin Clifford', who are one and the same person! See articles in *Horizon*, May 1940, and *Summer Pie*, summer 1944.

quite different from anything else now existing in English literature. A couple of extracts will do as illustrations. Here is one from the *Magnet*:

'Groan!'
　'Shut up, Bunter!'
　'Groan!'
Shutting up was not really in Billy Bunter's line. He seldom shut up, though often requested to do so. On the present awful occasion the fat Owl of Greyfriars was less inclined than ever to shut up. And he did not shut up! He groaned, and groaned, and went on groaning.

Even groaning did not fully express Bunter's feelings. His feelings, in fact, were inexpressible.

There were six of them in the soup! Only one of the six uttered sounds of woe and lamentation. But that one, William George Bunter, uttered enough for the whole party and a little over.

Harry Wharton & Co. stood in a wrathy and worried group. They were landed and strandled, diddled, dished and done! etc. etc. etc.

Here is one from the *Gem*:

'Oh cwumbs!'
　'Oh gum!'
　'Oooogh!'
　'Urrggh!'
Arthur Augustus sat up dizzily. He grabbed his handkerchief and pressed it to his damaged nose. Tom Merry sat up, gasping for breath. They looked at one another.

'Bai Jove! This is a go, deah boy!' gurgled Arthur Augustus. 'I have been thwown into quite a fluttah! Oogh! The wottahs! The wuffians! The feahful outsidahs! Wow!' etc. etc. etc.

Both of these extracts are entirely typical; you would find something like them in almost every chapter of every number, to-day or twenty-five years ago. The first thing that anyone would notice is the extraordinary amount of tautology (the first of these two passages contains a hundred and twenty-five words and could be compressed into about thirty), seemingly designed to spin out the story, but actually playing its part in creating the atmosphere. For the same reason various facetious expressions are repeated over and over again; 'wrathy', for instance, is a great favourite, and so is 'diddled, dished and done'. 'Oooogh!'

'Grooo!' and 'Yaroo!' (stylized cries of pain) recur constantly, and so does 'Ha! ha! ha!', always given a line to itself, so that sometimes a quarter of a column or thereabouts consists of 'Ha! ha! ha!' The slang ('Go and eat coke!', 'What the thump!', 'You frabjous ass!', etc. etc.) has never been altered, so that the boys are now using slang which is at least thirty years out of date. In addition, the various nicknames are rubbed in on every possible occasion. Every few lines we are reminded that Harry Wharton & Co. are 'the Famous Five', Bunter is always 'the fat Owl' or 'the Owl of the Remove', Vernon-Smith is always 'the Bounder of Greyfriars', Gussy (the Honourable Arthur Augustus D'Arcy) is always 'the swell of St Jim's', and so on and so forth. There is a constant, untiring effort to keep the atmosphere intact and to make sure that every new reader learns immediately who is who. The result has been to make Greyfriars and St Jim's into an extraordinary little world of their own, a world which cannot be taken seriously by anyone over fifteen, but which at any rate is not easily forgotten. By a debasement of the Dickens technique a series of stereotyped 'characters' has been built up, in several cases very successfully. Billy Bunter, for instance, must be one of the best-known figures in English fiction; for the mere number of people who know him he ranks with Sexton Blake, Tarzan, Sherlock Holmes and a handful of characters in Dickens.

Needless to say, these stories are fantastically unlike life at a real public school. They run in cycles of rather differing types, but in general they are the clean-fun, knock-about type of story, with interest centring round horse-play, practical jokes, ragging masters, fights, canings, football, cricket and food. A constantly recurring story is one in which a boy is accused of some misdeed committed by another and is too much of a sportsman to reveal the truth. The 'good' boys are 'good' in the clean-living Englishman tradition – they keep in hard training, wash behind their ears, never hit below the belt etc. etc. – and by way of contrast there is a series of 'bad' boys, Racke, Crooke, Loder and others, whose badness consists in betting, smoking cigarettes and frequenting public-houses. All these boys are constantly on the verge of expulsion, but as it would mean a change of personnel if any boy were actually expelled, no one is ever caught out in any really serious offence. Stealing, for instance, barely enters as a motif. Sex is completely taboo, especially in the form in which it actually arises at public schools. Occasionally girls enter into the stories, and very rarely there is something approaching a mild flirtation, but it is entirely in the spirit of clean fun. A boy and a girl enjoy going for bicycle rides together – that is all it ever amounts to. Kissing, for instance, would be regarded as 'soppy'. Even the bad boys are presumed to be completely sexless. When the *Gem* and *Magnet* were started, it is probable that there was a deliberate intention to get away from the guilty sex-ridden atmosphere that pervaded so much of the earlier literature for boys. In the 'nineties the *Boys' Own Paper*, for instance, used to have its correspondence columns full of terrifying warnings against masturbation, and books like *St Winifred's* and *Tom Brown's Schooldays* were heavy with homosexual feeling, though no doubt the authors were not fully aware of it. In the *Gem* and *Magnet* sex simply does not exist as a problem. Religion is also taboo; in the whole thirty years' issue of the two papers the word 'God' probably does not occur, except in 'God save the King'. On the other hand, there has always been a very strong 'temperance' strain. Drinking and, by association, smoking are regarded as rather disgraceful even in an adult ('shady' is the usual word), but at the same time as something irresistibly fascinating, a sort of substitute for sex. In their moral atmosphere the *Gem* and *Magnet* have a great deal in common with the Boy Scout movement, which started at about the same time.

All literature of this kind is partly plagiarism. Sexton Blake, for instance, started off quite frankly as an imitation of Sherlock Holmes, and still resembles him fairly strongly; he has hawklike features, lives in Baker Street, smokes enormously and puts on a dressing-gown when he wants to think. The *Gem* and *Magnet* probably owe something to the old school-story writers who were flourishing when they began, Gunby Hadath, Desmond Coke and the rest, but they owe more to nineteenth-century models. In so far as Greyfriars and St Jim's are like real schools at all, they are much more like Tom Brown's Rugby than a modern public school. Neither school has an O.T.C., for instance, games are not compulsory, and the boys are even allowed to wear what clothes they like. But without doubt the main origin of these papers is *Stalky & Co.* This book has had an immense influence on boys' literature, and it is one of those books which have a sort of traditional reputation among people who have never even seen a copy of it. More than once in boys' weekly papers I have come across a reference to *Stalky & Co.* in which the word was spelt 'Storky'. Even the name of the chief comic among the Greyfriars masters, Mr Prout, is taken from *Stalky & Co.*, and so is much of the slang; 'jape', 'merry', 'giddy', 'bizney' (business), 'frabjous', 'don't' for 'doesn't' – all of them out of date even when *Gem* and *Magnet* started. There are also traces of earlier origins. The name 'Greyfriars' is probably taken from Thackeray, and Gosling, the school porter in the *Magnet*, talks in an imitation of Dickens's dialect.

With all this, the supposed 'glamour' of public-school life is played for all it is worth. There is all the usual paraphernalia – lock-up, roll-call, house matches, fagging, prefects, cosy teas round the study fire, etc. etc. – and constant reference to the 'old school', the 'old grey stones' (both schools were founded in the early sixteenth century), the 'team spirit' of the 'Greyfriars men'. As for the snob-appeal, it is completely shameless. Each school has a titled boy or two whose titles are constantly thrust in the reader's face; other boys have the names of well-known aristocratic families, Talbot, Manners, Lowther. We are for ever being reminded that Gussy is the Honourable Arthur A. D'Arcy, son of Lord Eastwood, that Jack Blake is heir to 'broad acres', that Hurree Jamset Ram Singh (nicknamed Inky) is the Nabob of Bhanipur, that Vernon-Smith's father is a millionaire. Till recently the illustrations in both papers always depicted the boys in clothes imitated from those of Eton; in the last few years Greyfriars has changed over to blazers and flannel trousers, but St Jim's still sticks to the Eton jacket, and Gussy sticks to his top-hat. In the school magazine which appears every week as part of the *Magnet*, Harry Wharton writes an article discussing the pocket-money received by the 'fellows in the Remove', and reveals that some of them get as much as five pounds a week! This kind of thing is a perfectly deliberate incitement to wealth-fantasy. And here it is worth noticing a rather curious fact, and that is that the school story is a thing peculiar to England. So far as I know, there are extremely few school stories in foreign languages. The reason, obviously, is that in England education is mainly a matter of status. The most definite dividing line between the petite-bourgeoisie and the working class is that the former pay for their education, and within the bourgeoisie there is another unbridgeable gulf between the 'public' school and the 'private' school. It is quite clear that there are tens and scores and thousands of people to whom every detail of life at a 'posh' public school is wildly thrilling and romantic. They happen to be outside that mystic world of quadrangles and house-colours, but they can yearn after it, day-dream about it, live mentally in it for hours at a stretch. The question is, Who are these people? Who reads the *Gem* and *Magnet*?

Obviously one can never be quite certain about this kind of thing. All I can say from my own observation is this. Boys who are likely to go to public schools themselves generally read the *Gem* and *Magnet*, but they nearly always stop reading them when they are about twelve; they may continue for another year from force of habit, but by that time they have ceased to take them seriously. On the other hand, the boys at very cheap private schools, the schools that are designed for people who can't afford a public school but consider the Council schools 'common', continue reading the *Gem* and *Magnet* for several years longer. A few years ago I was a teacher at two of these schools myself. I found that not only did virtually all the boys read the *Gem* and *Magnet*, but that they were still taking them fairly seriously when they were fifteen or even sixteen. These boys were the sons of shop-keepers, office employees and small business and pro-fessional men, and obviously it is this class that the *Gem* and *Magnet* are aimed at. But they are certainly read by working-class boys as well. They are generally on sale in the poorest quarters of big towns, and I have known them to be read by boys whom one might expect to be completely immune from public-school 'glamour'. I have seen a young coal-miner, for instance, a lad who had already worked a year or two underground, eagerly reading the *Gem*. Recently I offered a batch of English papers to some British legionnaires of the French Foreign Legion in North Africa; they picked out the *Gem* and *Magnet* first. Both papers are much read by girls,[1] and the Pen Pals department of the *Gem* shows that it is read in every corner of the British Empire, by Australians, Canadians, Palestine Jews, Malays, Arabs, Straits Chinese, etc. etc. The editors evidently expect their readers to be aged round about fourteen, and the advertisements (milk chocolate, postage stamps, water pistols, blushing cured, home conjuring tricks, itching powder, the Phine Phun Ring which runs a needle into your friend's hand, etc. etc.) indicate roughly the same age; there are also the Admiralty advertisements, however, which call for youths between seventeen and twenty-two. And there is no question that these papers are also read by adults. It is quite common for people to write to the editor and say that they have read every number of the *Gem* or *Magnet* for the past thirty years. Here, for instance, is a letter from a lady in Salisbury:

I can say of your splendid yarns of Harry Wharton & Co. of Greyfriars, that they never fail to reach a high standard. Without doubt they are the finest stories of their type on the market to-day, which is saying a good deal. They seem to bring you face to face with Nature. I have taken the *Magnet* from the start, and have followed the adventures of Harry Wharton & Co. with rapt interest. I have no sons, but two daughters, and there's always a rush to be the first to read the grand old paper. My husband, too, was a staunch reader of the *Magnet* until he was suddenly taken away from us.

It is well worth getting hold of some copies of the *Gem* and *Magnet*, especially the *Gem*, simply to have a look at the correspondence columns. What is truly startling is the intense interest with which the pettiest details of life at Greyfriars and St Jim's are followed up. Here, for instance, are a few of the questions sent in by readers:

'What age is Dick Roylance?' 'How old is St Jim's?' 'Can you give me a list of the Shell and their studies?' 'How much did D'Arcy's monocle

---

1   There are several corresponding girls' papers. The *Schoolgirl* is companion-paper to the *Magnet* and has stories by 'Hilda Richards'. The characters are interchangeable to some extent. Bessie Bunter, Billy Bunter's sister, figures in the *Schoolgirl*.

cost?' 'How is it that fellows like Crooke are in the Shell and decent fellows like yourself are only in the Fourth?' 'What are the Form captain's three chief duties?' 'Who is the chemistry master at St Jim's?' (From a girl) 'Where is St Jim's situated? *Could* you tell me how to get there, as I would love to see the building? Are you boys just "phoneys", as I think you are?'

It is clear that many of the boys and girls who write these letters are living a complete fantasy-life. Sometimes a boy will write, for instance, giving his age, height, weight, chest and bicep measurements and asking which member of the Shell or Fourth Form he most exactly resembles. The demand for a list of the studies on the Shell passage, with an exact account of who lives in each, is a very common one. The editors, of course, do everything in their power to keep up the illusion. In the *Gem* Jack Blake is supposed to write the answers to correspondents, and in the *Magnet* a couple of pages is always given up to the school magazine (the *Greyfriars Herald*, edited by Harry Wharton), and there is another page in which one or other character is written up each week. The stories run in cycles, two or three characters being kept in the foreground for several weeks at a time. First there will be a series of rollicking adventure stories, featuring the Famous Five and Billy Bunter; then a run of stories turning on mistaken identity, with Wibley (the make-up wizard) in the star part; then a run of more serious stories in which Vernon-Smith is trembling on the verge of expulsion. And here one comes upon the real secret of the *Gem* and *Magnet* and the probable reason why they continue to be read in spite of their obvious out-of-dateness.

It is that the characters are so carefully graded as to give almost every type of reader a character he can identify himself with. Most boys' papers aim at doing this, hence the boy-assistant (Sexton Blake's Tinker, Nelson Lee's Nipper, etc.) who usually accompanies the explorer, detective or what-not on his adventures. But in these cases there is only one boy, and usually it is much the same type of boy. In the *Gem* and *Magnet* there is a model for very nearly everybody. There is the normal athletic, high-spirited boy (Tom Merry, Jack Blake, Frank Nugent), a slightly rowdier version of this type (Bob Cherry), a more aristocratic version (Talbot, Manners), a quieter, more serious version (Harry Wharton), and a stolid, 'bulldog' version (Johnny Bull). Then there is the reckless, dare-devil type of boy (Vernon-Smith), the definitely 'clever', studious boy (Mark Linley, Dick Penfold), and the eccentric boy who is not good at games but possesses some special talent (Skinner, Wibley). And there is the scholarship-boy (Tom Redwing), an important figure in this class of story because he makes it possible for boys from very poor homes to project themselves into the public-school atmosphere. In addition there are Australian, Irish, Welsh, Manx, Yorkshire and Lancashire boys to play upon local patriotism. But the subtlety of characterization goes deeper than this. If one studies the correspondence columns one sees that there is probably *no* character in the *Gem* and *Magnet* whom some or other reader does not identify with, except the out-and-out comics, Coker, Billy Bunter, Fisher T. Fish (the money-grubbing American boy) and, of course, the masters. Bunter, though in his origin he probably owed something to the fat boy in *Pickwick*, is a real creation. His tight trousers against which boots and canes are constantly thudding, his astuteness in search of food, his postal order which never turns up, have made him famous wherever the Union Jack waves. But he is not a subject for day-dreams. On the other hand, another seeming figure of fun, Gussy (the Honourable Arthur A. D'Arcy, 'the swell of St Jim's'), is evidently much admired. Like everything else in the *Gem* and *Magnet*, Gussy is at least thirty years out of date. He is the 'knut' of the early twentieth century or even the 'masher' of the 'nineties ('Bai Jove, deah boy!' and 'Weally, I shall be obliged to give you a feahful thwashin'!'), the monocled idiot who made good on the fields of Mons and Le Cateau. And his evident popularity goes to show how deep the snob-appeal of this type is. English people are extremely fond of the titled ass (cf. Lord Peter Wimsey) who always turns up trumps in the moment of emergency. Here is a letter from one of Gussy's girl admirers:

I think you're too hard on Gussy. I wonder he's still in existence, the way you treat him. He's my hero. Did you know I write lyrics? How's this – to the tune of 'Goody Goody'?

> *Gonna get my gas-mask, join the A.R.P.*
> *'Cos I'm wise to all those bombs you drop on me.*
> > *Gonna dig myself a trench*
> > *Inside the garden fence;*
> > *Gonna seal my windows up with tin*
> > *So the tear gas can't get in;*
> *Gonna park my cannon right outside the kerb*
> *With a note to Adolf Hitler: 'Don't disturb!'*
> > *And if I never fall in Nazi hands*
> > *That's soon enough for me*
> > *Gonna get my gas-mask, join the A.R.P.*

P.S. – Do you get on well with girls?

I quote this in full because (dated April 1939) it is interesting as being probably the earliest mention of Hitler in the *Gem*. In the *Gem* there is also a heroic fat boy, Fatty Wynn, as a set-off against Bunter. Vernon-Smith, 'the Bounder of the Remove', a Byronic character, always on the verge of the sack, is another great favourite. And even some of the cads probably have their following. Loder, for instance, 'the rotter of the Sixth', is a cad, but he is also a highbrow and given to saying sarcastic things about football and the team spirit. The boys of the Remove only think him all the more of a cad for this, but a certain type of boy would probably identify with him. Even Racke, Crooke & Co. are probably admired by small boys who think it diabolically wicked to smoke cigarettes. (A frequent question in the correspondence column: 'What brand of cigarettes does Racke smoke?')

Naturally the politics of the *Gem* and *Magnet* are Conservative, but in a completely pre-1914 style, with no Fascist tinge. In reality their basic political assumptions are two: nothing ever changes, and foreigners are funny. In the *Gem* of 1939 Frenchmen are still Froggies and Italians are still Dagoes. Mossoo, the French master at Greyfriars, is the usual comic-paper Frog, with pointed beard, pegtop trousers, etc. Inky, the Indian boy, though a rajah, and therefore possessing snob-appeal, is also the comic babu of the *Punch* tradition. (' "The rowfulness is not the proper caper, my esteemed Bob" said Inky. "Let dogs delight in the barkfulness and bitefulness, but the soft answer is the cracked pitcher that goes longest to a bird in the bush, as the English proverb remarks" ') Fisher T. Fish is the old-style stage Yankee (' "Waal, I guess" ', etc.) dating from a period of Anglo-American jealousy. Wun Lung, the Chinese boy (he has rather faded out of late, no doubt because some of the *Magnet*'s readers are Straits Chinese), is the nineteenth-century pantomime Chinaman, with saucer-shaped hat, pigtail and pidgin-English. The assumption all along is not only that foreigners are comics who are put there for us to laugh at, but that they can be classified in much the same way as insects. That is why in all boys' papers, not only the *Gem* and *Magnet*, a Chinese is invariably portrayed with a pigtail. It is the thing you recognize him by, like the Frenchman's beard or the Italian's barrel-organ. In papers of this kind it occasionally happens that when the setting of a story is in a foreign country some attempt is made to describe the natives as individual human beings, but as a rule it is assumed that foreigners of any one race are all alike and will conform more or less exactly to the following patterns:

FRENCHMAN: Excitable. Wears beard, gesticulates wildly.

SPANIARD, MEXICAN, etc.: Sinister, treacherous.

ARAB, AFGHAN, etc.: Sinister, treacherous.

CHINESE: Sinister, treacherous. Wears pigtail.

ITALIAN: Excitable. Grinds barrel-organ or carries stiletto.

SWEDE, DANE, etc.: Kind-hearted, stupid.

NEGRO: Comic, very faithful.

The working classes only enter into the *Gem* and *Magnet* as comics or semi-villains (race-course touts, etc.). As for class-friction, trade unionism, strikes, slumps, unemployment, Fascism and civil war – not a mention. Somewhere or other in the thirty years' issue of the two papers you might perhaps find the word 'Socialism', but you would have to look a long time for it. If the Russian Revolution is anywhere referred to, it will be indirectly, in the word 'Bolshy' (meaning a person of violent disagreeable habits). Hitler and the Nazis are just beginning to make their appearance, in the sort of reference I quoted above. The war-crisis of September 1938 made just enough impression to produce a story in which Mr Vernon-Smith, the Bounder's millionaire father, cashed in on the general panic by buying up country houses in order to sell them to 'crisis scuttlers'. But that is probably as near to noticing the European situation as the *Gem* and *Magnet* will come, until the war actually starts.[1] That does not mean that these papers are unpatriotic – quite the contrary! Throughout the Great War the *Gem* and *Magnet* were perhaps the most consistently and cheerfully patriotic papers in England. Almost every week the boys caught a spy or pushed a conchy into the army, and during the rationing period 'EAT LESS BREAD' was printed in large type on every page. But their patriotism has nothing whatever to do with power-politics or 'ideological' warfare. It is more akin to family loyalty, and actually it gives one a valuable clue to the attitude of ordinary people, especially the huge untouched block of the middle class and the better-off working class. These people are patriotic to the middle of their bones, but they do not feel that what happens in foreign countries is any of their business. When England is in danger they rally to its defence as a matter of course, but in between-times they are not interested. After all, England is always in the right and England always wins, so why worry? It is an attitude that has been shaken during the past twenty years, but not so deeply as is sometimes supposed. Failure to understand it is one of the reasons why left-wing political parties are seldom able to produce an acceptable foreign policy.

The mental world of the *Gem* and *Magnet*, therefore, is something like this:

The year is 1910 – or 1940, but it is all the same. You are at Greyfriars, a rosy-cheeked boy of fourteen in posh tailor-made clothes, sitting down to tea in your study on the Remove passage after an exciting game of football which was won by an odd goal in the last half-minute. There is a cosy fire in the study, and outside the wind is whistling. The ivy clusters thickly round the old grey stones. The King is on his throne and the pound is worth a pound. Over in Europe the comic foreigners are jabbering and gesticulating, but the grim grey battleships

---

1   This was written some months before the outbreak of war. Up to the end of September 1939 no mention of the war has appeared in either paper.

of the British Fleet are steaming up the Channel and at the outposts of Empire the monocled Englishmen are holding the niggers at bay. Lord Mauleverer has just got another fiver and we are all settling down to a tremendous tea of sausages, sardines, crumpets, potted meat, jam and doughnuts. After tea we shall sit round the study fire having a good laugh at Billy Bunter and discussing the team for next week's match against Rookwood. Everything is safe, solid and unquestionable. Everything will be the same for ever and ever. That approximately is the atmosphere.

But now turn from the *Gem* and *Magnet* to the more up-to-date papers which have appeared since the Great War. The truly significant thing is that they have more points of resemblance to the *Gem* and *Magnet* than points of difference. But it is better to consider the differences first.

There are eight of these newer papers, the *Modern Boy*, *Triumph*, *Champion*, *Wizard*, *Rover*, *Skipper*, *Hotspur* and *Adventure*. All of these have appeared since the Great War, but except for the *Modern Boy* none of them is less than five years old. Two papers which ought also to be mentioned briefly here, though they are not strictly in the same class as the rest, are the *Detective Weekly* and the *Thriller*, both owned by the Amalgamated Press. The *Detective Weekly* has taken over Sexton Blake. Both of these papers admit a certain amount of sex-interest into their stories, and though certainly read by boys, they are not aimed at them exclusively. All the others are boys' papers pure and simple, and they are sufficiently alike to be considered together. There does not seem to be any notable difference between Thomson's publications and those of the Amalgamated Press.

As soon as one looks at these papers one sees their technical superiority to the *Gem* and *Magnet*. To begin with, they have the great advantage of not being written entirely by one person. Instead of one long complete story, a number of the *Wizard* or *Hotspur* consists of half a dozen or more serials, none of which goes on for ever. Consequently there is far more variety and far less padding, and none of the tiresome stylization and facetiousness of the *Gem* and *Magnet*. Look at these two extracts, for example:

Billy Bunter groaned.

A quarter of an hour had elapsed out of the two hours that Bunter was booked for extra French.

In a quarter of an hour there were only fifteen minutes! But every one of those minutes seemed inordinately long to Bunter. They seemed to crawl by like tired snails.

Looking at the clock in Class-room No. 10 the fat Owl could hardly believe that only fifteen minutes had passed. It seemed more like fifteen hours, if not fifteen days!

Other fellows were in extra French as well as Bunter. They did not matter. Bunter did! (the *Magnet*)

After a terrible climb, hacking out handholds in the smooth ice every step of the way up, Sergeant Lionheart Logan of the Mounties was now clinging like a human fly to the face of an icy cliff, as smooth and treacherous as a giant pane of glass.

An Arctic blizzard, in all its fury, was buffeting his body, driving the blinding snow into his face, seeking to tear his fingers loose from their handholds and dash him to death on the jagged boulders which lay at the foot of the cliff a hundred feet below.

Crouching among those boulders were eleven villainous trappers who had done their best to shoot down Lionheart and his companion, Constable Jim Rogers – until the blizzard had blotted the two Mounties out of sight from below (the *Wizard*).

The second extract gets you some distance with the story, the first takes a hundred words to tell you that Bunter is in the detention class. Moreover, by not concentrating on school stories (in point of numbers the school story slightly predominates in all these papers, except the *Thriller* and *Detective Weekly*), the *Wizard*, *Hotspur*, etc., have far greater opportunities for sensationalism. Merely looking at the cover illustrations of the papers which I have on the table in front of me, here are some of the things I see. On one a cowboy is clinging by his toes to the wing of an aeroplane in mid-air and shooting down another aeroplane with his revolver. On another a Chinese is swimming for his life down a sewer with a swarm of ravenous-looking rats swimming after him. On another an engineer is lighting a stick of dynamite while a steel robot feels for him with its claws. On another a man in airman's costume is fighting barehanded against a rat somewhat larger than a donkey. On another a nearly naked man of terrific muscular development has just seized a lion by the tail and flung it thirty yards over the wall of an arena, with the words, 'Take back your blooming lion!' Clearly no school story can compete with this kind of thing. From time to time the school buildings may catch fire or the French master may turn out to be the head of an international anarchist gang, but in a general way the interest must centre round cricket, school rivalries, practical jokes, etc. There is not much room for bombs, death-rays, sub-machine guns, aeroplanes, mustangs, octopuses, grizzly bears or gangsters.

Examination of a large number of these papers shows that, putting aside school stories, the favourite subjects are Wild West, Frozen North, Foreign Legion, crime (always from the detective's angle), the Great War (Air Force or Secret Service, not the infantry), the Tarzan motif in varying forms, professional football, tropical exploration, historical romance (Robin Hood, Cavaliers and Roundheads, etc.) and scientific invention. The Wild West still leads, at any rate as a setting, though the Red Indian seems to be fading out. The one theme that is really new is the scientific one. Death-rays, Martians, invisible men, robots, helicopters and interplanetary rockets figure largely; here and there there are even far-off rumours of psychotherapy and duct-less glands. Whereas the *Gem* and *Magnet* derive from Dickens and Kipling, the *Wizard, Champion, Modern Boy*, etc., owe a great deal to H. G. Wells, who, rather than Jules Verne, is the father of 'Scientification'. Naturally it is the magical Martian aspect of science that is most exploited, but one or two papers include serious articles on scientific subjects, besides quantities of informative snippets. (Examples: 'A Kauri tree in Queensland, Australia, is over 12,000 years old'; 'Nearly 50,000 thunderstorms occur every day'; 'Helium gas costs £1 per 1,000 cubic feet'; 'There are over 500 varieties of spiders in Great Britain'; 'London firemen use 14,000,000 gallons of water annually', etc. etc.) There is a marked advance in intellectual curiosity and, on the whole, in the demand made on the reader's attention. In practice the *Gem* and *Magnet* and the post-war papers are read by much the same public, but the mental age aimed at seems to have risen by a year or two years – an improvement probably corresponding to the improvement in elementary education since 1909.

The other thing that has emerged in the post-war boys' papers, though not to anything like the extent one would expect, is bully-worship and the cult of violence.

If one compares the *Gem* and *Magnet* with a genuinely modern paper, the thing that immediately strikes one is the absence of the leader-principle. There is no central dominating character; instead there are fifteen or twenty characters, all more or less on an equality, with whom readers of different types can identify. In the more modern papers this is not usually the case. Instead of identifying with a schoolboy of more or less his own age, the reader of the *Skipper, Hotspur,* etc., is led to identify with a G-man, with a Foreign Legionary, with some variant of Tarzan, with an air ace, a master spy, an explorer, a pugilist – at any rate with some single all-powerful character who dominates everyone about him and whose usual method of solving any problem is a sock on the jaw. This character is intended as a superman, and as physical strength is the form of power that boys can best understand, he is usually a sort of human gorilla; in the Tarzan type of story he is sometimes actually a giant, eight or ten feet high. At the same time the scenes of violence in nearly all these stories are remarkably harmless and unconvincing. There is a great difference in tone between even the most blood-thirsty English paper and the threepenny Yank Mags, *Fight Stories, Action Stories,* etc. (not strictly boys' papers, but largely read by boys). In the Yank Mags you get real blood-lust, really gory descriptions of the all-in, jump-on-his-testicles style fighting, written in a jargon that has been perfected by people who brood endlessly on violence. A paper like *Fight Stories,* for instance, would have very little appeal except to sadists and masochists. You can see the comparative gentleness of the English civilization by the amateurish way in which prize-fighting is always described in the boys' weeklies. There is no specialized vocabulary. Look at these four extracts, two English, two American:

When the gong sounded, both men were breathing heavily and each had great red marks on his chest. Bill's chin was bleeding, and Ben had a cut over his right eye.

Into their corners they sank, but when the gong clanged again they were up swiftly, and they went like tigers at each other (*Rover*).

He walked in stolidly and smashed a clublike right to my face. Blood spattered and I went back on my heels, but surged in and ripped my right under the heart. Another right smashed full on Ben's already battered mouth, and, spitting out the fragments of a tooth, he crashed a flailing left to my body (*Fight Stories*).

It was amazing to watch the Black Panther at work. His muscles rippled and slid under his dark skin. There was all the power and grace of a giant cat in his swift and terrible onslaught.

He volleyed blows with a bewildering speed for so huge a fellow. In a moment Ben was simply blocking with his gloves as well as he could. Ben was really a past-master of defence. He had many fine victories behind him. But the Negro's rights and lefts crashed through openings that hardly any other fighter could have found (*Wizard*).

Haymakers which packed the bludgeoning weight of forest monarchs crashing down under the ax hurled into the bodies of the two heavies as they swapped punches (*Fight Stories*).

Notice how much more knowledgeable the American extracts sound. They are written for devotees of the prize-ring, the others are not. Also, it ought to be emphasized that on its level the moral code of the English boys' papers is a decent one. Crime and dishonesty are never held up to admiration, there is none of the cynicism and corruption of the American gangster story. The huge sale of the Yank Mags in England shows that there is a demand for that kind of thing, but very few English writers seem able to produce it. When hatred of Hitler became a major emotion in America, it was interesting to see how promptly 'anti-Fascism' was adapted to pornographic purposes by the editors of the Yank Mags. One magazine which I have in front of me is given up to a long, complete story, 'When Hell Came to America', in which the agents of a 'blood-maddened European dictator' are trying to conquer the U.S.A. with death-rays and invisible aeroplanes. There is the frankest appeal to sadism, scenes in which the Nazis tie bombs to women's backs and fling them off the heights to watch them blown to pieces in mid-air, others in which they tie naked girls together by their hair and prod them with knives to make them dance, etc. etc. The editor comments solemnly on all this, and uses it as a plea for tightening up restrictions against immigrants. On another page of the same paper: 'LIVES OF THE HOTCHA CHORUS GIRLS. Reveals all the intimate secrets and fascinating pastimes of the famous Broadway Hotcha girls. NOTHING IS OMITTED. Price 10c.' 'HOW TO LOVE. 10c.' 'FRENCH PHOTO RING. 25c.' 'NAUGHTY NUDIES TRANSFERS. From the outside of the glass you see a beautiful girl, innocently dressed. Turn it around and look through the glass and oh! what a difference! Set of 3 transfers 25c.', etc. etc. etc. There is nothing at all like this in any English paper likely to be read by boys. But the process of Americanization is going on all the same. The American ideal, the 'he-man', the 'tough guy', the gorilla who puts everything right by socking everybody else on the jaw, now figures in probably a majority of boys' papers. In one serial now running in the *Skipper* he is always portrayed ominously enough, swinging a rubber truncheon.

The development of the *Wizard, Hotspur*, etc., as against the earlier boys' papers, boils down to this: better technique, more scientific interest, more bloodshed, more leader-worship. But, after all, it is the *lack* of development that is the really striking thing.

To begin with, there is no political development whatever. The world of the *Skipper* and the *Champion* is still the pre-1914 world of the *Magnet* and the *Gem*. The Wild West story, for instance, with its cattle-rustlers, lynch-law and other paraphernalia belonging the 'eighties, is a curiously archaic thing. It is worth noticing that in papers of this type it is always taken for granted that adventures only happen at the ends of the earth, in tropical forests, in Arctic wastes, in African deserts, on Western prairies, in Chinese opium dens – everywhere in fact, except the places where things really *do* happen. That is a belief dating from thirty or forty years ago, when the new continents were in process of being opened up. Nowadays, of course, if you really want adventure, the place to look for it is in Europe. But apart from the picturesque side of the Great War, contemporary history is carefully excluded. And except that Americans are now admired instead of being laughed at, foreigners are exactly the same figures of fun that they always were. If a Chinese character appears, he is still the sinister pigtailed opium-smuggler of Sax Rohmer; no indication that things have been happening in China since 1912 – no indication that a war is going on there, for instance. If a Spaniard appears, he is still a 'dago' or 'greaser' who rolls cigarettes and stabs people in the back; no indication that things have been happening in Spain. Hitler and the Nazis have not yet appeared, or are barely making their appearance. There will be plenty about them in a little while, but it will be from a strictly patriotic angle (Britain *versus* Germany), with the real meaning of the struggle kept out of sight as much as possible. As for the Russian Revolution, it is extremely difficult to find any reference to it in any of these papers. When Russia is mentioned at all it is usually in an information snippet (example: 'There are 29,000 centenarians in the U.S.S.R.'), and any reference to the Revolution is indirect and twenty years out of date. In one story in the *Rover*, for instance, somebody has a tame bear, and as it is a Russian bear, it is nicknamed Trotsky – obviously an echo of the 1917–23 period and not of recent controversies. The clock has stopped at 1910. Britannia rules the waves, and no one has heard of slumps, booms, unemployment, dictatorships, purges or concentration camps.

And in social outlook there is hardly any advance. The snobbishness is somewhat less open than in the *Gem* and *Magnet* – that is the most one can possibly say. To begin with, the school story, always partly dependent on snob-appeal, is by no means eliminated. Every number of a boys' paper includes at least one school story, these stories slightly outnumbering the Wild Westerns. The very elaborate fantasy-life of the *Gem* and *Magnet* is not imitated and there is more emphasis on extraneous adventure, but the social atmosphere (old grey stones) is much the same. When a new school is introduced at the beginning of a story we are often told in just those words that 'it was a very posh school'. From time to time a story appears which is ostensibly directed *against* snobbery. The scholarship-boy (cf. Tom Redwing in the *Magnet*) makes fairly frequent appearances, and what is essentially the same theme is sometimes presented in this form; there is great rivalry between two schools, one of which considers itself more 'posh' than the other, and there are fights, practical jokes, football matches, etc., always ending in the discomfiture of the snobs. If one glances very superficially at some of these stories it is possible to imagine that a democratic spirit has crept into the boys' weeklies, but when one looks more closely one sees that they merely reflect the bitter jealousies that exist within the white-collar class. Their real function is to allow the boy who goes to a cheap private school (*not* a Council school) to feel that his school is just as 'posh' in the sight of God as Winchester or Eton. The sentiment of school loyalty ('We're better than the fellows down the road'), a thing almost unknown to the real working class, is still kept up. As these stories are written by many different hands, they do, of course, vary a good deal in tone. Some are reasonably free from snobbishness, in others money and pedigree are exploited even more shamelessly than in the *Gem* and *Magnet*. In one that I came across an actual *majority* of the boys mentioned were titled.

Where working-class characters appear, it is usually either as comics (jokes about tramps, convicts, etc.), or as prize-fighters, acrobats, cowboys, professional footballers and Foreign Legionaries – in other words, as adventurers. There is no facing the facts about working-class life, or, indeed, about *working* life of any description. Very occasionally one may come across a realistic description of, say, work in a coal-mine, but in all probability it will only be there as the background of some lurid adventure. In any case the central character is not likely to be a coal-miner. Nearly all the time the boy who reads these papers – in nine cases out of ten a boy who is going to spend his life working in a shop, in a factory or in some subordinate job in an office – is led to identify with people in positions of command, above all with people who are never troubled by shortage of money. The Lord Peter Wimsey figure, the seeming idiot who drawls and wears a monocle but is always to the fore in moments of danger, turns up over and over again. (This character is a great favourite in Secret Service stories.) And, as usual, the heroic characters all have to talk B.B.C.: they may talk Scottish or Irish or American, but no one in a star part is ever permitted to drop an aitch. Here it is worth comparing the social atmosphere of the boys' weeklies with that of the women's weeklies, the *Oracle*, the *Family Star, Peg's Paper*, etc.

The women's papers are aimed at an older public and are read for the most part by girls who are working for a living. Consequently they are on the surface much more realistic. It is taken for granted, for example, that nearly everyone has to live in a big town and work at a more or less dull job. Sex, so far from being taboo, is *the* subject. The short, complete stories, the special feature of these papers, are generally of the 'came the dawn' type: the heroine narrowly escapes losing her 'boy' to a designing rival, or the 'boy' loses his job and has to postpone marriage, but presently gets a better job. The changeling-fantasy (a girl brought up in a poor home is 'really' the child of rich parents) is another favourite. Where sensationalism comes in, usually in the serials, it arises out of the more domestic type of crime, such as bigamy, forgery or sometimes murder; no Martians, death-rays or international anarchist gangs. These papers are at any rate aiming at credibility, and they have a link with real life in their correspondence columns, where genuine problems are being discussed. Ruby M. Ayres's column of advice in the *Oracle*, for instance, is extremely sensible and well written. And yet the world of the *Oracle* and *Peg's Paper* is a pure fantasy-world. It is the same fantasy all the time; pretending to be richer than you are. The chief impression that one carries away from almost every story in these papers is of a frightful, overwhelming 'refinement'. Ostensibly the characters are working-class people, but their habits, the interiors of their houses, their clothes, their outlook and, above all, their speech are entirely middle class. They are all living at several pounds a week above their income. And needless to say, that is just the impression that is intended. The idea is to give the bored factory-girl or worn-out mother of five a dream-life in which she pictures herself – not actually as a duchess (that convention has gone out) but as, say, the wife of a bank-manager. Not only is a five-to-six-pound-a-week standard of life set up as the ideal, but it is tacitly assumed that that is how working-class people really *do* live. The major

George Orwell

facts are simply not faced. It is admitted, for instance, that people sometimes lose their jobs; but then the dark clouds roll away and they get better jobs instead. No mention of unemployment as something permanent and inevitable, no mention of the dole, no mention of trade unionism. No suggestion anywhere that there can be anything wrong with the system *as a system*; there are only individual misfortunes, which are generally due to somebody's wickedness and can in any case be put right in the last chapter. Always the dark clouds roll away, the kind employer raises Alfred's wages, and there are jobs for everybody except the drunks. It is still the world of the *Wizard* and the *Gem*, except that there are orange-blossoms instead of machine-guns.

The outlook inculcated by all these papers is that of a rather exceptionally stupid member of the Navy League in the year 1910. Yes, it may be said, but what does it matter? And in any case, what else do you expect?

Of course no one in his senses would want to turn the so-called penny dreadful into a realistic novel or a Socialist tract. An adventure story must of its nature be more or less remote from real life. But, as I have tried to make clear, the unreality of the *Wizard* and the *Gem* is not so artless as it looks. These papers exist because of a specialized demand, because boys at certain ages find it necessary to read about Martians, death-rays, grizzly bears and gangsters. They get what they are looking for, but they get it wrapped up in the illusions which their future employers think suitable for them. To what extent people draw their ideas from fiction is disputable. Personally I believe that most people are influenced far more than they would care to admit by novels, serial stories, films and so forth, and that from this point of view the worst books are often the most important, because they are usually the ones that are read earliest in life. It is probable that many people who would consider themselves extremely sophisticated and 'advanced' are actually carrying through life an imaginative background which they acquired in childhood from (for instance) Sapper and Ian Hay. If that is so, the boys' twopenny weeklies are of the deepest importance. Here is the stuff that is read somewhere between the ages of twelve and eighteen by a very large proportion, perhaps an actual majority, of English boys, including many who will never read anything else except newspapers; and along with it they are absorbing a set of beliefs which would be regarded as hopelessly out of date in the Central Office of the Conservative Party. All the better because it is done indirectly, there is being pumped into them the conviction that the major problems of our time do not exist, that there is nothing wrong with *laissez-faire* capitalism, that foreigners are unimportant comics and that the British Empire is a sort of charity-concern which will last for ever. Considering who owns these papers, it is difficult to believe that this is unintentional. Of the twelve papers I have been discussing (i.e. twelve including the *Thriller* and *Detective Weekly*) seven are the property of the Amalgamated Press, which is one of the biggest press-combines in the world and controls more than a hundred different papers. The *Gem* and *Magnet*, therefore, are closely linked up with the *Daily Telegraph* and the *Financial Times*. This in itself would be enough to rouse certain suspicions, even if it were not obvious that the stories in the boys' weeklies are politically vetted. So it appears that if you feel the need of a fantasy-life in which you travel to Mars and fight lions barehanded (and what boy doesn't?), you can only have it by delivering yourself over, mentally, to people like Lord Camrose. For there is no competition. Throughout the whole of this run of papers the differences are negligible, and on this level no others exist. This raises the question, why is there no such thing as a left-wing boys' paper?

At first glance such an idea merely makes one slightly sick. It is so horribly easy to imagine what a left-wing boys' paper would be like, if it existed. I remember in 1920 or 1921 some optimistic person handing round Communist tracts among a crowd of public-school boys. The tract I received was of the question-and-answer kind:

Q. 'Can a Boy Communist be a Boy Scout, Comrade?'
A. 'No, Comrade.'
Q. 'Why, Comrade?'
A. 'Because, Comrade, a Boy Scout must salute the Union Jack, which is the symbol of tyranny and oppression.' etc. etc.

Now, suppose that at this moment somebody started a left-wing paper deliberately aimed at boys of twelve or fourteen. I do not suggest that the whole of its contents would be exactly like the tract I have quoted above, but does anyone doubt that they would be *something* like it? Inevitably such a paper would either consist of dreary uplift or it would be under Communist influence and given over to adulation of Soviet Russia; in either case no normal boy would ever look at it. Highbrow literature apart, the whole of the existing left-wing Press, in so far as it is at all vigorously 'left', is one long tract. The one Socialist paper in England which could live a week on its merits *as a paper* is the *Daily Herald*: and how much Socialism is there in the *Daily Herald*? At this moment, therefore, a paper with a 'left' slant and at the same time likely to have an appeal to ordinary boys in their teens is something almost beyond hoping for.

But it does not follow that it is impossible. There is no clear reason why every adventure story should necessarily be mixed up with snobbishness and gutter patriotism. For, after all, the stories in the *Hotspur* and the *Modern Boy* are not Conservative tracts; they are merely adventure stories with a Conservative bias. It is fairly easy to imagine the process being reversed. It is possible, for instance, to imagine a paper as thrilling and lively as the *Hotspur*, but with subject-matter and 'ideology' a little more up to date. It is even possible (though this raises other difficulties) to imagine a women's paper at the same literary level as the *Oracle*, dealing in approximately the same kind of story, but taking rather more account of the realities of working-class life. Such things have been done before, though not in England. In the last years of the Spanish monarchy there was a large output in Spain of left-wing novelettes, some of them evidently of anarchist origin. Unfortunately at the time when they were appearing I did not see their social significance, and I lost the collection of them that I had, but no doubt copies would still be procurable. In get-up and style of story they were very similar to the English fourpenny novelette, except that their inspiration was 'left'. If, for instance, a story described police pursuing anarchists through the mountains, it would be from the point of view of the anarchist and not of the police. An example nearer to hand is the Soviet film *Chapaiev*, which has been shown a number of times in London. Technically, by the standards of the time when it was made, *Chapaiev* is a first-rate film, but mentally, in spite of the unfamiliar Russian background, it is not so very remote from Hollywood. The one thing that lifts it out of the ordinary is the remarkable performance by the actor who takes the part of the White officer (the fat one) – a performance which looks very like an inspired piece of gagging. Otherwise the atmosphere is familiar. All the usual paraphernalia is there – heroic fight against odds, escape at the last moment, shots of galloping horses, love interest, comic relief. The film is in fact a fairly ordinary one, except that its tendency is 'left'. In a Hollywood film of the Russian Civil War the Whites would probably be angels and the Reds demons. In the Russian version the Reds are angels and the Whites demons. That is also a lie, but, taking the long view, it is a less pernicious lie than the other.

Here several difficult problems present themselves. Their general nature is obvious enough, and I do not want to discuss them. I am merely pointing to the fact that, in England, popular imaginative literature is a field that left-wing thought has never begun to enter. *All* fiction from the novels in the mushroom libraries downwards is censored in the interests of the ruling class. And boys' fiction above all, the blood-and-thunder stuff which nearly every boy devours at some time or other, is sodden in the worst illusions of 1910. The fact is only unimportant if one believes that what is read in childhood leaves no impression behind. Lord Camrose and his colleagues evidently believe nothing of the kind, and, after all, Lord Camrose ought to know.

Where Engels Fears to Tread

From Oscar to Stalin. A Progress by Christian de Clavering
(The Clay Press)

At last the authentic voice of a generation! 'You are all a lost generation,' remarked Gertrude Stein of us post-war age-groups, and now, thanks to Mr Christian de Clavering, we know who lost us. Let me try and tell you all about this book while I am still full of it. First thing you know you have opened it, and there is the dedication:

TO THE BALD YOUNG PEOPLE

Then comes a page of fashionable quotations all in German. The middle part by Kafka, the fringes by Rilke and Hölderlin. The rest by Marx. Impeccable! And the introduction.

'Why am I doing this, my dears? Because I happen to be the one person who can do it. My dears, I'm on your side! I've come to get you out of the wretched tangle of individualism that you've made for yourselves and show you just how you can be of some use in the world. Stop worrying whether he loves you or not; stop wondering how you will ever make any money. Never mind whether the trousers of your new suit turn up at the bottom; leave off trying to annoy Pa. We're on to something rather big. The Workers' Revolution for the Classless Society through the Dictatorship of the Proletariat! Yes! It's a bit of a mouthful isn't it! We're used to words of one syllable, words like Freud, Death, War, Peace, Love, Sex, Glands, and, above all, to Damn, Damn, Damn! Well, all that's going to be changed. Morning's at seven, and you've got a new matron.

'I'm told Mr Isherwood is writing a book about the 'twenties.

Mr Isherwood is a Cambridge man, and we who made the 'twenties do not wish them looked at through the wrong end of a cocoa-tin. Through either end. My precious 'twenties! He shan't have them! Avaunt. Avanti!'

(And so the autobiography starts. I will quote a few of the dazzling vignettes. For the reasons with which the author concludes, I have refrained from comment.)

Home. Background. Mother.

'Mother, who is that horrible old obesity with the black chin? I believe he's following us.'

'Hush, that's Daddy.'

And so dawned my second birthday.

Home.

'Mother, where is home this time? Heliopolis? Hammamet? Ragusa? Yalta?'

'Guess again.'

'I know. Prinkipo.'

'Warm.'

'Monte Carlo.'

'Very warm.'

'Has it got a clever coastline? I know! Cannes!'

And home for the next two months it was.

'Mother – what does Father do?'

'He has his business, boy o' mine.'

'And what is that?'

'He's a sort of accountant.'

'On Change?'

'On the Turf!'

'Poor Mother, poor darling Mother – but we needn't see him, need we?'

'Of course not, precious, but I thought you were old enough to know.'

I pulled the hood down and for a moment it was very stuffy inside the pram . . .

Children's Party.

'What is your father, Christian?'

'He's interested in racing – my mother is the Honourable. What is *your* father, Edelweiss?'

'A mediatized prince. What sort of racing?'

'Oh, never mind now – let's ask Mother to play some *Rimsky.*'

But I realized I couldn't stay on in Montreux Territet.

My mother an angel. My father a bookie!

'And don't forget, my boy, a tenner for every little nob you bring home with a handle to his name.'

Eton. Henry's holy shade. An impression, above all, of arches, my dears, each with its handsome couple, and study fireplaces always full of stubs of Balkan Sobranie. And the naughtiest elms! While the battle of Waterloo was being fought all round me, I just sat still and watched my eyelashes grow. There were books, of course. Pater, Alma Pater, with his worried paragraphs. His prose reminded me of stale privet – and Petronius, who made me long to know more Latin. (I only learnt two words, curculio and vespertilio, a bat and a weevil, but they got me everywhere, afterwards, on Mount Athos.) And Compton Mackenzie as he then was, and Huxley, before he had acquired his Pope and Bradley manner, and Verlaine of course, Rimbaud, Mallarmé, Baudelaire.

'What is that book, de Clavering?'

'*Les Chansons de Bilitis*, sir.'

'And what is this lesson?'

'You have the advantage, sir.'

'What do you mean, boy?'

'Ah, sir, fair's fair. I told you what my book was. You must tell me what's your lesson.'

'Elementary geometry.'

'But it sounds fascinating! Then this delicious piece of celluloid nonsense is – I know, sir, don't tell me – a set-square?'

'I have been teaching it for twenty years, and never met with such impertinence.'

'Twenty years, and still at Elementary! Oh, sir, what a confession.' And it was a very purple face one glimpsed behind the blackboard. Ah, those Eton masters. I wish I could remember any of their names, for I was really sorry for them. What tragedies went on under their mortar-boards! Some of them were quite young, and one often got the impression that they were trying, inarticulately, to communicate; would have liked, in fact, to share in the rich creative life that already was centring round me. They used to teeter round my Baksts, and once I caught my housemaster sniffing at a very special bottle made up for me by Max of Delhez, and gingerly rubbing some on his poor old pate. Worldlings, yet deprived of all worldly grace, of our rich sex-life how pathetically inquisitive! They are all there still, I suppose, and I often wonder, when I motor through Switzerland in summer, if one will not find a bunch of them spawning round some mouldy *arrête*, in their Norfolk jackets, like eels in the Sargasso Sea.

The boys of course took up most of my time. I soon found that it was easy to get on with them by giving them presents, and making them laugh. A dozen of claret here, a humidor of Coronas there, a well-timed repartee, and persecution was made impossible. It was easy to find the butts and make rather more skilful fun of them than anybody else. In fact I give this advice to those of my readers who are still at school. In every group there are boys whom it is the fashion to tease and bully; if you quickly spot them and join in, it will never occur to anyone to tease and bully you. Foxes do not hunt stoats. But always defer to the original teasers, and hand your prey over to them for the *coup de grâce*. And boys like expensive presents, though they are genuinely embarrassed by them. All the same they were a provincial lot. I never felt very safe unless I had several of them round me, in coloured caps and gaudy blazers, puffing away at my cigarettes and looking for dirty jokes in the *Vie Parisienne*. By cultivating all the Captains of Games in this way I found my afternoons were left free. I would watch them troop away with their shinpads to some mysterious district on the way to Slough, and saunter up to Windsor with a book – on the bridge I would wave to any who seemed to be pushing a particularly big boat underneath it. Happy river of Eton-Windsor! I have always been very vague about its name, but I often pictured it winding away past Reading Gaol and into the great world somewhere – the world of the Ballet and the Sitwells, of Cocteau and the Café Royal.

'Hello, Faun, what a way to spend your *Après-midi*.'

It was Hubert, my most uneasy disciple.

'I was just thinking that summer made a noise like the rubbing together of biscuits.'

'Yes, it is hot,' he replied. 'If it goes on like this I shall have to buy some FLANNELS.'

'And be mistaken for Peter Fleming?'

'Oh, you're cruel. But seriously, what *shall* we do?'

'Well, there's Tull's, and I haven't eaten a lobster patty since this morning – or one might buy a gramophone record – or a very cool Braque of half a dozen ash-blonde oysters – then there's that place one goes to London from.'

'You mean the G.W.R.?'

'Thank you – and by now the school library will probably have heard of William Morris – or one might try the arches and see what one could pick up.'

'Or the Castle.'

'I'm bored with bearskins – but, my dear, that man – he's touched his cap – so familiar.'

'You mean the headmaster?'

It seemed an evil omen.

Then there was the Corps. I quickly joined the signal section. You didn't have to carry rifles. It was there that I first met intellectuals, dowdy fellows mostly, who went in for Medici prints and had never heard of Picasso. I realized for the first time what a gap separated cultured and cosmopolitan art lovers like myself, people who cared equally for music, painting, and literature, from those whose one idea was to pass examinations; literature is a very different thing to a poet and to someone who has to make a living out of it. 'What do you think of Apollinaire?' I asked one of them. 'Good God, we won't get a question on that – he's well outside the period.' 'On the contrary, he's very much of it. His book on Sade is vital.' 'I thought you meant Sidonius Apollinaris.' I could make no contact with them. But signalling was delightful. One sat for hours beside a field-telephone while little figures receded into the distance with the wire. 'Can you hear me?' 'No.' 'Can you hear me now?' 'No.' 'Well, try this.' 'This' was the morse-code machine, and nimbler fingers than mine would fill the air with a drowsy song. Iddy

iddy umpty umpty iddy umpty iddy . . . However, all things come to an end, and there were tiresome scenes – long waits in redbrick classrooms looking at huge sheets of paper – 'write only on one side of the page'. But which side? and the precious minutes were wasted. Suddenly a lot of people one had always been willing to avoid seemed to have no object in life but to try and see me. They would cluster round some old cannon outside New-Schools, gowns fluttering and tassels wagging. One afternoon, when the place was looking more Raphael Tuck than ever, I went upstairs, and unforgivable things were said. It seemed one was suspected of all the alluvial vices, in fact one was not getting the best out of the curriculum. For the last time I crossed the bridge over the mysterious river, past Tom Browne's, where rather a good pair of 'sponge bags' were being created for me for Ascot, past Hills and Saunders, who had turned out some passable groups of my tea-parties. 'These people are my friends,' I would implore the photographer, 'I want them to look fresh and good-looking and aristocratic and rich.' 'But, sir.' 'Remember, they are not the Shooting Eight, or Mr Crace's Old Boys, and I don't want to sit in the middle with folded arms and a football. I shall stand rather over to the side and at the back, and the only way you will know I am the host is by this enormous cocktail shaker.'

'Oh, my boy, my boy, 'ere am I sweating away on the Turf to edicate you and just when I 'ope you'll bring the nobs in you go and get sacked. Sacked from Eton!'

'Not sacked, supered.'

But my father could never appreciate an academic distinction.

Before one can understand Oxford one must have lived in Capri, and it was there that I spent the next few months, cramming. Mother had taken a quiet villa with a view of the funicular. At seventeen it was rather odd to figure fairly recognizably in five novels in three languages. But Monty and Norman were insatiable. 'No one would think it absurd if you sat to five painters,' they remonstrated, and I retorted that I had a jolly good mind to – but I was too busy at that time, sitting for Fersen.[1] It was my first introduction to *les paradis artificiels* (not counting Tidworth) and with all a boy's healthy craving for novelty I flung myself down on the Count's couches and sampled poppy after poppy through his amusing collection of Chinese pipes. When the time came for my Oxford viva, I was older than the rocks and my eyelids were definitely a little weary. I could not decide. Magdalen and *Sinister Street*, Merton and Max, Balliol and Gumbril? or the House – Peers and Peckwater? Max had praised my eyelashes. Hubert said Balliol was perfect for case-histories like mine, but I realized I should find it madly ungay. That Buttery! Finally it was the House I chose, two vast eighteenth-century rooms which I did up in pewter and cinnamon. Hubert supplied wax fruit, and antimacassars for the Chinese Chippendale chairs, I added incense, brass trays and Buddhas, and Robert a carpet from the Victoria and Albert, the Yacht, not the museum.

My father had become reconciled to me. ''Appiest days of your life, my boy, and don't forget, a pony for every youngster you bring 'ome with a 'andle to his name. Good for the business.' I was worried about my father. 'Mother,' I said, 'don't you think Daddy is looking definitely *blafard*?' 'Is he,' she replied. 'You're sitting on the Continental Bradshaw.'

Most of my Eton friends had also come up to the House, and as my father had taken a flat in Bicester ponies and monkeys came rolling in. I spent them on clothes and parties, on entertaining and on looking entertaining. Parties! 'Are you going to de Clavering's tonight?' and woe betide the wretch who had to say no. Nothing much happened at the time but he soon felt he was living on an icefloe, drifting farther and farther from land, and every moment watching it melt away. De Clavering's tonight! The candles burn in their sconces. The incense glows. Yquem and Avocado pears – a simple meal – but lots and lots of both, with whiskey for the hearties and champagne for the dons. Have a brick of caviare, Alvanley? More birds' nest, Gleneagles? There's nothing coming, I'm afraid, only Avocado pear

---

1   The Marsac of *Vestal Fires*.

and hot-pot. 'Hot-pot!' 'Christian, you're magnificent!' 'Caviare and hot-pot – Prendy will be blue with envy!' And then dancing, while canons go home across the quad, and David stomps at the piano. I took care at these parties to have a word and piece of advice for everyone.

There was an alert young man in a corner, looking rather shy. 'I know – don't tell me,' I said to him, 'it's your first party.' 'Yes.' I pinched his cheek. 'Si jeunesse savait!' I laughed. It was Evelyn Waugh.

Another merry little fellow asked me if I could suggest a hobby. 'Architecture,' I gave in a flash. 'Thank you.' It was John Betjeman.

'And for me?'

'Afghanistan.'

It was Robert Byron.

'And me?'

'Byron,' I laughed back – it was Peter Quennell.[1]

And Alvanley, Gleneagles, Prince Harmatviz, Graf Slivovitz, the Ballygalley of Ballygalley, Sarsaparilla, the Duc de Dingy, the Conde de Coca y Cola – for them, my peers, I kept my serious warnings.

'These bedroom slippers, Dingy? I flew them over from my *bottier*.'

'You ought to look a little more like a public school prefect, Alvanley. The front cover of *The Captain*, it's rather more your *genre*. There! Wash out the honey and flowers, and try a fringe effect. I want to see a pillar of the second eleven.'

'Good jazz, Gleneagles, is meant to be played just a little bit too slow.'

'Graf Slivovitz, this isn't the *Herrenclub* in Carpathian Ruthenia, you must take off your hat. Yes – that green growth with the feudal feathers.'

'Sarsaparilla, only the King rouges his knees when he wears a kilt, and then only at a Court ball.'

'Harmatviz, I can smell that Harris a mile away. What on earth is that terrifying harpoon in the lapel?'

1   All of whom, I am told (autumn, 1937), still keep afloat.

'That, de Clavering, is a *Fogas* fly.'[1]

'More Yquem, Ballygalley?'

'What's that?'

'That – if you mean the thing under your elbow – is how I look to Brancusi; the other is a kind of wine. Stand him up, will you, Ava?'

'Before the war we heard very little of the Sarsaparillas – he would not dare wear that tartan in Madrid.'

'Before the war I hadn't heard of you, Coca y Cola, either; Count, this is a democratic country.'

'I am democrats, we are all democrats, *vive le roi*.'

'Thank you, Dingy, you must have been reading *Some People*. Now I want all the Guinnesses and the Smiths to go into the next room and get a charade ready. Alvanley, Gleneagles, Harmatviz and Slivovitz – you will drive quickly over with me for a few minutes to Bicester to say good-night to father.'

'No I don't think.' – 'My price is ten guineas.' – 'Jolly well not unless we go halves.' – 'Where is my hat and gotha?' – and madcap youth was served.

My crowning moment. The Summerville Grind. Peers and their mothers and sisters in mackintoshes and shooting-sticks. My mount. A huge animal whose teeth need cleaning. For the first time in my life I wear a bowler hat. And my racing colours. White silk shirt with a broad blue stripe – but zigzag! Alvanley and Gleneagles on each side of me – off! I was petrified, my dears; the first fence was enormous and my animal seemed hours getting over it. There was time for me to get down, and I rolled over. On it thundered, its great ugly stirrups banging together. A man leant over me. 'Not hurt, are you?' he said. And then, *plus fort que lui*, 'Where *did* you get that shirt?' It was on a sigh that I answered, as I lost consciousness, 'Sire, at Charvets.' It was the Prince.

And there was talk – all kinds – the banter of my friends.

'Ah, de Clavering, if you were only of the nobility. I would ask you to stay at Dingy. What a pity you are not a real goodfellow.'

---

1   An amusing fish from the Balaton.

'Apfelstrüdel! He is coming to Schloss Slivovitz with Pryce–Jones, is not that good enough for you?'

'Slivovitz – how picturesque it must be. But at Dingy we have to consider the *convenances*, my aunt Doudeauville, my Uncle Sagan . . .'

'She 'appens to be *my* aunt Doudeauville, too.[1] Her mother was of the German branch.'

'I can find no Harmatviz on Madame Sacher's tablecloth.'

'Rosa Lewis says the Claverings are an old Scotch family.'

'Sarsaparilla would know that.'

'Before the war we heard very little of the Sarsaparillas, now it appears . . .'

'Ah, bonjour, Coca y Cola, how is the Alvis?'

'Very well, would you like to look under the bonnet?'

'Haw, haw, haw, what a suggestion.'

'But seriously de Clavering – you are rich, you are intelligent, why have you no titles? Have you spoken to the King?'

'He may have no title, but I would trust him with my waist-coats.'

'And I shake him by the hand – and say – "Well, what the hell, who cares?"'

'Bravo, Harmatviz, it's a democratic country. *Vive le roi!*'

Then there was brilliant conversation at Balliol, where the food makes very long journeys to the dowdy sitting-rooms, under tins.

'We were discussing, de Clavering, whether it was more correct to say Theophylactus Simocattes or Simocatta –'

'You should consider yourself very lucky to be able to say either.'

'And what the collective noun is for a group of pelicans; there is a gaggle of geese, of course, and a pride of lions.'

'A piety of pelicans, I suggest.'

'Thank you – how delightfully Thomas Browne. I shall repeat that.'

'I don't know which I dislike most, people who repeat my

---

1 By the marriage of Graf Hubertus Mary von and zu Slivovitz-Slivovitz with Katarina Auburn-Cord.

Cyril Connolly

epigrams or people who copy my ties – and, by the way, I hope you don't mind. I've brought Raymond Radiguet.'

'Where's he up?'

'He's not up. He lives in Paris.'

'Paris! If I get an All Sogger I am determined to go there. It's right on the way to the British School.'

'I know a very nice little hotel near the *Bibliothèque Mazarine*.'

'I can't see why they don't build an arcade from Brick Top's[1] to the Ritz.' Nobody laughs. As usual, one can find no contact with them.

My twenty-firster. Fifty people in fancy dress. The orchestra from the *Grand Ecart*. A large silver waste-paper basket. 'To Christian de Clavering, the Great Commoner – Alvanley, Alba, Ava, Abercorn, Andrassy, Aberconway, Argyll, Auersperg' – you can imagine the signatures. As the college barge, which I had taken for the occasion, glided up the Cher, life's goblet seemed full to brimming. But Nemesis pursued me. The dons descended. I suppose they hadn't had enough invitations. It appears that those afternoons which I spent under some hot towels in Germers were full of goings-on, lectures, tutorials, Heaven knows what. Divinity seemed a prominent element in the City of Lost Causes. I went down. Oxford, like Eton, had never really 'given'.

London at last.[2] The 'twenties. Parties. Parties. Parties. And behind them all an aching feeling. – Was it worth it? What is it all for? Futility . . .

'Christian – you must dine with me tonight!'

'Gawain – I can't – I've engaged myself to the *'Derries*.'

'Are you the manager?'

'Yes, sir.'

'My name is de Clavering. I should like to say I have never eaten such a disgusting meal. *Même à la Cour*. But haven't I seen you before?'

'Oui, monsieur, je vous connais depuis l'Eldorado.'

1   Always my favourite nightbox.
2   A London then when everybody knew everybody and we all squeezed into one telephone book!

'Es usted el cuadro flamenco?'
   'Si.'
   'Si.'
   'Si.'
   'Si.'

'Beverley, my dear, such a gaffe! I've just gone up to the old Dowager of Buck-and-Chan and mistaken her for the old Dowager of Ham-and-Bran!'
   '*Christian!*'

'She's got what the Americans call "that".'
   'What?'
   'What the Americans call "that".'
   'What's that?'
   ' "That" – that's what she's got.'
   'But what the Americans call what? I don't even know that.'
   'Oh, my dear Duchess!'
   For it was sometimes my privilege to give instruction to a very great lady.

'M. Picasso – Mr Hemingway. M. Hemingway – Señor Belmonte. Mr Nicolson – Mr Firbank – and now shall we begin? I'm starving.'

'I can't decide whether to stay with Lorenzo in Taos or Crowley in Cefalu – where *does* one go in August?'

'Dear Evelyn, *of course*, put me in to it!'

'Voulez-vous téléphoner à Mr Proust de venir me trouver dans les bains de la rue de Lappe?'

'Herr Reinhardt ist zuschloss?'

'You know Diaghileff, of course, Dingy?'

'I've found the title for you, Breton – *Surréalisme.*'

'And for this rather brusque poem, Osbert, I shall need the "meg".'[1]

1   A megaphone, and such small ability as I may have acquired with it, now constitute my 'platform manner'.

Parties. Futility. You can read of most of them in old gossip columns. I still remember my tropical party, when a punkah was heard for the first time in Egerton Crescent. Palms and bananas decorated the rooms. The central heating (it was in July) provided the atmosphere. Some stewards from the P. & O. worked away at the punkahs, or at distributing reistafel and planters' punch. The guests wore shorts, sarongs, stingah shifters or nothing at all.

'But this is *me*,' I remember saying, holding up a slim volume. 'Why haven't I been told about this before, Dadie? Who is this T. S. Eliot?'

'He works in a bank, I believe.'

'Works in a bank – and writes *The Waste Land*! But he should be here, at my Tropical Party! Go and fetch him.'

But there is a new disturbance, and Bolitho, our butler, is at my elbow.

'Some young people, sir.'

'Their names?'

'The *Blackbirds*.'

'Ask them to come up. We shall want some more room. Patrick, help me spread Elizabeth somewhere else. Ronald, come out from under that sofa, you're hunching the springs.[1] Fallen out of the window, you say, with Brenda? Never mind, for the moment. I want to be alone. I want to read this book.'

And then the blow fell. A summons, next day, to the Royal Automobile Club. 'I'm ruined, my boy. I'm ruined. 'Aven't got a penny left. Those pals of yours, Alvanley and Gleneagles. They've skinned me. You'll 'ave to earn your own living from now on. Oh, your poor mother!' 'It's poor me, you old banana. I've no intention of earning my own living, thank you.' – 'Ow, wot a boy, wot a boy.' And I flung out. Tears. Consultations.

'I can always sell my Gris.' 'But what will you do then?'

'Oh write – paint – don't fluster me.'

'And we were to have gone to the Londonderry del Vals!'

'Poor Mother.'

One thing stood out with terrible clarity in those dark days.

---

1   Firbank's shyness was proverbial.

The old life was over. I could never associate any longer with those friends who had been used to look to me for advice, loans, old clothes, and entertainment. They would see to that. The Ritz, the Blue Lantern must know me no more.

Exile. A few months in Paris – but Montparnasse, now, my dears, *Montparnasse*; a few offers for my memoirs; then Berlin, Munich – and finally, Greece. There, 'in the worst inn's worst room', I existed, miserably, on fried goat and raki. To write or to paint – to work – but how? Write only on one side of the page. But which side? It was the old dilemma. A wandering exile, the quays of the Piraeus knew me, as did the bars of Terreno, the Dôme and the Deux Magots, Bohême and Silhouette, and that place in the Marokaner Gasse. I ate rose-leaf jam with the good monks of Holy Luke, and fried locusts with the dervishes of Moulay Idris. And one crazy 4th of June, lobster salad with my housemaster! My slim figure lingered, winter-bound, in dim cathedrals, and there were beaches where summer licked me with its great rough tongue. Ah, summer! There's a crypto-fascist for you! The spring I never cared for. It held nothing but a promise, and I, too, was promising. The autumns I adored; they smelt of cassia. But poverty was crippling. To whom life once had been a bed of roses – no, of *Strawberry-leaves*, there remained only the 'Welcome' at Villefranche, the old Bœuf in the Boissy D'Anglas, the Pangion. It was not good enough. I came back to live with my mother.

It was then that I saw the light. One day I wandered into a little book shop near Red Lion Square. It was full of slim volumes by unfamiliar names – who were Stephen, Wystan, Cecil, and Christopher? Madge? Bates? Dutt? These blunt monosyllables spoke a new kind of language to me. I looked at the books. Not at all bad, and some of these young poets, I realized, had even attended my university! One quatrain in particular haunted me.

> *M is for Marx*
> *and Movement of Masses*
> *and Massing of Arses*
> *and Clashing of Classes.*

It was new. It was vigorous. It was real. It was chic!

Cyril Connolly

> Come on Percy, my pillion-proud, be
>   camber-conscious
> Cleave to the crown of the road

and

> It was late last night when my lord came home
> enquiring for his lady O
> The servants cried on every side
> She's gone with the Left Book
>   Study Circle O!

And everyone was called by their Christian names! So cosy! From that moment I've never looked back. It's been pylons all the way. Of course they didn't want me, at first. The meetings behind the Geisha Café – they suspected me of all sorts of things I'm afraid – I said quite frankly: 'I realize I shall never understand eclectic materialism but I'm terribly terribly Left!' And I showed them one or two things I'd written for the weekly reviews, all among the waffle-receipts and the guest-house advertisements.[1] And I called myself Cris Clay. Then on a drizzling February morning came the procession. It was for me a veritable *Via Crucis*, for we had to march up St James's Street – past Locks, and Lobbs, and Briggs, and Boodles. All my past was spread out before me. There weren't very many of us, and it was difficult to cheer and shout our slogans

> One, two, three, four
> Pacifism means War.

I raised my eyes to White's bow-window.

Yes, there they were – Alvanley and Gleneagles, with their soiled city faces and little moustaches, their bowlers and rolled umbrellas – and, good heavens, there were Peter, and Robert, and Evelyn! I never felt more ridiculous. When suddenly something made me look around. 'De Clavering, old horse!' 'Well I'm spifflicated.' 'You old *finocchio*!' '*Spinaten*!' It was too good to be true.

'But Harmatviz – I see you don't know the first thing about the cut of a corduroy.'

[1]   Soon to be published under the title of *I Told You So*.

'Not a red shirt, Slivovitz – a red tie if you must.'

'And you, Coca y Cola – you look like a scarecrow.'

'These are good workmen's pants, de Clavering, real dunga-ree!'

We gave a boo to the bow-window that made the *Tatlers* rattle in their holders.

'But how did you get here?'

'I was expelled for plotting against the Regent in favour of the traitor Otto.'

'I was turned out for lack of enthusiasm for the present régime and communicating with the traitor Wilhelm.'

'I wanted to annoy Sarsaparilla.'

'Anyhow, we're all good anti-fascists,' cried Comrade Graf Slivovitz.

I wanted to say something more – that I had even been told by the Party that I should be more useful outside it, but I couldn't speak. Old friends had met, travelling a stony road, coming to the same hard conclusions, and together.

And that's about all. There are one or two things I've left out, the War, the slump, the general strike, and my conversion to Catholicism, because I'm so vague about dates. But I think this will remain – A Modern Pilgrimage. And now for the reviewers. I think they'd better be careful. They'd better be very careful indeed. A line is being drawn. I'm going to say it again, and very slowly. A line is being drawn. Quite quietly at present – just a few names jotted down in a note-book – one or two with a question mark after them. They have another chance. And the rest don't. Those lines mean something. Tatatat! Yes, my dears, bullets – real bullets, the kind of bullets they keep for reviewers who step across the party line. One day you're going to see something rather hostile. It will make you feel, perhaps, a little uneasy. It's heavy – and stubby – and rather pointed. Guess? Yes. A machine-gun. POINTED AT YOU. And behind it, with his hand on the trigger, Comrade – no COMMISSAR – Cris Clay. Did you write such and such an article? Yes (No). It doesn't matter which. Tatatat. It's no good then bleating about how you voted in the last election, or where your sympathies have always been. We don't want your sympathy. We don't want you at all.

You subscribed to the *News-Chronicle*, did you? I am afraid you will be under no necessity to renew that subscription.

You wrote for the *New Statesman*? What did you write about? 'Gramophone records.'

'To sit on the fence is to be on the wrong side of it – line him up, Gollancz.'

'Yes, Commissar.'

'And you – what were you?'

'Turf-Accountant.'

'Your face seems vaguely familiar – but that doesn't make it more pleasant – line him up, Stephen.'

'It was no accident, Pryce-Jones, that you have lived near three royal palaces.'

'But –.'

But I am anticipating. There are two ways to review a book like mine, a right and a wrong. The wrong way is to find fault with it, for then you find fault with the book clubs behind it, in fact, with your advertisers. And if I seem too clever it's because you're too stupid. Think it over. The right way is to praise it, and to quote from it in such a way that you all can learn my lesson. I stand no nonsense. Remember, my dears, a line is being drawn. Tatatat. See you at the Mass Observatory.

> *Something is going to go, baby,*
> *And it won't be your stamp-collection.*
> *Boom!*

And that I think could particularly be meditated by the fascist Connolly.

CRIS CLAY
PARIS – BUDAPEST – PARTON ST
1936–1937

Malcolm Muggeridge

from *The Thirties*

Popularity is achieved by making manifest the contemporary mood, as Lord Northcliffe well understood when he made an immediate success of the *Daily Mail* by setting out to give the public what they wanted, rather than what they ought to want, or what would be good for them. Since then others have copied his prescription, and as so often happens, outdone its original application; and the *Daily Mail* has come to have a distinctly old-fashioned flavour.

The contemporary mood touches everything and everyone, like the light of the declining sun spreading the same glow over faces, houses, trees, motor-cars, slag-heaps and pylons. It may be seen in hikers noisily making for the countryside, their knees bare, males and females scarcely distinguishable; in road-houses, strangely named (the Monkey Puzzle, the Spider's Web), urban to the country, rural to the town; in beauty-treatment, much developed, filling whole newspaper pages, inquiries being invited and profusely received, women's page editors (not always women) ruefully surveying a mountain of letters all asking for advice about intractable complexions, pores, arm-pits, eye-brows.

From eton-crop to permanent wave covers the same distance as from Ramsay MacDonald to Mr Neville Chamberlain, or from D. H. Lawrence to Mr Hemingway, or from Charlie Chaplin to Walt Disney, or from Mr Beverley Nichols, cottager, to Mr Beverley Nichols, patriot. This author is notably susceptible to the contemporary mood's fluctuations. Its slightest shift in direction or abatement of intensity is registered by him. In 1930, he was still praising the delights of rural retirement; in 1934 turned his attention to the iniquity of war and of armament manufacturers, many who had previously scoffed at him becoming respectful; in 1936 God was his preoccupation, and in 1938,

England. There for the time being he has come to rest, his cottage sold, after probably the most profitable occupancy of a rural property on record, the local village shop participating in the harvest by selling picture postcards, for instance, of Mr Nichols's dog, inscribed: 'I just want him to be his own woolly self', and of a statue in Mr Nichols's garden, inscribed: 'The sweet country rain washed his limbs, and the wind played about him.'

Even sentimentality, though never diminishing, gushes and burbles differently at different times. Once Mr James Douglas might legitimately have been regarded as sentimentalist-in-chief, but now he has been superseded. It is not that his hand has lost its cunning, or his tear-ducts run dry, but that the hearts he once touched have changed and no longer respond to his treatment. What is his dog, Bunch, now deceased, compared with the one Mr Nichols just wants to be his own woolly self, or with Mr Godfrey Winn's Mr Sponge? 'I wish I could keen or howl,' Mr Douglas wrote in the *Daily Express* on the occasion of Bunch's death, 'like a woman or a girl or a child or a dog, but a man can't howl or keen.' That was where Mr Douglas was wrong. A man can howl or keen, a man does. 'He had rickets, you know, as a puppy,' Mr Winn has written of Mr Sponge, 'and though he is much better these days, he still wobbles sideways a bit.' On another occasion, Mr Winn 'said to Mr Sponge, pointing with my gardening scissors between the chopping: "Look at that rose, old man. An hour ago it reminded me of a woman in full bloom – wearing a pale pink dress at a party, knowing she was what is called the cynosure of every eye. Now? Her petals are falling. Softly, gently, one by one, in the noon-day heat. In another hour she will be nothing but a barren, blighted stalk." ' Bunch did well to die. His day was done.

Mr Winn, reputed to be the highest paid journalist in Fleet Street, has indeed captured the sentimentality market. In his own words, he 'set his pen high', and his salary mounted with it. His writings provide his readers with their own romanticized version of life. Beside by-pass roads are many mansions, mansions of light and love. It would be a good thing, Mr Winn thinks, 'if a law compelled all employers and employees, wherever it was compatible with public safety, to change places for one working day once a year'; 'charm is the plain girl's lifebuoy,' he writes, and to hearten a friend who is 'waiting patiently for that event which, though this is an age of sex-emancipation, still remains the most important and memorable moment in the lives of most women', quotes a remark of Carole Lombard's: 'I live by a man's code, designed to fit a man's world, yet at the same time I never forget that a woman's first job is to choose the right shade of lipstick.'

The same recipe as Mr Winn uses, but with different baking, is used by Mr H. G. Wells, whose film *The Shape of Things to Come* also holds out the prospect of a world full of charm, correctly shaded lipstick, and interchangeable employers and employees. Golden youths and maidens in white silken shorts and open-necked shirts live delectable, amorous lives, provided by science with innumerable conveniences and playthings, shooting through the air at immense speed, falling without self-consciousness into one another's hygienic arms, with no jealous squall or inward groan to disturb their bliss – this seen from plush seats across intervening darkness, typewriters all still, orders all taken, washing-up done.

In Mr Wells, too, the contemporary mood is made manifest. He has succeeded in giving the harsh materialism in which his own life is rooted, a glow of righteousness and joy. Prosperity, once regarded as an end in itself, he has endowed with transcendental qualities, adding unto it benevolence and eroticism. Bank balances dissolve into embraces, factory chimneys blossom like flowers, and company directors discard their black coats and put on white silk, take off their top-hats to twine bay leaves in their hair. The black-coated worker becomes white-coated. This romantic materialism, this sense that faulty technique, which might be corrected, rather than any fundamental fallacy, has prevented increased wealth from resulting in increased happiness, has also been popularized by religious teaching, which has tended to become increasingly chiliastic, choosing rather to stress the Kingdom-of-Heaven-on-Earth than expectations beyond the grave. Denunciations of slums from the pulpit have been more common than denunciations of sin, and the Church

Assembly has become animated, if at all, over derelict ecclesi-astical properties and the inequality of livings, rather than over derelict souls and the equality of dying.

In a film, directed by Professor Julian Huxley, the evolutionary process was demonstrated, culminating in radiant and nude youths and maidens floating heavenwards, the decencies being ingeniously safeguarded by a light, but opaque, mist which floated round their nether-portions; and a Pageant of Parliament portrayed the growth of constitutional liberties and social pro-gress. The performers were mostly amateurs, among them society ladies, débutantes, much photographed, whose names were frequent in gossip paragraphs. From Magna Charta onwards the tale unfolded, until the Industrial Revolution. Then the stage was darkened, and the débutantes appeared, whim-pering and wretched, dressed in rags, to represent miserable children condemned to work underground in mines, or in insani-tary factories. After a short performance in this role, they van-ished, soon to reappear beaming, and, as the programme put it, 'in clean white pinnies', to attend school in charge of a kindly Froebel teacher. All the lights were put on to suggest sunshine. Tennis-players, cyclists, hikers, athletes, boy scouts and girl guides assembled, and to invigorating music went through suit-able motions. This was the grand finale.

The same spirit is apparent in a rather different form, in the only successful revivalistic enterprise of recent years – Buch-manism, about which both Mr Nichols and Mr Winn, though not Mr Wells, have written sympathetically. This charac-teristically American importation has managed, by calling itself the Oxford Group, to acquire snob appeal, and to get vaguely associated with Newman and Pusey. Its founder, Dr Frank Buchman, looks like a successful business man of the Rotarian sort, and when in London stays at Brown's Hotel, which was also Kipling's favourite hotel. From this quiet and select, but expensive, headquarters, he directs his organization, which has attracted a number of dons, bishops, retired Army and Navy officers, athletes, and even politicians, besides enthusiastic teams of young men and women mostly belonging to the middle and upper classes. An efficiently produced, illustrated periodical made its appearance in 1938, in technique identical with all forms of photographic propaganda, whether *The U.S.S.R. in Construction* or the little leaflets wrapped round constipation cures – that is, showing smiling faces, varied, male and female, but alike in that they all smile. House parties are organized, at which sins, usually of an economic, but sometimes of a sexual, character, are publicly confessed; and occasionally there are large gatherings in the Albert Hall. The platform is decorated with flags; while the audience assembles the organ plays tunes like 'Land of Hope and Glory', and speeches are delivered by speakers representing as wide a social range as possible. Each, whether country gentlemen acknowledging that he has been in the habit of using bad language to his stable boys, or mill-worker acknowledging that he has sometimes neglected to work when the foreman's eye was not on him, or housewife acknowledging that she has been responsible for unpleasantness at the breakfast table, have the same message – life was dull and unprofitable until the Groups came along, and then was happy and prosperous. These successive testimonies, so eager, so spontaneous and yet never faltering, create a growing excitement. Each member of the audience recognizes himself in one or other of the testifiers; wonders – Might not I also smile, become self-confident and prosperous, testify even? The country gentleman is genial, the mill-worker in his Sunday best, the housewife serene. Thus it might be always – everyone smiling, in Sunday best, untroubled ...

The logical end, perhaps the *reductio ad absurdum*, of romantic materialism is some form of utopia. If heaven is transferred from Eternity to Time, from beyond the skies to earth, then it must come to pass; and if it refuses to come to pass, then what has come to pass must be called heaven, and woe unto those who question its celestial pretensions.

Two rival heavens-on-earth have been put on the market whose protagonists hurl abuse at one another, and are only united in despising whoever will not admit the momentousness of their rivalry. Many attempts have been made to define the conflict between them. Mr Wyndham Lewis, for instance, sees it as a clash between nationalism and internationalism; others have demonstrated that it is between Christianity and atheism, dictatorship and democracy, capitalism and communism, tyranny and freedom, bourgeoisie and proletariat. Even the nomenclature used is uncertain, Left and Right, Fascist and anti-Fascist, meaning one thing at one moment and another at another; and to add to the confusion, the two factions have tended to range themselves behind two existent régimes, the U.S.S.R. and the Third Reich, and have therefore felt bound to justify the acts of the one, whatever they may be, and to abhor those of the other, whatever they may be. Since, in practice, these acts have borne a marked and increasing resemblance to one another, the lot of their rival admirers and detractors has been hard indeed, and was made appreciably harder by the German–Soviet Pact, surprisingly concluded in 1939. When a Rothschild was spoiled of his possessions in Vienna, socialists must complain; patriots found their hearts glowing when British ships were bombed off the coast of Spain, and fulminators against imperialism groaned when Gibraltar was threatened; the extermination by Stalin of his revolutionary associates caused those who most disapproved of the deceaseds' activities when alive, to complain, and won delighted approval from those whose heroes they once were ...

If Mr Wells is the prophet of romantic materialism, Mr Nichols and Mr Winn its two most competent publicists, the *Daily Express* its most marketable, and contending political ideologies its most formidable, versions, D. H. Lawrence may be regarded as its poet. At the beginning of 1930, he lay dying at Vence, in the hills above Antibes, bearded and cadaverous, *Lady Chatterley's Lover* written and published, realizing according to its publisher, Mr G. Oriole, a profit of £1,615 18s. 3d.; his last work, *Apocalypse*, unfinished, and dealing, significantly, not with purifying sensuality but with power ('As a collective being man has his fulfilment in the gratification of his power sense ... If his country mounts up splendidly to a zenith of splendour and power, he will be all the more fulfilled ...'), and curiously recalling another work, *Mein Kampf*, more profitable even than *Lady Chatterley's Lover*.

He had wandered restlessly about the world looking for satisfaction and finding none, recruiting derelict ladies to found a new social order, impotently railing against Mind and its miseries, impotently exalting Flesh and its ecstasies; his death surely a fitting prelude to the years which were to come, full of mindless ecstasy, of new social orders and dark unconsciousness.

After his death, Lawrence's influence continued to be considerable, thumbed copies of *Lady Chatterley's Lover* to circulate widely, and his associates and disciples to wrangle, most writing books about him, and their relations with him and with one another. These books constitute one of the curiosities of literature, perhaps the gem of the collection being Mrs Dodge Luhan's *Lorenzo in Taos*. Their cumulative effect was to bore even those who did not read them; and gradually scenes in which a hero or heroine is spiritually refreshed by protracted embraces, vanished from contemporary fiction, the Dark Unconscious transforming itself into the Dark Class-Conscious as easily as, in the Pageant of Parliament, rags were transformed into white pinnies . . .

A great shifting of power has taken place; and when power shifts, men shift with it. Power is their everlasting pursuit. They follow it lovingly from place to place, from person to person, from idea to idea, sometimes with resultant confusion. When power shifts rapidly, the most practised power-diviners falter. By the time they have made up their minds to ingratiate themselves with, for instance, the legatees of the Russian Revolution, most of these are shot as spies and traitors; by the time they have accustomed themselves to the idea that Captain Röhm must be counted among the great ones of the earth, he is put to death. Now a Tsar Nicholas is powerful and requires adulation; now a Stalin is powerful, and also requires adulation, largely the same. The mighty are continually being put down from their seats and the humble and meek exalted, to become mighty in their turn and fit also to be put down.

When the Thirties began, Europe was dominated by France, with an elaborate system of alliances sustained by loans in Central and Eastern Europe, with a Maginot Line in process of being completed, deeper, stronger and more comfortable than any fortifications hitherto constructed, and with a Gold Reserve stored away which amounted to nearly a third of the total supply of gold in the world; as the Thirties proceeded, Europe was increasingly dominated by Germany, whose Führer's speeches were anxiously awaited, if angry, spreading panic, if mild, engendering a feeling of relief comparable to that of a prisoner who, expecting a term of imprisonment, is only bound over. After one such mild speech in the early part of 1939, the *Daily Sketch* reported that all the florists in London were sold out, though whether to provide wreaths or bouquets or household decorations was not explained. 'The great security for peace at the present moment,' Lord Grey of Falloden said in 1933, 'is that Germany is not armed, and not in a position to go to war.' He, dying soon afterwards, did not live to see how soon and how easily this 'great security for peace' was to be lost. At midnight on 4 August 1914, he had sadly reflected: 'The lamps are going out all over Europe. We shall not see them lit again in our lifetime'; on the morning of 3 September 1939, six years after his death, they would have gone out once more if any had been alight. There were none to go out then. Put out the light, when the light had already been put out; lamps extinguished before, were extinguished again.

Each generation has its hero, one in whom are embodied all prevailing trends and aspirations, whose very features are what his contemporaries would wish to see when they look into a mirror, whose character and achievements represent in the eyes of others what they would wish theirs to be. Heroes are mortal, like men. They die and are forgotten, lingering on, if at all, in the pages of books, in the glamour of a remembered name.

They expire with their validity, sometimes continuing to exist in the flesh, ghostly; more often expiring as heroes and as men simultaneously, like Colonel T. E. Lawrence, whose death in 1934 as a result of a motor-bicycle accident seemed inevitable, to himself and to others. His genius had left him, he wrote to a friend. The circumstances in which it could flourish no longer existed. Other wars were brewing, requiring other heroes.

At the beginning of the decade, the War book, and the War

play were still popular, *Journey's End* still running, *All Quiet on the Western Front* still selling. The War was far enough away to be romanticized, the prospect of another war sufficiently remote for the subject to be congenial to circulating-library subscribers. Men who had been heroic explained that they were sensitive, men who were sensitive explained that they had been heroic. Mr Robert Graves, Mr Richard Aldington, Mr Siegfried Sassoon, Mr Ernest Hemingway, Mr Edmund Blunden and others, published their War experiences, finding many readers. The fashion was for the soldier-poet, agonized at having to shed blood, listening to birds singing when the guns paused, with his Keats or Shakespeare's Sonnets in the pocket of his tunic; yet not less courageous and effective in action for that; if anything, more.

T. E. Lawrence filled this part perfectly, provided a perfect compromise between the conscientious objector to whom it was felt some amends were due, and Lord Kitchener whose glory had faded. He was the conscientious consenter; the successful man of action who wrote fine prose and the successful man of letters who won battles. As the War receded into the past, he alone emerged as its hero. Not even controversy over Earl Haig's equestrian statue, and the attacks of Mr Lloyd George on his generalship, could make him interesting. Two rival biographies by Lady Haig and Mr Duff Cooper were by no means bestsellers, whereas the public thirst for information about T. E. Lawrence seemed insatiable. Books about him were many, and his own books, *Revolt in the Desert*, and later *The Seven Pillars of Wisdom*, were much read and discussed.

His modesty and delight in fame pulling him in opposite directions; his passion for publicity which, like Greta Garbo's, took the extremely effective form of ostentatiously shunning it; his refusal of important posts and insistence on joining the Air Force as an aircraftsman under an assumed name, thereby attracting more attention to himself than any colonial administrator, however successful; his poverty which, as Sir Ronald Storrs has pointed out, did not prevent him from indulging in expensive luxuries like speed-boats; his achievements, so remarkable, yet coming to nothing, bearing no fruit; his reputation for endurance and feats of strength combined with a slight physique, an unathletic, unhearty appearance – all this fitted him to be the hero of the years during which all desire to hang the Kaiser had gone and a desire to hang Hitler not yet manifested itself. Mr Stephen Spender provided the Left Book Club with a statement of his political faith called *Forward from Liberalism*. In the same way, one of the many books on T. E. Lawrence might have been entitled *Forward from Kipling*.

The hero provides a pattern after which many aspire. His influence seeps down, evoking remote imitations, dreams. He appears in many guises; in living men, and in imagined characters. An age may be known by its hero, its Rousseau or Byron or Walt Whitman. Even the dead are made to conform to his lineaments, furbished up to look like him. Thus Sir James Barrie, shortly before his death, undertook the difficult task in his play *The Boy David* of presenting King David as a Prince Charming, a youthful soldier whose war-memoirs would have resembled Mr Sassoon's. The enterprise defeated him. He was too old for it; his technique out-of-date, the right moment past. The early, not the late, Thirties was the time for it; before, not after, German rearmament. It was a pre-Hitler enterprise. Mr Auden might have succeeded, stressing David's early proletarian sympathies when 'everyone that was in distress, and everyone that was in debt, and everyone that was discontented, gathered themselves unto him', perhaps detecting in Absalom's revolt a popular protest against his father's later authoritarian propensities; but not Sir James Barrie.

Not even the fame of Miss Elizabeth Bergner, who played David, equipped for the part by her face if not by her sex, sufficed to save the play from failure. She came to it fresh from her triumphant appearance in *Escape Me Never*, a dramatization of one of Miss Margaret Kennedy's several sequels to *The Constant Nymph*; a Bohemian fantasy or Café Royal idyll of the sort that has never failed to appeal since it became the fashion for young women with incomes, great or small, earned or unearned, to live their own lives in front of their own gas-fire. The combination of a Margaret Kennedy heroine and *Peter Pan* dialogue failed to convey the character of David. Perhaps it would have been easier but for the Bible.

It is commonly observed that there is an average or type produced by particular circumstances at a particular time. Everyman's appearances have ranged between Morality Plays and furniture advertisements; Strube's Little Man, battling with Income Tax demands and frightened of his wife, is one of his contemporary impersonations, another is the Man in the Street whom journalists and politicians constantly invoke. If, however, such an average man exists, he cannot be identified. When he is known he is no longer average. If the identity of the Unknown Soldier were discovered, it would be necessary to replace his bones by others, still unidentified. He is only the average soldier who died in the War as long as he is nameless and characterless.

Everyman is an abstraction, a dream figure who may evoke pity like Charlie Chaplin, laughter like Mr Chips, or fear and adoration like Hitler, but who cannot be said truly to exist. The popularity of Charlie Chaplin, which in *Modern Times* and *City Lights* survived even the talkies, has been due to his convincing impersonation of this abstraction, this average man, and consequent releasing in each individual breast of the self-pity contained there. Hitler has performed a similar feat, with Europe for his set and mankind for his audience, and with the finale still to come – the minute, lonely figure forlornly trudging along a winding road until he vanishes into the sunset, though perhaps in Hitler's case this finale may be reversed, and the sunset forlornly vanish into him. In a story by Mr James Hilton, Hitler would be Mr Hits.

Intuition makes possible such impersonations of the average man. He may also be synthetically produced – as the Economic Man of nineteenth-century economists, or Rousseau's Natural man, or the Marxists' Proletarian Man. These are symbols merely, used to balance an equation or populate a utopia. Attempts to give them a semblance of life as fictitious characters invariably fail, and when those who accept their validity look for them in the flesh, they are always disappointed – like Tolstoy, who heard a peasant curse him as he passed by, and turned to remonstrate: 'But I'm Tolstoy!' only to have more furious curses called down upon him.

If, however, there is no average man, but only men, each

Malcolm Muggeridge

to himself the centre of an incomprehensible universe, certain characteristic traits, a characteristic mental development, physiognomy even, may at all times be detected; but more easily in the distant past than yesterday. The distant past is like a strange land whose characteristics are at once noticeable, whereas yesterday is still familiar and therefore difficult to explore; the dead who tell no tales, may be understood, but the living who tell many, are full of mystery. Nor has the prevailing fashion for unreticent autobiography altered this. Frankness is usually more uncommunicative than reticence. By pretending to tell everything, what is not told is more securely hidden. The subtlest politicians, like Mr Baldwin at the time of the abdication of King Edward VIII, put all their cards on the table; and outspoken autobiographies by burglars, waiters, taxi-drivers, convicts, undergraduates, society ladies, diplomats, journalists, restaurateurs, politicians, down-and-outs, monarchs, all conditions of men and women, turn out to be no more than essays in self-dramatization. The burglar is a choice spirit out of the common run of burglars – for instance, Mr Mark Benny, who has described in *Low Company* how when he was on a job, cultural aspirations impelled him to fill his bag with *objets d'art* rather than with common-or-garden silver spoons. A small bust of Beethoven or a Hogarth print was irresistible, even though a fruit salver might be taken. Such a predilection, it may be assumed, is rare among burglars. In the same way, the waiter devotes his scanty leisure to intellectual pursuits; the monarch is never so happy as away from court formalities, and the prostitute imbibes culture from a Bloomsbury clientèle. Even Hitler, in *Mein Kampf*, makes the general observation that as a poverty-stricken youth in Vienna he read voraciously though without specifying what. He, too, though he exalts averageness, is reluctant to admit that his tastes are average ones.

These so diverse autobiographies have in common only the egotism which inspires them, and that is a constant, unvarying at all times and in all circumstances. If Rousseau had happened to be a burglar, his Confessions would have been very like *Low Company*, if an American journalist, very like *The Way of the Transgressor*. Burglars and prostitutes and queens have always aroused curiosity among those oppressed by a sense of the ordinariness of their lives; but when authentic burglars and prostitutes and queens set about satisfying this curiosity, they inevitably assume it is directed rather towards themselves than towards their unusual circumstances. The average burglar or prostitute or queen, like the Unknown Soldier, is necessarily anonymous; and the insatiable thirst for contemporary auto-biography is due rather to a desire to experience vicariously the excitement of an exceptional life than to acquire information about ordinary people in whom the reader may recognize his like. Each autobiographer is concerned to portray himself, not as he is, but as he would wish to be – experienced and travelled, yet innocent and eager; fond of a kiss and fond of a guinea; given equally to piping through the valleys wild and to *wagons-lits*, tough enough to kill, and tender enough to love, and err, and expose injustices, and espouse righteous causes. If it would be idle to look for a burglar in *Low Company*, or even for Mr Benny, it contains Mr Benny's conception of himself and of burglary at their noblest and best. From the abundance of contemporary autobiography dealing with high- and low-, but seldom with middle-life, a generation's aspirations may be deduced; all they would have wished to be and are not, all they might have experienced and have not. Like toreadors, Mr Bruce Lockhart, Mr Negley Farson, Mr Vincent Sheean, perform in the arena; and the onlookers, lolling in their seats, sucking oranges, applauding, feel that they too have been adventurous, they too have seen men and cities.

This vogue for self-dramatization has opened up a lucrative career for down-and-outs, convicts, and other former social outcasts. A term of penal servitude has its compensations when it may later produce abundant royalties; the prostitute on her weary search for a client may take comfort from the thought that one day her reminiscences may be marketable. Pockets which once had to be picked or left intact, will freely disgorge when a pickpocket's inner life is made available at ten-and-six net; those be edified who formerly had to be preyed upon, and Miss Rebecca West throw in her blessing with, 'He writes like an angel.' Nor have the upper classes neglected to participate in this profitable trade. If low-life has strange secrets to disclose, has not high-life, too? If social outcasts easily weep, and read Proust and Shelley, do not Aristocrats, too? The halls of fashion are as enthralling as doss-houses are, and Lord Castlerosse also has a tale to tell . . .

Washing down bacon-and-egg with hot tea, an eye on the clock; rocking along five a side between Croydon East and London Bridge, or packed together between Holborn and Chancery Lane, people absorb the contents of newspapers. Headlines surprise them, large print gets into the blood-stream, and little print lingers round the heart. The kingdoms of the earth are spread out before them, and all human activity.

Some country or town or mountain peak, formerly a name, perhaps not even that, is suddenly made familiar – a remote Greenland ice-cap, where Mr Augustine Courtauld spent seven months alone and in darkness in a little snow hut, when removed thence stating that he found this solitary mode of life not uncongenial; Abyssinia, where the lately crowned Emperor conferred on his grateful subjects a bi-cameral legislature, and abolished slavery in his kingdom, announcing his virtuous decision to the Anti-Slavery Society in a letter which began: 'The Conquering Lion of the Tribe of Judah, Hailé Selassié the First, the Elect of God, King of the Kings of Ethiopia, may this reach the President of the Anti-Slavery Society'; Dusseldorf, where a murderer was active, at his trial coolly explaining that he had made a point of mingling with the crowd which collected round his victims when they were discovered, this greatly interesting the many psychiatrists who assembled to observe him, and who suggested that his brain might, like Lenin's, profitably be dissected after his execution; Manchuria, where a Japanese invasion began, resistance being offered by Chinese War Lords, among them, Feng, a Christian one, whose soldiers sang hymns as they marched along, thereby pleasing missionaries; Chicago, where the Mayor, Big Bill Thompson, proclaimed his intention of 'landing King George V one on the snoot' if he attempted any interference with Chicago's affairs.

A name becomes momentarily prominent, a face picked out

from among innumerable other faces, as when a searchlight plays on a crowd, catching one face, white, staring, and then passing on to another – Miss Amy Johnson, who flew solo from England to Australia in twenty days, tumultuously welcomed on her return, a song made about her and a triumphal procession organized along the Strand and Fleet Street, she standing up in a car and all cheering as she passed, the *Daily Mail* presenting her with £10,000, and in its columns greatly extolling her as a manifestation of the unconquerable spirit of Youth; Lord Kylsant charged with 'drawing up and circulating a prospectus, the contents of which he knew to be false in an important particular', and sentenced to a year's imprisonment in the second division, after six months released, soon to die; Texas Guinan refused permission to land at Marseilles when she arrived there with a 'party of lovely kids', even then some of the lovely kids unaccountably missing when she started on her return journey; the Bishop of Birmingham in dispute with some of his High Church clergy who refused to abandon practices which he contemptuously dismissed as magic; Miss Millie Orpen, a typist who, acting as a common informer under the Sunday Observances Act of 1781, was awarded £5,000, this sum being later remitted and by her forgone; Professor Piccard who ascended ten miles into the stratosphere, and Zaro Agha who claimed to be 150 years old, and a Mrs Stocks who moved a resolution at a meeting of the National Society for Equal Citizenship protesting against the fashion of longer skirts, finding in this fashion a dangerous reversal to male ascendancy.

Place-names become momentarily familiar, different moods are awakened – desire, fear, hatred, grief, cupidity; like the conductor of an orchestra with his baton stirring up sound and stilling it, calling forth a little sentimental tune or a roar of passionate music. All that happens is digested, each morsel broken down by the requisite juices; what is nourishing absorbed into the blood-stream, and waste products discharged. Each event has its corresponding emotion as each note on an organ keyboard has its corresponding sound; and the play of these emotions, between gulps of food and drink and puffs of tobacco smoke, constitutes public opinion ...

A sweepstake, organized in Dublin for the benefit of Irish hospitals, proved popular, its prize-fund reaching £1,181,815. The tickets were shaken up in a large drum, and extracted by young women dressed as guardsmen; and newspapers prominently announced the list of winners, some with much personal detail. Outside the café of Emilio Scala, who won the first prize, a little crowd collected, looking up reverently at its shuttered windows; and the suggestion was made that a similar sweepstake organized in England would relieve the hospitals of increasing financial strain. Opposing this suggestion, Sir Reginald Poole wrote: 'I do not suppose that the poor fail altogether to realize that it is largely the money of the well-to-do which really enables the hospitals to exist, or that the poor are ungrateful. This lottery scheme would certainly put an end to any such sentiment of gratitude, for after all there would be no question of gratitude as the well-to-do would have no reason to subscribe.' Whether Sir Reginald Poole's or some other argument proved convincing, the suggestion was dropped . . .

The results of a census taken in April 1930 were published, showing that the population of England and Wales was slightly under 40,000,000, that the birth-rate had enormously fallen, and that London was steadily growing, soon to have 9,000,000 inhabitants, the largest number of human beings so far collected together in one place; at the same time a builder announcing that in his experience it was garages, not nurseries, which were in demand . . .

Sir Oswald Mosley carried his revolt further by founding the New Party, whose policy mainly aimed at reforming constitutional procedure, and a weekly, *Action*, first edited by Mr Harold Nicolson, later Member of Parliament for Leicester in the National Labour interest; the Pope broadcast for the first time, the Holy Father's voice being heard in all parts of the world; Mr Eugene O'Neill excelled himself by producing a play, *Strange Interlude*, whose performance lasted five hours without one laugh; and the *New Statesman*, a Socialist weekly, originally Fabian, amalgamated, first with the Liberal *Nation*, then with the *Week-End Review*, whose editor, Mr Gerald Barry, had formerly been editor of the *Saturday Review*, but had fallen out with its proprietor on a question of policy, and started the *Week-End Review* by way of protest. This confused situation in due course sorted itself out. Under the editorship of Mr Kingsley Martin, the *New Statesman* and affiliated periodicals became the chief organ of Left-Wing intellectuals; Mr Gerald Barry became editor of the *News-Chronicle*, sole relic of Liberal daily journalism; and the *Saturday Review* fell into the hands of Lady Houston, appearing until her death in 1937 with a Union Jack and a Red Flag and the legend 'Under Which Flag?' on the front cover, a cure for colds devised by Lady Houston herself on the back cover, and in between much patriotic matter.

Cross-word puzzles became daily instead of weekly features in most newspapers; air mails to all parts of the world were instituted, and the activities and internecine feuds of American gangsters were followed with interest, Al Capone, Jack Diamond and others becoming better known than most politicians, new words and expressions like 'racket', 'bumped off', 'taken for a ride', coming into common usage, and gangster plays, novels and films proving increasingly popular; for instance, *On the Spot*, a play believed to be based on the great Al Capone himself, which had a long run and provided Mr Charles Laughton with the first of many successful and lucrative gangster parts. This literature, whose theme was violence and crime, whose style reproduced the rattle of machine-guns, or at any rate of type-writers, and in which there was only action and appetite, owed its popularity to the relief it afforded from the boredom and deso-lation of mechanized life. It represented the poetry or mysticism of mass-production, the craving for violence and bloodshed, set up by days spent in exhausting but monotonous activity; unnecessary when, as in the U.S.S.R. and Germany, the same craving is catered for by State organized and publicized terrorism. Its leading purveyor was Edgar Wallace, a genial, rather pathetic figure, frenziedly pouring out words into a dictaphone, frenziedly making and getting rid of money, appearing at Black-pool in a yellow Rolls Royce as a Liberal candidate in the 1931 General Election, and dying exhausted and in debt a year later, having written in all 150 novels, eighteen plays, and innumerable short stories and newspaper articles; of words, many millions.

Evelyn Waugh

Awake My Soul! It is a Lord

'*I'm not on business. I'm a member of the House of Lords.*' These moving and rather mysterious words were uttered on my doorstep the other evening and recorded by the leading literary critic of the Beaverbrook press. They have haunted me, waking and sleeping, ever since. I am sometimes accused of a partiality for lords; whatever touches them, it is hinted, vicariously touches me. Certainly the nobleman who tried to insinuate himself into my house half an hour before dinner that evening has become a nine days' obsession.

Does anyone, I wonder, remember *Young England*, the drama of more than twenty years ago, which was taken up as an esoteric joke, soon became a popular saturnalia, but never failed to enchant? Here across the years came an authentic echo of that production; and the speaker, too, bald and overgrown though he was, had all the artless bearing of that inimitable troop of Boy Scouts.

But to explain his presence. The popular papers, I conceive, are fitfully and uneasily aware that there are spheres of English life in which they hold a negligible influence. The fifty or sixty thousand people in this country who alone support the Arts do not go to Lord Beaverbrook's critics for guidance. So it is that artists of all kinds form part of the battle-training of green reporters. 'Don't lounge about the office, lad,' the editors say, 'sit up and insult an artist.' Rather frequently writers, among others, are troubled by the telephone asking for interviews. When these are refused, the journalist goes to what in a newspaper office is lightly called 'the library', takes the file of his predecessors' misstatements, copies it out, adds a few of his own, and no one suffers except the readers of the popular press, who must, I should think, be getting bored with the recitation of old, false anecdotes. That is the normal routine – unless there is a lord handy, who is not subject to the conventions of the trade.

On the morning of the visit my wife said: 'An *Express* reporter and a lord wanted to come and see you this afternoon.'

'You told them not to?'

'Of course.'

'What lord?'

'Noel someone.'

'Has Noël Coward got a peerage? I'd like to see him.'

'No, it wasn't anyone I had heard of.'

There, I supposed, the matter ended. But that evening, just as I was going to prepare myself for dinner, I heard an altercation at the front door. My poor wife, weary from the hay-field, was being kept from her bath by a forbidding pair.

The lady of the party, Miss Spain, has recorded in two columns their day's doings. They were on what she called a 'pilgrimage'. This took them, uninvited, to tea with the Poet Laureate. 'Lord Noel-Buxton just walked into the house,' she writes, while she trampled the hay. The poet was 'silent, dreaming back in the past', thinking, no doubt, that in all his years before the mast he had never met such tough customers. He gave them oat-cake. Then he brightened, 'his blue eyes danced'. The old 'darling' had thought of a way out. He urged them on to me. ' "See you? Of course he'll see you." ' On they came to the village where I live which, curiously, they found to be a 'straggly collection of prefabricated houses' (there is not one in the place), and entered the pub, where they got into talk with its rustic patrons. I have since made inquiries and learn that they somehow gave the impression that they were touts for television. Members of the village band sought to interest them in their music, and the cordiality, thus mistakenly engendered, emboldened the two pilgrims. They attempted to effect an entry into my house and wrangled until I dismissed them in terms intelligible even to them.

Lord Noel-Buxton seems to have been unaware of having done anything odd. 'Oh, Nancy, do stop!' he is said to have cried, when I went out to see that they were not slipping round to suck up to the cook. 'He's coming to apologize.'

A faulty appreciation.

What, I have been asking myself ever since, was Lord Noel-Buxton's part in the escapade? He is not, I have established, on the pay-roll of the *Daily Express*. All he seems to have got out of it is a jaunt in a motor-car, an oat-cake and a novel he can hardly hope to understand. Who, in the popular phrase, does he think he is?

Well, I looked him up and find that he is the second generation of one of Ramsay MacDonald's creations. To the student of social stratification this is significant. Is there, in our midst, unregarded, a new social sub-class? The men who bought peer-ages from Lloyd George believed they were founding aristocratic houses, and there was, indeed, then a reasonable supposition that a generation or two of inherited wealth might refine the descendants of the gross originators. But the men who were put into ermine by MacDonald believed that the order they were entering was doomed. That statesman's bizarre appointments in the Church of England are eliminated by time, but the Upper House stands and the peerages he created survive. Are there, I wonder, many such orphans of the storm which blew itself out? Here, at any rate, was one specimen in full plumage on my doorstep.

I asked a secretarial agency, who sometimes helps me, to find out something about him. All they could say was that he is not strong, poor fellow, and was invalided out of the Territorial Army at the beginning of the war. Now, when he is not on a literary pilgrimage, he appears to spend much time paddling in rivers.

He clearly cannot have met many other lords. Students of *Punch* know that from the eighties of the past century until the thirties of this there was a standing joke about the distressed descendants of Crusaders who were reduced to retail trade. Now the thing is commonplace; not perhaps at the Co-operative Stores where, presumably, Lord Noel-Buxton does his shopping; but it is hard to believe that nowhere in the purlieus of the Upper House has he ever been approached with an advantageous offer of wine or clothing. But we must believe it. 'I'm not on business. I'm a member of the House of Lords.' The two ideas, in the mind of this naïve nobleman, are axiomatically irreconcilable.

We have many sorts of lord in our country: lords haughty, who think that commoners all seek their acquaintance and must be kept at a distance; lords affable, who like mixing with their fellow-men of all degrees and know the conventions of good society by which introductions are effected; lords lavish and leisurely; and dead-broke lords eager to earn an honest living. In Lord Noel-Buxton we see the lord predatory. He appears to think that his barony gives him the right to a seat at the dinner-table in any private house in the kingdom.

Fear of this lord is clearly the beginning of wisdom.

Evelyn Waugh

The Gentle Art of Being Interviewed

Was it a peculiarity of my own, or do you, Gentle Reader, as I once did, keep a black list of public characters? Mine grew longer every year. It comprised men and women, quite unknown to me except through the newspapers, for whom, nevertheless, I had a sharp personal dislike.

In a few cases, no doubt, the trouble was visual – a smirk in the photographer's flashlamp, a jaunty step in the news-reel, a hat; sometimes it was aural – adenoids at the microphone; but the vast majority of the people, at any rate on *my* list, were there for intellectual offences. It was something they were reported to have said to the press.

I refer, of course, to those utterances which seem to gush out spontaneously, washing away the patient camouflage of years in a great cataract of self-revelation. These people are kind in the home, good at their jobs, but when there are reporters about something comes over them, and it is then that they make their atrocious, unforgettable utterances – or so I used to think, when I watched them chatting to the men with the notebooks, posing for the men with the cameras.

The classic ground for the sport is a liner arriving in New York. New Yorkers still retain a friendly curiosity about their foreign visitors – indeed, believe it or not, a bulletin is printed and daily pushed under your door in the chief hotels, telling you just what celebrities are in town, where they are staying, and nominating a Celebrity of the Day, an introduction to whom is often included among the prizes in radio competitions.

To satisfy this human appetite, the reporters come on board with the first officials and have ample time before the ship finally berths to prosecute their quest. They are not got-up to please.

Indeed, their appearance is rather like Poe's Red Death – a stark reminder of real life after five days during which one has seen no one who was not either elegantly dressed or neatly uniformed. American papers have at their command most prepossessing creatures of both sexes, but they choose only those who look like murderers to greet visitors. They are elderly and, one supposes, embittered men. They have not advanced far in their profession and their business is exclusively with the successful. Their revenge is a ruthless professionalism. They look the passengers over and make their choice, like fish-brokers at market. One of their number, the grimmest, stalks into the lounge, breaks into a distinguished group, taps an ambassador on the arm and says: 'The boys want a word with you outside.'

I have often watched the process and decided that the fox, on the whole, rather enjoyed it. Eminent people get the feeling of moving everywhere among flashlamps and questions, and miss them if they are not there, as dog-lovers like to be greeted by a hairy, dribbling, barking herd whenever they enter their own house. I suppose it is like being an officer in the army. One's first day in uniform one was embarrassed at being saluted; after a short time one expected it. Anyway, I used to think, as I saw the distinguished goats segregated from the sheep and hustled away so brusquely, that they would greatly have resented being left out, and I read the results with stony heart. How they gave themselves away, I thought.

But I have become altogether a softer man in this matter since last year when, for one ghastly afternoon, I found myself one of the victims – not, I need hardly say, in the open competition of the first-class deck of a Cunarder, but in far more modest but equally disturbing circumstances.

It was shortly before it became a criminal offence to travel abroad. I made a last-minute rush to a country which I will call 'Happiland'; a small, friendly country never much visited by the English, and last summer quite deserted by them, so that my arrival was, to that extent, remarkable.

I came by air. We landed at what should have been lunch-time, at what indeed *was* lunch-time for the various officials whose consent was necessary for our entry. This is no season in which to expect a sympathetic hearing of vexations of travel. We will all go through hell cheerfully nowadays to get abroad. I did not repine, but I was weary when at length some hours later I reached my hotel. It was a stuffy afternoon; Happilandic trams rattled below the window. I shut out their sound, and with it every breath of fresh air. I lay down on the bed, lit a cigar, and before I had smoked half an inch was asleep. It was still in my fingers when I awoke at dusk; there was ash all over me, a hole in the top sheet and a smell of tobacco and burned linen. There was a strange figure in my room. It turned on the light and revealed itself as a young woman dressed as though for sport – not 'le sport' of Mr Michael Arlen; athletics, putting the weight, most likely.

'Good night, Mr Wog,' said this apparition. 'Excuse please, I must make a reportage of you.'

I sat up and began slowly to remember where I was; much more slowly than in detective stories the heroine comes round from chloroform.

'I am of . . .' said my visitor, uttering some deep Happilandic gutturals, 'our great liberal newspaper.'

'Do sit down.' I waved to the armchair; then noticed that it was full of my clothes. 'I am sorry to receive you like this.'

'How you are sorry to receive me? I represent all anti-Fascist intellectual activities.'

'Ah, well; do you smoke?'

'Not too much.'

She sat on my clothes and looked at me for some time without noticeable interest.

'Well,' I said at length, 'I suppose this is really worse for you than for me.'

'Excuse please?'

'I simply said this was worse for you than for me.'

'In what directions, please?'

'Well, perhaps it isn't really.'

'I am not understanding what is worse, Mr Wog.'

'No, it meant nothing.'

'So.'

There was another pause in which I began slowly to regain

my self-possession It was a game of snakes and ladders. The next throw set me back six squares.

'Mr Wog, you are a great satyr.'

'I assure you not.'

'My editor says you have satirized the English nobility. It is for this he has sent me to make a reportage. You are the famous Wog, are you not?'

'Well, I'd hardly say that. Some of my books have been fairly popular . . . a very ordinary Wog, you know.'

'I know, like the great Priestley.'

'No, much more ordinary. Quite different.'

'How different, Mr Wog? You have said "Fairly", "Popular", "Ordinary". I have those words written down. I understand well. You believe in social justice, you write for the people, yes? You represent the ordinary man? That is why you satirize the nobility. They abuse you?'

'Yes, come to think of it, some of them do.'

'Of course. In Happiland we are having many such proletarian writers. But since we have no nobility, they must satirize the secretaries of the trades unions. Do you also satirize the secretaries?'

'No, I can't say I do. You see, I've never met one.'

'They are high people?'

'Yes, very high.'

'So. I find you are a timid man, Mr Wog, to be afraid of the secretaries. In Happiland are many jokes about them.'

She seemed cast down by her memories of Happilandic humour and sat silent for some time. When she next spoke it was in the *plume de ma tante* tradition.

'Mr Wog, how are your pens?'

I did not try. I simply said, 'Very well, thank you.'

'Here are many pens. I am not a pen. My editor has been an international pen in Swissland. Were you an international pen, Mr Wog?'

Light broke. 'The Pen Club? I'm afraid I am not a member, myself.'

'How can that be? In Happiland all the great authors are pens. There is much jealousy to belong. Some say the elections are by intrigue, but it is not so. It is all by merit. Is it not so in England?'

'Yes, I am sure it is.'

'How then, please, are you not a pen? Do the great English writers scorn you?'

'That's exactly it.'

'Because you are a proletarian?'

'I expect so.'

'Oh, Mr Wog, how I will satirize them in my reportage! It will enrage my editor. He will protest to the International Committee of Pens.'

'Jolly decent of him,' I said, perhaps rather weakly.

She wrote busily, in longhand, covering several leaves of her notebook. Then she said: 'Mr Wog, you have come here to satirize Happiland?'

'Certainly not.'

'Why then have you come?'

'Oh, just for the change.'

'That is interesting me very much. You think Happiland is greatly changed?'

'I mean for myself.'

'In what directions, please, do you wish to change?'

'In all directions.'

'So. And you come to Happiland for these changes? Because of the new Age-Spirit?'

That was a long snake, leading me back half-way down the board. 'Yes,' I said, contemptibly.

'And your school? That will change too?'

'Oh, I expect so. All the schools are changing every day, I'm told ... I know what you're going to ask; in what directions? Well, not so much classics, you know, modern languages, more stinks.'

This seemed a ladder.

'I am not understanding stinks, Mr Wog.'

'That's what we used to call science at my school.'

'Yes, yes, now I understand you. It is an American idiom. Science stinks, yes? You suffer the cosmic despair because of the atom bomb. You antagonize the sciences. In Happiland we are having many such desperate intellectuals. And to express this world-sorrow you are leading your school of proletarian satyrs to new language-forms away from the classics. Mr Wog, this will be a fine reportage. I must go with it to my editor.'

She was gone, and as I lay back among the singed bed-clothes I felt deep gratitude that none of my friends read Happilandic and deep compunction for the injustice which for years I had been doing a number of suffering fellow humans.

Think of this more or less true story, Gentle Reader, when you next feel moved to intolerance. It may be your turn next.

Lord Kinross

Laughter in the Kitchen

As his century advances and common man grows more so, landmarks arise from time to time to mark his progress. One such, in the world of Art, has occurred. It was the jubilee of the most popular, hence most eminent English painter of the century, a water-colourist named Mr Donald McGill. Since he sold his first painting close on fifty years ago, some hundred million reproductions of his work have found their way into English homes. For Mr McGill is the creator of the English comic postcard.

The jubilee of Mr McGill coincided with his eightieth birthday. He is a courtly old gentleman, scrupulous in costume, with delicate hands and well-made feet. He started life as a draughtsman in an engineer's office which had formerly nurtured Linley Sambourne. But since his secret hobby was anthropology, the study of man as an animal, the anatomy of the machine failed to inspire him. Starting to draw on the backs of postcards for the amusement of nephews and nieces, he soon stepped downwards, in the direction of fame, to amuse uncles and aunts and mums and dads instead. His first printed postcard bore the caption:

Eminent Dog-fancier (on being shown the twins): And now which one are you going to keep?

Since then, with a vulgarity worthy of Shakespeare or Hogarth, Mr McGill has depicted, in eleven thousand masterpieces, half a century of Common English life. His work reflects an uninhibited English world of dazzling colour and Rabelaisian wit. Its ladies, saucy-eyed, flaunt Rubensian contours in skin-tight garments of imperial purple, royal blue, and pillar-box red, breaking exuberantly into spots and stripes. Their fashions, designed exclusively by Mr McGill, never die, displaying the human figure to provocative advantage with a permanent skirt-line several inches higher than Mr Dior's highest. They wear perms, small hats with frivolous bows, pointed, high-heeled, patent leather shoes, nylon stockings and gaily coloured underclothes.

The men of the species reflect in their costume the special distinctions of a less Common period. The Worker (still quaintly called Workman) is walrus-moustached, in cloth cap, kerchief and waistcoat without jacket. The Gentleman of Leisure is beady-eyed, in purple-striped suit, yellow waistcoat, straw boater or bowler, carrying gloves and a cane or rolled umbrella. The Professional Man is owlish in correct black coat, butterfly collar and pin-stripe trousers. The Vicar wears pince-nez, the Blimp striped pyjamas. Taste in house decoration favours mauve curtains, green easy chairs and tomato rugs.

The inhabitants of this world are primarily interested in – hence amused by – their anatomy and that of others, their natural functions, honeymoon couples, henpecking wives, philandering husbands, childbirth and nudism. There are certain basic axioms. Vicars don't know the facts of life. Window-cleaners are experienced lovers. Typists are never virtuous. ('You really must learn to use the typewriter. The people in the office are beginning to talk.') Servant girls (still in cap and apron) are either flirtatious or half-witted, old maids lascivious, office-boys pert. ('When I was your age I'd saved £100.' 'Well, there weren't no cash registers in those days, sir.')

Foreigners – fortunately scarce – wear floppy ties, long hair and beards, like the celebrated violinist 'Seenyor Lallapalooza' ('Not mine, 'e ain't'). They are confined to Europeans, except for the kangaroo, a native of Australia ('Good heavens! My poor niece married one of them'), and the Chinaman in pigtails, remarking on a lady who has fallen out of a window into a dustbin: 'Velly wasteful people, these English, to throw away a woman like that. She's good for another ten years yet.' The Scots are quite foreign enough, their kilts and what they wear – or don't wear – under them a source of greater interest than their thrift. The kilted bridegroom turns angrily on the train-bearer: 'Not mine, you little twerp, hers!!'

Mr McGill sorts his postcards into three categories: mild, medium and strong. The mild depict chiefly the antics of kiddies, and have the lowest sale. But there is a notable exception: the best-seller of all time, first drawn in 1916, re-drawn three times, and still outselling both medium and strong. In a bedroom (with striped green wallpaper of the style now known as Eccles Regency) a puppy tugs at the nightgown of a small girl saying her prayers, provoking the interpolation, 'Please, Lord, excuse me a minute while I kick Fido!!' To-day the next-best seller is the thin man with the handle-bar moustache, stripped for examination by a doctor, who says: 'I'm afraid you'll have to have it off – it's sapping your strength!' As a rule the Awful Child sells better than the Devout:

'Now go to sleep, dear – the dustman's coming.'

'All right! Two bob and I won't tell father.'

Animals are anthropomorphic, in conversation and behaviour. Storks are the favourites, then cats. There is the refined tabby, stalked by a prowling black tom, who says: 'I do not think one is justified in bringing kittens into such a world as this.' There is the hen who says: 'Oh Horace, I've something to tell you! I'm going to have an egg'; and the other, outside a poulterer's window, who advises her cock: 'Look the other way, Henry, we're passing one of those horrible nudist camps.' There is the vast sow, feeding her young, of whom a latecomer enquires, 'May I ask Jimmy to stay to lunch, Mum?'

Drunks conventionally lose their equilibrium, slur their words, develop red noses, and drop their gloves and umbrellas in the gutter. One, at a drinking fountain, complains: 'I keep on preshing Button B but nothing comesh out but water'; another, embracing a pillar-box, sobs: 'Darling, I love you even without your teeth in.'

Literary themes are rare. 'Do you like Kipling?' asks the spectacled young man, reading *Kim*. 'I don't know, you naughty boy,' she replies. 'I've never kippled!' Art is confined to statuary, with a preference for the classical nude. ('The Greeks had a word for it.')

Mr McGill's is a conservative world, strangely blind to all evidence of Progress, social or mechanical. Lord Beveridge is unborn. The blessings of a National Health Service have yet to come; doctors are still private practitioners in morning-coats. So have those of the Education Act: 'My old man's suffered from conscription ever since he was demoralized from the Army.' Language is still picturesquely class-conscious:

'Blimey, ain't that ruddy bus ever coming?'

'Willie, how often have I got to tell you not to say ain't?'

Entertainments belong to a more primitive age in which 'It wasn't half a posh affair – lots of the men wore collars.' Mr McGill's ladies have only once worn slacks, commenting on a kiltie: 'Nice bit of skirt, Gert.'

The design of cars is of the Harry Tate era. The telephone seldom appears. Television is left by Mr McGill to his rivals, of whom he has a number. (When Mr George Orwell wrote an essay on his work four Donald McGills wrote to thank him.) Broadcasting figures only once. ('I don't care if you *do* disagree with the referee's decisions, you're not going to throw bottles at the radio.') But Mr McGill admits that his 'strongest' jokes are borrowed from the B.B.C. Light Programme.

In these he is a master of words. The various parts of the human anatomy are described in terms of poetic euphemism, e.g., 'I've been busy washing my sitting-room curtains.' His is a whimsical world, rich with the varied images of aspidistras and truncheons, binoculars and canonicals, diplomas and seaweed, pears and budgerigars.

But above all it is a world of stalwart patriotism, loyal to Church and State. 'Adjudicator!' protests the judge at a beauty show. 'Certainly not, I'm Church of England.' Mr McGill's Britannia is a lady with an outsize back sitting-room, upholstered in scarlet, waving a Union Jack, beneath her the legend: 'British and proud of it!'

Graham Greene

A Hoax on Mr Hulton

No one, I suppose, will ever discover the authors of the odd elaborate hoax played on Mr Hulton, the elderly printseller of Pall Mall, in 1744; the story itself has been hidden all these years in an old vellum manuscript book I bought the other day from a London bookseller. With its vivid unimportance it brings alive the geography of eighteenth-century tradesman's London, the wine-merchants at Wapping, the clockmakers in Fleet Street, the carriers and printers and bust-makers, all the aggrieved respectable victims of an anarchic imagination, and in the background memories of Layer's conspiracy and the word 'Jacobite' and a vague uneasiness.

The story is told in letters and occasional passages of dialogue with notes in the margin on the behaviour of the characters. It might be fiction if these people did not all belong to fact. Who copied it out? It is hard to believe that any innocent person could have known so much. Mr Hulton suspected his apprentices, and the whole world; there was a young man called Mr Poet Rowzel, who knew more than he should have done; and an auctioneer, for some reason of his own, spoke of an upholsterer.

It began quite childishly on 21 January, 1744, with a letter which purported to come from Mr Scott, a carpenter of Swallow Street, who wrote that he had many frames to make for the Prussian Ambassador, that he was ill of the gout and his men were overworked, and would Mr Hulton call on him. Mr Hulton had the gout himself, but he limped to Mr Scott's house, when 'finding the whole was an imposition upon him and Scott, he hobbled back again muttering horrible imprecations against the letter-writer all the way'. Two days later the hoax really got under way. A stream of unwanted people arrived at Mr Hulton's shop;

Mr Hazard, a cabinet maker of the 'Hen and Chickens' in London's Inn, with a quantity of Indian paper; Mr Dard, a toy maker from the King's Arms in the Strand, who had received a letter from the pseudo-Hulton offering to sell him a curious frame; a surgeon to bleed him, and a doctor from Bedlam. It would take too long to describe the events of these crowded days; how a Mr Boyd brought snuffboxes and Mrs Hulton had to buy one to quiet him before her husband returned; how Mr Scarlett, an optician, arrived loaded with optic glasses, and was so ill-used by Mr Hulton that he threatened proceedings; how Mr Rutter, a dentist of Fleet Street, came to operate on an impostume, and was turned away by Mrs Hulton, who pretended her husband had died of it. Three pounds of anchovies arrived, and the printer of the *Harlaian Miscellany*, who was pushed roughly out of doors, and Mr Cock, an auctioneer in the Great Piazza, who 'muttered something of an Irish upholsterer', and a female optician called Deane – Mrs Hulton bolted the door against her, and spoke to her through the pane, which Mrs Deane broke. 'Mr Hulton at the noise of breaking glass came forth from his little parlour into the shop, and was saluted by a porter with a dozen of port wine.' By this time he was losing control, and when Mr Rogers, a shoemaker of Maiden Lane, wanted to measure him, 'Mr Hulton lost all temper ... and cursing, stamping and swearing, in an outrageous manner, he so frightened Mr Rogers that the poor man, who is a Presbyterian, ran home to Covent Garden without once looking behind him.' After that Mr Hulton shut up his shop, and went to bed for three days, so the man who had been told he had a peruke-maker's shop to dispose of failed to get him. Even when the shop reopened, Mr Hulton thought it safer to stay upstairs, and leave things to his son. His son too was choleric and what he did to a young oculist who thought his father needed spectacles is unprintable here.

On 2 February there is a break in the record, twenty-seven pages missing; but when the story begins again on 4 September Mr Hulton is still on the run. Three dozen bottles of pale ale arrived that day; Mr Hulton was obliged to pay for them, and 'Mrs Hulton and her maid were fuddled while it lasted'. We must pass over the incident of the silversmith's wife, who pulled off Mrs Hulton's nightcap, and the venison-pasty man who saw through the deceit, and enclosed the pseudo-Hulton's letter in piecrust and sent it to Mr Hulton (the crust was given to the dog Cobb as they suspected poison). A more subtle form of hoax was in train. It began with an illiterate letter to Mr Pinchbeck (son of Edward Pinchbeck, inventor of the alloy), accusing Hulton of having abused him 'in a monstrous manner' at a tavern, but this plot misfired; the two victims got together over a four-shilling bowl of punch.

It was then that the Reverend Aaron Thompson, of Salisbury, came on the scene (he who had baptized the conspirator Layer's child and allowed the Pretender to be a godparent by proxy). Somebody using his name ordered a number of articles which he said his agent Hulton would pay for – four canes with pinchbeck heads, a bust of Mr Pope, a set of *The Gentleman's Magazine*, 'the books (of which you know the titles) against Bishop Berkeley's Tar-Water', a complete set of Brindley's Classics, and even a chariot. This persecution caused Mr Hulton to write to Mr Thompson accusing him of being a Papist and a Jacobite and threatening him with the pillory, and the amazed Mr Thompson 'receiving this letter kept himself three weeks in a dark room lest he should see a letter of any kind: by the persuasion of his wife, he at length came forth; but wore a thin handkerchief over his eyes for about a month'. A lot of people's nerves were getting jumpy as the hoax enlarged its scope, taking in Bath and such worthy local characters as Mr Jeremy Peirce, author of an interesting little book about a tumour, and Mr Archibald Cleland, the surgeon who, it may be remembered, was concerned with Smollett in a controversy over the Bath waters. They all received letters from the pseudo-Hulton, Cleland being told that Thompson had libelled him and Peirce that Thompson had ordered him a set of *The Rake's Progress*. The real Aaron Thompson was by now convinced that he was the victim of a mad printseller, just as Hulton believed he was the victim of a mad clergyman, and they both – egged on by their pseudo-selves – appealed to a Mr Pitt of Salisbury, who assumed they both were mad. The story becomes inextricably confused with counter-

accusations, the pseudo-Hulton writing to the real Aaron
Thompson:

You write, you read, you muzz or muse as you call it, till you are fitter
for Bedlam than the Pulpit: poor man! poor Aaron Thompson. I
remember you in Piccadilly knocking at the great Gates and returning
bow for bow to the bowing Dean, your lean face, your awkward bow,
your supercilious nod of the head are still in my mind . . .

and the pseudo-Thompson would send the accusation flying
back, regretting to hear that Hulton and all his family had gone
mad, and recalling his strange way of walking about his shop
'and turning his thumbs one over another, a sure sign of madness'. And all the while goods continued to pour in, particularly
drink – three gallons of the best Jamaica rum from Wapping
New-Stairs, which Mrs Hulton drank and paid for, a gallon of
canary, a gallon of sherry, and a pint of Madeira.

We shall never know the end – the last pages are torn out with
any clue they might have contained to the hoaxer. It was an age
of practical jokes, and he may have been one of those who baited
Pinchbeck because he was a 'King's friend', mocking at his
nocturnal remembrancers and writing odes about his patent
snuffer. Perhaps Hulton, by his careful prosperity, had aroused
the same balked malice of men who sympathize with the defeated
and despise the conqueror and dare do nothing but trivial mischief to assert their independence – as next year proved when
Charles Stuart turned back from Derby.

Claud Cockburn

from *Bestseller*

The view from the shelves of the lending libraries included not only those deep blue lagoons, and the wide stretches of the Sahara, but also the Sea Coast of Bohemia. The prospect offered was varied indeed, and it would seem that the beaches of that shore catered for almost every type of tourist. Shifts in the meaning of words as a means of gauging the changing attitudes of those who use them are a well-known and valuable subject of study. 'Bohemian' is a word worth attention. Leaving behind the period when it meant simply a gipsy, it became a chameleon. It meant different things, not only at different times but often to different people at the same time. It could be used in a totally pejorative sense, indicating that the writer or speaker considered the 'Bohemian' a dissolute vagabond, immoral and dishonest, and possessing all the qualities which one would not wish to find in a man about to marry one's sister. At other times or to other people it suggested the picture of a person or a family who might be outsiders as far as properly established and well-conducted members of the community were concerned, but at the same time could be decent, jolly, amusing, and even – in their peculiar way – have certain insights, into the problems and perplexities of humanity. From there the Bohemian could go on at a later date to develop into an enviable being, free of the tiresome restrictions which hemmed in more conventional people, but still a little dangerous, or even very dangerous, precisely on this very account. The helpless Bohemian could also be brigaded at will as a kind of cultural bank-robber engaged by the author to attack the intellectual strong-rooms of the bourgeoisie.

Although always, and by definition, an outsider, on the whole his character improved throughout the latter part of the nine-

teenth century. Even so, we may recall the alarmed reaction of
the vicar's daughter in *When It Was Dark* to the news that her
fiancé, the curate, was about to share chambers in London with
two bachelor friends. She was reassured by her father. 'The days
when you couldn't be a genius without being dirty are gone,'
said the vicar. 'I am glad of it. I was staying at St Ives last
summer, where there is quite an artistic settlement. All the
painters carried golf clubs and looked like professional athletes.'
Here the vicar made a joke. He said, 'They drink Bohea in
Bohemia now.'

Even at that date, not everyone wanted artists to look like
professional athletes and spend their time on the golf links. They
enjoyed a literary walk out with a gay, unconventional, free, even
irreverent type of Bohemian and in 1906 their needs were amply
satisfied by *The Beloved Vagabond*, a novel by W. J. Locke. The
blurb to the latest edition of this immensely popular work presents the ingredients of appeal in a few succinct lines:

The Beloved Vagabond is an irresistible story of the open road and the
free life. The hero is a 'wandering philosopher' who rescues a small
boy from poverty, adopts him and takes him on his wanderings through
Europe, educating him on the way.

This is a happy story of a ne'er-do-well whose fascinating life and
adventures on the roads of Europe make us realize how attractive the
unconventional life can be.

No harm in describing the plot as preposterous; preposterous
is clearly what it was intended to be. It is as visibly 'contrived'
as a musical box, and as predictable. This is not to say that the
contrivance cannot repeatedly and almost continuously produce
deeper notes evoking thoughts about the meaning of life, civilization, society, and the nature of love. The central figure is as
well-equipped a Bohemian as ever played the role. He is the son
of a French father and an Irish mother, a parentage which is
automatically seen to explain, and where necessary excuse, his
finest qualities and his defects. Indeed, he is not just French on
his father's side, but Gascon to boot. His real name is Gaston
de Nérac. But for the greater part of the book he roams freely,
philosophizes, plays the violin for a living (a wandering minstrel

he), and drinks a great deal of absinthe under the name of Berzelius Nibbidard Paragot.

The narrator is at the outset a small Cockney boy named Augustus Smith. Adopting him as his boy-of-all-work and pupil, Paragot changes the lad's name to Asticot. Early in their relationship, in Paragot's disreputable rooms in Tavistock Street, Asticot finds some papers stuffed into an old stocking. Reading them, he discovers a good deal about his master's past and his views. Evidently he was at one time in love with a beautiful lady named Joanna: '*pure et ravissante comme une aube d'Avril*'. Other notes scribbled by Paragot at one time and another help swiftly to draw his picture.

At Prague I made the aquaintance of a polite burglar who introduced me to his lady wife and to other courteous criminals, their spouses and families ... Granted their sociological premises, based on Proudhon, they are too logical. The lack of imaginative power to break away from convention, *their convention*, is a serious defect in their character. They take their gospel of *tuum est meum* too seriously. I do not inordinately sympathize with people who get themselves hanged for a principle.

Encouraging! In the same paragraph it is suggested that disciples of Proudhon are likely to be criminals and the reader is assured that he is not going to be asked to admire some seriously political subversive. The narrator notes:

I also see now, as of course I could not be expected to see then, that Paragot, being a creature of extremes, would either have the highest or lowest. In these troubled sketches, as he cannot go to Grand Hotels, I find him avoiding like lazar-houses the commercial or family hostelries, where he will foregather with the half-educated, the half-bred, the half-souled; the offence of them is too rank for his spirit. The pretending simian class, aping the vices of the rich and instinct with the vices of the low, and frank in neither, moves the man's furious scorn. He will have realities at any cost. All said and done, the bugs of Novortovshakaya did not masquerade as humming-birds, nor merry Giuseppi Sacconi of Verona as a critic of Girolami dai Libri.

Paragot is manager of a satisfactorily Bohemian club called the Lotus.

During the daytime it was an abode of abominable desolation. No one came near it till nine o'clock in the evening, when one or two members straggled in, took down their long pipes and called for whisky or beer, the only alcoholic beverages the club provided ... At eleven the cloth was laid. From then till half past members came in considerable numbers. At half past supper was served. A steaming dish of tripe furnished the head of the table in front of Paragot and a cut of cold beef the foot.

There were generally from fifteen to thirty present; men of all classes: journalists, actors, lawyers, out-at-elbows nondescripts. I have seen one of Her Majesty's judges and a prizefighter exchanging views across the table. They supped, talked, smoked and drank whisky up to two or three o'clock in the morning, and appeared to enjoy themselves prodigiously.

Losing his job as manager of the Lotus, and smashing a violin over the head of the mean-souled owner, Paragot takes off for France. He and Asticot wander for a year through Europe. Then, the following spring, they arrive in Savoy. Outside a village they encounter a peasant girl and an elderly man who are on their way to Chambéry, to play the zither and the violin at a wedding. Almost immediately, the old man dies of exhaustion. Paragot appoints himself his successor, takes the girl Blanquette under his wing, and the three wander on to Aix-les-Bains.

Not being content to having attached to his person the stray dog and a mongrel boy and rendering himself responsible to their destinies, Paragot must now saddle himself with a young woman. Had she been a beautiful gipsy holding fascinating allurements in lustrous eyes and pomegranate lips, and witchery in a supple figure, the act would have been a commonplace of human weakness. But in the case of poor Blanquette, squat and coarse, her heavy features only redeemed from ugliness by youth, honesty and clean teeth, the eternal attraction of sex was absent ...

Of course he saved the girl from a hideous doom. Thousands of kindly honest men have done the same in one way or another. But Paragot's way was different from anyone else's. Its glorious lunacy lifted it above ordinary human methods.

So many of your wildly impulsive people repent them of their generosities as soon as the magnanimous fervour has cooled. The grandeur of Paragot lay in the fact that he never repented. He was fantastic, self-indulgent, wastrel, braggart, what you will; but he had an exaggerated notion of the value of every human soul save his own. The destiny of the poor Blanquette was to him infinitely more important than that of the wayward genius that was Paragot. His point of view had struck me even as a child when he discoursed on my prospects.

'I am Paragot, my son,' he would say. 'A film full of wind and wonder, fantasy and folly, driven like thistledown above the world. I do not count. But you, my little Asticot, have the Great Responsibility before you. It is for you to uplift a corner of the veil of Life and show joy to men and women where they would not have sought it. Work now and gather wisdom, my son, so that when the Great Day comes you may not miss your destiny.' And once he added wistfully – 'as I have missed mine'.

And then in the romantic setting of the Restaurant du Lac at Lucerne a romantic thing happens. While Paragot is playing the violin and Asticot is going round with the tambourine used as a collecting box, the beautiful lady out of Paragot's past life is discovered sitting with companions at a table.

This beautiful lady, Joanna, converses with Asticot, cross-questioning him about Paragot's way of life, and finally tells him that she is the Comtesse de Verneuil. She gives him her address in Paris, telling him that if they are ever in trouble and she can help, she will do so.

After this encounter the trio wander on. They reach Budapest. Here Paragot breaks his ankle and also inherits a small patrimony from an aunt. He provides for Asticot to spend the next two years in Budapest, studying art. At the end of that time they are reunited in Paris, where Paragot has established himself as a sort of King Bohemian and super philosopher among the Bohemians of the Café Delphine. Meeting Joanna by accident, Asticot tells her of Paragot's presence in Paris. She seeks him out at the Café Delphine, and begs him to come to see her husband who is ill. He does so. He finds himself in anguished love again after all these thirteen years since he left Joanna for the first time. Then one night she comes to the café to find Paragot. He is drunk, but she and Asticot get him to her house. The Comte de Verneuil, desperately ill in an adjoining room, gives Paragot a document – which he is intended to destroy. But Joanna reads it. She finds it to be a contract, drawn up and signed thirteen years before, by which de Nérac (Paragot) binds himself in consideration of the payment of ten thousand pounds, to leave Joanna's flat and never approach her again.

Joanna is almost speechless with agony at this disclosure of her lover's perfidy. They part again.

This apparently fearful imbroglio is quickly cleared up. The Comte de Verneuil dies, and on his death-bed confesses all to Joanna. It seems that in London thirteen years ago, the Comte de Verneuil had been a crooked financial speculator. Joanna's father, Mr Rushworth, a solicitor in very fashionable practice, was also a company promoter and became the 'tool and dupe, and drawer in general of chestnuts from the fire, for the Comte de Verneuil and his backers'.

Soon the father is in danger not only of bankruptcy but of imprisonment for fraud. On the very night of the party held to celebrate Joanna's engagement to Gaston de Nérac the Comte de Verneuil draws Gaston aside and explains the situation to him.

Ten thousand pounds of his clients' money which Rushworth held in trust had gone in the failure of the company. If that amount was not at his disposal the next morning he was finished, snuffed out. It appeared that no one in Paris or London would lend him the money, his credit being gone. Unless M. de Nérac could find the ten thousand pounds, there was the gaol yawning with horrible certainty for M. de Nérac's prospective father-in-law. As Paragot's patrimony, invested in French Government securities, was not a third of this sum, he could do nothing but wring his hands in despair and call on Providence and the Comte de Verneuil. The former turned a deaf ear. The latter declared himself a man of business and not a philanthropist; he was ready, however, to purchase an option on the young lady's affections. Did not M. de Nérac know what an option was? He would explain. He drafted the famous contract. In return for Paragot's signature he would hand him a cheque drawn in favour of Simon Rushworth.

Faithful to the terms of the contract, de Nérac disappeared from Joanna's life. The blackguardly de Verneuil first poisoned Joanna's mind against her former fiancé, then told her that he was dead – an acquaintance had found him in a Paris hospital and had paid for his funeral. She believed him. Urged by her parents, she finally accepted to marry de Verneuil. Now, the Comte being dead and Paragot very much alive, the way is open for him to marry Joanna.

At this point there is going to be a question in the reader's mind as to whether Paragot, or even de Nérac, is a suitable husband for a woman who has already been described as 'exquisite', 'fragrant', and 'an English rosebud wet with morning dew'. Fourteen years earlier Gaston de Nérac could have been seen as a suitable man. But think of his subsequent life as Paragot. An associate of riff-raff, a hard-living Bohemian. A person of absolutely no fixed address. Readers who might have been worried about this were immediately reassured. They and the astonished Asticot suddenly learn that all along de Nérac has been a second cousin of Joanna's; he was at school at Rugby, he was a brilliant architect who actually won the *Prix de Rome*, which, as Asticot puts it 'to a Paris art student . . . is what a Field Marshal is to a private soldier, a Lord Chancellor to the eater of dinners in the Temple'. He is at least as acceptable as that Sheik Ahmed.

These insignia of ultimate respectability are the more necessary because Paragot is about to go to stay with Joanna's mother in her old Georgian house at the end of the High Street of Melford in Wiltshire. He is going to meet the County and bits of the hunting set. His strictures upon them are going to be severe, and his behaviour towards them verging on the uncouth. The sight of a genuine, hundred-per-cent-born-and-bred Bohemian relieving himself, spiritually speaking, on the carpets of nice people in Wiltshire might have been a little hard to take for some readers, a little rough. But since the fellow is in reality an Old Rugbeian one can safely and with a sense of cultural superiority take the side of the pseudo-Bohemian against this collection of inhibited snobs.

Locke has made admirable arrangements for his public to have it both ways. Thus, at one of Mrs Rushworth's At Homes, we find Paragot

talking to an elderly and bony female with a great beak of a nose. I wondered how so unprepossessing a person could be admitted into so fine an assembly and I learned later that she was Lady Molyneux, one of the Great Personages of the county. The lady seemed to be emphatic. So did Paragot. She regarded him stonily out of flint-blue eyes. He waved his hands. She raised her eyebrows. She was one of those women whose eyebrows in the normal state are about three inches from the eyelids. I understood then what superciliousness meant. Paragot raised his voice. At that moment one of those strange coincidences occurred in which the ends of all casual conversation fell together, and a shaft of silence spread through the room killing all sound save that of Paragot's utterance.

'But Great Heavens, Madam, babies don't grow in the cabbage-patch; and you are all well aware they don't, and it is criminal of your English writers to mislead the young as to the facts of existence. Charlotte Yonge is infinitely more immoral than Guy de Maupassant.'

Then Paragot realized the deadly stillness. He rose from his chair, looked round at the shocked faces of the women, and laughing turned to Mrs Rushworth.

'I was stating Zola to be a great ethical teacher and Lady Molyneux seemed disinclined to believe me.'

'He is an author very little read in Melford,' said the placid lady from her sofa cushions, whilst the two or three women with whom she was in converse gazed disapprovingly at my master. 'It would do the town good if it was steeped in his writings,' said he.

After the party Paragot expounds to Asticot the predictable views of a Bohemian observing the English 'County'.

My son ... as a philosopher and a citizen of the world you will find Melford needs a patient study as much as Chambéry or Budapest or the Latin quarter. It is a garden of Lilliput. Here you will see life in its most cultivated littleness. A great passion bursting out across the way will convulse the town like an earthquake. Observe at the same time how constant a factor is human nature. However variable the manifestation may be, the degree is invariable. In spacious conditions it manifests itself in passion, in narrow ones in prejudices. The females in and out of petticoats who were here this afternoon experienced the same thrill in expressing their dislike of me as a person foreign to their conventions, as the Sicilian who plunges his dagger into a rival's bosom. When I marry, my son, I shall not live at Melford ... I must have room, my son, for development of my genius. I must dream great things, and immortal visions are blasted under the basilisk eye of Lady Molyneux.

Naturally he has a thing or two to say about a church wedding. 'You must forgive me, *ma chérie*,' he says to Joanna, 'I am a happy Pagan and it is so long since I have met anyone who belonged to the Church of England that I thought the institution had perished of inanition.'

'Why, you went with me to church last Sunday.'

'So I did,' said he, 'but I thought it was only to worship the great British God Respectability.'

Paragot also, of course, falls foul of Major Walters – an Aunt-Sally-type British Military man.

'He is a man,' said Paragot, 'in that he is brave and masculine; in that he is intelligent, he is nought. He is a machine-gun. He fires off rounds of stereotype conversation at the rate of one a minute, which is funereal. I have the misfortune, my little Asticot, to be under the ban of Major Walters's displeasure. Your British military man is prejudiced against anyone who is not cut out according to pattern ... Do you know what he had the impertinence to ask me yesterday? What settlements I proposed to make on Madame de Verneuil. Settlements, mon petit Asticot! He spoke as trustee, whatever that may be, under her husband's will. 'Sir,' said I, 'I will settle my love and my genius upon her, and thereby ensure her happiness and prosperity. Besides, Madame de Verneuil has a fortune which will suffice her needs and of which I will not touch a penny.'

I smiled, for I could see Paragot in his grand French manner, one hand thrust between the buttons of his coat, and the other waving magnificently, as he proclaimed himself to Major Walters.

'I explained,' he continued, 'in terms which I thought might reach his intelligence, that I only had to resume my profession and my financial position would equal that of Madame Verneuil. And, Sir, said I, I will not suffer you to say another word. We bowed and parted enemies. Wherefore the conversation of the excellent Major Walters does not appeal to me as attractive.'

Before long the suffocating atmosphere of Melford becomes too much for Paragot.

'It came to a point where I must either expire or go. I decided not to expire. These things are done all in a flash. I was walking in the garden. It was last Sunday afternoon – I remember now: a sodden November day. Imagine a sodden November Sunday afternoon in an English country-town garden. Joanna was at a children's service. Ah, *mon Dieu*!

The desolation of that Sunday afternoon! The Death, my son, that was in the air! Ah! I choked, I struggled. The garden wall, the leaden sky closed in upon me, I walked out. I came back to Paris.'

'Just like that?' I murmured.

'Just like that,' said he. 'You may have noticed, my son, that I am a man of swift decisions and prompt action. I walked to the railway station. A providential London train was expected in five minutes. I took it. *Voila!*'

Paragot has realized that he and Joanna have 'escaped a life-long misery but on the other hand they had lost a lifelong dream ... The twain had been romantic, walking in the Valley of Illusion, wilfully blinding their eyes to the irony of Things Real. Love had flown far from them during the silent years and they had mistaken the afterglow of his wings for the living radiance. They had begun to realize the desolate truth.'

After a brief period of Bohemian debauchery in Paris, he decides to leave for the country.

'It is a city of Dead Sea apples. It has no place for me, save the sewer. I don't like the sewer. I am going away. I shall never come back to Paris again.'

'But where are you going, master?' I asked, in some surprise.

He did not know. He would pack his bundle and flee like Christian from the accursed city, like Christian he would go on a Pilgrim's Progress. He would seek sweet pure things. He would go forth and work in the field. The old life had come to an end. The sow had been mistaken. It could not return to its wallowing in the mire. Wallowing was disgustful. Was ever man in such a position? The vagabond life had made the conventions of civilization impossible. The contact with convention and clean English ways had killed his zest for the old order of which only the mud remained. There was nothing for it but to leave Paris.

At this point Asticot suggests to him that he should marry Blanquette, the ill-favoured but loyal girl who has of course been slavishly in love with him all the time. Asticot for his part immediately discovers that Blanquette is the solution to his own woman-problem.

But it was written, my son, Asticot. It was preordained. She is the one woman in the world to whom I need not pretend to be other than I am. She is real, *mon Dieu*! What she says is Blanquette, what she does is Blanquette and her sayings and doings would grace the greatest Queen in Christendom. But have you thought of it? I have come indeed to the end of my journey. I started out to find Truth, the Reality of Things. I have found it. I have found it, my son. It is a woman, strong and steadfast, who looks into your eyes; who can help a man to accomplish his destiny. And the destiny of man is to work, and to beget strong children. And his reward is to have the light in the wife's eyes and the welcome of a child's voice as he crosses the threshold of his house. And it cleanses a man.

He marries Blanquette and Joanna marries Major Walters. When Asticot next visits Paragot and Blanquette they are living on a farm and have an eighteen-months-old child. Paragot announces himself totally happy. And he concludes with the words: 'All that the wisdom of all the ages can tell us is summed up in the last words of one of the wisest books that was ever written: "We must cultivate our garden." '

It would be absurd to take the 'message' of *The Beloved Vagabond* more seriously than did the author. It would be equally absurd not to take it seriously at all. The writer reflects and plays cunningly with the daydreams of his huge middle-class British audience. He understands the different *nuances* of those daydreams. They are sometimes whimsical, laughable. But sometimes too, and this is heavily emphasized, they are to be regarded as a form of quite serious philosophizing, a consideration of the meaning of life. The daydreaming reader in London finds all the philosophical options left happily open. For Paragot is a kind of spiritual double agent. Asticot remarks that he had 'often seen pierce through Paragot's travesty of mountebankery or rags ... the inborn and incommunicable quality of the high-bred gentleman'. His gentlemanly instincts prevent him throwing himself entirely in with the cause of vagabondage; his high-toned and well-tuned sense of freedom prevent his accepting the conventions of the gentleman. He betrays, so to speak, each side in turn.

The repeated references to 'Reality' and 'Illusion' are characteristic of the period. It may be noted that the supposed teachings of Indian philosophers, tailored to Western taste by numerous gurus, were a popular fad among the British middle classes of the time, as indeed they had been for many years before and continued to be for many years after. It is more or less traditional that in this kind of philosophizing a woman such as Blanquette is more 'real' than a woman such as Joanna. Similarly the country is in some way more real than the town. When the country so described is the Sahara Desert, or a Pacific island, it is usual to assume that its 'reality' consists in the fact that it is not 'man-made' and by inference is God-made. But this explanation, curious though it be, is not valid. In *The Beloved Vagabond* and many other writings both in prose and verse, well-tended expanses of agricultural or horticultural land are, despite the visible evidences of human husbandry, nevertheless more real than Paris or London. Paragot escapes from the 'illusions' of conventional life on the one hand and Bohemian vagabondage on the other to the 'reality' and 'truth' of his farm. It would be oafish to enquire how, in his total ignorance of farming methods and techniques, he proposes to make a go of it. From a remark made by Blanquette about the necessity of getting up at five in the morning to cut the corn, one may deduce that Blanquette is his only farm-hand. The two of them will have to manage not only the agriculture but the livestock, for it seems that Paragot sets a good deal of store by his possession of pigs. It is reassuring to the reader, and no doubt to Blanquette, that after buying the farm Paragot still has a little left of his capital. In any case we are certainly not intended to stand about waiting for a rainy day in Paragot's bucolic dreamland.

But even the reader most confident that he can eat his cake and have it can hardly hope that beneath the 'mountebankery or rags' of the Bohemian he will always find 'the inborn and incommunicable quality of the high-bred gentleman'.

Informed circles realize that the Bohemian is often not only a bit of a boor, but a bit of a cad. There are plenty of books in which this caddishness is noted for what it is and the caddish Bohemian exposed as unworthy of sympathy, still less of imitation or serious attention when he utters his outlandish remarks. But the door once shut in the face of these gate-crashers, the

Claud Cockburn

party is still not always satisfactory. It may lack *élan*, for it cannot be denied that, at least in literature, the presence of Bohemians, outsiders, even cads, can do a lot to make the party go. It is not too late to discover that the gate-crashers might after all be worthy of admittance. Uncouth they may be. The young ladies and, for all one knows, some of the young gentlemen may be in danger from their lascivious advances across the Edwardian or Georgian drawing-room. It is a matter of urgency for the host or hostess to explain that these people are carrying a little some-thing extra under their unsuitable clothes. It may be just an Unconventional and Liberating view of Sex, or a Perception of Truth which no one else in the gathering happens to have about his person. More often, and more simply, what the Bohemians have is Genius.

It is certainly a mark of general respect towards Art and Culture that anyone who is demonstrably a Genius in those lines finds, on walking into the pages of a popular novel, that everyone else is expected to overlook or at least try to condone his social *gaffes* and spiritual clangers. So far so good. But 'demonstrably' is the word which must necessarily bother the novelist. How to demonstrate the fact that the Genius has genius? On stage or film, and provided that the Genius is a musical one, the problem is simple. A top-notch musician can be engaged to write some pieces which the man can then play over as his own compositions on an electric piano. Even on stage or film, artists are more difficult to deal with, and writers are non-starters. It is not always enough for the rest of the characters to keep chattering about the beauty of the man's paintings. It is best to have someone come on with the news that his work has just been crowned with some exotic prize, or has sold for many thousands of guineas. The author with a genius as a character is near the position of a man trying to explain that *Hamlet* is a pretty good play to a man who has never heard of it. It is of little use to say, 'Well, here he asks himself the question whether to be or not to be, and goes on to make a long and marvellously poetic, marvellously philo-sophical speech.' The other man says, 'Well, fine, but what does he actually say?' Even if the man who is trying to put *Hamlet* over has memorized that one, he is going to be in trouble when he gets to the gravedigger scene or seeks to explain the play within the play. It is going to sound a lot of nonsense to the man he is trying to educate, and will not weigh much in the latter's opinion against the reports of how Shakespeare behaved to his wife and all those rumours about Mr W. H.

For the novelist to portray credibly a musical genius, or rather to make the fact of his genius credible to the reader, is a task of extraordinary difficulty. Yet it has been found necessary for him to do so. For it is necessary to resolve, or at least to clarify, the conflict in the mind of the reader between the respect he genuinely feels due to art, culture, and in a general sort of way 'the spiritual side of life', and 'everyday life' which means – again in a general sort of a way – getting or keeping money. Admittedly the genius and the Bohemian are not inevitably identical. One may again recall those artists observed by the vicar at St Ives. Still, as the genius often is a bit of a Bohemian, the fact has to be explained to the thoughtful bourgeois. And in any case the Bohemian, the vagabond, whether beloved or not, gradually becomes to some extent a welcome or unwelcome symbol of that 'spiritual side of life'. This was achieved partially by a negative process: that is to say, in so far as the Bohemian seemed to reject the conventions of a money-making society it had to be assumed that he was motivated by some immaterial inspiration which might be either divine or devilish.

A. J. P. Taylor

Diary

These are troubled times. We have a strike of water workers. I have been worrying for weeks whether the water would continue to run out of the taps. I even laid in a stock of Perrier water. In London at any rate, the water still runs. As to the Perrier water, almost my favourite drink, I cannot allow myself to drink it until the situation becomes acute. Then there are the interminable talks over the limitations or even reduction of nuclear weapons. The outcome of these talks is easy to surmise: they will end with all the nuclear powers possessing more nuclear weapons than they did when the talks started. Once I would have worried about this also. Now I look forward to drinking the Perrier water even if the water talks succeed.

To speak the truth, not an invariable practice with me, I do not care in the slightest about the nuclear talks and their outcome, I do not even care very much whether water will run out of the taps. Something far graver weighs upon me day and night: my wife is in hospital.

She is not gravely ill, though the doctors have not yet found out what is the matter with her. In a few weeks' time, perhaps in a few days, she will be returned to me fit and well. This is no consolation for the devastation my wife's absence causes me. My problems begin early. As soon as I am dressed I have to make the bed and it is no joke making a double bed single-handed. I have to run from one side of the bed to the other and no sooner is one side smoothly tucked in than the other side gets out of order again. Making a single bed is easy: the problem of tackling the double bed alone is one I have never had to face before.

Then there is the problem of getting dressed. I can get dressed all right but normally I rely on my wife to tell me whether I have done it correctly. Now I can only rely on the mirror, which is pretty useless when I am trying to tie a bow tie – I think I am one of the few men in England who wears one on alternate days. Breakfast is the only safe time in the day: I have been making breakfast, whether for a large family or none at all, for the last fifty years. My routine has never varied: bacon and egg, bacon and mushroom, kipper, and so round again. Washing-up is rather a problem. I have always held that as the one who makes the breakfast I am automatically exempt from taking any share in the washing-up. Now my wife is not here, and if I do not wash up, the dirty dishes will still be there when I begin to make dinner in the evening.

The most acute problem for the solitary housekeeper is the shopping. For years past I have relied on my wife either to do the shopping or to give me a list of what I should buy. Now I have to make the list and nothing comes into my head. I check every single item to see whether we have any left. I make a list. On my way to the shops the idea comes into my head of things I might have forgotten. So I go back home to see whether there is a perfectly adequate supply already. When I finally reach the grocer's shop I wander desolately up and down the aisles of shelves seeking what I wished to purchase. My search is usually in vain. In my younger days when I used to go shopping a courteous grocer took my order without any of this search, and the goods I ordered were delivered the same afternoon. Now I have to pull my trolley laboriously homeward. Civilization is certainly breaking down – indeed, has already done so.

Cooking a solitary dinner is the worst of all. I understand the rudiments of cooking. You place the object to be cooked in a pan, light the gas under the pan and the rest answers for itself. But how long does the object take to be cooked? Apparently the objects vary one from another. I am told I should use the oven for some objects but I cannot find out how to light the oven, so I have given up that idea.

Well, that is enough of my domestic troubles. I turn to a more cheerful subject. During my solitary evenings I have been reading the two volumes of Thomas Hardy's biography by Robert Gittings. I have just finished it and this recalls to me Hardy's funeral at Westminster Abbey, which I actually attended: Or rather the funeral of most of him: his heart had been left behind in Dorsetshire. I suppose I was one of the 'gate-crashers' of whom Mr Gittings writes so disapprovingly. I entered by the north transept door merely by showing my visiting-card and was ushered into a choir stall just where the coffin came to a halt. The pallbearers or chief mourners were an odd assembly. First came the Prime Minister, Stanley Baldwin, and the Leader of the Opposition, Ramsay MacDonald. Baldwin had some idea what to do at an Anglican service: MacDonald was much at sea and missed some of his cues. Then came John Galsworthy and Bernard Shaw, presumably the literary kings of the time. Galsworthy behaved impeccably, doing everything absolutely right. Shaw got enjoyment by looking around most of the time. The next pair were Edmund Gosse and J. M. Barrie. Barrie had arranged the whole thing, so I suppose he was entitled to be there. Gosse had been a friend of Hardy's in earlier days, so there was an excuse for his presence too. But why Kipling and Housman had been chosen to wind up the procession is beyond me. Perhaps they were rewarded for literary merit. Altogether an old-fashioned conspectus of the Dean's literary taste. The rearguard was composed of the Vice-Chancellors of Oxford and Cambridge Universities, singular mourners of Jude's creator. The funeral was in January 1928. It now occurs to me that I may be the last survivor of those who attended it. At any rate I am the only one who has set down his impressions of this macabre occasion.

17–30 November 1983

My dear friend Gerald, Lord Berners, died in 1950. I thought that not more than half a dozen people remembered him. But the centenary of his birth has brought him back into attention. There have been concerts of his music, performances of his ballets and an exhibition devoted to his life on the fifth floor of the Festival Hall. His two best books have been reprinted in paperback: *First Childhood*, the first part of his autobiography, and *Far from the Madding War*, the best novel written about the Second World War, at any rate in Oxford. This last contains that inspired feature, Emmeline's war work. Emmeline, niece of the head of an Oxford college, had been told that war meant destruction. She bought a priceless 15th-century tapestry, set it up on a frame and unpicked a piece of it every day – the only rational piece of war work ever undertaken.

Gerald had a minor but very good talent, best as a composer but a good writer as well. He also painted on a high level and perhaps best of all he understood the art of living. He had a beautiful house at Faringdon, which he kept modestly open throughout the war. During the week he, too, did war work like Emmeline: he catalogued donations of blood in the basement of the Bodleian Library. At the weekends he had modest parties and superlative food at Faringdon. The coloured pigeons were no longer there, but one could look across the valley to a church tower protruding through the trees. The tower was the last folly in England, built by Berners to improve the view. There was no church and the entrance door was bricked up to avoid the payment of rates imposed by an indignant local council. A retired admiral also wrote to protest, saying that he had been surveying the neighbourhood through his telescope for the last thirty years and that the tower interfered with his view. Gerald wrote back: 'My dear Admiral, If you have been surveying the neighbourhood for thirty years, you must have seen many things that you ought not to have seen.' ...

My autobiography has now reached America. It has had some odd reviews. A writer in the *New York Review of Books* has condemned me sharply for never having visited the United States and what is more for not intending ever to do so. Very odd. I can think of no reason for my ever going to the United States. I visit foreign countries either for the buildings or for the food. Neither of these reasons would justify a visit to the United States. There are plenty of other countries that I have not visited and that I regret not having been to. China obviously and Turkey-in-Asia; the Inca areas of Peru; Iceland. Nowadays I prefer to stay at home. But even if I felt an urge to travel it would not be to the United States. Another feature of this same reviewer is that he makes wild statements about me. For instance, he says all my six children were at public schools. The correct figure is: one. It is true that the school was Westminster, which perhaps counts for six.

I suppose that I should make some comments on public affairs since my last appearance. We have had four party conferences, which seems too much. I doubt whether they interest anybody except those who attend them. Maybe the SDP will die before next time; there seem to be quite enough parties without it. I suppose that Dr David Owen now regrets going over to the SDP. If he had remained in the Labour Party he would now be its leader. The Liberals put on a spirited performance to as little effect as ever. The Labour Party Conference was overshadowed by the question of who was to become leader. I understood that the question was settled from the start and it seems a great waste of time to make delegates come from all over the country merely to decide what had been decided already. At all events, no other decision of any moment was made. In the old days a leader of the Labour Party took years to mature. This time the Conference had a leader imposed on it of whom I at any rate had never heard.

The Labour Conference also put on its usual performance of giving an evasive answer to the question of nuclear weapons. Unilateral abandonment of nuclear weapons is the only policy that makes any sense and should be applied at once. It is also a policy that will never win a majority at a general election. This is a sad conclusion. I have a record as a champion for CND that goes back over twenty years. I dare say I could deliver as powerful a speech now as I did in those days of long ago: no one would take the slightest notice. CND has just had its greatest demonstration ever, both here and on the Continent. Nothing is going to happen. Indeed new consignments of the most malignant weapons are due to arrive any day. There will be more demonstrations and the weapons will be installed. Every day that passes brings nuclear war nearer, though no one can say how much nearer. I am beginning to think that I shall beat the race for nuclear war and die before the weapons go off. At any rate I have closed my mind to the problem.

That leaves me with the Conservative Conference. This is not a topic for serious consideration. It was a run of knockabout comedy. I have not known any Conference which spent its time on such futility. But perhaps this is the best way to run a Conference. No subject of any moment was debated. No decision of any moment was reached. Yet the Conservatives have gone home joyful. There seems some chance that the Thatcher Government may run into trouble, but this is taking too cheerful a view of contemporary affairs. If the bombs do not blow us up economic chaos will bring ruin upon us. One way or another we must take cover.

1–21 December 1983

Six years have passed since I gave my last television lecture. I could not think of any new subject, and in any case I was not wanted – an outmoded technique, no doubt. After some years I thought of a subject and have been trailing it around for some time. My last series of television lectures was called *How wars begin*. There was still a gap which I now propose to fill: *How wars end*. This will be more complicated than its predecessor. Most wars start in the same way: tension, misunderstanding and then a war. Some end by abrupt surrender, some by prolonged negotiations, some by a mixture of the two. What is more, even when the fighting stops, the agreement of peace can take a long time. In 1814–15 the Congress of Vienna went on for almost a year after Napoleon's abdication ended the fighting. The Treaty of Versailles came six months after the armistice. The other peace treaties that followed the First World War took even longer. The peace treaty with Italy came in 1947, though there had been unconditional surrender by Italy in 1943. The peace treaty with Japan was not concluded until 1951. Peace with Germany has never been concluded at all for the simple reason that Germany in the old sense ceased to exist in 1945. What delightful complications lie ahead of me. I must sound one warning. I suffer among other things from nominal amnesia, a high-flown name for forgetfulness. Short-lived, I may say – the name or date comes back to me within a few minutes. But I can hardly stand staring at the camera for all that time. I can't think what to do. Make something up, I suppose.

There is a serious trouble in my life quite apart from Parkinson's disease: books are getting too long, and there are too many of them, usually at certain times of the year. For some months I had no books at all to review. Then monstrous tomes came in shoals. For instance, one day recently I received three books on Field Marshal Montgomery to review: one of four hundred pages, one of nearly five hundred and one of nearly nine hundred. It is an accusation commonly directed at reviewers that they do not read the books they get or at best pass their hands lightly over the cover and wait for inspiration. I am more conscientious. Having no regular occupation except shopping, I sit at home day after day going loyally through my assignment until I have read the lot. But it certainly leaves me with very little spare time. Now I thought the moment had arrived when I could get on with some other writing or even read a book for pleasure. I rejoiced too soon. What awaits me today? A book of virtually nine hundred pages on F. E. Smith, first Earl of Birkenhead, by John Campbell, has appeared on my desk this morning. John Campbell has written first-rate biographies. I even have a vague recollection that F. E. Smith, Lord Birkenhead, was once a figure of some political importance, probably a man just too clever to reach the highest point. I suppose I must settle down with the book for the next three weeks. But I can't. This morning a photographer is coming, I can't think why. Then I am recording my second instalment of *How wars end*. After that, some BBC agents are coming to record my views on the First World War, not that I have any. I have really reached the stage of asking about the First World War: 'What was that?' How terrible it seemed at the time, and how trivial it seems now compared with what is coming. I even have people ringing me up and asking what the Third World War will be like. I answer: 'Wait and see. When the Third World War comes you won't know. You'll be dead.' So I had better get back to F. E. Smith while I have time.

I have more serious complaints in life than the excessive length of books that I have to review. Among the most troublesome and certainly the most exasperating is noise. This is the price of living in modern times. One curse, rarely commented on, is the helicopters that fly persistently over North London. Not only do they fly over my garden: the same helicopter flies over it again and again. What are they doing? I am told that for some obscure reason they are observing the traffic and reporting where there are traffic jams. I don't believe a word of it. They fly around for sheer pleasure, happy in the knowledge that they are making life unbearable. But still worse is the music which goes on ceaselessly. For instance, this morning I was taken to the television studio in a hired car. There was canned music all the time, occasionally interrupted by conversations between the driver and his office, replete with mysterious assignments. Then the music starts again. My wife tells me that in Oxford Street the shops have canned music going on all the time, acute enough to threaten her with a heart attack. Then, on a more domestic level, there is on the other side of our street a family with three or four young men. They all have cars equipped with radios and the radios play all the time. If one of them comes home he parks his car outside my window and leaves the radio playing, sometimes all night. Since I sleep with my bedroom window open, I have a restless night. Occasionally they have a party, at least once a month. Then the radio plays until two o'clock in the morning. Soon I expect they will be playing their radios simultaneously on and on and on. If I try to escape the radios by walking on Hampstead Heath I am pursued, indeed surrounded, by young boys or girls carrying voluble radios with them in the quietest areas. I have known radios played in railway carriages and of course in public houses. Their public playing should be made illegal ...

I spent most of last Sunday watching the silent movie *Napoleon*, made by Abel Gance some fifty years ago. The scenes of the French Revolution seem to me very unlikely: the principal characters make very strange faces and wear very rough clothing. Napoleon specializes in rushing from the left-hand side of the screen to the right and back again: he always seems in a hurry, no doubt seeking a further opportunity to pull faces. The film is very funny and occasionally very dramatic. It is very exciting. But really it won't do. I may have been too corrupted by watching talkies to be able to tell, but I doubt whether it is a masterpiece even as a silent movie. Of course it is much better than most of the talking masterpieces we have been offered in recent times. You have only to think of *Reds* to appreciate what the cinema can now make of revolutions.

1–14 March 1984

I buy coffee about once a month. This involves an elaborate pilgrimage. First I take a bus almost to Piccadilly Circus, a pilgrimage in itself. Then I find my way by back streets to the head of Old Compton Street, pausing at an excellent fishmonger who has the best kippers in London. My objective is I. Camisa, the best Italian grocer in the area. The history of this goes back a long way. In 1931, when I first married, I began to buy No. 5 coffee from Legrain's in Gerrard Street. This was the best coffee I ever found. The shop was kept by two elderly French ladies, who also kept a French café next door.

After about five years the two elderly ladies sold out to two rather casual young men who kept the name of Legrain and the No. 5 coffee. This kept me going until the war, when the two young men first closed the café and then closed the shop. They found a home for the coffee in I. Camisa, who have been selling it ever since. I doubt whether anyone has remained as steadfastly loyal to Legrain's No. 5 as I have. On this fine January morning I followed my usual routine: bus to Piccadilly Circus, walk to I. Camisa and then across Old Compton Street, where I bought chicory at the Algerian coffee shop. After that I recrossed Old Compton Street, I cannot remember why. I was half-way across when I received a tremendous blow on my left thigh and found myself sprawled in great pain on the road. The car which knocked me out was driven by a Mr Shah, from whom I never received a word of regret.

I remember no more until I found myself in the Middlesex

Hospital. There I was told at first that I had received only a superficial wound and that I should be out of hospital in a couple of days. Gradually my injury got worse and worse. Now I have a fractured pelvis and no sign so far of any improvement. I walk with crutches and in great pain. I struggle on my crutches only when I need to go to the lavatory, and these are agonizing pilgrimages. At first I had a room to myself in the hospital. Then I had to make way for an elderly man of 91 who maintained an uproar of complaint and boasting day and night. The ward, though agreeable, was very noisy. The television was kept on until late at night, and radio still played when television was turned off. I slept but little. We had three cooked meals, substantial though commonplace. I put on considerable weight while I was there.

After three weeks I was sent home and here I have been for a further week and more. I still rely on crutches. My left leg is agonizingly painful when I try to use it. This is my first attempt to work. My typewriting tends to be inaccurate. My mind does not work very well. Twice a day I walk about ten yards along the road, first up and then down. Even ten yards are a painful struggle. Most of the time I sit reading. The most difficult time is when I have to struggle up or down stairs. It is not so bad when I can use the banisters, but these do not extend the whole way. Occasionally I reflect moodily on the ghastly fate that has befallen me. Visitors call and say how much better I am looking. I am not impressed. It seems to me that my condition has not changed at all. Altogether this is the worst catastrophe that has befallen me in all my life. I am approaching eighty and on my way out. I could well have done without this last mishap.

5 September 1985

Two activities have brought me pleasure throughout my life. The first is fell walking, as it is called in Lancashire. The second is the systematic visiting of churches. The first I have long renounced. No more scrambles across Kinder Scout pursued by gamekeepers. No more struggles through the mist on Coniston

Old Man. Worst of all, no more doing the round of Fairfield Horse Shoe. I doubt whether I could even get to the top of Latterbarrow. One day I must try.

Churches keep their appeal longer. It is possible to explore them even if one is reduced to a wheelchair. The written authorities on the two pleasures are of equal merit, but there is more in Pevsner than in Wainwright, and a wider range. I delivered an address to Pevsner shortly before he died. What is more, I now owe him a new debt of gratitude. The first volume of a series on the cathedrals of England has recently appeared. This volume covers all the diocesan cathedrals, Anglican and Roman Catholic, south of a line between the river mouths of the Severn and the Blackwater. To my surprise, there are more cathedrals to the north of this line than to the south of it. The book derives from the volumes on the buildings of England which Pevsner had virtually finished when he died. Priscilla Metcalf has enriched Pevsner's text and added a great deal.

This wonderful work has set aflame my zest for visiting churches and cathedrals. There is one great obstacle. Until recently I was without a driving licence. This was all my own fault, and a high-minded fault at that. This is how it happened. I had previously renewed my licence without difficulty whenever the time came. On the last occasion for renewal I noticed a warning that I should state anything which I thought might disqualify me from driving. I loyally revealed that I was suffering from Parkinson's disease, which at least raised a doubt. No answer followed, except that my licence was not renewed. Time passed. After a year or so I was summoned to a medical examination at the Ministry of Transport. After two or three hours I was told that everything about me was satisfactory except my sight, and, after an examination in Wigmore Street, that was pronounced satisfactory also. What is more, I was told that I could go ahead and drive as soon as I liked even though my licence had not yet been returned to me. But now I have encountered a fresh obstacle. It is more than three years since I drove a car even across the road. I have looked at my car. I have sometimes started up the engine and convinced myself that I could handle it easily. But I could not bring myself to do so. To judge by my present behaviour, I shall never drive again. Maybe I shall find a quiet road one day and start off again without apprehension. But this time seems long a-coming. Meanwhile I content myself with an occasional stretch of my legs up Parliament Hill and find even that hard going. My car engine would, I am sure, run excellently if I let it. My physical engine seems to be grinding to a halt ...

I am not much concerned nowadays to add to my literary production or indeed to productions of any kind. But there is one production to which I can claim to have made some remote contribution. And this is a new grandson. There he is: Carl Taylor, as flourishing as can be. I have other grandsons, a whole host of them. But none of them is called after one of the statesmen of modern times. I must confess that I have got nearly to overlooking Karl Marx as worthy of admiration. But of course he is. In my opinion, most of his most famous book is nearly unreadable, though patches of *The Communist Manifesto* have their merits and *The Civil War in France* is without faults. Now I have a grandson who shares his name. The news cheers me in my declining years.

20 February 1986

The late Professor Tate of Manchester University, I have been told, made his last ascent of Scafell Pike at the age of 93. I made my last ascent of Pillar at the age of little more than 70. I used to go abroad at least once a year and often twice. Now I have put all that behind me and have been content for a long time with Yarmouth mill in the Isle of Wight. Last summer I went to Swanage and spent my time in the lavish surroundings of the Grosvenor Hotel.

Swanage is unique, having little in common with Lytham or Folkestone except the sea, and even that is restrained. The sea at Swanage is not designed to swim in or to boat in. Its function is for you to sit by in a deck chair. When that palls you can escape to a hall equipped with slot machines, which do not furnish a profitable return, at any rate not for me. The inns are many, and unlike most inns they provide more food than drink.

I would not claim that the inn food is exceptional, but the Grosvenor Hotel has a high standard, which it keeps to throughout the summer. It also has the sensible arrangement of charging wine by the bottle as you drink it.

The surrounding country has some good churches and other attractions. Corfe Castle is said to have been designed by William the Conqueror. I do not warm to it. The most fascinating feature of the entire neighbourhood is the Cerne Giant. He is an ancient turf-cut figure, holding a knobbed club in his hand. Full justice is done to his male parts. The girls of the village strive to establish intimacy with him, and the more enterprising remove their knickers before approaching him. Certainly the Cerne Giant merits a visit.

I have been holding out against visits to the cinema, but have recently given way. My first experiment was with *The Package Tour*, which shows the charabancs of Hungarians sent to the murder camps established by German Nazis during the Second World War. Most of those murdered were Jews. Now those who visit the murder camps are Jews also. I suppose it is usual to visit the cemeteries of relatives, and that the camps are much the same sort of thing. And of course those who survived are entitled to do what they want in this respect. But the camps have become accepted as a suitable spot for picnics, and perhaps German Nazis will soon be asked to join in by those they wanted to torture and kill. It seems strange to me. Then I went to see *A Letter to Brezhnev*, the story of a Liverpool girl who had a love affair with a passing Soviet sailor. They get on well till it is time for the sailor to leave. The girl resolutely decides to follow him and to marry him in Russia. A civil servant from the British Foreign Office warns her that the sailor will cheat her when she is there. But she writes to Brezhnev and gets invited to Russia. An easy, gentle, sentimental film – of a sort that does no harm.

Of the great film artists who have recently died, Orson Welles, I suppose, led the field for a long time; *Citizen Kane* had no rival. It sounded as if it were really true, and perhaps it was. I was once asked to share a film with Welles. I wisely refused.

Greta Garbo reached the same high level. I can think of no film which surpasses *Ninochka*. It is beautifully natural and at the same time imaginary. Without doubt Garbo was the most beautiful of all film stars: and yet she seemed not to be setting herself a standard beyond that of other film stars. The revival of *Ninochka* on television the other evening was for me a boon beyond imagination. I often wonder what the high figures of the Soviet Union make of *Ninochka* – if they have ever heard of it. To the list of great films which I press upon my readers from time to time I must add *Closely Observed Trains* and Buster Keaton's railway film, *The General*.

Every day one is asked to sign something or other – pleas to champion good causes, proposals to form new joint actions. To sign protests or hail gallant leaders. In general, I never sign, still less do I contribute money. But a couple of days ago I signed without hesitation in a good cause. This was to resist the destruction of the Round Reading-Room in the British Museum. It staggers me beyond comprehension that anyone should plan to detroy this great monument. For over a century scholars from all countries have used this reading-room as their work-place and refuge. Karl Marx himself occupied seat G38. That alone should rally in protection of the Reading-Room. But there is a more concrete reason for defending it. It is the best place in England in which to read. And yet high-grade architects are shouting to tear the Reading-Room down at once. I am delighted to note that there is a flourishing organization to prevent this. Here is a cause to which everyone who believes in civilization should give his signature, and it would do no harm to send some money as well. I am even prepared to speak in defence of the Reading-Room if it comes to a public meeting.

I have recently enjoyed the society of an Indian boy, the son of our postmaster, who is preparing to take O levels. He is preparing for Russian and especially Soviet history, which is a strange world for him. What, he asked, did Lenin write on the train? What did Kiev write? And who was Kamenev? This last question rather caught me out as I had quite forgotten about Kamenev. The session showed what nonsense it is to teach Russian history even to boys who are quick-witted. I laughed so much that we both enjoyed our researches. I am glad to record that he is to come again next week. I am looking forward to his

A. J. P. Taylor

enquiries about Germany or perhaps even the United States. It all goes to show that the study of history is a great strengthener of character.

Louis MacNeice

Under the Sugar Loaf

'Dublin?' said a friend of mine after his first visit. 'Dublin! There's no such place. It's just one enormous pub.' This aspect of the city presses itself upon visitors thanks to traditional Irish hospitality, combined, one should add, with the pleasure of a new audience. Not all the citizens, of course, are pub-goers. AE and the late Sarah Pursar, mistress of stained glass and malice, made do with their own weekly salons, while W. B. Yeats, they say, went only once into a pub and did not like it at all. But the Dublin salon is a thing of the past and the pub remains the temple of talk. There are other hard-drinking cities – New York, Edinburgh, Accra – but it is the talk in Dublin that gives the drinking its very distinctive quality. If any Dublin alcoholic were to write an autobiographical novel in answer to Malcolm Lowry's *Under the Volcano*, it could well be called *Under the Sugar Loaf* (that conspicuous Wicklow mountlet): things are not going to end with an eruption, they are going to melt in the mouth.

Anyhow the pubs in Dublin were even more assertive than usual this 16 June, 'Bloomsday', when some of the more intellectual and tourist-conscious Irishmen were about to open (or should we say consecrate?) the new Joyce Centre in his old Martello tower at Sandycove described in the first chapter of *Ulysses*. For me the pilgrimage began at Davy Byrne's, which was Joyce's favourite pub though he might not now recognize it with its smart modern décor and fancy murals. We met at mid-morning and, though everyone complained of being 'frail', started at once dissecting the Old Master. 'Let's face it,' someone said, 'he must have been a terrible old bore. He had no talk in him at all.' Someone else said someone was writing it all up for the *Lancet*. And so on till someone said: 'What makes us a nation is we treat our heroes like human beings.' At this point who should walk in but James Joyce himself in a straw boater with a bright blue band, a spruce blue bow-tie to match, and a Charlie Chaplin walking-stick dangling from his forearm. It turned out he was a well-known promoter who happens to look like Joyce (he himself said he was the *tourist's* idea of him) and Bloomsday indeed was a promoter's dream; outside waiting for us beside the Creation Arcade were two freshly refurbished black and yellow four-wheeler horse cabs. The only difficulty was to get the jarveys to start driving. It seems they were waiting for the cameramen.

The day, everyone said, was 'too bright too soon' but their fears proved unfounded; in another sense, perhaps, it lasted too bright too long. Martello towers, built to keep out the French, are like great grey stone gasometers, an apt image, I suggest, for this one at Sandycove which should certainly provide a vent for what Dublin calls 'great gas'. Yet it is to be doubted whether its high rocky perch will ever again be the setting for such a large and mixed cosmopolitan assembly, with drinks in a marquee and cameras attempting to focus and microphones thrust like carrots into reluctant faces.

All the time Dublin Bay down below us refused to look as Joyce said it did on 16 June 1904. It was neither grey nor snotgreen but obstinately and unbelievably blue, this blue being emphasized by the little white sails that littered it as though someone had been running a paper chase on the water; to the north the Hill of Howth remained as anomalous as ever. Above us on the tower was a strange flag, newly hoisted by Miss Sylvia Beach, who was naturally the heroine of the day; it had been lifted from one of the best scenes in *Ulysses* – 'none of your Henry Tudor's harps, no, the oldest flag afloat, the flag of the province of Desmond and Thomond, three crowns on a blue field, the three sons of Milesius'. Certainly a memorable occasion, were one only to remember the half of it. Some cynics, downing their free drinks, wrote it off as a cultural gimmick but, if it is such, it is one to be welcomed. It was time Joyce was rescued from the campus laboratories.

If Joyce might be proud of his resurrected tower, he might

also be turning – with laughter – in his grave at something that had happened the day before. In Dawson Street opposite the Mansion House, a pretty white doll's house with blue facings and a cast-iron porch, something yet dollier has appeared, the Anna Livia Boutique. Some years ago Sybil Connolly, by using native materials and concentrating on line, put Ireland on the couturiers' map. She has been followed by other dress designers, prominent among whom is Kay Petersen of Anna Livia who cannily timed her first showing for 'Bloomsday Eve' of this year. Her hand-out explains that 'Understated elegance is the theme carried out in the exclusive hand-woven tweeds fashioned into impeccably tailored suits.' Among those present at this excellently stage-managed performance were Sylvia Beach, Madame Eugène Jolas and the Irish playwright-magistrate who was chief organizer of the Bloomsday ceremonies (another writer long ago labelled him 'that fellow whose name goes round and around – Donagh MacDonagh MacDonagh MacDonagh . . .'); there were also one English atonal composer and one English actor, while Dominic Behan got near the door but did not come in.

Thirty-nine models, all 'with Joycean titles' and some, such as 'Molly Bloom', intended as 'direct interpretations of Joyce's characters' – there was never a dull garment. There were also 'jars' (of champagne) before and after, five beautiful girls to do the modelling (all swan necks and false eyelashes), a background of gramophone music and a foreground of very suave commentary. 'All you Joycean scholars,' said the lady commentator, 'will appreciate for example "Finnegan": Kay Petersen calls it her igloo outfit.' And 'Martello', the 'stylized idea' of which should be as right 'for Joyceans as for fashion people'. And 'Proteus' (with reversible cape). And 'Sylvia Silence': 'Do you see the way it *links*?' And 'Calypso': 'tweed simulating knitting and it's all hand-smocked'. 'I'm sure by now,' the commentator said, 'you're beginning to get the Anna Livia idea.' We were but it was worth it. The billing of Molly Bloom gave rise to ribald cracks in the pubs but this 'evening dress in three brilliant tweeds' *as a dress* was a sheer feat, though not everyone of course could wear it. Kay Petersen has stood the concept 'tweedy' on its head.

Dress designing is only one element in the new Dublin. Another is Irish television, pronounced tellyfish. This is partly a state affair and partly commercial and is said to be paying its way; I was surprised and impressed to hear that the well-known Irish actress Sheila Richards is in charge of religious tellyfish. Certainly the forest of unusually high aerials has changed the skyline of Dublin. This new Dublin contains, compared with the old, a lower percentage of bugs and bowseys and a higher percentage of smoothies. Here are the headquarters of the people who arrange subsidies and cajole German firms into opening up industries in Ireland. This may well be necessary in Ireland's precarious economy. What is certainly undesirable and unnecessary is the commercial vandalism which is prepared, in the name of efficiency, to ruin the finest Georgian vista in the world, Fitzwilliam Street. There is also some smugness about.

Yet the old Dublin survives and still dominates, not only the astonishing light and the air that caresses and the gifts for the amateur photographer (impoverished doorways framed by Ionic pillars) and the screaming of the gulls and the newsboys and the shops of Religious Goods (Sick Call Sets included), but also – and more important – the paradoxes of the Dubliners themselves, their notorious charm, their natural courtesy and misleading bonhomie, and what Kate O'Brien calls their 'cold gaiety'. They seem always to have the virtues of their vices and vices versa. Their malice in a way is innocent, except when there is a chance of litigation. Their sex life is mainly inadequate but their bawdy talk is uproarious. Their women, who seem so much put upon, have not only a great ease of manner but look happier than most Englishwomen. Among them are many good blaspheming Christians and many decent fluthered puritans. They are famous wasters of time but possibly because they prefer ends to means. Above all they can mythologize and debunk themselves simultaneously.

Though I am not a Dubliner, I have always found the city a home from home. My grandfather lived there once with his family and my father and an uncle were alumni of Trinity so that, when I was first taken there as a child, even though what I chiefly noticed was a shopwindow with little souvenirs of bogoak and Connemara marble, I felt, as E. M. Forster might say, that the city and I had at least 'connected'. I like it of course more than it likes me: there was a time when they sang about me,

> *Let him go back and labour*
> *For Faber and Faber*

though even then I found that flattering. My memories over the years are as mixed as sea-shells. Visits as a small boy to the Zoo in Phoenix Park: very good lions and a voluble keeper. My first visit to Trinity College Library: one very good book – rhymed with bells? – and again a voluble keeper. Visits in the early Thirties to Lansdowne Road for rugby football and out to Rathfarnham for W. B. Yeats. The former kept me shouting, the latter kept me wondering. I was there with a Professor of Greek, so Yeats talked of nothing but spirits. 'I suppose you are like Burnet,' he said, 'and think the Ionian Physicists were physicists; they were not, of course, they were spiritualists.' When challenged, he reluctantly admitted he had never actually *seen* any spirits. Then he rallied and said: 'I have often smelt them.'

In the late Thirties I came to know Yeats's disciple, the late F. R. Higgins, who thought I was lacking in 'singing robes' but seemed pleased to let me beguile him away from the Abbey Theatre when he was supposed to be rehearsing the company; we used to meet other poets and borrow odd pounds from each other. At this period in the famous Bailey restaurant I encountered a madman in the Gents. He poured out a monologue to which I had no reply. 'D'ye know?' he said, glaring. 'I'm like O'Connell Bridge.' 'Why?' I said, feeling I must at last say something. 'I get angry,' he said, 'when I'm crossed.' And then at the end of the Thirties I remember that Third of September when England declared war. I went to Croke Park to see the All Ireland Hurling Final. An old woman stood near me selling bananas. Suddenly there came thunder and a deluge: it was like Saint Michael, with All Angels to help him, if they had been producing *King Lear*. I looked round at the old woman; her bananas had vanished into pulp. Well, I thought, Dublin may keep out of the war (and who would blame her?) but at least she's ushered it in with her well-known sense of theatre.

Such reminiscences must seem trivial but for me they add up to a chain which can lower an anchor when I need it. On this last visit I was lucky enough to stay in a farmhouse with cows just under the window and the Wicklow hills in the distance and huge poppies in the garden and laburnums weeping on the lawn: a typical Irish farmhouse and only four miles from the Pillar in O'Connell Street on which Nelson still, typically, stands. I treated the house, as they say, 'like a hotel' but my host and hostess made me feel I treated it like home. Sometimes they came into Dublin to see me and we found ourselves in a pub with the Father and Mother of All Behans (constants if ever there were such) drinking cheek by jowl with teenagers. Age and youth: Dublin remains constant and constantly variable. Just before I left the wind got up and lathered the moon with clouds and tangled it and tousled it in the trees of Stephen's Green. I was taken to a final party. It was a room with the lights out and people sitting on the floor and a young man with a guitar singing with a final delicacy.

Peter Fleming

Death and Mrs Dale

I find it difficult to define the attitude which I adopt towards events which happen in my own country while I am out of it. It is, I fear, a fundamentally arrogant attitude, and I should like to believe that others share it, that I am not the only person who, when he says, 'Ah, that must have been while I was abroad', seems to disassociate himself from whatever 'that' is. And not only to disassociate himself. A keen student of human nature, if he listened carefully to my voice, would detect other undertones. Why, these undertones ask, was I not consulted? I have, they suggest, no objection to my fellow-countrymen passing new laws, producing new plays or embarking on new controversies in my absence; but if they do so they can hardly expect me to take much interest in them, far less to approve of any changes which the community may have made in its arrangements while I was away. It is because the implications of this attitude are so unattractive that I hope others besides myself unconsciously adopt it.

I felt it working strongly in me the other day when, returning to England after a short journey, I switched on the wireless in the car and discovered that the BBC had altered the sub-title of *Mrs Dale's Diary*. It was no longer A Recording of the Daily Happenings in the Life of a Doctor's Wife; 'Family' had been substituted for 'Wife'. And as I pondered the dread consequences which, on a long-term view, this change must seem to portend, I heard of the death of the Dales' dog, Bosun, at the age of eighteen.

Although ignored by *The Times*, the demise of this imaginary dog attracted a good deal of attention in the national press on the following day; a real human being who had died, like Bosun, in his sleep would have had to be extremely distinguished to get half the amount of space devoted to him. The BBC, choking back its corporate sobs, described Bosun as a large brown mongrel, so that we actually know more about the personal appearance of Mrs Dale's dog than we know about the personal appearance of Hamlet.

This is all very well as far as it goes; but where, and how, is it going to end? Eighteen is a great age for a dog, and Bosun had to die. Sooner or later, by the same token, the Grim Reaper will have to call for Mrs Dale. Will the nation be able to stand it? This is not a frivolous question. Ahead of us looms a dilemma which no previous age has had to face. Already, the BBC estimate, between four and six million citizens regularly listen to Mrs Dale. The programme has been running continuously for nine years, and throughout that period the number of its devotees has steadily increased. Mrs Dale is now forty-nine. In another fifteen years it is reasonable to suppose that she will be playing a daily part – often a surprisingly important one – in the lives of more than a quarter of the adult population; and her *aficionados* will include, as they do today, a high proportion of old people and invalids. The repercussions of Mrs Dale's death on the health and spirits of her frailer fans would be, to say the least, imponderable.

There are, of course, alternatives to killing off Mrs Dale. The BBC might brace itself to face a nation-wide storm of protest and bring the programme to an end, though I find it extraordinarily difficult to visualize the turn of events recorded in the final episode. Or – and the recent change in the sub-title may point to this intention – Mrs Dale might (perhaps after Dr Dale's retirement) fade more and more into the background, leaving one of the next generation to take over the twin duties of heroine and *commère*. But Mrs Dale has still got, eventually, to die, and even if she dies off-stage, there has got to be a funeral; and I seriously doubt whether *everyone* could be relied on to survive the emotional shock. Even if she were lost at sea (thus avoiding the obsequies), it might be too much for some of the old, precariously balanced minds to whom she has been so real for so long.

It is possible that I am wrong – that if Mrs Dale (clearance
having first been obtained from the Transport Commission)
were run over by an imaginary bus, nobody would be any the
worse. But old, lonely people whose wits have begun to wander
are anchored to life by all sorts of small, habitual things ('She's
never been the same,' I heard it said the other day of an eighty-
year-old widow, 'since her landlord put that new stove in last
autumn'), and though I do not suggest that Mrs Dale's death
would be followed by a wave of heart failures and suicides, I
imagine that it is impossible for the BBC wholly to discount the
possibility that it might in some cases induce something more
serious than a passing sadness.

Among the (as it were) extracurricular problems with which
man's ingenuity has confronted him, that of Mrs Dale's quietus
hardly ranks among the most serious. It has, nevertheless, a
certain fascination. Our age is reputed sceptical, not easily
impressed by the wonders which it so lavishly produces. How is
it that so many of us fall so deeply under the very un-
Millamantian spell of Mrs Dale, a fictitious character mainly
distinguished (like the even more popular Archers) by a pains-
taking ordinariness?

It is not as though she made us laugh, or cry, or kept us – save
to an almost imperceptible extent – in suspense. (By 'us' I
mean her regular listening public, among whom I cannot, quite,
presume to include myself.) She can hardly be called escapist,
unless you call a stroll round the prison yard escaping; the story
of her life unfolds itself like an endless roll of part-worn linoleum.
And yet the fact remains that she has become so integral a part
of our national life that it would be a tricky, controversial and
even dangerous business to expunge her from it.

Millions of people know more about the history of the Dale
family than they know about the history of their own; if you
asked them to name five members of the Cabinet they would be
gravelled, but they could tell you all about everyone in Ambridge,
where the Archers live. The available evidence suggests that this
curious cult of shadow-worship will strengthen and widen its
hold on the community. I suppose it is a harmless enough trend.
The imaginations which Mrs Dale makes so effortlessly prisoner,

the fancies whose need to roam she sublimates, might otherwise be wandering along less rewarding trails, such as those which lead to the private lives of American film-stars or to the idiosyncrasies of Mr Gilbert Harding (a mounted policeman at whose funeral I have no wish to be). But there was, in the dark and backward ages, a time when such fancies had heroes and marvels as their quarry, when people dreamed and wondered about different things in different ways. I do not say that Mrs Dale makes it impossible for her five or so million devotees to do likewise; but I doubt if she can be said to stimulate the tendency.

POSTSCRIPT. A few months after this was written one of the characters in 'The Archers' met a violent though imaginary death. Large sections of the population were convulsed with grief, many indignant letters were written to the BBC and the newspapers, and flowers and other funerary tributes were sent to Broadcasting House.

P. Y. Betts

from *People Who Say Goodbye*

In the early months of the First World War, large numbers of Belgian refugees, fleeing before the German invaders, came pouring into London. Everybody seemed to know of a family of Belgian refugees but only those few who spoke French, let alone Flemish, understood what they were talking about. They came babbling to tea. My mother, whose education, it will be remembered, began and ended with the knowledge that the capital of Portugal was Lisbon (on the Tagus) did her best at making do with sign language, which she was not bad at. What she wanted to tell her Belgian guests was that her husband, who had been educated partly in France, spoke excellent French but he unfortunately was working late at the office because the auditors were there, so he would not be home until (tapping vigorously at her wristwatch) nearly eight o'clock. Whenever Mother tapped her wristwatch the Belgian ladies would become restive, making French twittering noises and half rising to their feet, when my mother would push them down again and offer them whatever was going, which might well be bread and dripping as she was not one to stand on ceremony with anyone, let alone foreigners.

The Belgian ladies had no husbands but they had children. These came to tea too. One of these was an exasperating child of my own age. It was not long before Christmas and my brother and I were making paper chains. We sat at the dining room table with the coloured strips of paper, gummed at the ends, in front of us. The thing was to pick a strip at random, moisten the ends with a damp sponge and link it through the previous ring, which must not be of the same colour. Red, blue, green, white, yellow, purple, pink – it was lovely work as the finished links piled rustling up. Our guest, not exactly loved but tolerated because we had a common enemy, sat beside us at the table and was free to take part in this blissful occupation. One would have thought that just seeing the thing done would have been enough for anyone, even deaf and dumb, to get the hang of it, but no, petite Mignon did not seem to cotton on at all. Again and again she kept picking up a strip of one colour and linking it on to a link of the *same* colour – red, red, red, etc., or green, green, green ... In vain we laid strips of differing colour alongside each other, nodding savagely and crying, 'OUI! OUI' then putting the same colour together, the same the same the same, and screaming, 'NON!' In vain. It made me mad. Paper chains were precious and she was wasting them. I thumped the table. 'NON!' My brother was a clever, thoughtful boy, five years older than I and advanced for his years, but not even his careful demonstration of how paper chains should be made, and his tentative '*Comme ça?*' had the slightest effect on our guest. Was she exceptionally stupid or plain obstinate? Were Belgian paper chains all made of the same colour and did she think our variegated ones crude and garish, vulgar tasteless British kitsch?

We were never to know. She did not come to tea again. Later that winter, aghast grown-up talk going on over my head revealed that she had fallen in the fire and was dead.

When my brother came in from school I told him the news. We agreed it was a good job she was dead. People who couldn't make paper chains properly had no future anyway. The fire was the best place for them.

Our suburb was a favoured one on account of its wide roads and many open spaces. Not only was there the Common, there was a nursery garden full of flowers, threaded with footpaths, there were enchanting glimpses through wrought-iron gates of the secret gardens of the big houses in the road between two commons where my grandparents lived. No wonder our estate, with its comfortable modern housing, pulled in youngish couples who were, they expected, going to get on in the world. There were so many trees. There was such abundance of fresh air. It was incidental that much of the fresh air blew in from the domains of madness, crime, wounds and death, each of which required a large acreage of living space, if living is the word.

Madness was accommodated in the large lunatic asylum with its own farm, not far from the Common. In the days of my youth there were no euphemisms for mental disturbance. If you were mentally ill you were mad and if you were mad you went to a lunatic asylum and no messing. If you were very, very mad they put you in a padded cell.

My mother of course had something to say about lunatic asylums because as a girl she had visited one. Her father had taken her when he went there on business. He was a Commissioner in Lunacy, whatever that may have been – something to do with committing patients, I suppose, as he was a Justice of the Peace. While he went off to attend to what may have been gruesome business she remained behind, engaged in conversation with a pleasant gentleman to whom she had been introduced. They were on an upper floor with a view of the hall below, and when in due course her father came in sight, talking to an official, my mother's companion walked with her to the head of the stairs, where he bowed and took his leave, explaining regretfully that he was unable to accompany her down the stairs as his legs were made of glass and might break.

(His glass legs were vivid in my mind. They were like the very solid chunky kind of cut glass tumblers that stood ranged on shelves in my grandparents' butler's pantry.) But my mother had a more disturbing story than this. It was about a woman in a padded cell. I doubt whether she had been invited to see for herself, more likely her father had told her about it, but its impact on my mind was powerful and lasting. The madwoman was raving, flinging herself at the walls of her padded cell and screaming that she was burning to death, burning to death ... This horrified me. It seemed to me that being deluded that you were burning to death was far worse than really being burnt to death, because being burnt to death would end, in death, but being burnt to death *in the head* would go on and on. It was merciless. It was an eternity of torment. It was hell itself.

Glass legs, comparatively, were a bagatelle. You could lead quite a happy life on one floor, preferably the ground floor.

But that was in the past. In my own day no especial horror

stories came out of the asylum. There were high walls round the grounds. Sometimes a happy band of more or less presentable inmates would issue forth in the care of their keepers, busily chattering. I liked to look at them though I was not supposed to. Their enjoyment was intense. They were mostly, if not all, female, with bright excited eyes and frizzy grey hair, darting jubilantly in and out of the parade of shops facing the Common, clutching small purchases.

'They always buy sardines,' my mother said, and it was true: fourpenny tins of sardines gleamed in their hands as they emerged, discarding paper bags, afternoon light blazing back from their shining eyes. My mother would point out that mad people usually had either lank hair hanging in dank hanks or fuzzy stuff frizzing up all over their heads, and the frizzy sort was more often seen.

The hair style of the happy lunatics came naturally. Their hair stood on end of its own accord. In my own generation, for people near the age of the century in its last decades, the chosen hair style of nearly all old women is a similar frizzy mop, more or less veiling the pink skin beneath. The only difference is that now their faces are not bright with joy as were those of the happy loonies of my early childhood, nor are they joyfully clutching tins of sardines.

The domain of crime was the prison which, with its ancillary buildings, was as big as a village, whole streets of warders' houses and big houses with gardens for the Governor, chaplain, doctor. There was a *cordon sanitaire* of open ground around it, leased off to bowls and tennis clubs. Opposite our house was a rough field with a footpath leading away into the prison hinterland, whence sallied forth at times a hooligan family of red-haired boys, warders' children, to terrorize clean little prep school boys in their grey flannels. Neighbours tut-tutted about these boys, who seemed ripe for imprisonment themselves. Occasionally an active prep school father would catch and beat one of the red-heads, as could be lightly undertaken in those days without fear of a suit for assault. Bad boys were not easy to catch, but once caught, they could be beaten – that was the way of it then.

Arthur Marshall

Christmas Reviews of Books For Girls

1935

Fifty-two Sports Stories for Girls edited by R. S. Lyons
(Hutchinson)
The Lower School Leader by Veronica Marlow
(Oxford University Press)
The Head Girl at Wynford by Winifred Darch
(Oxford University Press)
Nancy in the Sixth by Dorita Fairlie Bruce
(Oxford University Press)

Life in schools for girls is clearly an exciting business. They go the pace. Lights are put out in the cubicles and one would think that the girls, exhausted by the strain of ragging Miss Bellamy, would be ready for refreshing sleep. But all that the merry madcaps seem to want is the ginger-pop hidden under Bertha's bolster and a moonlight climb over the roofs. And doubtless the readers of these stories would not have it otherwise.

In *Sports Stories for Girls* there are several gripping yarns, among the best being *Gloria's Secret*, *Amy's Mix-up*, *Doreen's Ride*, *Gertie's Glider*, and *The Rivals of the Racquet*. In the last named there is a splendid pen-picture of the tennis final for the Chalfont Cup (missing from its case in Big Hall) between the head-girl, Monica Warren, and Rita Frazer, who has just won a scholarship to Girton.

'Whang!'

It was the first ball of the set, and on the return it banged from Monica's racquet just inside the base line, an unplayable shot.

But Rita did not lose her head.

She stayed back at base and let the high balls bounce. She ran in to the short ones and lobbed them back. In a word, she was all over the court, showing amazing speed and endurance.

And so to the closing moments of the match.

The ball landed, and Rita was on it like a flash. Whizz! The next shot went like a streak – *ping*! And the next, *Ping*!

Small wonder that after all that excitement poor Monica spends the night walking in her sleep round the school, returning the lost cup to its case, watched by the headmistress, a Miss Dacres, 'all in black marocain'.

In *The Lower School Leader*, Miss Veronica Marlow has not hesitated to make full use of realism and the scene where a stubborn junior called Margaret refuses to eat up her gristle is strangely powerful.

'But that's all gristle!' protested the junior, 'really it is.'

'Nonsense. Eat it up at once. There is nothing put before you in this school that is not entirely digestible,' snapped Miss Buckett.

But Margaret did not move, nor did she try to eat it.

'If you want me to be sick, I will,' she said, defiantly, 'but it's just cruelty to animals.'

This seemed to enrage Miss Buckett. 'Take her out, please,' she ordered; and immediately two prefects left their places and more or less dragged the junior by brute force off her chair and out of the dining-room

Never mind. Everybody has cheered up in time for the staff lacrosse match.

Already, filling the entire gap between the posts stood Miss Jellaby, the heavyweight music mistress. There could be no getting past Miss Jellaby unless the ball went right through her. Keenly watching the match were Miss Salt, the Oak House matron, still smelling strongly of lysol, and three of the younger mistresses just down from the 'Varsity, and out came a battery of cameras to take 'snaps' of them in their glory.

And finally comes Miss Buckett herself, clutching an umbrella 'though the sun did not look like going in'.

The Head Girl at Wynford introduces us to a charming school; indeed, as a visiting hockey player remarks:

'I never come over here but I envy you,' said Myra Jarvis, the Bingston captain.

'Why?' asked Betty, as they walked across the middle field.

'Your topping grounds! Your marvellous old school!'

But in spite of the scrumptious surroundings, there are the usual tiffs.

'I don't know what you are talking about,' Edmee observed coldly, and turned away.

Petronel looked after her. 'Pig!' she said, under her breath.

Miss Dorita Fairlie Bruce in *Nancy in the Sixth* excels in her choice of names. There are Desdemona Blackett, Geraldine Judkins, Ryllis Rutherford and Clemency Walton. The heroine, Nancy Caird, who is a ripping bat, is unable to get to the all-important match against the Lady Foresters.

Seated on the bank beside the useless bicycle, Nancy fumbled in the tool-bag, and one or two involuntary tears splashed in upon spanner and screwdriver before she was able to get to work on the flabby tyre.

Nancy is ambitious to win the Woodford-Leigh Organ Scholarship, but there are difficulties.

'That's what I thought!' burst out the organ-master explosively, 'but I didn't want to make any ill-founded accusations. When I asked Mrs Paterson as a very special favour to allow you to use her organ, I gave her an undertaking – a solemn undertaking – that neither of you would do it any damage. I told her that you could be trusted – you were not beginners; I practically pledged my honour that no harm would come to her instrument – and what has happened? This morning I get this note from her to say that she could hardly get through the morning service yesterday because some of her most important stops were completely out of action!'

Three of the above books bear the noble imprint of the Oxford University Press. Oh well, *il faut*, no doubt, *vivre*.

1936

Prefects at Springdale by Dorita Fairlie Bruce
(Oxford University Press)
A Schoolgirl in Switzerland by Kathlyn Rhodes (Harrap)
The Winifred Darch Omnibus, containing:
*For the Honour of the House, Cicely Bassett, Patrol Leader,
Margaret Plays the Game* (Oxford University Press)

Gusto streams from these packed pages and one reads breathlessly on and on.

In *Prefects at Springdale* there is a bizarre recluse called Miss Peters who enlivens her conversation with cries of 'Hoots toots' and 'Tits, lassies!' She offers a prize for the most go-ahead house. The girls are in a great flutter. What shall they do to be go-ahead?

'This idea at least,' said their house-captain triumphantly, 'is entirely my own. It came to me – just came to me – in a blinding flash. Girls, this house is going all out for domestic science.'

And they do too, eventually winning Miss Peters' prize, which turns out to be 'a pot of exquisite Eastern workmanship, containing a dwarf cedar tree, gnarled into a perfect miniature'. The names of the girls who receive this charming trophy are Marion Banister, Louise Sturges, Isolt Kingsley, Tibbie Macfie and Fearnelith Macpherson.

The girls are all fearfully keen on a ripping games mistress called Miss Stewart, and can one wonder? 'It isn't her beauty and her auburn colouring, but she's got that – that sort of glamour.' She abandons lacrosse momentarily in order to go for walks with a plucky little junior called Faith Kersey, who has 'eyes liked drowned violets' and is an 'undeveloped genius at throwing-in'. It is Faith who canoes down the flooded main street to the rescue of two girls who are singing hymns while imprisoned in a ruined tomb. Meanwhile, the plot requires the headmistress, a Miss Timmins, to try to shin up an extremely high wall. Need I add that she reaches the top?

A Schoolgirl in Switzerland is a riot of violent wiggings from the headmistress and stern punishments. Lucia, who has a Sicilian great-grandmother, is to dance the Tarantella at an hotel for charity, but she takes the wrong shoe-bag. Elma hurries after her with the correct one, gets caught in a storm, loses her purse and receives a tremendous reprimand, partly in French. Then Elma goes back for her Kodak, misses the bus at the St Bernard Hospice and is told to write out 'I must remember to wind my watch' a hundred times in French and English. Then Rosalie smacks Elma's face for having ruined her water-colour sketch when attacked by a savage goat and, refusing to apologize, is shut up in the sanatorium. Then Lucia is set upon by a lunatic in the Castle of Chillon and, soon after, Rosalie steals Gwen's flute and hides it in Elma's work-bag. Gwen is incensed ('She flung herself on Elma and snatched away the flute, recklessly pulling stitches out of Elma's beautifully knitted sweater'). And even in the holidays, Elma is found in a casino, heavily made up, and Lucia is seen dashing about on the beach in a bathing dress called La Sirène.

In *Margaret Plays the Game* the girls are extremely fond of theatricals and of the English mistress, Miss Rylands. Margaret, who lives in a house called Red Clamps, is a splendid little actress, who does not hesitate to let herself go.

'You were *it*, Margaret,' murmured Thetis Standen. 'I should have wept in another minute. But if you're going on being so intense all through the play, you'll be a rag at the end.'

Rosamund, a girl with 'red-gold plaits and dazzlingly fair skin', is head prefect, an unjustified appointment to some.

'Rosie carries being "all things to all men" a bit far. I often wonder what she'll do in a really tight place where pretty ways and book-cleverness would cut no ice.'

Quite so. Rosie can't even see that Doris Gilmour has heels more than three inches high.

'And though the Head was too old-fashioned to suspect the presence of powder, *teint Rachel*, not only on her *nose*, Doris had boasted that on Saturdays she used lipstick as well.'

1937

Dimsie Intervenes by Dorita Fairlie Bruce
(Oxford University Press)
The Dorita Fairlie Bruce Omnibus, containing:
Nancy at St Bride's, That Boarding-School Girl,
The New Girl and Nancy (Oxford University Press)
Elinor in the Fifth by Winifred Darch (Oxford University Press)
Audrey on Approval by May Wynne (Ward Lock)
Growing Up at St Monica's by Jessie McAlpine
(Oxford University Press)
Gillian the Dauntless by Frederica Bennett (Nelson)

What is up with the Girls of England? This year's batch of stories
contains far too many references to beauty culture. Are Hilda's
plaits as glossy as Thelma's? Where is Patience's bejewelled hair-
slide? Who has tampered with Eileen's cold cream? This is
unhealthy stuff, and let this be the last of it.

In *Dimsie Intervenes*, the headmistress has a hard time of
it: 'My dear, I am never off duty except when I'm in bed – and
not always then.' Some of the girls are keen on their appearances and purchase bath-cubes, freesia soap and bottles of
Anti-Freckle from Boot's. To counteract these, there are the
Anti-Soppists who troop down to the gym, anxious to practise
'those last leg movements of Miss Mallory's'. The Seniors
have a percussion band in the basement and the climax of
the story finds Dolly Ansell being laced into a pair of stays
in the lower music-room, where 'many dark deeds had taken
place'.

In *Nancy at St Bride's* there are Helga Grub ('a slim dainty-
looking Senior'), Betty Muffet ('wispish-looking') and Charlotte
Truscott, the head girl, who has 'exchanged the big glasses of
her younger days for a trim pair of pince-nez'. The dormitories
are named after fruits – Gooseberries, Apricots, Nectarines, etc.
Sybil 'takes up' Nancy, and even Christine, 'yellow hair' and all,
is 'drawn to her', but Nancy will have none of it: 'I think you're
a perfect pig, Christine Maclean! The horridest Senior in the
whole school!' Nancy is very wild and if she isn't upsetting

herself in a canoe or getting cigarettes from the pier, she is in trouble over her 'topsy-turvy drawers' or up at the 'skreigh of dawn' and painting a skull and crossbones on the school boat. And even before the story begins there have been troubles. One of the characters muses about the school's past history and utters the most remarkable sentence that I have ever found. 'It was the summer of the great gale when the san. crashed into the sea – stirring times.'

In *Elinor in the Fifth* there are some topping mistresses: Miss Vance, busily occupied with her cyclostyle, the gym mistress who does 'caterpillar crawl down the empty lower corridor to relieve her feelings' and favours a stiffish brew of tea, Miss Brown ('young, round and rosy') and the Head herself 'in the severely cut coat and skirt that she wore during all but the hottest weather'. There is a tremendous row between Elinor and Rosemary: 'She even called me all sorts of things and banged the Lab. door in my face.' And there is one unpopular mistress, Miss Ellis, who really gives the girls what for: 'Nobody would think you had just come from a gymnastic lesson. Look at your sitting postures now! Disgraceful!'

Audrey Trevorne of *Audrey on Approval* has a mother who 'is obviously a sport', the Trevorne eyes ('dare-devil blue') and an uncle who is a rich recluse. She visits him in Cornwall and comes in for a lot of Cornish dialect, bats (referred to as 'airymice'), and a dear old Cornish soul called Mrs Wherry, from the fishing world ('It's the prattiest sight to see t'mack'rel brought ben').

Audrey's uncle is overcome by fumes from fluids which 'have drenched the linoleum in his laboratory', but Audrey is thoroughly on the spot:

A towel lay beside a basin of water; she soaked it and flung it dripping round her head. The water trickled down her face and into her eyes, but she did not care.

And goodness me, how Miss May Wynne can write when given half a chance:

Who minded a scramble when sun-kissed wavelets were dancing over the golden sands. Evening mists were rising over the moors, drawing a mysterious curtain as though pulled by fairy hands, hiding the secrets of the Little People who love the heather and moonshine.

Those dear, dear moors! How *could* she leave them?

How indeed.

In *Growing Up at St Monica's*, the girls have 'a keen desire to know more about Nature' and there are some fascinating open-air botany lessons with Miss Telford:

'Ah, I see a sand-martin up by those rabbit-warrens.' Miss Telford put her field-glasses up to her eyes and focused them on a grassy knoll. 'And look, there is a puffin. Come, Agnes. Come, Vera. We mustn't lose sight of this elusive bird.'

In class too, Miss Telford never lets things lag:

'An order mark for both of you,' said Miss Telford grimly. 'Hang the map on the board, Kathleen. Marjorie, name the British colonies in Africa. Attention, everyone. Sit up straight.'

In a book rich in incident and characters we have Miss Denton, a wealthy neighbour, who is robbed of her 'dear old Russian leather handbag', Vera Winter, the school bowler, who is constantly 'loosening up her arm-muscles', and Meg Elliot, who practises Bach fugues on the boot-room piano and announces 'a common or garden spot forming on the side of my nose'. And Miss Jessie McAlpine can be thoughtful too:

Some people would laugh if you asked them to play a game of cricket by themselves, yet they think nothing of playing the game of life single-handed.

In *Gillian the Dauntless* we meet a highly strung Russian girl called Mystica Degris, given to 'long shuddering sighs that shook the girl from head to foot'. She is steeped in mystery, captured by Bolshevists in Paris and has eyes that make one think of 'vast forests with pathways strewn with countless years of pine needles'. She appears in four pictures – being tripped up by wire, examining a padlocked parrot's cage, peering nervously from a window, and being knocked down by a motor-car, in colours.

Girls, shie away your bath-cubes and freesia soap. A moonlight night and a rope ladder were all your mothers ever needed to make them happy. And give those stays to Mademoiselle.

1939

The Term of Many Adventures by May Wynne (Nelson)
The Rector's Second Daughter by Kathleen Conyngham Greene
(Harrap)
The St Berga Swimming Pool by Theodora W. Wilson (Nelson)
The Jolly Book for Girls (Nelson)

The Führer's reckless *démarche* occurred too late in the year
to enable our gallant authoresses to prepare for this Christmas such heartening yarns as *Madcap Monica of the Maginot
Line* or *Vivandière Vera*. So this year the girls' books are the
usual gay round of scrumptious study teas with that spiffing
Senior, Hyacinth Duggleby, rags in the cubies (and no quarter
with the bolsters) and diamond cut diamond on the lacrosse
field.

The Term of Many Adventures is well named. Mrs Hinford,
who has moved her school to an ancient Jacobean house and
brought 'her thirty lassies out into the wilds to develop', knows
a thing or two: 'Too easily assumed responsibility is hurtful both
to rulers and ruled. It creates that masterful spirit which we see
bringing chaos in adult life.' Quite so. So she abolishes prefects
and deals ruthlessly with any hanky-panky ('she trusted her girls
and expelled them if they failed her'). On the staff there is a
bogus widow called Mrs Lysden 'whose husband is at present a
convict in Dartmoor Jail' and after a successful literature class
she thanks her pupils with 'Girls, you have been sports.' She has
a son called Barry, 'such a friendly little chap' who is partial to
'a lubly brekkus wif an egg and storberry jam'. Prominent among
the girls is Mogs Gordon ('as jolly and sporty as any boy') who
will 'be a topping nurse for wounded soldiers when she's grown
up – do you know what I mean?' It is she who rescues little Barry
from the gypsies in a chapter called 'Mogs of the Loyal Heart'.
There is also a mysterious Indian who refers to the girls as 'The
Missie-Babas' and looks 'as though he might be a Thug', and a
Mrs Mingleton 'who made a very great point about being her
boys' "big comrade" and "elder sister Mum" '.

The Rector's Second Daughter is Nan Hawker, who has 'charm in her freckled face, in her smile, which showed one little crooked tooth, in the dimple at the corner of her chin' and should you be tempted to doubt it you can see her picture on the cover depicting Nan fresh, apparently, from the most demanding room in a Turkish bath and wearing an arresting blouse covered in mauve stripes.

The St Berga Swimming Pool begins dramatically with Pat receiving from her dying mother ('hot stuff in mixed tennis for years') advice on how to win the tournament: 'Grip – grip that racket. Never go flabby and slack.' So it was 'a quiversome moment' when Pat reached the school centre court, but 'she played all out to ramp through' and by dint of 'scooting in the right direction at the right moment' trounced a muscular strongly built girl named Maud Graham 'whose speciality was the 'cello'. In the end of term concert, Joan Chesterfield distinguishes herself by singing in *Night and Day*, 'a simple cantata which seems to have turned into an operetta'. Lady Chesterfield, Joan's grandmother, is not keen on her taking up singing and wants to keep her 'in prison in the Kensington flat', until the Vicar gives her a good talking-to, referring sombrely to 'The Prince of Fear'. Then Joan sings 'Come unto Me' at the Sunday concert and, as a novel encore, confesses to a cardinal misdemeanour and rushes from the room, the awkward pause being tided over by Miss Jordan ('Come Maud! We will have your 'cello solo'). Lady Chesterfield is a Daisy Ashford character who lives in Bellevue Mansions and 'indulges in very choice China tea at nine o'clock with cake which she has sent from Edinburgh'. She goes to a concert, faints and is carried out. She is recognized by the audience: 'That was Lady Chesterfield!' – that was.

The Jolly Book for Girls is very very jolly indeed and includes a gripping tale called *Fire!* by Betty Ferguson. Eileen and Cora are in the laboratory, experimenting with nitrogen, but Cora is nervous: 'Don't be so panicky, Cora,' retorted Eileen tartly and a moment later, of course, she is a mass of flames and being rescued by the headmistress. Then 'nasty little stories went round, hinting that Cora had deliberately allowed Eileen to burn'. However, when the stables catch on fire, it is Cora who frees the horses, lies 'burbling unintelligibly' in the San, and eventually emerges from Coventry surrounded by roses addressed 'To the Bravest Funk'.

1954

The School on the Precipice by Nancy Moss (Chambers)
Fourth Form Detectives by Nancy Breary (Blackie)
One Day Event by Josephine Pullein-Thompson (Collins)

Welcome, thrice welcome to Nancy Moss, a newcomer in the finest Brazil tradition. This is the real thing.

The school in question, Cliff House (headmistress Miss Pusey. Colours: maroon-and-cream), is somewhat riskily situated: 'the last fall of cliff took an acre or so of ground down with it', and indeed the major portion of the hockey field now forms part of the foreshore, forcing the school hockey aces, Irene Fletcher and Maud Draper, to join the local Ladies' Club ('There's television in the club-house, I've been told'). However, on the limited remaining terrain, a great deal happens. Susan Savage diverts from the cliff top a runaway horse bearing the head girl, Beryl Marston ('I won't try to thank you, dear'), and subsequently receives the Marston Award for Heroism, which turns out to be a brooch 'intrinsically valuable, being made of solid hall-marked silver and studded with a fine diamond', the *ensemble* being in the form of a rearing horse.

The headmistress has a barely satisfactory brother who drives the school shooting-brake down a disused tunnel as a preparatory move to dynamiting the school buildings and collecting the insurance money. This novel plot is foiled by Beryl Marston herself, who unselfishly misses the Rambling Club ramble to achieve it, and is witnessed by Susan Savage through Elsa Marling-Brown's telescope. There is the school wag, Cissie Carew ('Cissie was a tonic'), who is given to saying 'Cheerybuzzfuzz' and 'Bung-ho', and who sings the solo part in *The Ballad of the Singing Sands* ('That child has the voice of an angel') at the Kent County Festival, Miss Lonsdale being quite beside herself 'at the excellent quality of the vocal material under her baton'.

Then Susan wakes one morning to find that during the night her pigtails have been cut off ('Her face flushed with anger'), and Cissie, who is responsible, treats herself to a perm at Maison Raoul's. There is also a Fast Set who smoke scented cigarettes: 'you'll find them useful as a screen when you're nervous'.

The book contains a daring innovation. A needle match against a visiting team is not concerned with either cricket or net-ball:

'Check!' said the Cudham College girl. Ada Mackintosh gazed long and earnestly at the board, but she had no choice. There was only one move open to her. She made it. 'Check!' said the Cudham College girl, inexorably again. Almost despairingly, Ada glared at the board.

In *Fourth Form Detectives* we are at Merrilees Manor (headmistress: Miss Petrie. Colours: brown-and-scarlet), with girls called Loveday Scott, Rosemary Heathcote and Natalie Tottenham. The head girl is Gretchen Halstead ('her people are the Hampshire Halsteads, you know, and they have a glorious place in the New Forest'). Gretchen Halstead is also 'considered a cert for County hockey next year'. There is pleasantly varied activity, with the Posture Competition to decide on the best ladies-in-waiting for the Pageant (Prologue spoken by Gretchen Halstead. Epilogue spoken by Gretchen Halstead), the upsetting by Wanda Tottenham of Jill's violet toilet water, and the day when Gretchen Halstead invites Jill to bowl to her ('Send me along a few balls, will you?'). After a false report of damage to an exhibition *gouache* ('Still Life', by Gretchen Halstead), Jill is discovered to have remarkable ventriloquial powers (' "Your voice is really very funny," Gretchen Halstead encouraged') and plays Puck in the Pageant ('Jill was an absolute hoot, she really was').

'June hasn't turned up yet,' says a character in *One Day Event*, 'but I think I hear her hoofs', thus setting the tone for what follows. This is the ideal book for pony-maniacs as, when doubts and difficulties arise, there is always Major Holbrooke to make everything clear:

In other words, his head, neck and inside shoulder will be bent to the inside, his inside foreleg will be off the school track, his inside hindleg will follow in the track of the outside foreleg and his outside hindleg follows a track of its own. The horse's head is flexed in the opposite direction to the movement.

Got it? Better to make quite sure for we are in the world of Mrs Van Cutler (a novice judge), Susan Barington-Brown, Merry Hemlock-Jones, Maureen Painter, Mrs Cresswell (of 'Dormers') and Mrs Exeter, in a fashionable shade of carbon grey, who is getting on in years and 'finds herself landed with masses of half-broken Anglo-Arabs'. The Exeters aren't, alas, dressage-minded but there are lots of things to take the mind off this sad lapse: mucking out Spartan and Echo, for instance, or undoing the stud billets of your double bridle, or getting yet another canister of hoof oil, or saying 'I do so want a lovely dressage seat' or 'A dropped noseband will prevent evasions.' After a good bit of lunging, June Cresswell announces that 'everyone knows that too early use of the double bridle spoils the development of the horse's cadence'. Well, I knew it, of course, and I'm sure you did too, but ... *everyone?*

1957

The Cliff House Monster by Nancy Moss (Chambers)
If It Hadn't Been For Frances by P. M. Warner (Collins)
The Young Horse Dealers by Mona Sandler (Country Life)
Jump To The Stars by Gillian Baxter (Evans)
Excitements at the Chalet School by Elinor Brent-Dyer
(Chambers)

'It's ... it's uranium!' breathed Hilary, squatting behind the Pankhurst Pavilion and jabbing at the ominous grey substance with her lacrosse stick. So it had been true then, that little telltale twitch of her geiger counter during algebra, and Muriel watched enthralled as her chum deftly stuffed great handfuls of the valuable matter into her satchel. Then she tensed as Hilary's face, drained of all colour, swung towards her. 'There's only one way to make sure, though. Bung it into Miss Bellingham's reactor in Stinks Lab. We may ...' here she caught her breath for a space, 'we may vaporize ourselves, but . . .' Swiftly banishing the thought of forming yet another dreaded mushroom, the two youngsters darted off, pigtails flying, towards the stately yellow pile that was the Edythe Castleton Laboratory.

Stories for girls should by now be chock-a-block with passages such as the above, with radio-active headmistresses on every side and strontium in the porridge, but authoresses haven't yet responded to this exciting challenge and we might as well not have struggled into the atomic age at all.

But who can complain when there is another Nancy Moss to cheer us? Characters in *The Cliff House Monster* divide up roughly into those who have glimpsed the Monster (cave-dwelling and with eyes like giant red wine-gums) and those who have missed this treat. Clara Figgins has seen it ('Quite an experience'). Vesta Carnilly hasn't seen it but her father has, from the air. Pale-faced Lilian Purdey ('I feel all wobbly') sees it and faints dead away. Then, while Alerdyce Bell is trying to take a happy snap of the Monster by night, Cissie and Susan pedal along the shore to prevent a kidnapping and Susan is nearly decapitated by an aeroplane ('I'd rather not talk about it if you don't mind'). For tampering with prefects' togs, Susan is seized, put into a sack, and in a voice 'vibrant with menace', Irene Fletcher (the wickedest head girl in the business) announces a flogging. The startled Susan kicks gamely out and registers a stinger on Martha Cray's shin, but is overwhelmed.

'Leave her to me!' snapped a menacing voice, and Felix, almost in one bound, leapt upon Susan, who, restricted by the sack, collapsed under her weight. 'Now,' snarled Felix, 'get your canes ready.'

In the end, Maud Draper replaces the demoted Irene ('She soon made her influence felt. She suggested table-tennis as an indoor game'), and the Monster turns out to be a fuel-less car, the invention of Raymond Poyntz, run by springs and requiring a complete rewinding every thirty miles.

In *If It Hadn't Been For Frances*, Frances and Deborah take a sea trip ('I feel a bit weird') to Holland ('We're going to enjoy ourselves or bust'). Dutch surprises abound: there is Haarlem ('Coo! There's a nun on a bicycle!'), Alkmaar ('Horses with chequered behinds'), Noordwijk ('I do love canals'), and Amsterdam ('The *hugest* pansies'). And there is the excitement of getting home to the cat ('Put it down, Frances, do. It wants to settle') and Miss Baring (centre parting, with a twist of brown plaits at the nape: cinnamon wool dress: brown sandals). Stand-offish Diana Templeton ('What a pill!') comes to stay, hurls all her shoes at pussy ('Filthy things!'), slops about in slacks wondering where the servants are, wears her flowered organdie at the Fete, but helps to water the wallflowers ('You're a sport, Di'). Little Deborah gets quite thoughtful about the Morgans, 'a most troublesome family – but extremely interesting psycho-logically'.

How would it be, Deb's thoughts inquired of her, to be one of a family of nine, sleeping, somehow or other, on the top deck of an old bus? Mightn't it make you think differently, act differently, grow up, in fact, into a different kind of person?

See what you mean, Deb.

The Young Horse Dealers are Jean and Moyra, who invest Moyra's £200 ('Mummy, *please* don't stop us') in various quad-rupeds and off we canter into the world of Dawn Wind (which is a horse), the Handy Pony Class, and that nice Mrs Sykes calling people 'poppets'. Eventually even Daddy is won over and is saying 'I shouldn't mind a day out with the Boxford.' In that particular four-legged world, the following things appear to be desirable: sloping shoulders, heaps of bone, well let down hocks, dark dapples, and massive quarters. I can't quite make out whether 'plenty of feather on her legs' is nice or nasty. It doesn't *sound* very nice.

Jump To The Stars contains a devil-horse called Ember, with a Death notched up, who has thinly chiselled nostrils, through which he has the unlovely habit of snuffling out white froth over Helen's faultlessly cut jodhpurs. Never mind: there is a stallion at stud promisingly named Silver Fountain, and Mr Cooper-Smythe on Southdown Dragonfly, and saddle sores and girth galls and stable stains. Finally, the heroine is offered a job as a groom-instructress and, naturally enough, resigns instantly from the Bognor Regis Secretarial College.

Excitements at the Chalet School vary. There is an avalanche ('A whacker to judge by the sound of it'), a past headmistress (Miss Bubb), a landslide, Miss Annersley in her crimson twin set, and Margot Maynard (forget-me-not eyes), who 'fell into Lucerne last March'. You'll want to know the school officers for the term: Head of Games – Blossom Willoughby; Responsible for Stationery – Lala Winterton; Second Hobbies Prefect – Lesley Bethune. Conversation is partly in French ('*Voulez-vous des order-marks?*'). Matron ('Matey') leads locker-raids on the Pansy Dormitory and then has an emotional upset and takes to her bed ('Shove in a couple of bottles'). Charmian Spense switches off all the lights during plain sewing with Mademoiselle ('Be quiet, *mes filles*! A fuse has blown'), has to apologize to the entire school after Prayers, and souses her pillow in an agony of remorse. Poor Yseult Pertwee is besotted with elocution and wants to specialize, but Mrs Pertwee, lecturing in America on the Arthurian Legends, is against it:

Mother knows how much her big girly wants to give more time to verse-speaking and acting, but really, pet, your work is so poor in other subjects that I feel I must stiffen my upper lip and be *firm*. So the answer is no.

My answer isn't exactly no. But it's in the y-y-y-yes category.

James Cameron

Bertie's Booster

Now that most of the clotted cream and treacle has dripped off the eulogies to the Queen Mother for her eightieth birthday, I feel able at last to reveal the story of my brief association with the gracious lady many years ago. The indiscretion is unlikely to figure greatly in the official royal biographies, so it might as well figure momentarily in mine.

At the time the lady was on the phone, and I was in Sussex. Very late at night, I got a phone call from the foreign desk of a newspaper, which was not the *Guardian*. It was to this effect: would I go to India, and there was a plane booked at six next morning. Reasonably enough, it seemed to me, I asked why. The man on the phone said he had no idea; the Foreign Editor had gone home, leaving this urgent requirement.

Had it occurred to the Foreign Editor, I asked, that I had only that very morning got *back* from India, and I knew damn well there was no story? The hireling replied: 'All I know is it says here, "Get the 6 A.M. tomorrow".'

So, obedient to a fault, as I always am, I got it. In those days there was no question of 747s and soft seats; you travelled on horrible converted Yorks or Lancaster bombers; it was Hell, and it took forever. A lifetime later I decanted at Karachi, and found a feeder to Delhi. I cabled back asking, with respect, what the Hell I was supposed to do.

To which, in the fullness of time, my master gave reply. (He is still a friend of mine, or I would tell you his name.) 'Most sorriest,' he said. 'Didn't mean India, meant South Africa stop proceed Capetown soonest accompany royal tour.'

Anyhow, that is how I came for the first and last time to be part of a royal party. Never having been what you might call an over-enthusiastic monarchist, such a thing had not occurred to me. In the event, it turned out to be rather fun. We travelled in what we called the White Train, and in a style to which I have always vainly hoped to become accustomed: We went all over the place. South Africa is, mostly unfairly, a vividly beautiful country, and we were fed and watered profusely. There was practically nothing to do.

No two personalities could have been more different than those of the King and Queen. She was, then as now, composed, eager, on top of every situation; he was tense, unbearably nervous, alternating diffidence with bursts of temper. At the time there was a frightful cold spell in Britain; the papers were full of snowdrifts and power failures and freeze-ups; he kept saying he should be at home and not lolling about in the summer sun; never was a man so jumpy. The Queen kept smiling through.

Three or four times a day the White Train stopped at some wayside halt, where everyone was formally lined up. The King would stand shaking at the door of the train, dreading the inevitable encounters. The Queen would appear beside him, looking (the word is inescapable) radiant, or at any rate full of beans.

'Oh, Bertie, do you see, this is Hicksdorp! You know we've always so wanted to see Hicksdorp! Those people there with the bouquets – they must be the local councillors. *How* kind! And those people at the far, far end of the platform, behind that little fence – I expect they are the Bantu choir. How kind! We must wave, Bertie.'

And with a little nudge, the King found himself on terra firma, clearly wishing he were anywhere else on earth, with his wife just as clearly having waited all her life to see Hicksdorp.

One evening he called some of us press people along to his dining car, ostensibly because he had a communication to make, but more probably to relieve the deadly boredom of the Hicksdorps and the Bantu choirs. I believe it to have been the only royal press conference ever. We found him behind a table covered with bottles of all sorts of things, with which it would seem he had been experimenting, with some dedication.

'We must not f-forget the purpose of this t-tour,' he said, bravely, because his stammer was troublesome for him, 'trade and so on. Empire cooperation. For example, South African brandy. I have been trying it. It is of course m-magnificent, except that it is not very nice.' (It was in those days quite dreadful.) 'But,' he said triumphantly, 'there is this South African liqueur called V-Van der Humm. Perhaps a little sweet for most. *But*, now, if you mix half of brandy with half of Van der Humm . . . Please try.'

The South African journalists were ecstatic. They, and their fathers, before them, had used this brandy–Humm mix for generations; nevertheless they applauded the King for having stumbled on something as familiar to them as gin and tonic. Their stories could have done the South African liquor trade no harm.

We arrived one day at a place called Outshoorn. This was a centre of the ostrich feather trade, and ostrich feathers had suffered a sad decline since, I imagine, the days of Queen Alexandra. Our passage through this empty place was, I supposed, to stimulate it – to which end the King was detailed to nip a tail feather off a sacrificial ostrich for the cameras, presumably to create a renaissance of feather boas. The King was understandably more nervous than usual – the ostrich even more so, its head and neck buried in a long stocking-like thing, as if it were for an execution. The King fumbled the operation, and his tweezers nicked a quarter-inch off the ostrich's backside, at which the unlucky bird made a fearsome screeching hullabaloo, from which we all retreated in terror.

Enter the Queen, stage right, as usual in total smiling command. She took the clippers from her husband, and there and then did an absolutely expert featherectomy – snip. She spoke to the nearest bystander, who happened by chance to be me.

'We do a lot of gardening at home, in the Palace,' said the Queen. 'The King is good at the digging and the weeding. It is I who concentrate on the secateurs.'

Here endeth the first and last of my Monarchical Memoirs. Let me be the last to wish the old lady a happy birthday. The ostrich can look after itself.

Flann O'Brien

The Trade in Dublin

In the last ten years there has been a marked change in the decor of boozing in Dublin. The old-time pub was something in the nature of an Augean stable (it is true that Pegasus was often tethered there) with liberal lashings of sawdust and mopping-rags to prevent the customers from perishing in their own spillings and spewings. No genuine Irishman could relax in comfort and feel at home in a pub unless he was sitting in deep gloom on a hard seat with a very sad expression on his face, listening to the drone of bluebottle squadrons carrying out a raid on the yellow sandwich cheese. In those days a definite social stigma attached to drinking. It was exclusively a male occupation and on that account (and apart from anything temperance advocates had to say) it could not be regarded as respectable by any reasonable woman. Demon rum was a pal of the kind one is ashamed to be seen with. Even moderate drinkers accepted themselves as genteel degenerates and could slink into a pub with as much feline hug-the-wall as any cirrhotic whiskey-addict, there to hide even from each other in dim secret snugs. A pub without a side-door up a lane would have been as well off with no door at all.

Up to recent times the only improvement was the bar parlour, a dark privacy at the rear where any respectable bowler-hatted gentleman from the countinghouse of a large drapery concern could tinkle in peace at his hot mid-day whiskey. Such places were clean and comfortable enough, though often equipped with forbidding furniture of the marble-topped and iron-legged variety usually found in morgues and fish-shops. Latterly, however, we have had the Lounge, the Lounge Bar, the Select Lounge, the Oak Lounge, and Octagonal Lounge, and still more refined booze-shops called brasseries and butteries where obsequious servers in white coats will refuse point-blank to give you beer, even if your doctor has certified under his own hand that you will drop dead after one glass of spirits.

It is in such places that one can perceive in its full force the Reformation which has been spreading throughout the public-house congregations. The old-fashioned curate, the drinker's confessor and counsellor, is disappearing. His honest country face, his simple black clothes, his coatlessness, his apron and the gleaming steel armbands on his shirt-sleeves were almost supernatural symbols which invested the lowliest pub with a feeling of being-with-friends, a homeliness which many men fail to find in their own houses. He was the repository of every grain of knowledge which could be gathered from a lifetime of other people's drink-loosened conversations. In one small head he could contain an incomparable compendium of every known fact about politics, women, the G.A.A. and, tucked away in a separate compartment by itself, a thesaurus of horse-lore not entirely to be independently unearthed from the Form Book or the Calendar. Sensing the innate spiritual character of his calling, he served humanity well in his licensed parish.

The white-coated server who has ousted the curate in some pubs may be taken as a sign of the decline of faith. The Irish brand of humanity, expansive and voluble, is hardening and contracting under the hammer-blows of international mammon, dealt through the radio, press and cinema. Among the stupider section of the younger generation a shabby and rather comic 'smartness' may be discerned, even in the simple task of dealing with a bottle of brown stout.

Their cinema-going has taught them the great truth that William Powell does not walk up to a counter, bellow for a schooner or a scoop and ask Mick whether the brother is expected up for the match on Sunday. William is modern and drinks out of glasses with long stems in a cushioned corner with his doxy. His many imitators (what could be more flimsy than an imitation of a flat two-dimensional picture-house ghost?) have insisted on something similar, since they, too, have to go out with Myrna Loy. The Select Lounge has been the handsome answer of the trade in Dublin.

To-day there are many of these lounges in the city, even in those areas which people living elsewhere call 'tough quarters'. Some are very good, many are curious travesties of what may be regarded as the publican's conception of paradise. The better places are quiet and comfortable, softly lighted, and a boon to any sensible, tired person who wants a stimulant without being jostled and who does not concern himself with social trends or think that a well-dressed woman in a pub is an outrage that imparts a sourness to the drink.

The other places afford a pathetic insight into the meaning attached to the word 'modern' by many publicans. They think that it means just tubes – tubular chairs, repellent alike to eye and seat, tubular lighting, tubular effects in decoration. Those who have been to prison immediately recognize the lamentable simplicity of the decor and the severity of the furnishings. The ugliness of such a tavern cannot be completely offset by the fact that most of the customers appear to be film-stars or that the man who serves you is a bell-hop from New York.

Here let us digress to touch upon a very important irrelevancy. The lower orders (non-car-owners and the like) are excluded from all these lounges, sometimes by an impudent surcharge on the already extortionate price of drink, nearly always by out-lawing the pint, which is the only cheap nourishing light beer that can be had. Although probably more than half of the money amassed by any publican has been made from selling pints of porter, the pint-drinker is rigidly confined to his outer corral, far from the heat and the soft seats; he never even sees the fancy clock that has no numbers on its face, only a dot for each hour. Some publicans, equipped with the odious sham-gentility which money earned by astute trading confers on humble folk, justify this nonsense by a process of reasoning too tortuous to record. One well-known argument is that 'the lads would not go in there if you paid them'. In a country which is held to be democratic and in which writers and labourers are on the same economic plane, it is an impertinence which should be challenged by some public-spirited person at the annual licensing sessions, if only to make 'himself' explain his quaint social theories in public.

One wonders what Mr James Montgomery would think of it all. Mr Montgomery is one of the select band of Dublin gentlemen who knew the Dublin pub-life of the old days and who contributed his own big share of whatever ambrosial vitamin made that generation of drinkers and thinkers immortal. (We cannot help wondering, myself, the printer and the Editor, whether a compliment can also be a libel.) Other veterans, happily still encounterable, are Seamus O'Sullivan and famous Martin Murphy of the Gaiety Theatre. If they could be persuaded to tell the tale (or 'write it down' in the manner of people who summon their neighbours for using unmentionable language) they could fill THE BELL for many issues with material that would make it a standard work of reference for anybody who wants to dig under the calloused skin of Dublin.

They could tell about the beginnings of the United Arts Club, conceived in Neary's snug (or maybe in MacCormack's of South King Street) by the boisterous Count Markievicz. If you turn into Chatham Street to-day and mount the stairs inside the Neary hall-door, you will find yourself in a seductive den (Select Lounge is the correct term) probably never dreamt of by the Count. Here the authorities had the sense to employ a real artist, Miss Bradshaw, rather than a distant Japanese technician, to enliven the walls with pictures.

The only other public-house that comes to mind in this connexion is Higgins's Waterloo Bar at the bottom of Waterloo Road. Here the far-sighted proprietor, who also owns another pub in Pembroke Street and in person resembles Kreisler, had the enlightenment within him to retain Mr Brendan O'Connor to design his lounge and Mr Desmond Rushton to leave his mark upon the walls. The result is a combination of utility (functional something-or-other architects call it), comfort and restraint – but no pints. All sorts may be seen here of an evening, front and rear.

> *Sometimes carters slacken rein,*
> *Sometimes exiles come again,*

Or a pilgrim you will see
On the way to Mellary.

Davy Byrne's in Duke Street, the Bailey Restaurant nearly opposite, and the underground Bodega in Dame Street are licensed tabernacles sanctified by the past attendances of people with names like Orpen, Gogarty, Griffith, Murphy, Furlong, Montgomery, McKenna, even Joyce, not to mention the Toucher Doyle, the Bird Flanagan and his relative, the Pope. (Who will pretend that these are not ordinary surnames that can be borne by anybody?) All three still open their doors at ten o'clock and possibly shelter to-day the makings of a second fame – the same again. They are run by new if cognate personalities and none has found any necessity to have recourse to the blandishments of the Select Lounge. The premises bear openly the marks of their departed guests, like traces of fresh stout found in a glass by a policeman after hours; but they still look prosperous, not like banquet-halls deserted.

The bar of the Ormond Hotel and Barney Kiernan's down the quays were other centres of intellectual sodality. Barney's was a dim and venerable backwater where an argument could be pursued hour by hour without interruption, with casks all around to receive the resounding fist. Fanning's of Lincoln Place had and has a similar fame. Some of the distinguished guests in Fanning's, guzzling the uniformly good drink, will tell you that the intransigence of the distinguished boss's political beliefs can sometimes lend an unwelcome uniformity to his conversation.

To-day, as in the past, birds of a feather tend to flutter into the same snug. Grogan's of Leeson Street and Higgins's of Pembroke Street are noted for the punctilious attendances of students from 'National'; Trinity students have their names marked on the roll at Davy Byrne's. Mulligan's in the narrow street which runs alongside the Theatre Royal caters for painted ladies and painted men – the theatrical kind, often straight from the stage. Most people connected with show business make their way here, and Mr Mulligan has recently provided a new Lounge for their further entertainment and approval.

The Palace Bar in Fleet Street is the main resort of newspapermen, writers, painters and every known breed of artist and intellectual. Porter is served willingly everywhere in the house, and in fancy tankards. The clients range from the tiniest elfin intellectual to a large editor, alive and in good condition. Looking at the editor, one frequently sees the left hand flung out as if in demonstration of some wide generous idea; actually, however, it is merely a claw in search of a cigarette, a modest tax that is gladly paid by listening neophytes. The editor is unconscious of this mannerism; he is king in this particular Palace and merely exercises a ruling-class prerogative.

The partitioning-off idea which dominates the scheme of the lounges at Doran's of Marlboro' Street and O'Mara's of Aston's Quay seems to attract clients who have weighty secrets to exchange – lovers and the like. The Scotch House on Burgh Quay is famous for the mellowness and good colour of its whiskey and civil servants. It was stated officially recently in the newspapers that the Dolphin Hotel is noted for its 'sporting crowd' and 'racing people'; whatever about the horses, it abounds in suede shoes and jackets with two splits. Probably the oldest licence and the oldest pub in Dublin is the Brazen Head Hotel, an old coaching-house down the quays, one-time resort of Robert Emmet and the United Irishmen. Here the most random spit will land on ten centuries of antiquity. 'Professional gentlemen' as they are called by landladies – doctors, lawyers, architects and that ilk – do a lot of their drinking in the Metropole. The Red Bank, the Wicklow Hotel, the various Mooney's, Madigan's of Earl Street, and McArdle's of South King Street are popular with all creeds and classes.

When many of Ireland's staid rulers of to-day were younger and on the run, they ran sometimes towards Rathfarnham, frequently in the Parnell Street direction. Devlin's, Kennedy's and Kirwan's in that thoroughfare were places where Miss Ní h-Uallacháin was served without question, even though the lady no longer lived in her guardian's house and was wanted by the police. Michael Collins often drank a bottle of stout in the bar of Vaughan's Hotel. In Dan Dunne's of distant Donnybrook, as Batt O'Connor relates, he once, leaning back, touched a hanging bell-push with his head. The man of the house promptly cut down the bell-push and proudly showed it afterwards to customers as his most famous and cherished possession. Not even the jagged wire can be seen to-day, for Time, that bedfellow of all publicans, has erased the whole public-house.

At ten o'clock on week nights and at half-nine on Saturday the tide ebbs suddenly, leaving the city high and dry. Unless you are staying at a hotel or visiting a theatre, you may not lawfully consume excisable liquors within the confines of the county borough. The city has entered that solemn hiatus, that almost sublime eclipse known as The Closed Hours. Here the law, as if with true Select Lounge mentality, discriminates sharply against the poor man at the pint counter by allowing those who can command transport and can embark upon a journey to drink elsewhere till morning. The theory is that all travellers still proceed by stage-coach and that those who travel outside become blue with cold after five miles and must be thawed out with hot rum at the first hostelry they encounter by night or day. In practice, people who are in the first twilight of inebriation are transported from the urban to the rural pub so swiftly by the internal combustion engine that they need not necessarily be aware that they have moved at all, still less comprehend that their legal personalities have undergone a mystical transfiguration. Whether this system is to be regarded as a scandal or a godsend depends largely on whether one owns a car. At present the city is ringed round with these 'bona-fide' pubs, many of them well-run modern houses, and a considerable amount of the stock-in-trade is transferred to the stomachs of the customers at a time every night when the sensible and the just are in their second sleeps. Coolock, Tallaght, Templeogue, Santry, Lucan, Ballydowd, Cabinteely, Shankill, Fox-and-Geese and Stepaside are a few of the villages where there is revelry by night. Stepaside in recent years has been notable for the engaging personality of Mr James Whelan, who has now, however, forsaken the dram-shop for the farm. The Lamb Doyle's nearby, cocked high up near Ticknock, was a favourite point of pilgrimage of a summer Sunday for the boys of Casimir Markievicz's day. It is still there, though under new and female management.

To go back to the city: it appears that the poor man does not always go straight home at ten o'clock. If his thirst is big enough and he knows the knocking-formula, he may possibly visit some house where the Demand Note of the Corporation has stampeded the owner into a bout of illicit after-hour trading. For trader and customer alike, such a life is one of excitement, tiptoe and hush. The boss's ear, refined to shades of perception far beyond the sensitiveness of any modern aircraft detector, can tell almost the inner thoughts of any policeman in the next street. At the first breath of danger all lights are suddenly doused and conversation toned down, as with a knob, to vanishing point. Drinkers reared in such schools will tell you that in inky blackness stout cannot be distinguished in taste from Bass and that no satisfaction whatever can be extracted from a cigarette unless the smoke is seen. Sometimes the police make a catch. Here is the sort of thing that is continually appearing in the papers:

Guard — said that accompanied by Guard — he visited the premises at 11.45 p.m. and noticed a light at the side door. When he knocked, the light was extinguished, but he was not admitted for six minutes. When defendant opened eventually, he appeared to be in an excited condition and used bad language. There was nobody in the bar but there were two empty pint measures containing traces of fresh porter on the counter. He found a man crouching in a small press containing switches and a gas-meter. When he attempted to enter the yard to carry out a search, he was obstructed by the defendant, who used an improper expression. He arrested him, but owing to the illness of his wife, he was later released.

Defendant – Did you give me an unmerciful box in the mouth?

Witness – No.

Defendant – Did you say that you would put me and my gawm of a brother through the back wall with one good haymaker of a clout the next time I didn't open when you knocked?

Witness – No.

Justice – You look a fine block of a man yourself. How old are you?

Defendant – I'm as grey as a badger, but I'm not long past forty. (Laughter.)

Justice – Was the brother there at all?

Defendant – He was away in Kells, your worship, seeing about getting a girl for himself. (Laughter.)

Justice – Well, I think you could give a good account of yourself.

Witness – He was very obstreperous, your worship.

Witness, continuing, said that he found two men standing in the dark in an outhouse. They said they were there 'for a joke'. Witness also found an empty pint measure in an outdoor lavatory and two empty bottles of Cairnes.

Defendant said that two of the men were personal friends and were being treated. There was no question of taking money. He did not know who the man in the press was and did not recall having seen him before. He had given strict instructions to his assistant to allow nobody to remain on after hours. There was nobody in the press the previous day as the gasman had called to inspect the meter. The two Guards had given him an unmerciful hammering in the hall. His wife was in ill-health, necessitating his doing without sleep for three weeks. A week previously he was compelled to send for the Guards to assist in clearing the house at ten o'clock. He was conducting the house to the best of his ability and was very strict about the hours.

Guard — said that the defendant was a decent hard-working type but was of an excitable nature. The house had a good record.

Remarking that defendant seemed a decent sort and that the case was distinguished by the absence of perjury, the Justice said he would impose a fine of twenty shillings, the offence not to be endorsed. Were it not for extenuating circumstances he would have no hesitation in sending the defendant to Mountjoy for six months. He commended Guards — and — for smart police-work.

Not many publicans, however, will take the risk. If they were as careful of their souls as they are of their licences, heaven would be packed with those confidential and solicitous profit-takers and, to please them, it might be necessary to provide an inferior annex to paradise to house such porter-drinkers as would make the grade.

Lawrence Durrell

Case History

Last week, Polk-Mowbray's name came up again – we had read of his retirement that morning, in *The Times*. We had both served under him in Madrid and Moscow, while Antrobus himself had been on several missions headed by him – Sir Claud Polk-Mowbray, O.M., K.C.M.G., and all that sort of thing.

Talking of him, Antrobus did his usual set of facial jerks culminating in an expression like a leaky flower-pot, and said: 'You know, old man, thinking of Polk-Mowbray today and all the different places we've served, I suddenly thought "My God, in Polk-Mowbray we have witnessed the gradual destruction of an Ambassador's soul." '

I was startled by this observation.

'I mean,' went on Antrobus, 'that gradually, insidiously, the Americans got him.'

'How do you mean, "the Americans got him"?'

Antrobus clicked his tongue and lofted his gaze.

'Perhaps you didn't know, perhaps you were not a Silent Witness as I was.'

'I don't honestly think I was.'

'Do you remember Athens '37, when I was first secretary?'

'Of course.'

'Polk-Mowbray was a perfectly normal well-balanced Englishman then. He had all the fashionable weaknesses of the eighteenth-century gentleman. He fenced, he played the recorder.'

'I remember all that.'

'But something else too. Think back.'

'I'm thinking . . .'

Antrobus leaned forward and said with portentous triumph: 'He wrote good English in those days.' Then he sat back and stared impressively at me down the long bony incline of his nose. He allowed the idea to soak in.

Of course what he meant by good English was the vaguely orotund and ornamental eighteenth-century stuff which was then so much in vogue. A sort of mental copperplate prose.

'I remember now,' I said, 'committing the terrible sin of using the phrase "the present set-up" in a draft despatch on economics.' (It came back gashed right through with the scarlet pencil which only Governors and Ambassadors are allowed to wield – and with something nasty written in the margin.)

'Ah,' said Antrobus, 'so you remember that. What did he write?'

' "The thought that members of my staff are beginning to introject American forms into the Mother Tongue has given me great pain. I am ordering Head of Chancery to instruct staff that no despatches to the Foreign Secretary should contain phrases of this nature." '

'Phew.'

'As you say – phew.'

'But Nemesis,' said Antrobus, 'was lying in wait for him, old chap. Mind you,' he added in the sort of tone which always sounds massively hypocritical to foreigners simply because it is, 'mind you, I'm not anti-American myself – never was, never will be. And there were some things about the old Foreign Office Prose Style – the early Nicolson type.'

'It was practically Middle English.'

'No, what I objected to was the Latin tag. Polk-Mowbray was always working one in. If possible he liked to slip one in at the beginning of a despatch. "*Hominibus plenum, amicis vacuum* as Cato says", he would kick off. The damnable thing was that at times he would forget whether it was Cato who said it. I was supposed to know, as Head of Chancery. But I never did. My classics have always been fluffy. I used to flash to my Pears Encyclopedia or my Brewer, swearing all the time.'

'He sacked young Pollit for attributing a remark in Tacitus to Suetonius.'

'Yes. It was very alarming. I'm glad those days are over.'

'But Nemesis. What form did he take?'

'She, old man. *She*. Nemesis is always a woman. Polk-Mowbray was sent on a brief mission to the States in the middle of the war.'

'Ah.'

'He saw her leading a parade wrapped in the Stars and Stripes and twirling a baton. Her name was Carrie Potts. She was what is known as a majorette. I know. Don't wince. No, he didn't marry her. But she was a Milestone, old fellow. From then on the change came about, very gradually, very insidiously. I noticed that he dropped the Latin tag in his drafts. Then he began to leave the "u" out of words like "colour" and "valour". Finally, and this is highly significant, he sent out a staff circular saying that any of the secretaries caught using phrases like *quid pro quo, sine qua non, ad hoc, ab initio, ab ovo* and *status quo* would be transferred. This was a bombshell. We were deprived at a blow of practically our whole official vocabulary. Moreover as he read through the circular I distinctly heard him say under his breath: "This will pin their ears back." You can imagine, old fellow, I was stiff with horror. Of course, the poor fellow is not entirely to blame; he was fighting the disease gamely enough. It was just too much for him. I found a novel by Damon Runyon in his desk-drawer one day. I admit that he had the good taste to blush when he saw I'd found it. But by this time he had begun to suffer from dreadful slips of the tongue. At a cocktail party for instance he referred to me as his "sidekick". I was too polite to protest but I must admit it rankled. But there was a much more serious aspect to the business. His despatches began to take a marked transpontine turn. By God, you'll never believe it but I kept coming across expressions like "set-up", "frame-up", "come-back", and even "gimmick". I ask you – *gimmick*.' Antrobus blew out his breath in a cloud of horror. 'As you can imagine,' he went on after a pause, 'the F.O. was troubled by the change in his reporting. Worst of all, other Ministers and Ambassadors junior to him and easily influenced showed some disposition to copy this sort of thing. Finally it got to such a pitch that all despatches before being printed in Intel-summary form had to pass through a sieve: they established an office in the Rehabilitation section specially for deformed English. Then you remember the Commission on Official English and the book called *Foreign Office Prose – How to Write It*?'

'Yes. One of the worst written books I've ever read.'

'Well, be that as it may, it was the direct outcome of Polk-Mowbray's activities. It was a last desperate attempt to stop the rot, old man. It was too late, of course, because by this time that dreadful Churchill chap was wandering all over the globe in a siren suit waving a Juliet at everyone. I need hardly add that Mowbray himself ordered a siren suit which he referred to as his "sneakers". He used to potter round the Embassy grounds in them – a bit furtively, of course, but nevertheless ... there it was.' Antrobus paused for a long moment as he sorted out these painful memories. Then he said grimly, under his breath, and with dark contempt: 'Faucet, elevator, phoney. I *ask* you.'

'Yes,' I said.

'Hatchet-man ... disc-jockey ... torch-singer.'

'Yes. Yes. I follow you.'

'I was terribly sad. Poor Polk-Mowbray. Do you know that he went to a Rotary meeting in a hand-painted tie depicting a nude blonde and referred to it in his speech as "pulchritudinous"?'

'Never.'

'He did.' Antrobus nodded vigorously several times and took a savage swig at his drink. 'He absolutely did.'

'I suppose,' I said after a moment, 'that now he is retiring he will settle over there and integrate himself.'

'He was offered a chance to go to Lake Success as a specialist on Global Imponderables, but he turned it down. Said the I.Q. wasn't high enough – whatever that meant. No, it's even more tragic. He has taken a villa outside Rome and intends to summer in Italy. I saw him last week when I came back from the Athens Conference.'

'You saw him?'

'Yes.' Antrobus fell into a heavy brooding silence, evidently stirred to the quick. 'I don't really know if I should tell you this,' he said in a voice with a suspicion of choking in it. 'It's such a nightmare.'

'I won't repeat it.'

'No. Please don't.'

'I won't.'

He gazed sadly at me as he signed his bar slips, waiting in true Foreign Office style until the servant was out of earshot. Then he leaned forward and said: 'I ran into him near the *Fontana*, sitting in a little *trattoria*. He was dressed in check plus-fours with a green bush jacket and a cap with a peak. He was addressing a plate of spaghetti – and *do you know what*?'

'No. What?'

'There was a *Coca Cola* before him with a straw in it.'

'Great heavens, Antrobus, you are jesting.'

'My solemn oath, old man.'

'It's the end.'

'The very end. Poor Polk-Mowbray. I tried to cringe my way past him but he saw me and called out.' Here Antrobus shuddered. 'He said, quite distinctly, quite unequivocally, without a shadow of doubt – he said: "*Hiya!*" and made a sort of gesture in the air as of someone running his hand listlessly over the buttocks of a chorus girl. I won't imitate it in here, someone might see.'

'I know the gesture you mean.'

'Well,' said Antrobus bitterly, 'now you know the worst. I suppose it's a symptom of the age really.' As we sauntered out of his club, acknowledging the porter's greeting with a nod, he put on his soft black hat and put his umbrella into the crook of his arm. His face had taken on its graven image look – 'a repository of the nation's darkest secrets'. We walked in silence for a while until we reached my bus stop. Then he said: 'Poor Polk-Mowbray. In Coca Cola veritas what?'

'Indeed,' I said. There could not be a better epitaph.

Julian Maclaren-Ross

Good Lord, Jeeves

All unconscious of impending doom I was gnawing a solitary bone at the Drones Club and wistfully recalling that golden age when coves like Catsmeat Potter-Pirbright and Barmy Fotheringay-Phipps had reigned supreme, filling the air around with snappy dialogue and bread rolls bandied to-and-fro. I'd reached the point, after a few shots of cognac imbibed to assist the gastric juices, when a less reserved chappie would have burst into the chorus of 'Auld Lang Syne' or wondered, with the poet, where the jolly old *neiges* of *a*. had got to nowadays, and it was in this mellow mood that I became suddenly aware of two birds in formal attire bearing down on me from across the banqueting hall – now, alas, empty save for the last of the Woosters.

Though the advancing figures were clearly recognizable as Sir Roderick Glossop and Sir Watkyn Bassett CBE, JP, respectively, it took me some moments to realize that these knights were actually present in the flesh, and by the time it'd sunk in that they weren't mere shades conjured up from the mists of m. or the pages of a cheap edition chronicling some past kick of the heels, they were already standing over my table with expressions that betokened business.

Sir Watkyn was the first to give tongue, and at his tone of voice even my iron nerve began to describe a graceful arc. I felt a kinship with those private eyes of American lit., who glance up from a newly-discovered stiff to find the boys from the Homicide Squad standing around, idly swinging their black-jacks in preparation for a cosy chat about the case.

'Mr Wooster,' said the former bane of Bosher Street, 'we are from the Ministry of Rehabilitation. We were informed that the club secretary was to be found lunching in this room.'

'I'm the Hon. Sec., Sir Watkyn,' I said: an honest admission received by Sir Roderick with what brothers of the PEN qualify as a mirthless chuckle.

'A suitable nominee for an institution so named, do you not concur, Bassett?' he said.

'Especially apt in view of the establishment's future function,' Sir W. agreed. 'You are, of course, aware, Mr Wooster, that these premises have been requisitioned w.e.f. today's date as a State Home for the Mentally Deficient . . .'

'. . . and that I, as Governmental Psychiatrist,' said Sir Roderick, coming in pat on his cue, 'will be in charge of the scheme, which is to be implemented forthwith.'

'Here, I say,' I protested, rallying from the ropes, as one who recovers from a right cross, 'you can't do that, you know! The members won't stand for it!'

'There are no members, Mr Wooster,' Sir Watkyn said, planting another banderillo in the quivering hide. 'We've already ascertained that. And if it is the free board and lodging which as club secretary you receive here that causes your patent anxiety, why, you are in no danger of losing it. Sir Roderick, I am sure, will gladly sign the certificate insuring your future as an inmate of the Home – eh, Glossop?'

It was the KO delivered with full force to the softer parts of the anat. I had crumpled over the table, gasping for breath, when through the loud singing in my ears a familiar and well-loved voice spoke sharply, scattering the opponents to right and left.

'Gentlemen,' it said, 'I wish to have a word in private with Mr Wooster, if you please.'

The big fight was over. Before you could say Sugar Ray Robinson, Sir Roderick and W. Bassett had beaten it, murmuring 'Yes, Minister', and 'Certainly, Lord Jeeves', in the most obsequious of accents, and the hand, it seemed, of a ministering angel was holding a beaker of brandy to my lips.

'Jeeves,' I said fervently, 'lives there a man with soul so dead as to resist the incomparable Jeeves?'

'Thank you, sir. The tribute is much appreciated.'

'I merely quote from the *Daily Herald*. But wait a sec.,' I said, as full consciousness flooded back to the brain, 'didn't I hear

those two blighters address you as Minister? And Lord Jeeves?
Or was it a dream?'

'The Government has been kind enough to reward my trifling
services with a peerage, and also by inclusion in the Cabinet,
sir.'

'As Minister of Re-Thing?'

'Habilitation, sir. A little more brandy, if I might so suggest?
I feel this news has come as a grave shock to you, sir.'

'Worse than that, Jeeves. The loss of this job would be the last
straw.' I raised my measure on high. 'To your success, Jeeves,
which you dashed well deserve.'

'Thank you, sir. But you were saying about your position as
secretary here, and its importance to you . . .'

'Supreme importance, Jeeves, financially speaking. National-
ization and surtax have taken their toll. The Wooster millions
are, in fact, down the drain. Need I say more?'

'It is a plight shared by many in these times, sir. Your friends
are unable to assist?'

'Friends,' I echoed bitterly. 'Shall I show you the typed note
I had from Mrs Bingo Little's secretary? Or the stern refusal
received from Stiffy Byng's spouse, the Bishop of Blandings,
formerly the Rev. Stinker Pinker? The receipt of such missives
is souring to one's sunny nature, Jeeves.'

'Man is an ungrateful animal, sir. But perhaps I might be of
some little help, if you'd allow me . . .'

'How?'

'The offer of employment, sir?'

'What kind of employment?'

'I hesitate to say, sir.'

'Don't hesitate. Out with it. Beggars can't be c., Jeeves.'

'Well, sir, the post of secretary to the Junior Ganymede Club
has fallen vacant in the past week. I could confidently promise
you the appointment if you so desire.'

'But the Junior Ganymede's a club for gentlemen's personal
gentlemen. How could I get in?'

'By accepting a temporary position as my personal attendant,
sir . . . If I may say so, you would not find me too exacting an
employer.'

We Woosters are nothing if not adaptable. My hesitation was of the briefest. 'Jeeves,' I said, 'you're on! Let's drink to that!'

'Thank you,' said Jeeves, as I ladled out liberal portions. 'Er – . . . not all the soda, Wooster.'

'No, sir,' I said, falling without effort into the new role. 'I will endeavour to give you satisfaction, sir . . . I mean, m'lord.'

Patrick Campbell

A Boy's Best Bodyguard

When a fellow is faced by armed men it's my honest opinion that he should have his mother around, if the situation is not to descend into flurry and confusion.

Three times I have looked down the muzzle of a gun. On the first two occasions my mother was present, and an orderly conclusion was achieved. In her absence, the third time, I handled the business so maladroitly that even the police got it back to front. The lesson is plain.

My mother and I first started gun-slinging, as it were, in 1922. The Irish Civil War was in progress and one of its victims – or very likely to be if he didn't look slippy – was my father, then a member of the Cosgrave Government. He had returned once to our house outside Dublin with three perceptible bullet holes in the back door on his car, in no mood to share my mother's opinion, aimed at restoring his confidence, that the IRA had probably mistaken him for someone else. The shots had, apparently, been fired near Portobello Bridge. So sure was my father of their intended destination that he covered the three miles home in three minutes, and went straight to bed.

When, therefore, the thunderous banging came on the back door a few nights later it had the effect of freezing him to his armchair, in which he'd been reading the evening paper. It was my mother who went to the top of the kitchen stairs, to see what was afoot. I joined her almost immediately, a pale lad of nine, having been roused from my sleep by the noise. I'd been sleeping badly of recent weeks because it was nearly Christmas, and my whole soul was crying out to take possession of my first Hornby train.

'It's all right,' my mother said, taking her customarily steady view, 'it's only some men.'

We heard the bolts being shot on the back door, and then the voice of the cook raised in indignant surprise. She was a loyal retainer, who'd been with the family for some years. 'It's youse lot, is it?' she said. 'Janey, I thought yez wasn't comin' till half-eleven.' It was, in fact, only ten-fifteen.

A male voice said peevishly, 'Ah, don't be shoutin' ...' and then the first of the raiders came running up the stairs. I had a brief glimpse of a gun, then a face masked with a cap and a handkerchief. My mother stopped him dead. 'If there's going to be any murder,' she said, 'you can get back out of that and go home.'

More masked faces and caps appeared at the bottom of the stairs. Querulous voices arose. 'What's the matther, Mick?' 'Get on with it, can't ya?' But Mick was explaining the matter to my mother.

'Nobody's gettin' shot, mum. You needn't take on. We've orders to burn down the house, that's all.' He sounded injured by the false impression.

'You're sure of that?' my mother asked him, wishing to have the matter absolutely clear for the benefit of my father, in the event that he was still able to receive messages, in the next room.

'There'll be nobody shot,' said another raider impatiently. 'Now will you stand back owa that an' let's get on with it. We haven't all night.'

My mother remained firm. With the first matter on the agenda settled to her satisfaction, she passed to others, now of equal importance. 'What about all my lovely books?' she said. 'First editions, signed by Lawrence and Katherine Mansfield and Middleton Murry. And the pictures – Orpens, Gertlers, the little drawings by John ...'

The raiders, jammed on the stairs, were getting hot and angry. An exposed youth, still stuck in the passage, was being berated by the cook. He appeared to be a cousin of hers, and was refusing to carry her trunk out into the garden.

'All right, all *right* ...' said the first raider. The protracted conversation was causing the handkerchief to slip off his face.

'Take out annything you want, but for God's love hurry up about it.' He turned to the men behind. 'Who's got the pethrol an' the matches?' he wanted to know.

At this point my father appeared in the hall, unobtrusively, and still unsure of his welcome. The raiders appealed to him. 'Ask your missus to give us a chance, sir, will ya? Sure, we're only actin' under ordhers . . .'

He took command, in a voice slightly higher than normal, advising me to wake my sister, still peacefully asleep, and to put on some warm clothes. He then suggested to my mother that they should both try to save a few personal mementoes before we all withdrew to safety in the garden.

'And leave,' my mother cried passionately, 'all the children's Christmas toys behind? Certainly not!'

The possible outcome of the night struck home to me for the first time. 'Me train!' I cried. 'Don't let them burn me train!'

'Of course they won't,' said my mother. She rounded on two of the men. 'You,' she said, 'go to the cupboard in the bedroom and bring out all the parcels you can find. And look out for the doll's house. It's fragile.'

They shuffled their feet, deeply embarrassed. Several other men were throwing petrol around the hall. 'Well, go on!' my mother shouted at them. 'And leave your silly guns on the table. Nobody'll touch them.'

By the time the first whoosh of petrol flame poured out of the windows she had five of the men working for her, running out with armfuls of books and pictures, ornaments, and our Christmas toys. They'd become so deeply concerned on her behalf that they frequently paused to ask what should be salvaged next. 'Is the bit of a picture in the passage anny good, mum?' 'Is there ere a chance of gettin' the legs offa the pianna, the way we could dhrag it out . . .?'

When they disappeared into the night they left my mother, bathed in the light of the flames, standing guard over a great heap of treasures in the middle of the lawn, with Orpen's picture under one arm and the little drawings by John under the other – a clear winner on points.

Next time it was the IRA again. My unfortunate father was

now officially on the run – an appalling situation for a peaceful and dignified man – while the rest of us, being homeless, were staying with my mother's parents in Foxrock, a base that at first sight could not have been more neutral. But then, in the middle of the night, the caps and the handkerchiefs appeared again, and it turned out that we were sitting on a miniature arsenal, not, admittedly, of the first calibre, but undoubtedly containing weapons of war.

Once again it was probably the domestic staff who provided the link between the beleaguered fortress and its attackers, but – as is common in the uncertain art of espionage – they'd considerably exaggerated their report, in the interests of making it seem worth while.

After twenty minutes in the house the IRA were dissatisfied to find themselves in possession of two assegais, a knobkerry, a Gurkha knife, a 1914 bayonet and a pith helmet from the Boer War, trophies brought home from foreign service by my mother's numerous brothers. All these warriors, however, were now somewhere else, so that the depleted garrison put up no great struggle as the IRA ranged through the house, throwing open cupboards and peering under beds in search of the machine-guns and Mills bombs promised them by the cook.

While all this was going on I was standing on the rug beside my bed with a pillow between my knees, placed there by my mother. The burning of our house, followed by close proximity to my grandmother, who was a fast hand with a ruler, had brought my nerves to a low state. From the first crash on the back door my knees had been knocking together so rapidly that they were now severely bruised on the inside, making each new percussion an agony. The pillow, however, eased things considerably. I was holding it in position, fore and aft, when the raider burst into the room, waving a huge Service revolver, but I dropped it immediately when he shouted, 'Hands up!' The knees started rattling again, like castanets.

My mother went into immediate action. 'How can he put his hands up?' she shouted at the raider. 'Look at his little knees!' She slotted the pillow home again into position and returned to the attack.

'How dare you frighten the life out of a little child!' she cried. At the age of nine I was nearly six feet tall, but the principle was right. 'Give him your gun! Let him see it isn't loaded!'

As usual, the speed and directness of her assault bouleversed the enemy. He was a lumpish youth in the regulation cap and trench-coat, with a handkerchief over his face which looked as if it had recently been used for cleaning floors. He became placatory. 'I wouldn't frighten the little fella, mum. A'course it's not loaded. Amn't I only afther findin' it down below . . .?'

My mother pounced upon this new intelligence. 'That's Malcolm's revolver,' she cried. 'Put it back where you found it! Didn't he risk his life with it, defending you and all the other hooligans like you from the Germans?'

'Put it back, mum?' The proposition staggered him. 'I can't do that, mum. Sure, the commandant'll kill me . . .'

At this point my mother snatched the gun out of his hand. 'Let him hold it, anyway,' she cried. 'I'm not going to have any child of mine having nightmares over a filthy, silly revolver.' She thrust it into my hand.

I didn't want it at all. I only wanted to hold on to my pillow. I dropped it on the floor, with the pillow on top of it, and tried to put my hands between my knees.

In the midst of this confusion there was a hoarse shout from downstairs: 'Christy, come on owa that, willya! There's nothin' more here . . .'

Christy made a move towards the gun. My mother put her foot on it. They faced one another for a moment, with a thin, obbligato sobbing from myself. 'You'll be hearin' more of this,' said Christy unconvincingly. Then he turned and ran.

My mother put me back to bed, then she picked up the revolver by the muzzle and threw it into the bottom of the cupboard. 'I'll put it in the bank in the morning,' she said. 'Filthy, silly things. Don't you ever have anything to do with them.'

It was a piece of advice which I had no difficulty in following over the next thirty years, until I suddenly found myself staring down the barrel of a Mauser in a public house in Wapping, with no mother to guide me on a night of impenetrable fog.

I'd gone down to 'The Prospect of Whitby' to write a story about one of its familiars, a character known as Prospect Jock, who allowed customers to sign their names on his white suit. After an indeterminate interview with Jock, who could analyse his curious activities no more deeply than 'a bit o' sport', I fell into such a lengthy conversation with the landlord, Mr Broadbent, that I was still there at midnight when the man in the black hat, with the red muffler over his face, came rushing up the stairs, waving the gun.

Mr Broadbent had been talking for some time about the murky, early history of Wapping, and the glamour it certainly lent to the bright, present charms of his pub, so that when the figure in the red muffler appeared I immediately presumed that he'd been hired by Mr Broadbent, in the interests of publicity, to present some sort of masquerade of the bad old days.

It seemed to me to be an unnecessary elaboration, seeing that I was going to write about Prospect Jock anyway, and I rose to my feet to say so.

If, of course, my mother had been there she would have cut the proceedings short by telling the gunman to do the washing up, or get us another round of drinks, but I was on my own.

It was my intention to say, 'Come off it, cock – who do you think you're ...' but before a word of this stricture could be delivered the man in the muffler seized me by the front of the coat, hit me on the back of the head with his gun and threw me down a whole flight of stairs into the public bar. It was the swiftest transition from one state to another I'd ever known.

I should think I became unconscious, while passing down the stairs, though more from fear than the actual blow, because when I came to I found the floor of the bar littered with the bodies of a number of people whom I'd last seen upstairs in the restaurant. They included Captain Cunningham, the Mayfair oyster bar proprietor, and his guests, who'd been dining at another table. They weren't dead, but acting under the orders of three men who were stamping about with coshes, telling them to keep their heads down.

I found an empty space, and another one for my wife, and then, with some regard for the family tradition, I asked one of the gangsters if we could sit, rather than lie, as we were wearing our best clothes, and the floor was rather dirty. He replied by holding his cosh directly beneath my nose. We assumed a semi-recumbent position.

They worked swiftly. The junior representatives smashed the glass-fronted cash registers with their coshes, and filled straw fish baskets with the loose change. At the other end of the bar the man in the red muffler threatened Mr Broadbent with death if he didn't open the safe. Mr Broadbent obliged. The guests on the floor were invited to unload whatever valuables might be on their persons. We obliged, too. Ten minutes later the men were gone, leaving a deeply stricken silence behind.

Even at this late stage I wish it had been my mother who'd taken charge of the investigation, instead of Scotland Yard. With her steady record in matters of violence she would certainly have been able to prevent me identifying the wrong man, putting him in gaol for three weeks, and subsequently having to make a public apology from the witness box.

She might also have been able to prevent my wife from saying, in her evidence, that the bracelet of which she'd been robbed 'couldn't have cost more than £2 because my husband gave it to me for Christmas'.

She could also have induced me to put my personal loss higher than five shillings which, while it was true, stood up badly in a list beginning: 'Wm. Broadbent, £2,500; Captain Cunningham, £75', etc.

She could also have been there to put another pillow between my knees when I discovered that the man in the red muffler, who'd hit me with his gun, was no less a villain than Scarface Nobby Saunders, on the run from Parkhurst Gaol, who, ten days after dealing with me, shot a policeman in the eye during a warehouse raid, and got a life sentence in Dartmoor from the Lord Chief Justice himself.

If I'd known, that night in 'The Prospect of Whitby', that it was Scarface Saunders who was rushing up the stairs at me, I would not have risen to my feet, to ask him to come off it. I'd have jumped straight backwards out of the window into the river.

But there, it's what I always say. When the old equalizers come out every boy needs his mother around, if the situation is not to descend into shame, flurry and confusion.

Patrick Campbell

Doing the Cobblers' Trot

An absolutely dreadful thing happened last week to me and Nellie.

We were having this cycling holiday, you see, combined with adding to our collection of wild flowers, and to begin with it was most enjoyable.

Although we've been engaged for seven years we haven't had much opportunity to be alone together, because Nellie lives in Birmingham and I've got this job in Southend, so you can imagine it was quite a thrill for both of us as we set off awheel, side by side. Nothing 'naughty', of course, because we'd promised our parents we'd put up at separate lodgings at nightfall, and a promise is a promise, but all the same I won't be betraying any very big secret if I let it slip that a little 'light dalliance' might have taken place during our lunch breaks. Yum yum.

It was on the fourth day of our holiday that this dreadful thing happened. We were wheeling along near a little village called Patching, near Worthing in Sussex, when we turned a corner and ran into a lot of people who were queuing to get into a field.

Nellie – she's very keen on all kinds of outdoor sport – said, 'Oh, goody – it must be a cricket match. Do let's go in and have a look. Perhaps Prince Philip is playing.'

I demurred. The people who were trying to get into the field didn't look like cricket lovers to me. In fact, they looked pretty rum. Young fellows with long hair and musical instruments and nearly all the young ladies wearing dresses down to the ground. More like folk dancers, really. That kind of thing.

I pointed this out to Nellie, but she said she'd always been keen on folk dancing and if they did the Cobblers' Trot she'd like to join in. We were arguing a little about what to do when suddenly these dreadful-looking youths simply snatched our bicycles from us and threw them into a pond. We didn't know *what* they were. They were wearing German helmets and leather jackets and they had iron bars and screwdrivers and one of them had taken the chain off Nellie's bicycle, before throwing it away, and he was swinging it round in a most disturbing manner.

I said, 'You may perhaps be German soldiers but even if you are that does not give you the right to throw our bicycles away.'

The leader – he had enormous caps on his boots – said, 'Bikes is offensive weapons, mate. Not allowed at the Phun City Festival. Now split.'

He actually pushed me, so that I pushed Nellie, and all at once we were being hurried along in the middle of all these folk dancers towards a kind of stage thing in the middle of the field. There was a big sign above it: 'THE PHUN CITY FESTIVAL'. A band was playing on the stage but whatever they were playing it certainly wasn't the Cobblers' Trot. More like just yowling and banging, really.

When we couldn't go any further we sat down, like everybody else, and then we jumped to our feet again at once, because the most disgusting things were going on all round us. I mean, a lot of the young couples were actually – I mean, right in the middle of this English field, as if it was Paris, or somewhere like that. I put my coat over Nellie's head and we tried to fight our way back to the gate but it was hopeless, so we just sat down again and tried to keep our eyes on the ground, both of us under my coat.

About a minute later the coat was torn off us and it was the German-looking people again. 'Bad trip, cats?' the leader said. It sounded like a question, so I said as sternly as I could, 'We were enjoying our little outing to the full until you took away our bicycles. I shall inform the police.'

'No coppers here, mate,' he said. 'Us Hell's Angels is the law. Now cool it.' Suddenly he lashed out with his whip at a young woman who, we saw to our horror, had taken off all her clothes. 'You too, chick,' he said. She didn't even seem to feel the lash, being busy trying to do a kind of very slow dance, perhaps the

Merry Harvesters' Hoe-Down, except that she kept on moaning, 'Harry Krishner – Harry Krishner . . .' She seemed to have been hypnotized by him, whoever he was.

It was too much. Stumbling over prostrate bodies, we battled our way to the exit, where we were arrested by six uniformed police, waiting outside the gate. The Sergeant said, 'Any pot, grass, or L.S.D.?' When I said we had £1.16 between us for some reason or other they let us go.

Afterwards, Nellie said, 'You'd never expect that kind of thing to happen in an English field.'

'No, dear,' I said. 'And they couldn't even spell "fun".'

Dylan Thomas

How to Begin a Story

The way to begin a story depends not so much upon what you mean by a story as upon the story itself and the public for which it is intended. That this goes without saying need in no way deter me from saying it: these are notes in the margin of a never-to-be-written treatise and are free as the London air, though not so smutty.

It would, for example, be wrong, however pleasant, to begin a story for *Little Tim's Weekly* in the style of a sentimentally savage, gauchely cynical, American underworld novel salted with sex-slang, peppered with lead, sugared with stiffs and stiff with cigars and sugars: the kind of novel beneath whose hard and sinister shell lurks no embryonic bird of prey, great Chicago auk or fabulous Brooklyn roc, but a backward, shy and shabby backwood sparrow twittering for crumbs and buddies. Those flash, brash, cigar-mashing floozy-flayers and anti-social bad babies who, in recent gangster-films, confess, at some Ufa-lighted moment in abattoir, railway-siding, or condemned cell, that they have always been kinda unwanted and lonesome, even back in mid-western little Bloodville, and that it all began when their dipsomaniac second stepmothers put them on the fire for saying their prayers – these psychopathic gorillas coked to the gills have no place in Little Tim's cosmography, however much Little Tim would appreciate it, and the writer of children's stories should never, in any circumstances, emotional or atomic, begin with an expletive-packed and monosyllabic description of a raid by the vice-squad on a clip-joint for retired rod-men. It is legitimate to begin a children's story with a conversation between rats; but only between certain kinds of rats.

Neither should the writer of a story intended to command a

steady, unsensational provincial sale, and concerning the birth, education, financial ups and downs, marriage, separations, and deaths of five generations of a family of Lancashire cotton-weavers, begin with, say, the Joycean interior monologue of a moronic haberdasher trapped in a lift full of moths, or with a twee scene, in Hopskipandjump Town or Eiderdown Land, between Gruffums, the Lion, and Hold, that Tiger.

The man who begins a story for a girl's popular weekly – 'Myrtle's' or 'Pam's', or maybe it is 'Greta's' now, or 'Ingrid's' – with a subtle analysis of the state of mind of a neurotic young man of letters about to meet a phobia, socially, in a disused Nissen-hut, will never make the grade and is doomed to perpetual immurement in magazines with a circulation of seventeen poets and a woman who once met Kafka's aunt.

Now let us consider, most briefly, just a very few of the many favourite ways of beginning stories, and see if we can put a little new life into them.

School-stories first: not the dull ones about the repressions and urges of sensitive plants and backward sons, and the first dawning of love and Shelley on the awakening mind, but the good, or bad, old stories which are all about tea and muffins in the cosy study, midnight spreads by candlelight in the ill-patrolled dormitory, escapes by knotted sheets to out-of-bound circuses or fairs, the ruthless ragging and baiting of unpopular masters and impecunious buffoons, the expulsion of cads for smoking in the fives-court – poor little sallow Maltravers with the dark rings already under his *roué*'s eyes – and all the trivial tribal warfares of fantastic and ageless boys.

The onomatopoeic, gemmed and magnetic, time-honoured opening cannot be bettered:

'Leggo!'

'Geroff!'

'Yaroo!'

And then, of course:

'These stentorian cries echoed down the corridor of the Upper Shell.'

The novice should begin every school-story with exactly those words.

In the next sentence he must introduce his principal characters, a bunch of bold, breathless, exclamatory, ink-stained, beastly, Dickensian-surnamed boys with their caps awry, their lines undone, pets in their desks, paper-pellets in their pockets, and barbarous though innocuous oaths on their unrazored lips.

But let us introduce a new element:

'Leggo!'

'Geroff!'

'Yaroo!'

'These stentorian cries echoed down the corridor of the Upper Shell as Tom Happy and his inseparables, known to all Owlhurst as the "Filthy Five", lurched arm-in-arm out of Mrs Motherwell's fully licensed tuckshop.'

There you have a beginning at once conventional and startling. The reader is at your mercy. And you can continue, within the accepted framework and using only the loudest, minutest, and most formal vocabulary, to describe such goings-on as the formation, by Tom Happy, of the Owlhurst Suicide Club and the setting-up of a hookah in the boothole.

Then there is the story of rural life. I don't mean the depressing tale, told through four interminable seasons, of rugged toil and weather-beaten love on an isolated farm of that part of Sussex where you can't hear the thrushes for the noise of typewriters; nor the earthy, middenish record, stuffed with nature lore and agricultural information, studded – if that is the word – with all too precise observations of animal behaviour, whiskered with 'characters', riddled with unintelligible snatches of folk-verse and altogether jocular as a boot, of how a middle-aged literary man 'discovered' the country and his soul, price eight and six. No; I mean the kind of story set in a small, lunatic area of Wessex, full of saintly or reprehensible vicars, wanton maidens, biblical sextons, and old men called Parsnip or Dottle.

Let us imagine a typical beginning:

'Mr Beetroot stood on a hill overlooking the village of Upper Story. He saw that there was something wrong in it. Mr Beetroot was a retired mole-trapper. He had retired because he had trapped all the moles. It was a fine winter's morning, and there were little clouds in the sky like molehills. Mr Beetroot caught a rabbit, taught it the alphabet, let it go, and walked slowly down the hill.'

There we have firmly fixed the location and mood of the story, and have become well, if briefly, acquainted with Mr Beetroot, a lover of animals and addicted to animal education.

The common reader – legendary cretin – now knows what is coming to him: Mr Beetroot, that cracked though cosmic symbol of something or other, will, in the nutty village, with dialect, oafs, and potted sermons, conduct his investigation into unreal rural life. Everyone, in this sophisticatedly contrived bucolic morality, has his or her obsession: Minnie Wurzel wants only the vicar; the vicar, the Reverend Nut, wants only the ghost of William Cowper to come into his brown study and read him 'The Task'; the Sexton wants worms; worms want the vicar. Lambkins, on those impossible hills, frolic, gambol, and are sheepish under the all-seeing eye of Uncle Teapot, the Celestial Tinker. Cruel farmers persecute old cowherds called Crumpet, who talk, all day long, to cows; cows, tired of vaccine-talk in which they can have no part, gore, in a female manner, the aged relatives of cruel farmers; it is all very cosy in Upper Story. But so the reader – cretinous legend – thinks.

The beginner, beginning a story of this kind, would be wise to . . .

I see there is little, or no, time to continue my instructional essay on 'How to Begin a Story'. How to 'End a Story' is, of course, a different matter . . . *One* way of ending a story is:

ANNOUNCER: That was Dylan Thomas talking about 'How to Begin a Story'.

Anthony Carson

from *A Rose by Any Other Name*

A HOT BATH AT ROTORUA

I was twenty and still in New Zealand. I had given up learning how to farm. I could half shear a sheep, half milk a cow, and half fell a tree. I had tried house painting and had fallen half-way down a house. (The boss had kept me on and given me a bonus. 'You keep the men happy,' he had said.) So I decided to become a tourist and visit Rotorua in the North Island. I wrote to my parents, explaining that I wished to broaden my mind. 'Then,' I said, 'I will really settle down.' Eventually I received a sum of money and a letter telling me that as far as they were concerned, my mind was now quite broad enough. I bought a ticket and a new suit and set off for Rotorua.

I had heard many fantastic things about this township, and was half expecting to see a cluster of erupting volcanoes sur-rounded by steam. But when I arrived I found myself in a place like Frinton-on-Sea, except that most of the neat little houses (called Sans Souci and Bide-a-Wee) had corrugated iron roofs. But there was the same atmosphere. The patter of balls on hard tennis-courts, privet hedges, whist drives, and the Rotorua Dramatic Society giving a performance of *Iolanthe*. There was a huge Victorian Thermal Establishment purveying multi-col-oured baths, ranging from a sort of lemonade-colour to thick pea-soup, and each of them expensively foetid. Residential hotels with old ladies in the far corner turning the pages of their Agatha Christies. Curio shops with metal kiwis and Kia Ora embroidered on mats, and Welcome to Rotorua. American tour-ists with cameras and fishing rods.

But after walking a short way from the town I came across a

lake with steam rising all round it. I was quite alone. There was a sweet smell of sulphur and a drowsy whir of crickets. In the distance I could hear a gurgle, a watery cough and a bang, followed by a spurt of boiling water shooting up to the sky. As I walked further round the lake, I came to places where the earth was trembling. Pits in the ground were bubbling with boiling mud, and jets of steam whistled out of rocks. It was like a gigantic, inhuman fun-fair. Its gods, faintly and shiveringly apprehended, were gods beyond known time or human experience.

Perhaps that was why the residents of Rotorua kept all these phenomena at arm's length and hardly ever referred to them, except as grotesque and mad domestic servants who only did their duty in the thermal establishments. Here, with shower baths, white-coated attendants, bath-mats, and cups of tea, the terror of the gods was insulated. Of course it was different with the tourists. They wandered all over the forbidden area and the most distinguished ones even encouraged the geysers to explode, off duty, with bars of soap stuffed down their vents. They put coins in pools of water and watched them turn green. They paddled in rivers with cold water and hot bottoms, and probably didn't notice the malignant ineffable ghosts crouched behind the steaming rocks. And finally they visited the Maori reservation village at Whakarewarewa.

The reservation stretches for many miles beyond Rotorua, and is inhabited by the Arawa tribe, the finest and noblest looking type of Maori. Many of them carry on the same kind of lives as other New Zealanders, and are businessmen, doctors, shopkeepers, and farmers. They drive about in smart cars, wear expensive suits, and smoke cigars. They play games magnificently, and read books. But there is a tacit agreement that they go to the Maori village, probably in rota, take off their suits, and put on grass skirts. They plait mats, dance, and shout the thunderous Haka at illustrious visitors. There is even a Maori theatre where they enact legends, and where the dusky girls sway in the rhythm of the canoe dance.

It is a huge tourist enterprise, but by no means bogus, because the Maoris have a deep Pacific poetry in their blood, more powerful and nostalgic than all the lending libraries in New

Zealand put together. The Maori place-names sing like the surf of forgotten seas and blaze like hibiscus.

I put up in a small residential hotel and began, in a rather cowardly way, to play games of tennis and fumble at bridge. I was a decent chap. I read the *Rotorua Gazette* and even had a plunge in sulphuretted hydrogen at the thermal baths. But I am not built for such solid, unperforated living, and guiltily I stole away to Whakarewarewa and spent my time hanging about the village. I met a Maori princess. She sat on the ground outside a flax-weaving hut, wearing a grass skirt and beads. She seemed highly amused. 'I love sitting here and watching your people,' she said; 'it is such fun, and extremely educative. I simply don't need to travel. Why, an old lady gave me a peanut the other day.' Later I met her at one of the hotels, dressed in a smart evening gown and drinking a cocktail. She looked just as regal. 'There's a Deputation visiting the village tomorrow,' she told me. 'Do come. I'll be there, weaving flax.'

The next day I returned to Whakarewarewa, but I didn't see any Deputation. I strolled about, talking to various friends I had made, and arrived at a small lake near a bend of the road. While I was standing there a tall naked Maori ran out of one of the huts, holding a bar of soap and a towel, threw down the towel and dived into the lake. He swam out a certain distance, lay on his back and lathered himself. Then he plunged under the water, splashed about vigorously, and swam back to the shore. He clambered out.

'That looks good,' I said.

'It is good,' agreed the Maori. 'Try it yourself.'

I felt the water with my hand. 'But it's cold,' I said.

'It starts cold,' he said, 'but you swim out and it's warm and you swim out some more and it's hot. You swim out more and it's too hot. In the middle it's boiling. No good.'

'I'll have a go,' I said.

He lent me his soap and towel, and I took off my clothes and jumped in.

It was cold at first, but after I had swum out a bit it felt wonderful. I splashed about in the water and lathered myself and floated in my enormous hot bath, and looked up at the sky.

Then I began to swim back. At that moment I saw about thirty people lining the bank. Some of them were in uniform. One man, obviously the mayor, had a chain of office round his neck. Women were holding elaborate parasols, and somebody was making a speech. Wildly I struck back towards the centre of the lake, hit the boiling fringe, gave a shout and shot back again, treading water. The Deputation were still standing there, gazing towards me. Higher up the bank I could see a tall Maori waving and shaking with laughter.

He was wearing my suit.

LECTURE TO THE TROOPS

I went into the army. I knew it would be an uneasy relation. I had thought of pacifism. But the only sort of permitted pacifism I knew of was tied up with Jehovah, seeing your sister raped, and the sexless potato field. So there I was, brown and numbered, peering at enormous anti-aircraft guns. After preliminary training, I was transferred to Intelligence.

Just before my arrival at Winchester there had been an overhaul. Pasty men lolling back in armchairs reading Proust had been returned to their units. Gigantic guardsmen had arrived. Their terrible voices could be heard from the railway station. Also there were batches of gleaming, violent motor-bicycles. A general had come down, breathing flames. '*Mens sana in corpore sano*,' he had barked with some originality. 'Intelligence doesn't mean looking like a dog's vomit. It means this Corps will become the toughest, fittest, and best-disciplined in the Service. Even if it kills you.' This régime had produced a good supply of neurotics and invalids. A man had gone about for a time convinced that he was Goebbels. Later he acquired a commission. It was just about then that I reported there, was flung on to a snorting motor-bicycle, and pushed down a ravine.

Later there was square-bashing. It was so alarming that, as I tend to treat all crises, I half ignored it, rushing about from one parade to another, dropping belts and joining the wrong squad. On one occasion, during a monster parade I should have attended, when somebody important arrived on a horse, I walked through it in a pair of shorts.

'Where are you going?' shouted a purple-faced giant.

'To have a shower,' I replied in a tiny voice.

They could see I felt wretched about it. All that pomp and precision, and my ridiculous shower. There was only one thing left for me to do. An instinctive act of self-preservation. I put on an army concert. Later, in a sort of dream, I was transferred to another Intelligence unit, where I put on another concert. Finally I was returned to my unit.

Here, in miraculous fashion, I gained a corporal's stripes, and was sent to Cleethorpes. This at the best of times is an alarming experience. During the war it was like a second-class nightmare. Facing the sea was a façade of boarding houses, Sea-Views and Marine Villas, whose windows, divested of aspidistras, framed the shaving faces of sergeants. Decayed amusement arcades were converted into a ghastly bazaar of army blankets and webbing equipment. A hundred tea-shops served as rat-holes for the sick. I saw the C.O. and explained to him my uncertain attitude towards guns. 'Lecture the troops, Corporal,' said the C.O. contemptuously. When I got to the door, he called me back. 'No Red stuff, of course,' he said.

I started off my lectures as though I had suddenly been awarded a Fellowship at an ancient university. A sergeant stood by my side, glaring at the ranks of tea-mad soldiery. I was promoted by printed ABCA talks. Empire, Democracy, the Benefits of Discipline. But after a time I relaxed. I began to lecture about animals. Finally, I perfected a talk about the Amoeba which achieved a great deal of success. There was a little joke attached to it. 'To reproduce itself, the Amoeba merely has to split in two. Intensely labour-saving, but not much fun.' Old lags would stop me by the blanket bazaar, or waylay me in the tea-shops. 'Give us that Amoeba talk again, Corp.' Only the sergeants didn't approve. Their faces looked grimly before them. When the laugh came up over unicellular sex-life, they used to lunge forward to make charges, and I had to restrain them.

'They're *supposed* to laugh at that bit, Sergeant.'

'O.K., Corporal. As long as you're sure the bastards should be laughing.'

One day I was told to give a lecture in Grimsby.

'Rather a lot of chaps from all over the command,' said an officer. 'Captain Clock will be driving you there and back.'

I turned over various talks in my mind, and decided on the Amoeba. On the way to Grimsby Captain Clock said, 'We'll be interested to hear your talk, Corporal. I hear you have a good approach.' I stepped up on the platform and saw a sea of faces. I had expected nothing like it. More amazing still, many of the front rows were occupied by high-ranking officers. Everyone faced me with a sort of rigid, uncomfortable, yet respectful attention. As if I was some sort of apostle with a military appointment. I cleared my throat and began. 'Let us consider a low form of life . . .' I had rather expected a laugh, but didn't get it. Endless glazed eyes glared at attention. I began to sweat, sensing the baffled hostility behind the frozen attitudes. I wanted to run from the hall. My voice trembled. 'To reproduce itself,' I stammered, 'the Amoeba merely has to split in two. Intensely labour-saving, but not much fun.' I waited, feeling rather sick. The silence was shattered by an obscene guffaw. Everybody's head turned round accusingly and said 'Shush'. A sergeant appeared and led the offender out. Then the eyes engulfed me once more. Finally I staggered off the platform, without applause.

A bit later, Captain Clock drove me back to Cleethorpes. It was not till we got there that he broke the news. 'Jolly interesting talk, Corporal,' he said. 'Some of them were a bit shaken. You see, they'd been given a title beforehand. "British Way and Purpose, Part Two". Ought to have remembered to mention it earlier.'

THE WARDROBE

I was sent to arrange some business in Barcelona. I stayed in a small hotel, near the Ramblas, called the Cuba. It was an odd place, full of chandeliers – there was even one in the lift – and mirrors and tasselled cushions and improbable furniture. 'Like London, yes?' the proprietor had said when I had first signed my name in the book. He seemed attached to the idea, particularly as he had numbers of English clients, middle-aged and all looking mostly alike, who mainly came from the Midlands. 'How you like Barcelona?' the proprietor would ask them. 'Champion,' they would all reply. If it hadn't been for the chandeliers and a man whom nobody could stop singing in the kitchen, it might have been Leeds.

One of these tourists was a man called Bronson. His home was near Manchester, and he proudly showed me snaps of his wife, kids, and dog. 'The truth is,' he said, 'I'm on my own like. Having a bit of a change. Life in the old dog yet.' He nudged me in the arm and winked.

'I see,' I said. As a courier, I had handled hundreds of men like this. Sooner or later, in a museum, a crypt, a cathedral, they would come up to me and say, 'I expect you know all about the night-life here, eh?' and bring out their wallets.

'I expect you know all about Barcelona,' said Bronson.

'A bit,' I said.

'I'll bet you do,' said Bronson with meaning. 'We ought to go out one evening. What about it?'

So I took him around the Chinese quarter (where there are no Chinese), which sucks you down into the vortex of its squalid poetry. Then we went to various cabarets, ending up at the Baghdad, where we sat in the open air, under the stars, and watched dancing. It was derelict, tatty, and occasionally electric with beauty. Spain shambles through history, but can reach up and touch the sky.

Next morning I met Bronson having coffee and rolls. He didn't look very well.

'I had a bad night,' he said, picking up his cup with a trembling hand.

'What was wrong?' I asked.

'Something odd in my room,' he said. 'It was a creaking noise. Just before getting into bed, I was pouring myself a little nightcap of brandy. Immediately this thing started creaking.'

'What thing?' I asked.

'I'll get to that,' said Bronson. 'It went on creaking, rustling and sighing for quite a time. So I got out of bed, and hunted round the room. Eventually I found out what it was. It was a wardrobe.'

'A wardrobe?' I said.

'A wardrobe. A plain, harmless-looking wardrobe. I stood looking at it while it creaked at me. I was dead scared, and started to sweat. *There was obviously something inside it.* I took another swig of brandy and it began making a noise like sobbing. I opened the wardrobe door; there was nothing there except a few shirts. I got back to bed, but I couldn't sleep. I was waiting for the bloody thing to start again. Eventually I got out of bed and poured myself a drink of water. Almost at once the wardrobe started purring like a cat. It was purring this morning when I woke up. Gently.'

'I see,' I said, looking at Bronson carefully. He didn't look that sort of man who would get wardrobes to purr at him. 'Have you ever had this trouble with wardrobes before?' I asked him as casually as possible.

'Look here,' said Bronson angrily. 'I'm not the sort of man who imagines things. I'm a hard-headed businessman. I'm in good health, and there's no insanity in the family – yet. There *is* a wardrobe in my room, and it's got a down on me.'

'But why?' I asked.

'Don't ask me why,' cried Bronson. 'How on earth could I know why a wardrobe has a down on me?'

'You could change your room,' I said.

'I refuse to be made a fool of by a bloody Spanish wardrobe,' shouted Bronson angrily.

I didn't see Bronson all that day. I was busy, and when I got back to the hotel I was late for dinner: Bronson had already eaten and gone out. But next morning I was down to breakfast before Bronson and decided to wait for him. Eventually he appeared. His eyes were slightly bloodshot and he hadn't shaved.

'I'm getting scared,' he said, pouring out the coffee. 'The bloody thing moved last night. *Moved.* Mind you, I'd been waiting for something like that. I had it in mind all of yesterday. I had a rotten day, I can tell you. This wardrobe has ruined my holiday. Wherever I went, I thought to myself, "It's waiting for you." So I stoked myself up with a bit of booze in the evening and brought back a bottle to the room and sat in front of the wardrobe and put a few back. "So much for you," I said to it, and it started chattering at me. A sort of hollow chattering. I started to swear at it then. I said everything I could think of. And it began moving. *Moving.*'

'What did you do?' I asked.

'I hit it,' said Bronson. 'It made a terrible sound like whimpering. Listen, Carson, I haven't prayed since I was a kid. I'm not that sort. I don't say I don't believe in it, but I don't do it. But I did then. A sobbing, whimpering wardrobe, I mean. I prayed for quite a bit, and it quietened down and just breathed. But I've had enough. I'm going home. I'm leaving tomorrow, but I'm not going to spend tonight alone.'

'Could I see this wardrobe myself?' I asked him.

'Certainly,' he said. 'Come along. I'd like you to meet it.'

He led me upstairs to the third floor. His room number was 110. He opened the door and pointed dramatically to a plain black wardrobe standing in front of the bed.

'What do you think of it?' he said.

'It seems fairly ordinary,' I answered.

'Doesn't it seem to be frowning?' he asked. 'In any case, listen, *listen.*'

We stood there, listening. But there was no sound at all, just the tap dripping into the wash-hand basin.

'It approves of you,' said Bronson. 'Try hitting it. On the other hand you'd better not. You might wake it up.'

That night, after dinner, I set out with Bronson and we drifted from café to café and finally ended up in the Chinese quarter. At one o'clock in the morning, in a garish little café, I suggested going back.

'No. I won't come back yet,' said Bronson. 'Leave me here. I'll be all right here.'

I got a taxi and drove to the hotel.

At about five o'clock I was woken up by a crash, a door slamming, and someone clattering down the stairs. Then my door opened and I heard the sound of heavy breathing.

'Are you awake?' said the voice of Bronson.

'Yes,' I said. 'Turn on the light.'

He flicked the switch, and I saw he was wearing a dressing-gown. His hair was on end and he'd obviously been drinking a lot.

'May I stay here for an hour or two?' he asked. 'I'll sit in the armchair. Then I'll go up and pack and clear the hell out of it. I'm not staying in my room.'

'What happened?' I asked.

'I've had a fight with the wardrobe,' he said thickly.

'A fight?' I said, sitting up.

'Yes. I came back about an hour ago. With a girl. We went into the room and had a few drinks. Then I turned out the light. I've forgotten exactly what happened then, but suddenly this wardrobe gave a terrible groan and came down flop on the bed. The girl ran for her life. I got hold of the wardrobe and wrestled. It was panting, and seemed as if it wanted to hug me. At last, I managed to throw it down on its back. It's ticking over.'

He turned out the light and settled down in the armchair. When I woke up in the morning he was gone.

After breakfast I had a word with the proprietor. 'I'm rather interested in furniture,' I told him. 'You have quite a fine wardrobe in Room 110. There was an English gentleman staying there. Could you tell me anything about it?'

'The wardrobe in 110?' said the proprietor. 'Quite an ordinary wardrobe, I assure you. It came from a building near the Plaza de España. A convent for English ladies.'

Denton Welch

Sickert at St Peter's

I had been in Broadstairs for months, trying to recover some sort of health after a serious road accident.

My doctor, knowing that I was an art student, tried to persuade Sickert to come and see me, but he wouldn't. I was told that he stormed off down the street, saying: 'I have no time for district visiting!'

That was while I was still in bed. When at last I got up, someone engineered an invitation to tea on Saturday afternoon. So he did not escape me after all.

Just as I was about to leave the nursing home for St Peter's, Sister sailed into my room, closely followed by Gerald, an art school friend. He had evidently come all the way from London to see me.

I controlled my face as best I could and said: 'I'm going to tea with Sickert. What are you going to do? Can you wait here till I get back?'

He gave me one rapid glance and then said firmly: 'I'll come, too.'

I was horrified.

'But you haven't been asked!' I burst out.

'That doesn't matter. One more won't make any difference.'

Feeling powerless in my convalescent state against his strength of will, I let him climb up beside me in the aged taxi which bore us swayingly to 'Hauteville'.

Sickert had not lived long in the house and it was still being altered. One entered through what at one time had been the 'cloakroom'! I remember with vividness the slight shock I received on being confronted with a glistening white 'WC' as soon as the door was opened.

Mrs Sickert stood beside it, welcoming us charmingly, with great quietness. She led us into what must have been the original hall. It was now a sort of dining-room, furnished with a strange mixture of interesting and common-place things. An early Georgian mirror with flat bevelling and worn gilt frame hung over the Art Nouveau grate. Seen thus together, each looked somehow startling and new.

We left our coats and passed on into the much loftier and larger drawing-room. The first thing I noticed was that the floor was quite bare, with that stained 'surround' which makes the white boards in the middle look so naked. By the sofa stood a stringy man who was about to go bald. The pale gold hair was still there, but one could tell how thin the crop would be next year. He looked at us with piercing eyes and fidgeted with his teaspoon. Mrs Sickert only had time to tell us that her husband was still resting but that he would be down soon, before this man engaged her again in earnest conversation. She could only show us attention by pouring out cups of tea. My cup was of that white china which is decorated with a gold trefoil in the centre of each piece. Gerald's was quite different. It was acid-blue, I think, with an unpleasant black handle and stripe; but I noticed that both our spoons were flimsy and old. I turned mine over and saw, amongst the other hall-marks, the little head of George III winking up at me.

I looked at the other things on the table, at the brown enamel teapot, the familiar red and blue Huntley and Palmer's tin, and at the strange loaf which seemed neither bread nor cake. In spite of myself, I felt that at least I was seeing Bohemian life.

I was glad that the man was keeping Mrs Sickert so busy, for it gave me time to stare at everything in the room. I saw that along most of the walls ran narrow panels, almost in monochrome. They looked like bas-reliefs flattened by a steam roller. They were most decorative. Mixed with these, but standing on easels or resting on the floor, were some of Sickert's own paintings. Gwen Ffrangcon-Davies dressed in Elizabethan farthingale and ruff, with harsh white light on her face, looked out from a picture mostly green and red.

Toylike, bustled ladies and Derby-hatted men, all in soft greys and pinks, skated on a country pond. Pinned to the canvas was the original *Punch* drawing from which the composition had been taken.

Near the fireplace stood the long, brown haggard picture of the miner with his swinging lamp, just come up from the pit, grasping his wife fiercely and kissing her mouth.

As I was looking at this last picture, Sickert appeared in the door. My first sight of him was rather overwhelming. Huge and bearded, he was dressed in rough clothes and from his toes to his thighs reached what I can only describe as sewer-boots.

He had seen me staring at the picture and now said directly to me: 'That picture gives you the right feeling, doesn't it? You'd kiss your wife like that if you'd just come up from the pit, wouldn't you?'

I was appalled by the dreadful heartiness of the question. I found myself blushing, and hated him for making me do so.

Sickert came right up to me and looked me all over.

'Well, you don't look very ill,' he said. 'I thought you'd be in a terrible mess. Didn't you fracture your spine or something?'

I nodded my head.

He made an amusing, whining baby's face.

'Look here, I'm very sorry I didn't come and see you, but I can't go round visiting.' He waved his hand round the room. 'You see, I have to keep painting all these pictures because I'm so poor.'

He took up a position with his back to the fireplace. Mrs Sickert got up and carried a cup of tea to her husband. The stringy man also rose and floated to the door. He was still talking to Mrs Sickert over his shoulder, and the last words I heard as he left the room were: '. . . couldn't pass water for six days!'

This sounded so surprising that for one moment I forgot Sickert. Then I remembered him with a jolt, for he had begun to dance on the hearth in his great sewer-boots. He lifted his cup and, waving it to and fro, burst into a German drinking song. There was an amazing theatrical and roguish look on his broad face.

I could not believe that he always drank his tea in this way, and I felt flattered, because he seemed to be doing it especially for us.

I don't know how long the dance or the song would have lasted if the front door bell had not rung. Sickert suddenly broke off and waited, while Mrs Sickert hurried out of the room.

She returned with a Mr Raven, whom I had met once before. After giving him a cup of tea, she left him standing on the hearth beside Sickert. He sipped his tea in silence for a few moments; then he began to feel in his breast-pocket. At last he brought out a rather crumpled, shiny object, and I saw that it was a photograph.

'This is my mother,' he said, pushing it under Sickert's nose.

Sickert drew back perceptibly and gave a grunt which might have meant anything.

Mr Raven continued, unruffled. 'Interesting face, isn't it? If you'd like to do a painting of it, I'd be very pleased to lend you the photograph for as long as you liked.'

There was another grunt from Sickert.

When Mr Raven realized that this was the only answer he was going to get, he turned very red and hurriedly thrust the portrait of his mother back into his breast-pocket. He looked just as if he had been caught in the act of displaying an indecent postcard.

Gerald and I exchanged glances. I think we were both sorry for Mr Raven and yet glad that his efforts towards cheap immortality for his mother had been frustrated.

Sickert, evidently prompted by Mr Raven's action, opened a drawer in a cabinet and also produced a photograph.

'Isn't she lovely?' he said, holding it out to me.

I took the yellowing little 'carte-de-visite' between my fingers and saw that it was of some young woman of the 'eighties. She had her back to the camera, so that her face was seen in profile resting on one shoulder. She appeared to me quite hideous with a costive, pouchy look about the eyes and mouth.

I wondered who she could be. Perhaps she was someone famous; or perhaps she was one of Sickert's past wives or mistresses.

I felt in a very difficult position. Thinking as I did, I hated to be sycophantic and say: 'Yes, she's beautiful.' So I compromised very clumsily by answering:

'The photograph is so tiny that I can't see very much of her; but I love the clothes of that period, don't you?'

Sickert snatched the photograph from me.

'Tiny! What do you mean by tiny?' he roared.

He held the picture up and pointed to it, as if he were demonstrating something on a blackboard; then he shouted out in ringing tones for the whole room to hear.

'Do you realize that I could paint a picture as big as this' (he stretched out his arm like an angler in a comic paper) 'from this "tiny" photograph as you call it?'

Horribly embarrassed and overcome by this outburst, I smiled weakly and cast my eyes down so that they rested on his enormous boots.

I was not thinking of his boots. I was thinking of nothing but the redness of my face. But Sickert evidently thought that I was curious, for the next moment he had opened another attack with:

'Ah, I see that you're staring at my boots! Do you know why I wear them? Well, I'll tell you. Lord Beaverbrook asked me to a party, and I was late, so I jumped into a taxi and said: "Drive as fast as you can!" Of course, we had an accident and I was thrown on to my knees and my legs were badly knocked about; so now I wear these as a protection.'

In a dazed way, I wondered if he meant that he wore the boots to protect the still bruised legs, or if he meant that he intended to wear them as a permanent safeguard, in case he should ever again have an accident as he hurried to a party of Lord Beaverbrook's. I thought of the sensation they would create amongst the patent leather shoes.

By this time I was so exhausted that I was pleased when Sickert turned his attention to Gerald. He started to talk about politicians, and I thought it was clever of him to guess that Gerald had an enormous appetite for tit-bits about the famous.

As I sank down on the sofa beside Mrs Sickert, I heard them begin on Anthony Eden. Sickert was describing his good looks.

He must have sensed that I was still listening, for he suddenly turned his face on me, and his eyes were twinkling with fun and malice.

'Ugly ones like us haven't a chance when there's someone like Eden about, have we?' he called out across the room.

I was so surprised at being lumped together with Sickert in ugliness, as opposed to the handsomeness of Anthony Eden (who had never struck me as anything but middle-aged) that I took him quite seriously and could answer nothing.

I hurriedly tried to compensate myself for the humiliation by telling myself that, although it might not be saying very much, I was undoubtedly by far and away the best-looking person in the room, and this in spite of my long illness.

Mrs Sickert saw that I was ruffled and very kindly started to talk about my career. She asked me if I intended to go back to an art school when I was well enough. We discussed the various objects in the room. She told me that the two glittering monstrances had come from a Russian church. We went up to them and I took one of the sparkling things in my hands. The blue and white paste lustres were backed with tinsel. They were fascinatingly gaudy and I coveted them.

We sat talking together on the sofa for a little longer. Through our words I caught snatches of what Sickert was saying. Gerald evidently had got him on to Degas and anecdotes were streaming out. Gerald was drinking them up thirstily, while Mr Raven hovered rather uncomfortably at the edge of the conversation.

At last he decided to go. Coming forward, he coughed slightly and held out his hand to Mrs Sickert. Then, as he passed Sickert on his way to the door, he felt in his pocket and with almost incredible courage brought out the crumpled little photograph again.

Putting it down on the table, he said simply: 'I'll leave this just in case ...'

His voice tailed off as he saw the completely blank look on Sickert's face. I knew exactly what was coming and waited for it.

Sickert gave the same enigmatic grunt. It was somehow quite baffling and insulting.

Mr Raven crept unhappily to the door and Mrs Sickert followed swiftly to put salve on his wounds.

Immediately Raven was out of the room Sickert became boisterous. He started to dance again, thumping his great boots on the floor. Gerald and I caught some of his gaiety. We did not mention Raven, but I knew that we were all celebrating his defeat. It was pleasant to feel that Sickert treated us as fellow artists. I wondered how many people each year asked him to paint pictures for love.

As Mrs Sickert did not return, we went into the hall, where Sickert dragged on our coats as if he were dressing sacks of turnips. Then dancing and singing in front of us, he led the way through the 'cloakroom' to the front door. I half expected some remark about the shining flush-closet, but none came.

It was dark outside. We walked over the greasy cobbles. Sickert was leading us. He threw open the creaking stable-yard door and stood there with his hand on the latch. He looked gigantic.

We passed through and started to walk down the road.

'Goodbye, goodbye!' he shouted after us in great good humour. 'Come again when you can't stop quite so long!'

And at these words a strange pang went through me, for it was what my father had always said as he closed the book, when I had finished my bread and butter and milk, and it was time for me to go to bed.

Marghanita Laski

Cheap Clothes for Fat Old Women

Although the chief business of the fashion journalist is to find flattering alternatives to the phrase I have chosen for my title, the practised wielding of a new and esoteric language has now become instinctive with her. I am not speaking of those copy-writers in the daily press who offer Gowns for the O. S. Matron in a colour-range (*nigger, saxe, eau-de-nil*) that has elsewhere disappeared from the spectrum. My study is of the specialized grammar and vocabulary of the fashion-writer in the glossy monthlies whose language, while representing the quintessence of glamour to thousands of women, must still be virtually incomprehensible to millions more.

Her grammatical usages really merit special research, and here I will refer only to my two favourites. First, the Hypnotic Imperative *This season you will be wearing . . ., reading . . ., talking about . . .* The best example I ever met ran: *Because it's high summer you'll buy a new aeroplane painted blue to match the skies.* Second, the Omitted Conjunction in descriptions of intellectuals – *He lives in an old house in Essex, writes for 'Horizon', collects china cats . . .*

But it is in the bold misuse of our contemporary vocabulary that the art of the fashion-writer is seen at its best; and for those who may wish to penetrate into hitherto unexplored fields I append an all-too-short glossary. I should add that the abbreviation G. W. indicates a Glamour-Word, extremely evocative in the right context and of no real meaning whatsoever.

AMUSING: cheap.

BOLD: G.W.; e.g., *b. back-sweeping fullness.*

BRIEF, adj.: very short in length; e.g., *b. bolero, b. panties,* also briefest.

BULGE, UNSEEMLY: stomach fat.

CHARM, NOSTALGIC: G.W.

CLASSIC, n.: English garment (shoes, hat, suit) barely susceptible to fashion changes.

CRISP, adj.: G.W.; e.g., *a c. silhouette, c. touches of white.*

DEMURE: (of hats and hair-styles) those which symmetrically frame the face.

DERRIERE, n.: buttocks; e.g., *tuck in your d.*

DIGNIFIED: (i) of women: old; (ii) of clothes: for old women.

DRAMATIC: virtually unwearable, but photographs well.

-EST: intensive used instead of 'very'; e.g., *palest grey, softest and finest worsteds.*

EVERYWHERE: in a very few places; e.g., *sable stoles are e.*

FLATTERY: G.W.; e.g., *the f. of mink, diamonds, orchids against your skin.*

FRANKLY, adj.: would be ugly if we didn't tell you it wasn't; e.g., *a f. jagged hemline.*

FUZZ, UNSIGHTLY: superfluous hair on the legs.

GENEROUS: (i) the designer is making nothing out of the dress-length, e.g., *g. cuffs;* (ii) fat.

HAIRS, OBSTINATE OR RECALCITRANT: the un-wanted moustache; e.g., *tweak out those o. (or r.) h.*

HIGHLIGHT, n.: a noticeable accessory. Cp. SPOTLIGHT.

HUGGING: tight; e.g., *bosom-h, waist-h.*

HUSKY: suitable for out-of-door country wear.

IMPORTANT: G.W.

INDISPENSABLE: G.W.; e.g., *the i. pearl choker.*

-IZE: verbal suffix; e.g., slenderize, glamorize, accessorize.

JAUNTY: G.W.

LIGHTLY-BONED: of corsets (no corsets to-day are HEAVILY-BONED).

LIMITED INCOME, adj.: cheap.

MIDRIFF: stomach.

OLDER: (of women) old.

PUSH, vb.: fabric-fullness is *pushed* (occ. *pulled*) to the back, side or front; once arrived at the back, however, it becomes BACK-SWEPT (formerly used only of vertically ascending hair).

SIGNIFICANT: G.W.

SOFTLY: G.W.; e.g., *s. rounded, s. draped, s. knotted.*

SPOTLIGHT, vb.: to add a noticeable accessory, cp. HIGHLIGHT.

SUBTLE: G.W.; frequently *s. emphasis of . . .*

TEAM, vb.: to wear one thing with another; e.g., *t. your palest grey dress with the subtle flattery of a brief scarlet bolero.*

THAT, THOSE: adjs. of distaste and elimination; e.g., *eliminate t. unsightly bulge,* or, as above, *tweak out t. recalcitrant hairs.*

Finally I should, I suppose, give an example of the way in which my title, that epitome of the whole thing, can be translated. A professional could, of course, do better: I offer *Limited Income Clothes for Dignified Maturity.* You see what a different impression you get right away?

Honor Tracy

A Fresh Eye

With the first swallows of the year came Mr Bingham-Childs. A friend of us both had sent him along with a letter of introduction, begging me to show him Dublin. On reading it I gave a little whine of self-pity, for the immediate future seemed likely to be full of visits to Guinness's Brewery, the National Museum and other historic edifices in which no resident normally sets foot; but there was no need for anxiety. Mr Bingham-Childs merely wished to absorb the atmosphere and to meet Dublin intellectuals, of which he understood there were a great number.

He was a young man with a cheerful rosy face and blue untroubled eyes which he fixed unwinkingly upon me as he outlined his views on the Irish situation. Ireland has been explained to me by English visitors more times than I can remember, but the savour of it never grows any less. He had been in the country some forty-eight hours and was bemused with love and admiration. Further, he was obsessed with guilt at the sorrows of Irish history for which he appeared to feel in some way directly responsible. Mr Bingham-Childs so obviously could never have hurt a fly that I felt bound to intervene at this. Let him forget about Irish history, I urged, for the simple reason that Irish history did not really exist. People who cannot tell you accurately what happened next door last week have no history: they make do instead with legend and myth which are both more amusing and more advantageous.

I described to him a conversation I once had with a National teacher, over which I ponder to this day. The earnest young man had assured me that one of the great blessings of the English withdrawal from Ireland was that now at last, after centuries of mystification, history could be properly taught in schools.

Myth, propaganda, superstition – except that approved by the Church – all had been swept away, and wholesome fact had taken their place. I asked him at what moment in time he would begin the story of this land and he answered, gravely, from when the Phoenicians conquered it by weaving their magic spells.

And for my own part, I told Mr Bingham-Childs, sorrowfully wagging my head, I had too often watched the events of ordinary life around me gradually assume in reminiscence the colour and the radiance of a folk-tale to read the accounts of things far off with anything but a tranquil and pleasurable disbelief.

'Oh *but* . . .' said Mr Bingham-Childs.

His voice flowed easily on. I began to fear that as we moved about together he might involve us in awkward scenes. Once I had journeyed late at night from Killiney to Dublin in a crowded bus with a pair of English Mass Observers. The female, who was if anything slightly the more dotty, had been descanting on Irish wrongs and Saxon wickedness in exactly this strain and at the top of a voice that put one in mind of a cockatoo. We were at the rear of the bus; at the front and greatly the better for drink was an old I.R.A. gunman who, maddened by the English accent, presently made his way towards us. An altercation followed, with the I.R.A. man abusing the female Mass Observer for just these wrongs which, from the height of her parlour pinkery, she was so freely deploring. She saw herself as the lately emancipated victim of the same wicked forces as had plagued and tormented and beggared Ireland: he saw her as merely another quacking Saxon. Her sympathies were plainly modifying themselves as the discussion proceeded; and it ended, to my mingled joy and terror, with the debauched veteran falling heavily into her lap.

An evening at the Abbey Theatre seemed a good point of departure and Mr Bingham-Childs brightened as the suggestion was made. He remarked at once that one of his aims in visiting Dublin was to see at last some really good plays, after all the tawdry nonsense of the West End of London. Audiences, he gravely continued, were a factor of the highest importance too: he should welcome the opportunity of sitting in one that was really intelligent and critical. I began to feel as if our positions were reversed and it was he who was showing me around.

Both the title of the play we saw and the name of its author escape my memory but it was rich in P.Q. or Peasant Quality, an attribute hard to define but greatly prized by the theatre directors. The curtains went up on the dim smoky interior of a cabin in 'the wesht' with an aged crone huddled over the fire, passing remarks of a typically racy kind. Ragged figures came and went: a bottle circulated: there was a struggle. The upshot of it all, as I remember, was that somebody got the better of somebody else.

Mr Bingham-Childs greatly enjoyed the whole thing. A nice thing about the true-blue English visitor is that he not only approaches the Abbey expecting to see a worth-while play but leaves it convinced that he has done so. In the intervals we repaired to a neighbouring bar where we fell in with a jovial stranger who explained that England's wars had all been won, as her literature had been written, by Irishmen; with which my companion fully agreed. He stood erect with shining eyes for 'The Soldier's Song' at the end of the performance. He was a little disappointed to learn that Dublin could offer nothing in the way of a nocturnal life. He had expected apparently to find some kind of an Irish Montparnasse along the banks of the Liffey with a row of brightly lit cafés where the wit flashed back and forth in perpetual scintillation. But such was his equable and unassuming nature that he accepted a Milk Shake in one of the ice cream parlours along O'Connell Street, all that the city could offer at that hour, without a word of reproach.

My services were not to be required on the following day as he was beginning his round of the Dublin intelligentsia. He had made an appointment for coffee at eleven o'clock with a man whose distinguished name was so familiar to me that when at eleven-thirty a plaintive voice inquired for me on the telephone I was not in the least surprised.

'He said the Oriental Café in Grafton Street,' the voice explained. 'I suppose I *am* in the right place?'

He gave details of his position and I assured him there was no mistake.

'That's all right, then,' said the voice with relief in it.

At ten minutes past twelve it was back again, subdued and flattened, and asked what I was doing for lunch. Nothing, I said, and we made an appointment for half past one. Then I leaned back in my chair and fell into a meditation. Is there anything truly wrong in the little harmless white lies that bring peace and joy to honest men? Mr Bingham-Childs had sounded full of the dejection of a nice child whose toy has been snatched from its hand. His pleasure in Dublin ought not to be spoiled for want of a word from me. I picked up the telephone and, having got through to Davy Byrnes, inquired if by any chance the missing intellectual were on the premises. By a coincidence he was; and I begged him to tell me if he happened to know the whereabouts of a Mr Bingham-Childs.

'He's here incognito, scouting for the B.B.C.,' I said. 'Mind you, I've said nothing.'

A silence followed these words during which the very wire seemed to be vibrating with emotion.

'Did you say the B.B.C.?' the intellectual presently asked, with a suspicion of hoarseness in his voice.

'That's it. Only he doesn't want it to leak out. He believes he will get a better idea of who's who in Irish culture by informal contact. Or so I hear.'

There was another silence.

'Well, if I come across him I'll let you know,' said the intellectual, casually. 'I don't think much of the B.B.C. myself, as you know, but I should like to be of assistance.'

Twenty minutes later Mr Bingham-Childs telephoned in high feather to say there had been a mix-up and would I think him very rude if he suggested our lunching some other day.

'His American agent had cabled urgently for an essay,' said Mr Bingham-Childs in awed tones. 'He hadn't even the time to put me off. All he could do was hurl himself at his typewriter and compose.'

'Much of the best work gets done that way,' I said. 'Would you mind not telling him that you've been in touch with me?'

'Why ever not?'

'In this part of the world it is better when the left hand doesn't know what the right hand is up to.'

'*O how delightfully odd.*'

Nothing more was seen of him in the next days: serenely he had plunged into the uncharted morass of Dublin cultural life, supported only by faith and innocence. News trickled in: he had lunched here, dined there, boozed up somewhere else: he had been seen to purchase a copy of *The Face and Mind of Ireland* by Mr Arland Ussher: he was said to have been invited – and the rumour set my mind at rest completely – to the home of a celebrated literary lawyer.

I was impatient to learn what he was making of it all. For all his candour he gave the impression of being nobody's fool and at some moment the salient fact of Irish letters to-day must surely catch his eye: that in Ireland there are dozens of brilliant writers and few, quite remarkably few, manuscripts. The Englishman assumes that the existence of the first will lead to the production of the second, an attitude which reveals the gulf between English and Irish modes of thought. The Irishman deplores this vulgar insistence on achievement. He feels that it is a splendid thing to be a writer and that little or nothing is added to it by writing: even, indeed, that it might be a grave mistake.

There are of course modern Irish writers, and fine ones, who have so far broken with custom as to produce books; but they are not a patch on the others. And they have put their cards on the table, the last thing a man should do if he wants to keep a reputation in Dublin. It is all very well to fulminate briefly against every one and everything in the pages of an obscure and short-lived magazine from time to time. You can dismiss the Victorians or the Russians in a paragraph, you can in your haphazard little review describe *The Times Literary Supplement* as 'semi-literate' and still leave your own mysterious potentialities intact: you will be reverently quoted by members of your own coterie in further short papers and savagely assailed by the others and it is all great fun; but once you put pen to paper at length and for years on end you give the game away and expose yourself to withering blasts of scorn.

Other, graver snags lie in the path of the Irish writer. There is the difficulty of finding new subjects in a small empty country where everything seems to have been chewed over and over again to the point of nausea. There is the censorship and behind the censorship the hosts of wavering, impure minds that acquiesce in it and make it possible. It is in fact that horrid mentality, and not the small committee that sits in Dublin gravely adding title after title to an already fantastic list, that kills literature. A young man may produce a book that is perfectly honest and fresh and sincere and some pious yahoo may get hold of it, read it with but a partial understanding, mark a few passages that he deems perilous to faith and morals – of which he very likely has neither – and forward it with zeal to the censors. The words 'banned in Ireland' are something of a joke abroad but it is not so easy to smile them away at home. There may be social unpleasantness and repercussions in business affairs for the author; and in any case his natural and proper audience has gone. It is true that banned books can be ordered directly from England and will in all likelihood come safely through the Customs, but that is possible only to people with the means and, as it were, in the know: there is a touch of the black market about it. Such books will not be found in Irish bookshops or in public libraries; and they will be read by the wrong people for the wrong reasons, passed lovingly and furtively from hand to hand like those treasured copies of muck-raking Sunday newspapers that Irish servant girls in England send home to their fathers, hidden away in the leaves of the *Catholic Herald*.

The first unexpected brush with that rancid Irish puritanism, that fear and hatred of life, is a bitterly wounding experience and one that may even sour a new talent into silence. And if the young author tries again one of two things may happen, both detrimental. He can give in and work his passage back to respectability by saying what he doesn't mean. Or he can 'give them something to bloody well ban me for' which is another way of saying what he doesn't mean and so of spoiling his work. In the latter case his public henceforward will be mainly English and American, that is to say, cannot really know what he is talking about; and there is a danger of his ending up as a buffoon or a whimsical purveyor of 'Oirish' charm. The most difficult thing for an Irish writer to do is to go calmly on and say what he wants to say without troubling himself as to whom it will please or annoy.

This has all been noted before, of course, and will be noted again at frequent intervals for centuries to come.

Mr Bingham-Childs telephoned again: he had just been talking to the Irish La Rochefoucauld.

'Such wit! A mind like a rapier! If his books are anything like his conversation . . .'

'He hasn't written any.'

'No? Really? How extraordinary. Teeming with ideas . . . so refreshing . . . some of his conceptions are amazing. He said the universe will come to an end presently because no one will believe in it any longer. Or stop, was it that? No, hang it, I've got it wrong. But he had me spellbound . . . spellbound . . .'

In the evening he telephoned again to say that in his opinion Dublin was the Athens of the modern world. From then on indeed he telephoned every day afresh, bubbling over with the joy of his discoveries: and with each preposterous statement I was able to stick another little flag mentally on the map of the battlefield.

One of the things that he may have enjoyed the most, as an utter change from the sober intellectual habits of his own country, was the note of positive affirmation. It is to be met with not only in Dublin but through the whole of Ireland, is indeed one of the strongest and happiest of Irish attributes. The newspapers breathe it out in great rosy puffs: the clergy fan it on every possible occasion: among the nationalists it rises to a pitch that leaves one speechless with wonder. For instance, you may read in a pamphlet advocating the spread of the Irish language and the boycott of English books and papers that the Gaelic culture is the supreme achievement of Europe. Many of us will be on delicate ground here, for we may not be as familiar with Gaelic culture as, evidently, we ought to be. We shall no doubt have heard the language spoken at odd times: the occasional careful halting speech in the Dáil, a gossip in a bus between two Christian Brothers carried on with a maximum of self-consciousness and – as one Gaelic scholar avers – a minimum of proper syntax, or the rough talk of peasants in the west. 'Patois rauque, exhumé du fonds des siècles,' wrote a Frenchman after an experience of the kind, but that is simply the view of one man. Not all of us are qualified to consider the claim of the militant Gael nor to weigh his culture against that of Greece or Rome, of mediaeval Christendom or the Italy of the Renaissance. And certain special obstacles often lie in the way of any one attempting to do so. Once I read, in no nationalist leaflet but a restrained and judicious textbook, that the old Irish music was the finest and sweetest in the world and, old melomaniac that I am, pricked up my ears in joyous anticipation: but they dropped again at once. 'Unfortunately,' the writer went on to say, 'not a single note of it has been preserved.' There would be nothing for it but to accept the supremacy of Irish music by faith, as clearly the writer had done, but this is possible only for certain types of mind. All this is not to the point, however; our ignorance, our doubts, our hesitations are neither here nor there: the beauty of the thing and the special grace of this fiery Gael lie in the fact that he is as unaware of the other elements in European culture as we of his and yet, simply and superbly, he arranges them in their order of precedence.

And here perhaps a tribute should be paid to the liberating influence of the Catholic education. The other side of the picture is only too familiar: the repression, the cramping effect of dogma, the staleness created in men's minds when they feel themselves in possession of the final and absolute truth. Yet the Catholic enjoys a mental freedom unknown to members of other sects and, above all, to those who describe themselves as free-thinkers. From his childhood he has been wont to accept without exam-ination statements that on the face of them are absurd. His mind is free from those habits of scrutiny and analysis which shackle the brains of other men. When therefore the patriot utters his declaration on Irish music or Gaelic culture: or if an eminent ecclesiastic should state, not as a matter of conjecture but of fact, that the Virgin Mary was five foot seven inches, weighed seven stone, had blue eyes and hair that was a 'class of mahog-any': he is simply offering a truth which has been revealed to him and he would as soon think of arguing it out with a sceptic with all the tedious concomitants of fact and figure as he would of questioning the infallibility of the Pope.

When Mr Bingham-Childs telephoned next, I asked if he was ever likely to have an evening free.

'Oh yes: I've seen much less of you than I should have liked. But you do understand? This has been such a wonderful experience . . . welcomed everywhere . . . never thought it possible . . .'

'I want to take you to the Pearl Bar. It's where the cream of Dublin intelligence assembles. You can see them all together at once.'

'And you know them all?' cried the eager voice.

'More or less.'

'Ah!'

The lounge of the Pearl Bar was not yet very full as we climbed up to it the following evening. It looked indeed fuller than it was, owing to the presence of the editor of the *Irish Times*. This huge gentleman possessed the gift not only of creating by himself the sense of a party but of bestowing on the whole bar a distinguishing air: without him, it became something quite different. Vast, genial, he would sit there by the hour, his comfortable frame shaking with laughter at the sallies of his companions, and draw sagely at his pipe; but should one enter whom he really wished to avoid this seemingly inert, apparently rooted, mass would suddenly vanish, now here, now gone, with the amazing finality of a Bodily Assumption.

'Who's that?' whispered Mr Bingham-Childs.

No introduction could be made for the moment since, near the large friendly editor, sat another of a different kind. His paper was the most widely read and perhaps the sourest of all the Catholic publications in Ireland. Moral reprobation was a feature of it; and once indeed I had been mildly vexed to find myself described in it by a clerical gentleman as 'a mouth spewing obscenity and blasphemy'. The worthy cleric, who was no doubt of a practical rather than a literary bent, had failed to grasp the point of something I had written and was unable to contain himself. To me it seemed that the little episode released us from all mutual social obligations, a view which the editor, to judge from his effusiveness on the sole occasion that I was trapped into meeting him, did not share. Nor was it in fact a properly Dublin view. There is a peculiar frivolity about the whole of life in Dublin; nothing matters, nothing is serious, least of all what any one thinks or says. And this is perhaps as it should be, since no one thinks what he says or says what he thinks. It was suggested to me, for that matter, in defence of this individual that he possibly never meant what he said or allowed to be published. A lively discussion had followed as to whether this would make him worse or better, and ended inconclusively.

I steered Mr Bingham-Childs to a table, avoiding corners – one should never let oneself be cornered in the Pearl – and choosing a site from which a fast retreat would be possible and which yet afforded a wide view of the room.

One of Dublin's major poets immediately joined us, with a thirsty look on his face. He was glad to depend on our kindness that evening because the confidence he felt in certain racehorses had turned out to have been misplaced. This in no way reflected on his judgement: as a wise old lady once observed, in Irish racing the things to consider are the owner, the jockey and the horse and you need to know what is passing in the minds of all three before you lay down a shilling. Yet the pain of the loss itself had cast a shadow over his mind and he launched, in his beautiful voice, a diatribe against Ireland and all her works, her passion for mediocrity, her crucifixion of genius: he lamented the passing of his best years among marshmen and Firbolgs: he threatened to shake the dust of her off his feet and to seek his living henceforward in strange places among foreign men.

Mr Bingham-Childs murmured something about oases of Christian culture in a world distracted by materialism and the voice was hushed and over the craggy peasant face stole a look of infinite compassion. Its owner applied himself without uttering again to his Guinness as being of its own nature permanently and unassailably good and left as soon as he had finished it.

An unknown young man came up and waved a wad of grimy paper at us.

'I've written a pome,' he remarked. 'Will I read it?'

'By all means,' said Mr Bingham-Childs, companionably. I began almost to wish he had been the more usual kind of tourist.

'But you will sign me up?' proceeded the youth.

'I beg your pardon?'

'Sign me up. The way you signed **** up. Didn't you sign **** up?'

'I haven't signed any one up. I don't think I know what you mean.'

'Then isn't he the biggest bloody liar in the world?' and the stranger flounced indignantly away.

Seeing myself poised, as so often before, on the brink of exposure I began hurriedly to explain what might have been in the poet's mind. The word of my friend's presence was sure to have gone round Dublin and it was likely that some people might have put a wrong construction on his interest in cultural affairs. The belief that in Ireland a rich vein of talent was waiting to be opened up was very persistent abroad, and publishers and agents were in the habit of coming over in relays to scout for themselves. They would stay a week or so and leave delightedly, fed with promises of dramas, poems, novels and brilliant new interpretations of James Joyce. Perhaps it had been assumed that Mr Bingham-Childs was one of them? since a pure disinterested love of Irish letters was new in Dublin experience. If so, I urged, the thing to do was to play up in order not to cause disappointment and give offence: did he agree?

To my relief Mr Bingham-Childs, laughing merrily, agreed. Yet even as he laughed there was a gleam in his eye that was not of pure amusement, or rather it was of an amusement extended some little way beyond the immediate joke and, therefore, disquieting. One of the many articles of Irish faith to which I have never subscribed is that all Englishmen are very very simple. I had seen that gleam in English eyes before and most often indeed as they rested on an Irish object.

The familiars of the Pearl were making their appearance one by one. In trotted a gnome with a face like a bottom and his hair *en brosse*, celebrated even in Dublin for the malignant venom of his attacks on all and sundry. Next came an Anglo-Irishman of letters with a mad light in his pale eyes, carrying with an air of decision and importance a briefcase that bulged with sandwiches and pyjamas. A literary editor with an air of gentle, refined melancholy about him. More poets. Some playwrights. Lawyers. One gaolbird. Civil Servants. Some of this crowd showed signs of incipient persecution mania, due to their having in fact at one time or another been persecuted. A drunk reeled from one table to the next trying to find some one who would listen once more to the tale of an ancient wrong. A little haze of cigarette smoke settled over the room. The bar boys ran hither and thither with their trays like men distracted.

Gradually, imperceptibly, yet steadily, a tide was flowing our way. My companion seemed to possess a kind of lunar attraction. People I barely knew strolled up and complained that it was a long time since we had met. Drinks were bought in a freehanded style unparalleled in my memory. Invitations to lunch and dinner were issued for any day, any time, and with the proviso that my nice English friend should come as well. It was in the nature of a small triumph.

I became engrossed for some little time in an anecdote, muttered by a neighbour into my ear, concerning the Archbishop of Dublin and when I turned back to the party as a whole it was to find that Mr Bingham-Childs was throwing himself into the game with an abandon of which one would have supposed him incapable. He was, if not by Dublin standards drunk, noticeably elated; and with a splendid lunatic gravity was dishing out contracts right and left. In nothing did he reveal his subtlety, equally unsuspected heretofore, so much as in the fact that he left the exact nature and scope of these contracts undefined. Each of his victims clearly believed himself to have been 'signed up'; yet at no moment did Mr Bingham-Childs make any concrete proposal or volunteer any information as to whom he was allegedly representing. It was a masterpiece, a *tour de force*: it proved once again that when an Englishman puts his mind to it he can be more wickedly Irish than anything that ever came out of Ireland: and at the end of the evening, as the lights went up and down and the cries of 'Now, gentlemen, please!' grew even more urgent, the honest blue eyes were wide and calm as before.

Humbled, as we all must be in the presence of a master, I crept through the dark streets at his side. The following day was to be his last among us: we therefore took leave of each other.

'I only wish I could have done more to enliven your stay,' I told him.

'But you did a great deal, a great deal! More than I had any right to expect,' he cried, expansively.

Then he gave a deprecating little giggle.

'I may be silly, you know, but I'm conscious!'

It was precisely as I had feared, all the way along.

Kingsley Amis

Age-old Ceremony at Mumbles

'Now, let's see, you must be Mr Ames,'[1] the manager said, looking at one of the pieces of paper in the large sheaf he held.

'Amis is my name,' I said for perhaps the five thousandth time in my life. Often, of course, I just let it ride, depending on how I feel.

'Right, now this is Mrs Roberts,' he said. A plump smiling lady in an orange hat shook my hand. 'Like you to meet Mr Ames,' he added.

This time I let it ride, especially since somebody was giving me a glass of whisky at that moment.

'Shall we have a look at the forms?' Mrs Roberts said. 'It's quite straightforward. We mark them for General Appearance, Beauty of Face and Teeth, Attractiveness and Beauty of Hair (I'm going to keep my highest marks for the natural blondes, I don't know about you), then Figure (that's where you men come in, isn't it?) and Deportment. They do that downstairs.'

'What sort of marks do we give them?' I asked. 'Supposing we get an absolute smasher, how many –?'

Mrs Roberts vigorously explained to me what ten out of ten meant, and how it came about that five such sets of marks gave

---

1   The late Evelyn Waugh shared the manager's view of the pronunciation of my surname. An acquaintance told me how he once asked Waugh: 'What do you think of Kingsley Amis?'

'Ames,' said Waugh.

'Amis, actually.'

'You mean Ames.'

'Look, I happen to know him, and he pronounces it Amis.'

'The man's name is Ames,' said Waugh, so firmly that the discussion of my works was broken off at that point.

a possible maximum of fifty. I then met the other three judges. By the use of great cunning I wormed out of them what their occupations were, for I had already decided, naturally, that the occasion of the selection and crowning of the Mazda Queen of Light (Swansea Heat) would have to be written up. The trio who confronted me were the editor of a South Wales newspaper, the wife of a police sergeant and the wife of a director of the Casino Ballroom, Mumbles. This last structure was the scene of tonight's competition, and the office of its manager, the small earnest man with rimless glasses who had known at the start what my name was, had been set aside for the judging and the preliminary drinking in which I was now engaged. The room was small and meagrely furnished, except for a table, five chairs and a great number of bottles.

The manager got us sitting down, drove some of the supers from the room and brought the contestants in to pick their numbers. 'It'll give you a kind of preview, you see,' he told us.

'What do you think of them?' I muttered after a minute to the editor.

'Well, there's nothing to start a riot there, eh?' he said.

It was true. With exceptions, the entrants were such as to arouse mild wonder that they were indeed entrants for a beauty contest. (The same thought struck me last night while I was watching the selection of Miss World on television. None of the six finalists, as far as I could tell, would have looked much out of their element in, let us say, first-year English at the University College of Swansea.) All this lot were blondes, as they had to be to enter at all. This was less rigorous than might appear, since, in the words of the hand-out, 'you could decide to become blonde for the contest or you could have changed to blonde because it suited you', though Condition 6 added rather grimly: 'Competitors must agree to remain blonde for 12 months following the contest.'

This hand-out was informative in other ways, too. Until reading it I had no idea that in 1956 there will have been forty-eight preliminary heats, six regional finals and a Grand Final in this business, with over a thousand pounds in cash prizes. And before 1956 – but I cannot do better than recall the author of the hand-out and allow his historical sense and knowledge of the development of ritual to speak for themselves:

'The competition was first held in this country in 1954 when it reintroduced a popular ancient custom after a gap of hundreds of years ... The source and inspiration of the competition was originally provided by the fact that for thousands of years the blonde races of the North chose a "Queen of Light" each year to preside over their feasting on December 21 – the "shortest day and longest night" – when the old year turned its face to the coming spring. As with many other ancient customs, the churches eventually adopted the ceremony and "Queen of Light" celebrations were popular in Merrie England and continued without a break as national custom in Sweden.'

'I'll start bringing them in now,' the manager said. While we waited I first reflected that, in South Wales at any rate, 'now' is going the same way as 'presently' did in the seventeenth century, and then read through the forms on which the girls had entered some personal details. Ages ranged from seventeen to twenty, no further, though crones of up to thirty were admissible under the regulations. Occupations included salesgirl, cashier, secretary, typist, housewife, advertising and consigning clerk, and clerk. Favourite hobbies were the best. There was singing, dancing, swimming, dancing, ballet and ballroom dancing, dancing, swimming, and swimming and dancing. (Honest, now. That is the order I copied down on the ruled feint lines of my Challenge tablet.)

The girls started coming in. All were constrained in manner, and stood awkwardly smiling while the manager put them through a little rigmarole he had devised, first assuring them that they were among friends and then putting a string of questions to which 'Yes' was the almost invariable answer. 'It's really to show off their teeth, you see,' he explained during an interval. I had guessed that several of the girls would have made it a habit to go round beauty contests picking up what prizes they could, and this was confirmed, but their demeanour was notably at variance. 'You wouldn't think that that one was thirty-nine, would you?' Mrs Roberts said at the departure of the girl I had liked best. 'Oh no, sorry, that's her hips.'

There was a pause while the Deportment was being got ready in the ballroom itself. Hastily comparing notes, I found some evidence that the girls at present in the lead were those who came closest to the appearance of models in the women's magazines: neat, refined, underweight, on or over the brink of insipidity, over elegant as to hair. Sexual attractiveness, what there was of it, was not doing so well. 'That's the trouble when you get a crowd of women on the judges,' the editor murmured when I showed him my findings. 'I knew this would happen.'

For the Deportment the five of us sat at separate little tables spaced round the dance floor while the girls, after an inexplicable delay reminiscent of procedure in the Armed Forces, paraded about us. The girl I had liked best walked briskly round in the manner of someone going to catch a bus. I marked her up for that. All the others produced mild imitations, with varying embarrassment potential, of the film-star wiggle or the mannequin's slow march. I marked them all down for that. This part was accompanied by the band playing 'A Pretty Girl is Like a Melody', oddly enough, and by almost continuous applause, recommended over the loudspeakers by the manager and set going by a man in a maroon jacket who seemed virtually crazed with amiability. Eventually our mark-sheets were collected and handed to the local knight who, with his wife, had turned up to perform the actual coronation.

This ceremony I did not see, being unforewarned and in the bar at the time, but the editor was able to assure me that immediately afterwards the crown had fallen off the queenly head and bent itself slightly. This did not much recompense me for my chagrin at seeing the three leading women's magazine incarnations – none of them with a Swansea address and one from as far away as Barry – receiving their prizes of ten pounds, five pounds and three pounds and being marshalled for their photographs. The editor and I shook our heads in sad unison. 'Always the same when you get a crowd of women on the judges,' he said.

Back in the manager's office, where my wife and six friends were having a drink or two while they waited, I worked out from the mark-sheets that the girl I had liked best had come bottom and the girl I had liked next best had come next to bottom. This made me feel guilty and humiliated in some way. I looked up to see a man, doubtless one of the Mazda representatives, looking round the room with the expression of one about to ask just who the hell all these people were. Instead of that he said: 'Now has everybody got a drink they fancy?' In case they had not he pulled a fresh bottle of whisky out of a fuse-box.

Rather later I was summoned on to the balcony of the ballroom to have my photograph taken congratulating the new Queen of Light. 'Don't look at her, Mr Ames, look at me,' the manager said. 'Then it'll look as if you're looking at her, you see.'

'Let's have it a bit more informal,' the photographer said, pushing the Queen's stole down off her shoulders. 'That's more like it. Now stand a bit closer to her, would you? Put your arm round her waist. No, I don't think we need you quite as close as that.'

With the Queen standing as if carved out of dough, with myself grinning mindlessly at the manager, and to the accompaniment of hundreds of feet thundering in the veleta and the crashing of chairs being piled, the photograph was taken. 'Where will it appear?' I asked diffidently.

'Oh, nowhere,' somebody said. 'It's just for records, that's all.' This was untrue. A few days later the photograph appeared on the front page of the *Swansea Voice*. It shows the Queen as quite a sweet girl and myself as a broken-down comedian in the grip of satyriasis – looking, moreover, quite unmistakably at something out of the frame. But perhaps that is just as well.

If any blonde clerk or typist of eighteen with a passion for swimming and dancing is reading this, I can put her in the way of an easy ten pounds. As I write there are still quite a few heats to run. And there's always next year.

1956

POSTSCRIPT 1970: The interested will find a version of this incident in the poem 'Maunders' (cf. 'Mumbles'), in my verse collection *A Look Round the Estate* (Cape, 1967). The various dissimilarities between the two accounts, plus the nine-year gap between the dates of composition, afford a useful lesson on the relations of life and art.

Alan Ross

from *Coastal Lights*

Henry and Bill were long-time friends, but I doubt whether they ever had a meal together on their own initiative. They lived on opposite sides of London and were the kind of people, solitary in their work, who needed prodding from others to budge. Henry was by seven years the older of the two and in literary terms belonged to another generation. At the end of the war Henry was forty, Bill thirty-three. By the time Bill acquired some sort of public recognition, with his first novel, *The Body*, published in 1949, Henry had already written his best books and begun to run out of material. Between 1945 and the appearance of the first novels of Kingsley Amis and Alan Sillitoe, and of the plays of John Osborne, Bill was among the most prolific and admired of writers whose careers began during the war.

It was only after he had joined the fire service as a full-time fireman on the outbreak of war that Bill had started writing. He had worked briefly as a bank clerk, as an advertising copywriter and as a pianist in a club, so he said. He always seemed to me a terrible pianist, making whatever he played sound exactly the same, but perhaps the customers weren't fussy. Bill's father had been a naval architect, designing ships for the Russians as well as the Germans, and as a boy, before and after a spell at Uppingham, Bill had travelled all over Europe with him. I have on my desk as I write a silver anchor, given to me by Bill, a souvenir of one of his father's enterprises.

I must have first met Bill at John Lehmann's. He was then living in Swiss Cottage, at Buckland Crescent, and I, having left the Vaughan-Minton household, was nearby in Cavendish Avenue. My flatmate Vera was a friend of the fashion artist Ruth Sheradski, with whom Bill spent weekends. Bill's ground-floor flat opened on to a large garden, the lawn of which he rarely cut. As a result it was like looking on to a Douanier Rousseau jungle, through which at dusk bare-breasted women sometimes stalked. The flat itself was infested with snails, whose slimy trails left Jackson Pollock-like markings all over his floorboards.

Whatever deprivations in the way of cooking, comfort and company Bill may have suffered during the week were amply compensated for when he was with Ruth at her home in Chelsea. She gave elaborate dinner parties, encouraged his latent dandyism and was never other than sweetly solicitous and gentle. The fashion world in which Ruth moved – inhabited by designers such as Bunny Roger and Digby Morton, and by photographers like John French and Peter Rose Pulham – was never much to Bill's taste and he ended up becoming increasingly drunk and truculent. Sadly for all their friends their long relationship ended abruptly; Bill left Ruth Sheradski on a Saturday morning to go shopping and never returned. He rang us up that night at 1 a.m. to announce rather drunkenly that he was getting married. 'I'll put you over to Ruth,' he said, handing the telephone, so I thought, to Ruth Sheradski. But it was another Ruth who spoke, also rather drunkenly: an actress called Ruth Grundy. Bill did indeed marry her, and for a while they seemed very happy. They moved to Hamilton Terrace, had a son and generally prospered. But Ruth, though initially attractive and lively, unfortunately became as heavy a drinker as Bill, who would veer between complete abstinence and alcoholic bouts lasting several days. Soon the fur began to fly, and long before Bill died they were tearing each other to pieces. The last time I saw him, when he was in hospital with various complaints including terrible ulcers on his legs, he showed me a note left for him with the ward sister. It was from Ruth. 'I have torn up and thrown away all your notebooks, diaries and manuscripts, so if you ever come out you won't find anything.'

Of the more interesting writers of his generation Bill has suffered the most severe eclipse. I am not sure why this should be so, except that he was rather mannered in much, though not all, of his work. His early volumes of stories, *Fireman Flower* and *Something Terrible, Something Lovely*, were certainly influenced from *Coastal Lights*

by Kafka, a sense of undefined threat hanging over many of the characters. But with each book the Kafka resemblance diminished, Bill's own loving eye for topographical detail, his pleasure in the macabre and the bizarre, his delight in unusual words and people, combining to produce a flow of stories quite unlike anyone else's. His prose was cumulative in effect, the result of minute observations recorded in not quite the way one would expect.

In 1949 Bill published his first novel, *The Body*, which had a jacket by Ruth Sheradski. This part-hilarious, part-tragic study of a hairdresser driven crazy by jealousy became the *Evening Standard* Book of the Month, taking Bill into quite a different readership. He began to write more simply, often very comically; menace and disquiet were now replaced by quirkiness of behaviour, oddness of predicament. In a Sansom story setting counts for as much as character and it is scrutinized and described with a miniaturist's passion. The characters tend to be conventional, rather dull people, whose humdrum lives are totally changed by a sudden slight shift of circumstance. I don't recall Bill ever writing about men or women of much worldly consequence; certainly not about intellectuals, artists or high-powered professional people. What his characters are, in fact, rarely matters, what count are the intense feelings which they harbour and which drive them to uncharacteristic and strange acts. All writers are to an extent voyeurs, but Bill, in his concentrated, pressurized way, was more so than most; he was sleuth-like in his efforts to pick up clues, relentless in his pursuit of evidence.

Bill always carried a notebook and he was not shy of producing it to jot down something he had just thought of, heard or seen. When he was writing he would jig one foot up and down, like a Bengali tailor or bazaar vendor. I used to do the same.

After the success of *The Body*, Bill began to get lucrative commissions for travel articles. His fare paid, he managed to use these journeys also to write fictionalized travel sketches. These were collected in two volumes, *South* and *The Passionate North*, both remarkable for their skill in suggesting light, climate and landscape, and at the same time telling a convincing story with convincing foreign characters.

By the early 1960s Bill had written three more novels, more travel pieces, a book of ballads, and a large number of stories. These last were collected in a volume called *The Stories of William Sansom* and published in 1963 with a long introduction by Elizabeth Bowen. 'The writer has taken,' she wrote, 'and shown himself right in taking, a succession of calculated risks. He is not writing *for* effect, he is dealing *in* it, and masterfully.'

By now only V. S. Pritchett was comparable in talent as a writer of stories. There were two more collections, *The Ulcerated Milkman* and *The Marmalade Bird*, published seven years apart, but apart from the wonderful story 'Down at the Hydro', the stories of his last years lacked the strangeness and tension, the hallucinatory quality of his best work. The tone became obtrusively whimsical, playful in the faintly tiresome manner that Bill put on when he was getting drunk.

His behaviour in a bad mood was boring and indefensible. At one stage he was always being sick. During the brief reign of Malcom Muggeridge at *Punch* I undertook to do a piece on the Miss World contest and foolishly took Bill along to the ceremony. At the crucial moment, after the rattle of drums and in the silence before the announcement of the winners, I was appalled to hear the unmistakable preliminaries to Bill's throwing up. For about ten seconds there was no other sound in the place. Then, the vomit neatly deposited in his brown bowler, he was as right as rain and ready for the action. The ushers were less well disposed, and politely but firmly we were requested to leave. Only Philip Toynbee threw up more often and in more places than Bill.

It was not always as bad as that. I had to go into the London Clinic about the same time for a minor operation and Bill insisted on accompanying me. First, we would go to some fish place where there was singing and there were waitresses in black silk stockings and they made wonderful apple tart. It would be his treat.

We got there in good order, and the fish, the singing and the black silk stockings were all as promised. But the tart was off. By now Bill had drunk enough for any inadequacy or provocation to call for immediate retribution. Nothing on earth would stop him from sending for the head waiter, the manager, the proprietor, the landlord. He himself had declined the fish and the tart, saying he only wanted baked beans, which of course they did not have. Then he demanded *one* Brussels sprout, which, when produced, he ignored. As a consequence of this turbulence the dinner took a long time, and the situation was not enhanced by Bill's efforts to pull the waitress's knickers down each time she leaned over.

At last we were ready, the account settled. It was now long past the Clinic's requested admission time, but despite my protest Bill insisted that he himself would explain the reasons when we arrived. I knew what that would be like. Still, we sought out a taxi and set off. I tried to persuade him to take the taxi on but he would have none of it, it was his responsibility to see me safely in.

Once he had stumbled out of the taxi, the cool air must have gone to his head, for he suddenly plunged forward, grasping the revolving doors at the entrance. Under his full weight they gave way, propelling him at some speed into the foyer. There he slid to a stop, apparently out to the world, his brown bowler at his side. Simultaneously, the lift doors opened and an elderly, much made-up patient gingerly emerged, to be confronted with what seemed to be a corpse. A stretcher had to be found, for Bill had struck his head and was unconscious.

He appeared a day or two later at my bedside, in full Arab dress. Most of the clinic's patients at that time were Arabs, whose retinues squatted silently in the corridors. Since the Arabs tended to be rich rather than poor and paid lavishly, they were well looked after. I expressed some trivial complaint about the service to Bill, whereupon, breathing fumes of gin, he took it upon himself to give the nurses a severe reprimand in phoney Anglo-Arabic. They appeared impressed, especially since he had claimed princely status. On one occasion when he was with me we were interrupted by a piercing yell from the corridor. It turned out to be an Iraqi Brigadier returning from an unsuccessful visit to the lavatory; he had been operated on for piles the day before and forbidden to have a motion for at least forty-eight hours. Now he was stranded and in distress. The Floor

Sister came out and upbraided him for his disobedience. In pain though he was, the Brigadier, helped to his feet by Bill, himself in Arab dress, replied with some asperity, 'My dear lady, it has been my habit, every day of my adult life, to go to the Mess at noon, drink three martinis, lunch, and then have a shit, and I'm not going to change my habits now.' 'Then you're a very naughty boy,' the Sister replied, wagging a bony finger at him, 'and if you don't obey my orders you won't get another shit for at least a week.'

Bill's brown bowler: in the end it became part of him, like his checked, waisted suits, high-cut, lapelled waistcoats, elastic-sided boots. His suits were made in Newbury to a style and pattern of his father's, and he looked, with his neat beard and rather florid complexion, like a character out of Chekhov. On his bad days he could be taken for a bookmaker drowning his sorrows.

John Mortimer

from *Clinging to the Wreckage*

'Why have you such a slope-shouldered, belly-protuberant, stooping and deformed appearance? Answer me that, oh ye faithless and hunchbacked generation!'

The headmaster of my prep school looked very much like God. He had long, white, slightly curly hair, and was old and beautiful. He wore a dark suit which had shortish trousers showing the tops of his highly-polished black boots. He also spoke in God's prose, a mixture of the Old Testament and Rudyard Kipling's *Just So Stories*.

'Draw nigh and hearken to me, oh litter of runts and weaklings. I say unto you that you are round-shouldered through the wearing of braces! Unbutton your braces and cast them from you. Each boy to acquire a dark-blue elastic belt with a snake buckle, to be slotted neatly into the loops provided at the top of school shorts.'

'Dear Mummy,' I wrote, in the compulsory letter home, 'I don't like it here at all. I know it said braces on the clothes list, but we're not allowed braces any more. In fact we have to cast them from us. Noah told us this in assembly' (we were expected to call the staff by their nicknames; the headmaster's was 'Noah'). 'Could you send me a dark-blue belt with a snake buckle as quickly as you can?'

'What, gasping for breath, ye red-faced and pop-eyed generation?' Noah looked at us with amused contempt at the following week's assembly. 'Why do you show such clear signs of stomach contraction? Why are you an offence to the eye, all tied up like parcels? I say unto you, there will be no more belts or the wearing thereof. Abandon belts! Each boy to equip himself with a decent pair of sturdy elastic braces!'

'Dear Mummy,' I wrote, 'I still don't like it here. Would you please send me a new pair of braces as soon as you can? I cast mine aside and now I can't find them. And now I have to cast aside my belt ...'

Noah was also tremendously keen on iodine lockets. These were small china bottles, full of iodine, tied to a tape which, if worn round the neck at all times would, he was persuaded, prevent any known disease from bunions to botulism. We were all issued with these charms, which we used to fight with like conkers.

'I have noticed that some boys,' Noah looked sadly around him at assembly and sounded puzzled, 'have taken to wearing small pieces of broken china slung about their necks on a ribbon. I take this to be a primitive superstition, and calculated to ward off the evil eye. "Ham" will be giving us a talk with lantern-slides on African tribes who still cling to such irrational beliefs. This school is a Christian community. Cast aside the amulets, resist the mumbo-jumbo, or behold I will strike ye with my rod and terrible will be the striking thereof!'

I can't remember Noah taking a great part in our education. He bought a little carillon of bells which he hung outside the dining-room, and he used to summon us in to Sunday supper by playing tunes on them. He enjoyed this exercise and long after supper was over, indeed long after lights had been turned out, he would stand in the passage in his dark suit and highly-polished boots, delicately picking out tune after tune with a small hammer, smiling benevolently.

For its period the prep school was progressive. As I have said, we knew the staff by their nicknames. 'Shem' was the head-master's son, 'Ham' taught Latin and Greek to the top class, 'Japhet' played expertly on the banjolele and sang songs such as *Here we sit like birds in the wilderness* and *We left your baby on the shore*. He also taught us ballroom dancing and I spent a good deal of time being pushed steadily backwards by 'Japhet' to the tune of *Smoke Gets in Your Eyes* as he shouted, '*Chassé*, boy! *Chassé*, damn you!' Ham had shrapnel stuck in his head, which caused him to go periodically out of his mind and strafe us with textbooks and blackboard rubbers, attacks for which he was profoundly apologetic when he came to himself and the armistice was signed.

We were allowed many liberties: we could bicycle round the town and take boats out on the river. I early developed a pronounced allergy to any sort of organized sport which has been with me ever since. Perhaps it's because I was an only child, but I never have felt any sort of team spirit. Loyalty to the school to which your parents pay to send you seemed to me like feeling loyal to Selfridges: consequently I never cared in the least which team won, but only prayed for the game to be over without the ball ever coming my way. In the cricket season I learned there was a safe and far-away place on the field called 'deep' which I always chose. When 'Over' was called I simply went more and more 'deep' until I was sitting on the steps of the pavilion reading the plays of Noël Coward, whom I had got on to after Bulldog Drummond. All I wanted then was to be a star of musical comedy and come tap-dancing down a huge staircase in white tie and tails. I got a theatrical costumier's catalogue and wrote up for a silver-topped ebony cane and a monocle.

Future experience was to show me that my early distrust of sport was well founded. I was told of a public school where the lascivious butler used to change into games clothes and crouch behind a bush from which he would leap during the muddy confusion of a 'scrum down' and covertly join the game for the purpose of fondling the boys in an intimate manner. Sport, as I have discovered, fosters international hostility and leads the audience, no doubt from boredom, to assault and do grievous bodily harm while watching it. The fact that audiences at the National Theatre rarely break bottles over one another's heads, and that Opera fans seldom knee one another in the groin during the long intervals at Covent Garden, convinces me that the theatre is safer than sport. In my case the masters at my prep school agreed to the extent of sending me to the local repertory theatre with a bar of Fry's Mint Chocolate. In this way I saw most of the plays of Bernard Shaw, which must have been better than playing cricket.

*

At the beginning, when I was away at school, I was extremely lonely. Loneliness, however, the birthright of the only child, held no particular terrors for me. In the holidays, having built his new house near to our old country cottage, my father devoted almost all his spare time to a large garden, and as his eyes failed and the flowers and vegetables faded from his view, his gardening became more dedicated, until, when he could no longer see the results of his labours, but had to rely on my mother or me to describe the health of a dahlia or the wilt of a clematis, he spent every possible hour pricking out, or potting on, or groping for dead heads and trying to get a correct aim with his secateurs. He never welcomed visitors and would often ask my mother to lead him away into the undergrowth if they appeared at the gate, so a month or so would pass without our seeing anyone at all. My segregated education seemed to have driven some sort of wedge between me and Iris and the Mullard boys, so holidays were a solitary pleasure which I tried to carry on at school.

Being alone was easier, I had long ago discovered, if you became two people, the actor and the observer. The observer was always the same, the actor played many parts: an officer in the Foreign Legion, for instance, or a ruthless private detective with rooms in Half Moon Street, or a Brigadier in Napoleon's army. 'There he goes,' I was able to say about myself, even in the deeply unhappy days when I lolloped about a frozen football field, keeping as far as possible from the ball, 'cantering across the burning sands with his crack platoon of Spahis (ex-murderers, robbers and at least one Duke disappointed in love, but whoever asked questions of a Legionnaire?) in search of the tents of Mahmoud Bey, and a levelling of the score after the disgrace of Sidi Ben Oud.' Later my character became more sophisticated, as I came more under the influence of Noël Coward and Dornford Yates.

'*Sic vos non vobis mellificatis apes.* Translate, Mortimer.'

'Thus you don't make honey for yourselves, you apes, sir.' Mortimer drew a flat gold cigarette-case from the breast pocket of his immaculate grey, double-breasted jacket. He was bubbling with suppressed laughter: the answer had been deliberately misleading. With a tap the heavy case sprang open and he offered it to the bewildered little man at the blackboard. 'Turkish this side,' he said, 'and Virginian the other.'

Later still, when I made a friend, we inflicted our lies on each other. Childhood is a great time for lying. Later in life you may be able to boast of some real achievement or some extraordinary adventure, in childhood all must be supplied from the imagination. So I told my friend that I was the son of a Russian aristocrat, smuggled out of Moscow during the revolution, and had been kindly taken in by the simple English lawyer with whom I happened to live. I had a long story, a rare sporting fantasy, about walking along the tow-path at Hammersmith when the cox of the Oxford crew had a heart attack and, being then of the appropriate weight, steering the eight to victory in the Boat Race. More consistently, I pretended that my parents never stopped going to cocktail parties, bickering, throwing 'White Ladies' and 'Manhattans' into each other's faces and would soon be getting a divorce. If I had one clear ambition during those years it was to be the child of a broken home.

My friend was Bill Mann. I can't remember exactly how we met and when we found each other. Recently, standing side by side in the Gents of a London hotel, we at first failed to recognize each other, yet our relationship was very close. We were in business together and our business was the theatre. At first we merely talked about the plays we had seen. My father went to the theatre regularly, usually after consuming a leisurely four-course dinner at the 'Trocadero', which would mean his being led into the entertainment followed by me in a state of acute embarrassment and an Eton suit, somewhere about the middle of the first act. We always occupied seats in the front row of the stalls, so our arrival never passed unnoticed, either from the stage or the audience. Failing vision and a late start made the plots of new plays extremely hard for my father to follow and the show would be punctuated by deafening whispers of, 'What's happening now, Kath? Go on, paint me the picture!' With Shakespeare of course he had no problem and could remember all the quotations and say lines aloud and with great relish seconds before the actors. Once a year we would go to Stratford and see all the productions. We stayed at an hotel in which the bedrooms were called after plays and decorated with ancient engravings of blood-curdling scenes from the major tragedies. One night I was kept awake by a violent quarrel coming from 'Romeo and Juliet' next door. On another I was frozen with fear at a curiously ghoulish engraving of the witches in *Macbeth*. I turned my eyes from the picture to the wardrobe mirror only to be stricken to a more permanent immobility by the sight of a frightful phantom, product, no doubt, of the witches' cauldron, consisting only of two pale spindly legs and white hooded blur. I had been standing for a long while before I realized that I was looking at the reflection of myself taking off my shirt.

So I had a good many theatrical experiences to discuss with Bill Mann. I could tell him much about the plays I had seen and even more about those I hadn't. As a future music critic of *The Times*, he could tell me about concerts and operas which were then, and remained for many years, a subject of total mystery to me, my father's idea of a musical experience being to repeat Shakespearean quotations or sing several verses of *Pretty little Polly Perkins of Paddington Green*.

After long theatrical discussions, during which we drew out the seating plans for most of the London theatres, we decided to put on plays at my home during weekend visits. This excitingly entailed writing off for review sketches and printed paper scenery from Samuel French Limited, but there were several dangers in inviting my friend home. He would inevitably be exposed to certain disgraceful facts about my family which I had been at pains to conceal, such as the immovable solidity of my parents' marriage, the glaring absence of a cocktail-shaker and my father's growing blindess. These things must have been obvious to Bill Mann, but he was too polite to mention any of them. However I noticed him staring at my mother's finger-nails, which I had described to him as very long and painted green, and taking in the fact that they were rather blunt and chipped from a good deal of potting up.

We put on a review we had written called *Champagne Cocktail* and one we bought from Samuel French called *Airy Nothings*. We stood on the dining-room stairs in bedspreads and pink paper shakos and sang selections from Ivor Novello. We did a play I wrote where we acted the ghosts of two young subalterns killed on the Somme. Whenever she heard that we were going to do what my father called 'An entertainment' my mother would give a little cry of horror at the thought of all the clearing up. When we played the two ghostly officers we laughed so much that we felt compelled to run into the kitchen to eat cold roast potatoes smeared with honey, a dish we thought would be disgusting enough to bring us to our senses.

Back at school the theatrical productions were better regulated and very well done. Each year we did a Shakespeare play and a Gilbert and Sullivan opera, and by a process of extreme democracy, of which the left wing of Equity would approve, the plays were cast by popular vote. In our last year Bill Mann was elected to play Bunthorne and I won Richard II. By that time the school had become, for me, a place of glorious excitement. I lay awake at night repeating:

> For God's sake, let us sit upon the ground
> And tell sad stories of the death of kings

and hardly slept. The masters either attacked us savagely or put on concerts for us, evenings when we drank cider-cup and they sang, to the unaccompanied banjolele, *Olga Pulloffski the Beautiful Spy, Abdul the Bulbul Ameer* and *Gertie the Girl with the Gong*. I fell violently in love with a tow-haired small boy called Jenks who reminded me of the signed photograph of Annabella I had written up for. He promised to be faithful to me forever, but when I last saw him he was with his wife and four children at London airport. No time in my life was ever as exciting or triumphant as the term I put up for Richard II and won the election.

Through all this excitement Noah moved in a mysterious way. He had to deal with a major problem. A boy called Ramsden, who never said much in class, put a tin chamber-pot on his head and no one could get it off. To avoid public derision Ramsden was moved from the dormitory to the sanatorium. The doctor was sent for and the school carpenter, but no solution was found.

In order to subdue public disquiet Noah would issue a bulletin at almost every meal about the progress of the crisis.

'Ramsden may think he has done something extremely clever,' Noah boomed sadly. 'He may think he has drawn attention to himself in some unusual and original manner. Oh ye of little judgement, would you laugh at Ramsden? What he has done is just very silly and dangerous. He is missing lessons, which will put him well behind for the School Cert. He is causing the unhappy couple who gave birth to him needless anxiety. So I say unto you, go about your daily business, work hard and do your best in the class-room and at school sports. Do not pay Ramsden the compliment of whispering about him in corridors. His exploits are best forgotten.'

In fact Ramsden, when we peered at him through a crack in the sanatorium door, presented an unforgettable spectacle. He was sitting bolt upright in bed, wearing striped flannel pyjamas, his ears flattened by a huge chamber-pot of chipped enamel, his face decorated by a grin that was at once sheepish and proud. At a subsequent meal Noah reassured us. 'A man has been sent for,' he announced. 'Expert in these matters. It is to be hoped that in due course Ramsden will be released. Every boy to remember, this is no subject for laughter!' That afternoon a man in dungarees with a bag of tools drove up in a van, and later on an uncrowned Ramsden rejoined the class and resumed his habitual 'low profile'.

Gerald Durrell

from *My Family and Other Animals*

We threaded our way out of the noise and confusion of the Customs shed into the brilliant sunshine on the quay. Around us the town rose steeply, tiers of multi-coloured houses piled haphazardly, green shutters folded back from their windows, like the wings of a thousand moths. Behind us lay the bay, smooth as a plate, smouldering with that unbelievable blue.

Larry walked swiftly, with head thrown back and an expression of such regal disdain on his face that one did not notice his diminutive size, keeping a wary eye on the porters who struggled with his trunks. Behind him strolled Leslie, short, stocky, with an air of quiet belligerence, and then Margo, trailing yards of muslin and scent. Mother, looking like a tiny, harassed missionary in an uprising, was dragged unwillingly to the nearest lamppost by an exuberant Roger, and was forced to stand there, staring into space, while he relieved pent-up feelings that had accumulated in his kennel. Larry chose two magnificently dilapidated horse-drawn cabs, had the luggage installed in one, and seated himself in the second. Then he looked round irritably.

'Well?' he asked. 'What are we waiting for?'

'We're waiting for Mother,' explained Leslie. 'Roger's found a lamp-post.'

'Dear God!' said Larry, and then hoisted himself upright in the cab and bellowed, 'Come *on*, Mother, come on. Can't the dog wait?'

'Coming, dear,' called Mother passively and untruthfully, for Roger showed no signs of quitting the post.

'That dog's been a damned nuisance all the way,' said Larry.

'Don't be so impatient,' said Margo indignantly; 'the dog can't help it . . . and anyway, we had to wait an hour in Naples for *you*.'

'My stomach was out of order,' explained Larry coldly.

'Well, presumably *his* stomach's out of order,' said Margo triumphantly. 'It's six of one and a dozen of the other.'

'You mean half a dozen of the other.'

'Whatever I mean, it's the same thing.'

At this moment Mother arrived, slightly dishevelled, and we had to turn our attentions to the task of getting Roger into the cab. He had never been in such a vehicle, and treated it with suspicion. Eventually we had to lift him bodily and hurl him inside, yelping frantically, and then pile in breathlessly after him and hold him down. The horse, frightened by this activity, broke into a shambling trot, and we ended in a tangled heap on the floor of the cab with Roger moaning loudly underneath us.

'What an entry,' said Larry bitterly. 'I had hoped to give an impression of gracious majesty, and this is what happens . . . we arrive in town like a troupe of medieval tumblers.'

'Don't keep *on*, dear,' Mother said soothingly, straightening her hat; 'we'll soon be at the hotel.'

So our cab clopped and jingled its way into the town, while we sat on the horsehair seats and tried to muster the appearance of gracious majesty Larry required. Roger, wrapped in Leslie's powerful grasp, lolled his head over the side of the vehicle and rolled his eyes as though at his last gasp. Then we rattled past an alley-way in which four scruffy mongrels were lying in the sun. Roger stiffened, glared at them and let forth a torrent of deep barks. The mongrels were immediately galvanized into activity, and they sped after the cab, yapping vociferously. Our pose was irretrievably shattered, for it took two people to restrain the raving Roger, while the rest of us leaned out of the cab and made wild gestures with magazines and books at the pursuing horde. This only had the effect of exciting them still further, and at each alley-way we passed their numbers increased, until by the time we were rolling down the main thoroughfare of the town there were some twenty-four dogs swirling about our wheels, almost hysterical with anger.

'Why doesn't somebody *do* something?' asked Larry, raising his voice above the uproar. 'This is like a scene from *Uncle Tom's Cabin.*'

'Why don't *you* do something, instead of criticizing?' snapped Leslie, who was locked in combat with Roger.

Larry promptly rose to his feet, snatched the whip from our astonished driver's hand, made a wild swipe at the herd of dogs, missed them, and caught Leslie across the back of the neck.

'What the hell d'you think you're playing at?' Leslie snarled, twisting a scarlet and angry face towards Larry.

'Accident,' explained Larry airily. 'I'm out of practice ... it's so long since I used a horse-whip.'

'Well, watch what you're bloody well doing,' said Leslie loudly and belligerently.

'Now, now, dear, it was an accident,' said Mother.

Larry took another swipe at the dogs and knocked off Mother's hat.

'You're more trouble than the dogs,' said Margo.

'Do be careful, dear,' said Mother, clutching her hat; 'you might hurt someone. I should put the whip down.'

At that moment the cab shambled to a halt outside a doorway over which hung a board with Pension Suisse inscribed on it. The dogs, feeling that they were at last going to get to grips with this effeminate black canine who rode in cabs, surrounded us in a solid, panting wedge. The door of the hotel opened and an ancient bewhiskered porter appeared and stood staring glassily at the turmoil in the street. The difficulties of getting Roger out of the cab and into the hotel were considerable, for he was a heavy dog, and it took the combined efforts of the family to lift, carry, and restrain him. Larry had by now forgotten his majestic pose and was rather enjoying himself. He leapt down and danced about the pavement with the whip, cleaving a path through the dogs, along which Leslie, Margo, Mother, and I hurried, bearing the struggling, snarling Roger. We staggered into the hall, and the porter slammed the front door and leant against it, his moustache quivering. The manager came forward, eyeing us with a mixture of apprehension and curiosity. Mother faced him, hat on one side of her head, clutching in one hand my jam-jar of caterpillars.

'Ah!' she said, smiling sweetly, as though our arrival had been the most normal thing in the world. 'Our name's Durrell. I believe you've got some rooms booked for us?'

'Yes, madame,' said the manager, edging round the still grumbling Roger; 'they are on the first floor ... four rooms and a balcony.'

'How nice,' beamed Mother; 'then I think we'll go straight up and have a little rest before lunch.'

And with considerable majestic graciousness she led her family upstairs ...

For some time Mother had greatly envied us our swimming, both in the daytime and at night, but, as she pointed out when we suggested she join us, she was far too old for that sort of thing. Eventually, however, under constant pressure from us, Mother paid a visit into town and returned to the villa coyly bearing a mysterious parcel. Opening this she astonished us all by holding up an extraordinary shapeless garment of black cloth, covered from top to bottom with hundreds of frills and pleats and tucks.

'Well, what d'you think of it?' Mother asked.

We stared at the odd garment and wondered what it was for.

'What is it?' asked Larry at length.

'It's a bathing-costume, of course,' said Mother. 'What on earth did you think it was?'

'It looks to me like a badly-skinned whale,' said Larry, peering at it closely.

'You can't *possibly* wear that, Mother,' said Margo, horrified, 'why, it looks as though it was made in nineteen-twenty.'

'What are all those frills and things for?' asked Larry with interest.

'Decoration, of course,' said Mother indignantly.

'What a jolly idea! Don't forget to shake the fish out of them when you come out of the water.'

'Well, *I* like it, anyway,' Mother said firmly, wrapping the monstrosity up again, 'and I'm going to wear it.'

'You'll have to be careful you don't get waterlogged, with all that cloth around you,' said Leslie seriously.

'Mother, it's *awful*; you can't wear it,' said Margo. 'Why on earth didn't you get something more up to date?'

'When you get to my age, dear, you can't go around in a two-piece bathing-suit ... you don't have the figure for it.'

'I'd love to know what sort of figure that was designed for,' remarked Larry.

'You really are *hopeless*, Mother,' said Margo despairingly.

'But I *like* it ... and I'm not asking you to wear it,' Mother pointed out belligerently.

'That's right, you do what you want to do,' agreed Larry; 'don't be put off. It'll probably suit you very well if you can grow another three or four legs to go with it.'

Mother snorted indignantly and swept upstairs to try on her costume. Presently she called to us to come and see the effect, and we all trooped up to the bedroom. Roger was the first to enter, and on being greeted by this strange apparition clad in its voluminous black costume rippling with frills, he retreated hurriedly through the door, backwards, barking ferociously. It was some time before we could persuade him that it really was Mother, and even then he kept giving her vaguely uncertain looks from the corner of his eye. However, in spite of all opposition, Mother stuck to her tent-like bathing-suit, and in the end we gave up.

In order to celebrate her first entry into the sea we decided to have a moonlight picnic down at the bay, and sent an invitation to Theodore, who was the only stranger that Mother would tolerate on such a great occasion. The day for the great immersion arrived, food and wine were prepared, the boat was cleaned out and filled with cushions, and everything was ready when Theodore turned up. On hearing that we had planned a moonlight picnic and swim he reminded us that on that particular night there was no moon. Everyone blamed everyone else for not having checked on the moon's progress, and the argument went on until dusk. Eventually we decided that we would go on the picnic in spite of everything, since all the arrangements were made, so we staggered down to the boat, loaded down with

Gerald Durrell

food, wine, towels, and cigarettes, and set off down the coast.
Theodore and I sat in the bows as look-outs, and the rest took
it in turn to row while Mother steered. To begin with, her eyes
not having become accustomed to the dark, Mother skilfully
steered us in a tight circle, so that after ten minutes' strenuous
rowing the jetty suddenly loomed up and we ran into it with a
splintering crash. Unnerved by this, Mother went to the opposite
extreme and steered out to sea, and we would eventually have
made a landfall somewhere on the Albanian coastline if Leslie
had not noticed in time. After this Margo took over the steering,
and she did it quite well, except that she would, in a crisis, get
flurried and forget that to turn right one had to put the tiller
over to the left. The result was that we had to spend ten minutes
straining and tugging at the boat which Margo had, in her
excitement, steered on to, instead of away from, a rock. Taken
all round it was an auspicious start to Mother's first bathe.

Eventually we reached the bay, spread out the rugs on the
sand, arranged the food, placed the battalion of wine-bottles in
a row in the shallows to keep cool, and the great moment had
arrived. Amid much cheering Mother removed her housecoat
and stood revealed in all her glory, clad in the bathing-costume
which made her look, as Larry pointed out, like a sort of marine
Albert Memorial. Roger behaved very well until he saw Mother
wade into the shallow water in a slow and dignified manner. He
then got terribly excited. He seemed to be under the impression
that the bathing-costume was some sort of sea monster that had
enveloped Mother and was now about to carry her out to sea.
Barking wildly, he flung himself to the rescue, grabbed one of
the frills dangling so plentifully round the edge of the costume,
and tugged with all his strength in order to pull Mother back to
safety. Mother, who had just remarked that she thought the
water a little cold, suddenly found herself being pulled backwards. With a squeak of dismay she lost her footing and sat
down heavily in two feet of water, while Roger tugged so hard
that a large section of the frill gave way. Elated by the fact
that the enemy appeared to be disintegrating, Roger, growling
encouragement to Mother, set to work to remove the rest of the
offending monster from her person. We writhed on the sand,

helpless with laughter, while Mother sat gasping in the shallows, making desperate attempts to regain her feet, beat Roger off, and retain at least a portion of her costume. Unfortunately, owing to the extreme thickness of the material from which the costume was constructed, the air was trapped inside; the effect of the water made it inflate like a balloon, and trying to keep this airship of frills and tucks under control added to Mother's difficulties. In the end it was Theodore who shooed Roger away and helped Mother to her feet. Eventually, after we had partaken of a glass of wine to celebrate and recover from what Larry referred to as Perseus's rescue of Andromeda, we went in to swim, and Mother sat discreetly in the shallows, while Roger crouched nearby, growling ominously at the costume as it bulged and fluttered round Mother's waist.

Robert Robinson

from *Prescriptions of a Pox Doctor's Clerk*

OUR BETTERS

In 1950, royal asides at public functions were printed in newspapers with the verbal elisions carefully subbed out. No royal person was allowed to say 'that's' or 'it's', they were always heard to speak the words in full. So that when – during his visit to the South Bank Exhibition – the King was handed a weather report which rather unnecessarily pointed out that it was raining, the *News Chronicle* got him down as saying, 'That Is Certainly Accurate.' On the same occasion, the Queen ('fascinated immediately by the 74-inch telescope') was heard – at least by the *Chronicle* man – to remark, 'What A Pity It Is Not Working.'

The words are recorded as though they aren't examples of speech so much as plucky imitations of it. Royalty has to talk (so the *Chronicle*'s message seems to go) because that's the primitive way you and I do it: left to themselves, they'd probably communicate by osmosis (an extension of the myth, rife among schoolboys, that the King and Queen never engaged in sexual congress, but produced children by methods that were very much more polite). But just because, by a wild act of graciousness, not to mention ventriloquial skill, they managed to adapt to our style, this was no excuse for listening too closely and overhearing those touches of the vernacular which might make a decent person feel he had startled his father by coming across him too suddenly in the lavatory.

The obligation felt by sub-editors to preserve this kind of

distance, while at the same time pretending it was all going down verbatim, led to the concoction of royal ad libs that sounded as if they were being delivered over the public address system at a railway station. When Queen Elizabeth copped a deserter who had had the bad luck to stray into her bathroom at Windsor Castle, the *Sunday Pictorial* told its 1950 readers that she said, 'What Are You Doing Here?' and in case they missed the point, added that she said it 'without losing the natural poise and dignity associated with her' (an MVO, one might have thought, for the amanuensis hiding behind the door). Having got him nicely in her sights, the Queen (according to the *Pic*) then sent the following impromptu ringing round the white tile: 'And now I will press this bell and have you turned over to the Castle guard. I advise you to serve your punishment like a man – and then serve your country like one.' A clear case (if you took the *Pic*'s account literally) of a malefactor being cornered by a Speak-Your-Weight machine.

Perhaps the style was set by the royal speech writers. In 1950, it was still mandatory on royal persons to make statements that could be guaranteed to yield no meaning. 'When you leave school,' Princess Margaret was heard to say at a 1950 Speech Day, 'you will all go your different ways. But I know that each one of you will give something towards upholding and cherishing the great traditions which you have inherited.' It was a strange runic idiom, bearing little relation to human speech. Indeed, it was anti-speech, since its object was to insulate the speaker against the possibility of communication. 'Free men everywhere,' Princess Elizabeth disclosed to President Truman on arrival at Idlewild, 'look towards the United States with affection and with hope. The message which has gone out from this great capital has brought help and courage to a troubled world.' But on this occasion the distinction between royal rhubarb and ordinary words was splendidly highlighted by the President's reply: 'I thank you, dear.'

There was no hint of discrimination in the reporting of royal 'news'. In 1950, the *Daily Mail* found space to tell its readers that Prince Charles had changed his parting ('from left to right'), and the *News Chronicle* revealed that the King owned two tartan dinner-jackets. 'For some time he has kept them a close secret,' the *Chronicle* added importantly, in case you hadn't realized it was a scoop. Pressed to say more, the tailor who had made these interesting garments was alleged to have replied, 'My lips are sealed.' A solemn aldermanic note was maintained, no doubt because the subs sensed that if the obligation to keep his face straight wasn't placed squarely on the reader, he might make a rude noise. 'News of a carefully kept secret was given at a distinguished gathering at London's Savoy Hotel last night. Princess Anne has been enrolled by the Automobile Association as its millionth member.' By making it perfectly clear that this information was not being offered to the infidel, the *Mail* was hoping to distract the reader from any suspicion that – since Princess Anne was only two months old – the Automobile Association may have slipped a few of its cogs.

No discrimination, no irony. When Queen Juliana and Prince Bernhard gave a dinner for the King and Queen at Claridge's, fifty boxes of gold plate were sent on from Holland, along with seven chefs, one Master of the Royal Household, two silver-room staff, two under-florists and a wardrobe man – an advance party later reinforced by thirty-one Dutch waiters, a clutch of footmen, and the royal florist. Three thousand freshly cut flowers were flown in, and the meal began with pâté de fois gras, turtle soup, went on to sole and capon, and ended with iced meringue and fruit. To drink, there were several wines. At the time these events were being placed on record, a number of papers were carrying an advertisement for a dish called Brown Betty, a sinister compound conjured (in those days of austerity) from Weetabix and marmalade, and this ad could sometimes be seen flanked by another urging you to lay hands on a bottle of Rajah pickle 'and pep up your cheese sandwiches'.

Even so, the *News Chronicle* – culturally the most progressive of the popular dailies – made obeisance to the vulgarity of the Dutch state visit as though it had been Mr Pecksniff himself. The paper went so far as to print (with every sign of endorsing its premises) a hand-out prepared for the occasion by Claridge's Hotel: 'Reporters meet very polite but very complete barriers between them and people they want to see, and after wasting some time generally go quietly away, infected by the spirit of quiet good manners that abounds at Claridge's.' Purified by his contact with the hotel staff, the *Chronicle* man went down to Victoria where amid the loyal huzzas of the taxpayers, one royal family met the other. 'This moment,' reported the *Chronicle* man, still reeling from the cleansing influence of Claridge's, 'had all the warmth of delighted friends saying: "It's lovely to see you."' And manfully banishing from his recollection the fifty cases of gold plate and the thirty-one waiters, the reporter – a credit to hotel diplomacy, if ever there was one – added: 'The Queen and her Prince are such a homely couple.'

Having it both ways was a feature of royal reporting in 1950. The *Mirror* wanted to make it clear, or clearish, that although Princess Margaret had been known to buy a new dress, 'ball gowns are retrimmed and renovated, and so are hats'. Just in case you thought royalty was mostly engaged in the exhausting business of having a damn good time, the papers liked to draw your attention to homely economies. For instance, the Yeomen of the Guard: 'As the Yeomen retired,' reported the *Mail*, 'the king simply could not afford to replace them. There should be 100 Yeomen – now there are only 76.' Dashing a suspicious moisture from his eye, the 1950 reader was only too pleased to learn that 'the £40,000 the Yeomen and the Gentlemen-at-Arms cost will be met by the government'.

In case, from time to time, a subscriber was besieged by the thought that the business of waiting on royalty was anything other than an enviable pastime, magazines like *Woman* were alert to disabuse him: 'I often think,' wrote a correspondent in 1950, 'what fun it must be to be on the staff of Buckingham Palace. How proud you'd be to think if it wasn't for you, Princess Margaret wouldn't have had that boiled egg.' And the task of convincing the readership that royalty was having a hard time of it was intimately associated with that other branch of double-think, the proposition that if they hadn't devoted themselves to opening bazaars, they might well have soared to the top of any profession you cared to name. The *Chronicle* man's line on the Queen's visit to the South Bank – 'She was instantly fascinated by the 74–inch telescope' – is a little classic in this vein. Here, the reporter hints at a natural aptitude for astronomy that would have left Galileo standing at the gate.

In 1950, any indication that royalty wasn't wound up like clock-work was greeted by Fleet Street with open-mouthed incredulity. This was due both to a natural commercial disinclination to let an easy source of copy evaporate too quickly, and to a dull conviction that the readers shared the social prejudices of their scribes. The *News Chronicle*, in attendance at the birth of Prince Charles, swore public fealty to what the subs secretly believed in, when it announced that 'a ghillie carried the good news to the King'. And borrowing a hazel-twig from the news editor, the *Chronicle* man divined that to the crowd outside Clarence House 'the birth of a royal baby is a needed symbol of national stability in an uncertain world'. This left the *Times* leader-writer free to strike a note of arcane bonhomie in allowing that 'as a future sovereign, Prince Charles may now look forward to exercising himself in the art of government at the head of his own nursery'. It was as though the newspaper-and-radio age of 1950 thought communications was a picture you looked at, instead of a window you looked through. How else account for the fact that when the *Mail* reported that Princess Margaret had been ticked off by Queen Mary for wearing a head-scarf and the old Queen had said, 'You look like a house-maid', the *Mail* seemed to accept her premise, without at all convincing you it had noticed the implication.

OH, MOSES, MOSES, YOU STUBBORN, SPLENDID, ADORABLE FOOL

I wonder what it is that everyone enjoys about really bad films? It doesn't make sense, since good ones are what you're paying to see, but when a film is *exactly* bad, the pleasure is intense.

Perhaps my all-time favourite is the one where at HQ CMDF (Combined Miniature Deterrent Forces) they are briefing Stephen Boyd. He is to be shrunk to microbe size and injected (along with a submarine and a crew of four) into the circulatory system of a master-scientist who lies unconscious from a head injury.

Boyd's orders are to navigate upstream to the brain, and there dissolve a blood-clot that is short-circuiting the injured man's capacity to pass on a new idea that will save mankind. 'Well,' chuckles Boyd, as if he didn't want anyone to think he hadn't had his leg pulled before, 'that's a wild one!' But having paused for sober reflection – about three seconds – he decides his suspicions are provincial.

'Prepare for miniaturization!' The sub gets smaller and smaller and is sucked up into a syringe. Crew member Donald Pleasance, overcome by a touch of claustrophobia, dashes spiritedly for the conning tower. 'You'll feel better once we're under way,' nods the senior surgeon, played by Arthur Kennedy. Red and white blobs hang around the pulmonary conduit as the craft slides easily downstream.

'What are they?' enquires Boyd. 'Corpuscles,' replies the surgeon, with a hint of asperity. Physicist and paramour, Raquel Welch dotes on the scenery. 'I never dreamed it could be like this,' she breathes. But Donald Pleasance is knitting his brow. 'We're in the carotid artery,' he mutters thoughtfully, 'dammit, we should be in the jugular vein.'

Back at HQ two generals are contributing to the enterprise by pacing the control-room with mugs of coffee in their hands. 'How long can we stop the heart for?' rumbles one. His companion whips out a slide-rule, consults it shrewdly and replies, 'As short a time as possible.' Meanwhile, the sub's propellers are tangled up in lymphatic sea-weed and the craft has run aground in the inner ear. 'What about turbulence?' Aye, what indeed. As to flatulence, Surgeon Kennedy is supplying us with all we need – 'The meedeeval philosophers were right,' he says, staring with visionary eyes at Disneyland outside, 'man *is* the centre of the universe ...'

I suppose a really bad film offers a holiday from the responsibilities imposed by the authentic. Our sensitivities are not put to the test, and we know we are looking at something we shall easily feel better than. The dialogue in particular operates like valium, dissolving anxiety. For instance, in the epic *Solomon and Sheba* the Temple has fallen in on Gina Lollobrigida, she's been stoned by disaffected extras dressed in tablecloths, and a dreadful thunderstorm is augmented by the voice of God handing down six months without the option for everybody. Whereupon the High Priest, played by Raymond Massey, raises his eyes to the heavens and mumbles, 'It's been a hard day for all of us.'

The bathos is reassuring. A bad film – a precisely bad film – lets us off. A bad film is not good for the character because it turns experience into foolishness and we are freed of all obligation. *Africa – Texas Style* was essentially an earnest travelogue into which a little genteel Pinewood romance had been decanted. What gave pleasure was the way neither element had been absorbed into any sort of whole, and the script's efforts to stay conversational while dropping lumps of zoology into the storyline was specially enjoyable.

'Yes, you can see them now,' says John Mills, squinting down at the bush from his light aircraft, 'moving in their typical wedge-shaped formation. We'll hear more about them later.' Ronald Howard plays the pipe-smoking cold-fish scientist. 'The contents of that eland's stomach,' he volunteers, 'will yield valuable information.' Valuable information is being yielded all over the place. 'What are those?' enquires a visitor to John Mills's game-farm. 'Flamingoes,' his host replies, indulgently.

The film switches to romantic mode. 'There's a balance of nature out here,' cries tempestuous Adrienne Corri, clasping the chest of Hugh O'Brian as though it were the north face of the Eiger, 'and you're upsetting the whole thing!' The girl is troubled – she is affianced to the cold fish. 'All you ever think about,' she taunts him, 'is your old microscope.' 'Pass me another slide, Fay,' the swot rebukes her. 'Slides!' exclaims the girl, defiant in her khaki-drill, 'I couldn't *look* at another slide.'

A rascally cattle-farmer releases all the wild animals that have been carefully rounded up for scientific study, but has not reckoned with the beasts' natural devotion to John Mills. Twice, they're let out, twice they come back under their own steam.

'Jim, they're coming home,' yelps Fay, then adds (as in all decency she is bound to), 'I still don't believe it.'

Sometimes a genre accommodates absurdities, and must take the blame for the Bad Films its conventions inspire. *Dracula, Prince of Darkness* was but one film of many in which a sinister butler fags up umpteen flights of stone stairs to bang on the door of the guest-room. Since it's the middle of the night and no one has summoned him, what's he doing glowering at the man who opens the door, asking in sepulchral tones, 'Is there anything more you require, sir?' Students of the genre will immediately reply, 'He is announcing that he is a vampire', and if you should ask them what the guest's response is likely to be they will tell you, quite accurately, that he shakes his head cannily and says to his wife, 'Queer fellow, that.'

The guest appears in all such films, but seldom to such pure effect as in this one. Offered a lift by riderless horses, locked in a deserted castle by an unseen agency, and confronted by a table mysteriously set for four, he might have been expected by the uninstructed to say something on the order of 'What the bloody hell's going on?' In fact, he rubs his hands, looks at the table, and says, 'Dinner sounds like a good idea.'

As ever, the crucifix is used as an early form of six-gun, but the special brand of the prosaic that this sort of film deals in is raised to its apogee when the butler picks up the box containing Dracula's ashes, sprinkles them inside his empty tomb, then pours on blood to reconstitute him like packet-soup. The butler's name is Klove, but the director didn't take the hint.

Occasionally, the witheringly serious film can be more grotesque than the commercial turkey. When I reviewed a Japanese offering called *The Pornographer* none of the hacks present was left in any doubt as to the film's high purpose, since famed sexologists Phyllis and Eberhard Kronhausen did the pre-screen warm-up, and we settled back in our seats reassured that what we were about to see would not breach the high standards of the Cinephone, Oxford Street.

The hero of the story was a Mr Ogata who, in addition to being a big importer of rhino horn from Hong Kong, runs a blue film and dirty book business, while enterprisingly slipping tape-recorders into the bedrooms of his neighbours. He is not one of your nine-to-five men, for on his return home he is regularly dragged into his landlady's bed and obliged to make love to her under the gloomy eye of a pet carp in a glass tank on the sideboard. Every time Mr Ogata gives his landlady an extra hard squeeze the fish turns a moody somersault, thus confirming the landlady's suspicion that it is the reincarnated spirit of her dead husband.

What with the fish and the flesh, Mr Ogata's nerves are under siege. Dashing a volume of his own merchandise from the hands of his daughter, he exhorts the girl to bone up on the works of Dr Schweitzer. The landlady is carted off to hospital with a heart-attack, where she offends the other inmates by sitting up in bed and singing indelicate songs. Already worried by the police, the protection rackets, and the expense of buying a new enlarger, Mr Ogata doesn't know which way to turn. The landlady goes mad, and the fish does double-Axells all round the tank.

We fade into the final sequence. Mr Ogata has retired from the hurly-burly of retail sex and spends his time on a small houseboat, working diligently at his masterpiece. This is to be a rubber landlady complete with central-heating. As we watch, the houseboat sheers its moorings and in a shot that must be included in any list of the great non-sequiturs, floats out into the Pacific, with Mr Ogata crooning heedlessly as (a stickler for detail) he stitches the last of the hairs into the armpit of the inflatable chatelaine.

Yes, you're right, you couldn't make it up. Phyllis and Eberhard loved it, but I seem to remember I took a gloomier view and predicted a split week at Scunthorpe.

Wrong Notes

I have said this before, and I have no doubt that I shall say it again. Meanwhile, I am saying it today. I went to the Festival Hall to hear Abbado and the L.S.O. do the Mahler Fifth, preceded by Pollini playing the Schoenberg Piano Concerto, a work which put me powerfully in mind, and with rather more objective justification, too, of Rossini's celebrated remark to the effect that the overture to *Tannhäuser* would sound just as well played backwards. (The concerto is supposed to be in four movements, but it ended – or more precisely left off – after twenty minutes or so without my having noticed any particular alteration in the nature or quality of the sounds.) The Mahler was very exciting, though it left me, as Mahler almost invariably does, quite unmoved, whereas Bruckner's almost equally spacious symphonic wrestlings find me deeply involved in his struggle. Bruckner universalizes; Mahler doesn't.

But that is not what I am about this morning. What I am about is the programme notes for the concert, by Ates Orga, who sounds like an anagram, possibly, of O, EAT RAGS, which is what Marie Antoinette *really* said, or AARG! TOES!, which is what the startled policeman said when he found a horrid clue in the case of the gentleman who had dismembered his wife, or A RAT GOES, which will be the headline on my obituary of a certain politician, or simply GOAT-ARSE, a term of abuse common among Cypriots, I believe.

Anyway, Mr Orga, in his guide to the evening's music, amply bore out the truth enshrined in the definition of such writing that I first put forward many years ago: those who can understand it don't need it, and those who need it can't understand it. As witness:

Bernard Levin

this Adagietto functions to some extent as an introduction – in the present case to a predominantly linear, stratified Rondo-Finale of immense scope in which the structural parameters of sonata-rondo and variation are combined with a masterful display of fugal and imitative texturing worthy of late Beethoven, not to say the Mozart of the *Prague* or the *Jupiter*, in the toughness and cohesion of its procedure.

Now a man who can write drivel like that about Mahler will obviously be inspired to even greater efforts when it comes to Schoenberg, and so he is, with this result:

In the 40s, Schoenberg reinterpreted this trait in harmonic rather than textural terms, contrasting instead the anti-gravitational equality of serialism with the gravitational inequality of diatonicism. With the Piano Concerto such tendency gives rise to several passages of seemingly retrogressive nature. In the long term, however, these prove paradoxically to be not so much backward-looking as anticipant of the future. At this mature moment of his development (as we have suggested) Schoenberg's art had reached that point when many of those rigid features typical of his technique in its formative stages could now actually be discarded without the overall serial logic of the whole suffering. Thus ['Thus' is a fine word in the circumstances, I must say] the Piano Concerto freely encourages the appearance of diatonically/tonally implicit or [*sic*] combinations, the often frequent application of the *Grundgestalt* in vertical (chordal) rather than horizontal (melodic) form, the use of pedal points, a relative simplification and elucidation of rhythmic structure, and so on.

In the name of Saint Cecilia and all her harp-playing angels, what use is that to any human being alive? Note that I do not ask what it *means*; it doesn't mean anything, but even if it did, and there were someone who understood every word of it, in what way would it add to the total of such a paragon's happiness or knowledge?

It is true that Mr Orga is attempting one of the most difficult tasks that language can set its users. He is trying to convey the essence of music in words, whereas the essence of music does not lie in words, and if it were possible to catch the musical essence verbally composers would all be novelists, or at the very least poets. But the solution to this insoluble problem is not to write gibberish; it is to accept that the programme-note writer's function is a humbler one: to guide the listener who needs guidance through a piece of music in a way which enables him to hear more clearly how the composer is reaching his effects. How he is reaching them, mind; what the effects *are* is something that altogether bypasses such ratiocination, and they stir us in ways which are not dependent upon reason at all, and could not stir us at all if they were, or even if they tried to be. (Have you ever shed a tear at a concert of the music of Satie or Webern – unless, perhaps, from the thought that you could have been having dinner instead? Come to think of it, though, where does that leave *The Art of Fugue?*)

Such a guide will not waste time on pseudo-erudite twaddlings about the *Grundgestalt* or parameters; he will point out the way in which the main themes are introduced and developed, draw attention to contrasts of melody or tempo that the composer stressed, touch upon the quality of the scoring, indicate which instruments are prominent at which significant points, refer to useful parallels or analogies which may be presumed to lie within the listener's experience, and then shut up and let art do the rest. For in the end, as we all know, art is magic, and magic in its purest form, too, which must not yield to one of woman born.

Now at this point, Mr Orga, or his lawyers, may ask me whether I can provide any evidence that what I demand can be done, let alone that it has been. As it happens, that's easy; there are half a dozen regular writers of concert-notes today who do exactly what I have demanded above, our own Mr Mann, I am happy to say, prominent among them. But a study of what is at present available in London's concert halls may be thought invidious; let me then offer an example of what I mean from a somewhat earlier day. Perhaps some of my older readers will recognize the style – by its simplicity, its honesty, its straight-forward, practical helpfulness – from their own first steps on the journey into music, and certainly they, and many others who do not know who the writer is, may also recognize what music is here being written about, which is a good deal more than anybody could do with Mr Orga:

Bernard Levin

The long slow movement (*Larghetto*) is happily designed to contrast with the virile energy of the *Allegro*. The strings start with a melody of eight bars, reechoed by the woodwind. The character of the theme is melancholy, but tender rather than poignant. The second subject (also eight bars) is treated in the same way as the first by the strings and woodwind. A syncopated melody for the first violins seems to be leading us away from the restrained sadness of the opening theme, and presently the second violins and cellos bring in a new figure, distinctly cheerful in character. The first subject is repeated in the minor, developed with fanciful ingenuity, and passed to and fro among the various groups of instruments. There is a modification of the lighter figure alluded to above. The movement ends with a restatement by the full orchestra of the opening strain.

That is an account of the slow movement of Beethoven's Second Symphony, by the great Rosa Newmarch, and I do not believe that the job has ever been done better, or indeed that it can be. Certainly it provides true nourishment for the concert-goer, in a way that the work of Mr Ates Orga does not. A matter, you might say, of TEA OR GAS.

Brigid Brophy

Henry Miller

Tropic of Cancer by Henry Miller (Calder, 1963)

Henry Miller is a commonplace personality whom we have all met several times. I am referring, by the way, to the hero and first-person narrator of *Sexus* and the now published in England *Tropic of Cancer*, who, by a Proustian device which makes a far from Proustian effect, bears the same name as the author. I shall distinguish between them by calling the character Henry Miller and the author Mr Henry Miller.

I first saw Henry Miller when I was fourteen. It was in Kensington Gardens, and he was playing baseball for a United States Army team. Whenever the ball was scooped up really high, Henry Miller would run to where he thought it was going to descend, stretch up his hands (he wore enormous gauntlets like a knight in armour) and scream 'I got it, I got it, I got it'. The other players cleared a holy circle round him. In the sky – that sharp blue wartime sky – the ball seemed to halt for solid minutes. Henry Miller started screaming he had got it long before he could, let alone did, have it, and he did not stop until it actually fell – sometimes wide of him, sometimes plumb on his gauntlets. Not once, wherever it fell, did he catch it. Not once was he abashed by the failure. It seemed that in his mental world to assert he had the ball was as good – was the same – as having it. With hindsight I suspect some of the other players were deceived into inhabiting Henry Miller's world: after the game they remembered only his assertion, and forgot whether it tallied with the facts. Probably Henry Miller had a reputation for catching – perhaps even among men who themselves sometimes caught the ball.

Since the war I have seen him in many parts of Europe, usually in the evening and in a café. He is loud-mouthed, bodily coarse and dressed in ugly clothes designed visibly to mop up his sweat. He is drunk – on incredibly little alcohol, if you bother to check up – and may be going to vomit on the floor. He is boasting to the other Americans he is with (he is always with other Americans), and boasting inaccurately. He may be tipping them the wink about the places which are the real thing, where tourists don't go – in which case he is quite likely to name the Folies Bergère. He may be detailing, as being in the Uffizi, the pictures which are in fact in the Pitti. Evidently he does not know either museum is open to the public, since it has never crossed his mind the pictures have been seen by anyone else. As it gets darker and he gets drunker (not necessarily through taking in any more alcohol), he starts to grab at every female buttock that passes. Eventually he persuades a pair of them to sit in his lap. If it is a French prostitute he has got hold of, you can predict the evening will evaporate without any sexual event taking place, because there will be a stalemate between her meanness and his. The way Henry Miller demonstrates he is an habitué of Europe is to baulk at the price of everything, including sexual inter-course. In Italy he always gets hold of that sad girl of whom there is one in every Italian small town – half nymphomaniac, half half-wit; her conversation runs skittishly along just beside the point, and her shoulder strap straggles just below her sleeve; as she sits in Henry Miller's lap, she giggles, puts her hand affectedly up to her mouth, and reveals the thick black hair in her armpit. With her you can guess Henry Miller will end the evening in a ditch just outside the town. He will boast about her for months afterwards, getting her name slightly wrong: his ear is unattuned to Italian syllables and he has never grasped that girls' names in Italian are more likely to end —a than —o.

In other words, Henry Miller is THE (not the typical but the noticeable) American in Europe: quintessentially, the American in Paris. When he turns writer (the character called Henry Miller is a writer, too – the books in which he is a character are his work), he wants to epitomize his emotions towards Paris. His emotions can be described as warm, human and from the guts.

He does not believe in the discipline of art but writes in a near-automatic state, as though taking down dictation from his guts. He is confident the results will be valuable, because he has a deep faith (the faith which persuaded him no one else had ever visited the Uffizi/Pitti) in his originality. In his creative trance, he rolls the paper into the machine and, convinced no one else has ever brought forth any such idea, types: '*Tropic of Cancer*, p. 209. Paris is like a whore.'

From well before p. 209, Henry Miller has been at his old game of asserting 'I got it, I got it, I got it' – in this case, genius. O, and a penis. We'll come back to the second, which he probably has got. Genius he has not. Like an amateur doing the crawl, he kicks up a terrific foam, but actually he has been hanging on to the rail all the time. He is exuberant, but lacks energy. His narrative, without direction and equally without form, potters from anecdote to anecdote. It neither creates an imaginary nor re-creates a real-life world. The Paris of *Tropic of Cancer* is indistinguishable from the America of *Sexus*, and almost as exclusively populated by Americans. For all his boasting how he loves it, Henry Miller has really only one thing to say about Paris – 'Miller was here.' To chalk that and a few rude words on the walls of Paris is what *Tropic of Cancer* amounts to.

It is not the intensity of his inner life which makes Henry Miller a failure at reportage. His anecdotes are wholly concerned with externals: accounts of the acrobatics of copulation; accounts, leadenly told ('my fear turned my legs to lead'), of down-and-out life; rambling accounts of eccentric 'characters', in which the characterization is many rungs below Saroyan ('He is big and tender, a man every inch of him, but with a woman's heart'). People who live without definite income and with an indefinite connection with the arts make Henry Miller palpitate like any Du Maurier or Murger. His are scenes from the vie de Bohême with more sex but less charm – and even scrappier. The only passages of inner life come when Henry Miller spills his warm, human guts at our feet. His guts turn out to consist of the rhetoric of Walt Whitman (whom he idolizes), an unaimed invective perhaps inspired by Nietzsche, some of the more banal images of surrealism, plus Henry Miller's own persistent image

Brigid Brophy

of human excrement, which he relies on to shock and soil our minds at each repetitive encounter, quite as though he did not know it is a substance we all produce every day. (Perhaps he believes this, too, is an originality on his part.)

Now and then a phrase splashes up (in the sheer gush it could scarcely, on the law of averages, help it) which does lodge in the mind – or, rather, which would, if it were not unfeelingly pounded out again by the next noisy phrase. As a tactician with words, Henry Miller is so clumsy as repeatedly to get himself into a rhythm which serves no artistic purpose in the first place and which he then cannot get out of: '. . . the fumbling fingers, the fox-trotting fleas, the lie-a-bed lice, the scum on his tongue, the drop in his eye, the lump in his throat, the drink in his pottle, the itch in his palm, the wail of his wind . . .', ti tum ti ti tum, etc. etc. (I've quoted only about a third) – I've known a train be more subtle. There might be a childish point if Henry Miller were evoking a train. But he's not. Still, just as it's possible to be a famous catcher without being able to hold the ball, it's possible to make a reputation by writing like a train, provided you do it loudly enough. One of the Sunday critics actually said you can open any of Henry Miller's books at any page without finding a clumsily written sentence.

The monotony of his style and images extends to Henry Miller's behaviour. In _Sexus_ he remarks to a friend (for once he is making his friends the receptacle of an apology instead of a boast) 'You can't fuck every woman you run into, can you?' But to do him justice he has a pretty good try. Or perhaps it's just that he doesn't notice the woman he runs into and doesn't fuck. Not that he really _notices_ the ones he does. He becomes aware of their psychological characteristics at the moment when he is about to do something to them, but the idea of a woman as a personality by whose autonomous existence he might feel moved is beyond him. Curiously enough, so is the idea – the sexual idea – of the female body. Proclaiming that sex is everywhere, he seems insensitive to sexuality, so blunted that nothing less than a primary sex characteristic can force itself on his attention. He is no sensualist. He might have made a mechanical engineer. He sees the female body as an assembly of knobs, pipes and

362

slots. The connecting passages of flesh mean nothing to him except as a containing wall, on which he might well chalk – he really feels no more about any woman than about that whore, Paris – 'Miller was here.' Monotonously, he records his monotonous behaviour. Lacking D.H. Lawrence's puritanism, he lacks the effect of literary fastidiousness which puritanism, perhaps by accident, lent to Lawrence. Henry Miller does not even understand that if you are going repeatedly to use 'fuck' in its proper meaning you will debase that meaning out of it if you also repeatedly use it as a swear-word. Henry Miller holds himself up to us to be admired on the grounds that he is for ever fucking: and yet the strongest diatribe he can fling at the world in general is that it's a fucking world.

When he is not boasting his untutored genius, Henry Miller is boasting the high cultivation of his knowledge and taste. With a snootiness Bloomsbury never touched, he tells us that his difficulty as an employee is to avoid the boss's intellectual envy: Henry Miller has to 'play' the moron and take care not to use polysyllabic words – but, even so, 'I knew too much. It leaked out now and then, despite all the precautions I took.' For verisimilitude's sake, it is a pity that Henry Miller's own style is often semi-literate (he prefers 'commence' to 'begin', and 'prior to' to 'before') or illiterate (he thinks 'effluvia' is a singular and gives the impression he thinks 'exhaustive' means 'tiring'). As for taste, his insight into art is almost as valueless as his attempts at it. He can be merely scatty – he insists at length there is a close similarity between Matisse and Proust; and he can descend to a banality truer than truism – he mentions Uccello and adds 'That fascinating world of perspectives!'

It might be that Mr Henry Miller had written vernacular novels which brilliantly caught Henry Miller the character, pretentiousness, bathetic performance, self-unawareness and all. But that is not supported by the real-life Mr Henry Miller who stated in an interview that his first-person novels are autobiographical and that his literary method was his salvation. Evidently Mr Henry Miller is not outside and seeing all round the character but right down in there with him: he seems to subscribe to Henry Miller's fantasy that shouting 'I got genius' is equivalent to having it. Mr Henry Miller does not claim it exactly for himself, because he subscribes also to Henry Miller's theory that writing is a matter of taking down dictation from another personality inside, but Mr Henry Miller does not hesitate to number the results of his own stenography among the great books. 'Listen,' he says, explaining and justifying the dictation-theory. 'Who writes the great books? It isn't we who sign our names.' The coincidence of Henry Miller and Mr Henry Miller is finally established by *The Colossus Of Maroussi*, in which the American in Europe reaches Greece. The 'I' of this book must be the real-life Mr Henry Miller – indeed, the book can hardly be fiction, since the other important character in it is Mr Lawrence Durrell who, I am told, is a real-life person, too. The sexual tone is here muted (which leaves nothing but boredom for the reader), but otherwise the author of *The Colossus Of Maroussi* has exactly the same literary manner as the character Henry Miller of the earlier books – even to the point ('Durrell, whom I could see now was caving in with fatigue . . .') of failing to distinguish between 'whom' and 'who'.

Mr Henry Miller has declared himself in favour of obscenity, which he calls 'forthright', and against pornography. This is just as well, because Henry Miller lacks the skill of the commercial pornographer. The sensibility which is blunt to the poetry of the erotic cannot exploit the erotic either. His descriptions of sexual intercourse do (though more in *Sexus* than in *Tropic of Cancer*) make an effect, as any tolerably graphic descriptions of it will; and it is a subject on which it is easy for an author to be graphic, since the reader usually meets him halfway. Perhaps the reader is inclined to be ungrateful afterwards, as he is to any book which depends wholly on excitement: as soon as the mystery is solved, one may turn contemptuous of the thriller which gripped one all afternoon. But Henry Miller cuts across any self-accusation on the reader's part. He will go on and *on*, over-earning the reader's gratitude by proffering after the reader is surfeited: 'forthright' indeed – to the point of garrulity. Almost the only claim of Henry Miller's which is justified is that he is honest about sex. No one could accuse him of making it falsely attractive to the reader for whose natural susceptibilities he shews so little consideration. To his credit, neither does he use sex to seduce the reader into sadism, such violence as he describes being of the legitimate, purely erotic kind which occurs between consenting – indeed craving – adults. It is not in writing about sex, it is sheerly in *writing*, that honesty proves an insufficient policy. All very well to be so literal-mindedly honest that you disdain to learn the skill necessary to making an artistic effect: but then your honest course is not to write. What makes Henry Miller not a mere neutral but an enemy of art is that he disdains the skill and yet screams unskilfully that he has succeeded in becoming a great writer without really trying.

It is almost always dangerous to state *one* of your opinions. If I say I think Coventry Cathedral ugly, I risk being congratulated by the circles which hold that all sacred building should be in suburbs gothic; and I can cause nothing but hurt feeling when I add that actually I like 'modern architecture' and don't consider churches sacred. Let me therefore be explicit. In my opinion, *Tropic of Cancer* is without literary value, but I do not mean anyone should be prosecuted for publishing it – or for publishing any book, even one whose intentions are purely pornographic and whose execution fulfils them. The notion that writing about sex is O.K. provided the sex is alloyed with a certain percentage of 'literary merit' is – as well as a philistine misprizing of art – one of the law's quaintest asininities. It is as absurd as it would be to require that any food which is not strictly nourishing should come in an 'artistic' packet. A taste for pornography is as legitimate as a sweet tooth, and none of the law's business. If people want to be corrupted and depraved, they have a perfect right to seek to be – though in point of fact I doubt if even the best executed pornography is capable of doing it. If anything could deprave, it would not be Henry Miller's bad language but his bad use of language: but anyone with twenty-five shillings and a taste for either has a perfect right to indulge it. Pornography is a false problem. Obscenity is no problem at all. There are obscene actions, like capital punishment, but no obscene words. Thought ceases if I cannot refer to capital punishment, though it may be only to call it obscene, without myself committing an obscenity. Certainly a word cannot be *more* obscene than the thing it signifies. 'Shit' chalked on a wall has exactly the same meaning as the paragraphs of a laxative advertisement (and the literary advantage at least of terseness). Of course advertiser and chalker have different intentions: the one wants to make money out of you, whereas the other hopes to shock – that is to hurt – you. However, his assault is not carried out in the real world. The word in itself can no more really hurt or dirty you than the laxative advertisement which means precisely the same thing. The chalker is only expressing his wish to hurt; he is casting spells. To call upon the law to stop him is to make an ass of the law and yourself. It implies you believe witchcraft works.

Penelope Gilliatt

Miz Peggy

The Road to Tara: The Life of Margaret Mitchell
by Anne Edwards (Hodder, 1983)

From Anne Edwards's biography of Margaret Mitchell, we know
that Peggy Mitchell had 'sailor-blue eyes'. We also know that
she stood four feet eight, which is mighty small for the militant
author of *Gone with the Wind*. At this size she mounted, or
climbed up a ladder to, a large horse. Wheeling him (fervently:
her whole life was led in adverbs) and crying 'Look at me!'
to the South in general, she fell off. The horse landed on top
and she had a leg injury that forced her into orthopaedic shoes
for the rest of her life. She wore a bow on one side of her
hair for the premiere of her film: infant star, around forty. By
this time, her book was well over a thousand pages long, but
she was no taller. Even if this Minnie Mouse of a figure was
wearing stiletto heels under her orthopaedic shoes, which one
suspects in the light of her many disguises, she would never
have stood more than four feet eight. She liked dancing the
tango in those shoes, in a black satin dress slit up to her knees.
One wishes there were a photograph of this wild Depression
sight.

She absolutely hated writing. Accident-prone as she was, one
of her many accidents included a car falling on top of hers,
leaving her to live in a back-brace. The back-brace hurt her
when she was typing. When it gave pain she gratefully flung a
bath-sheet over the typewriter and went out in search of mini-
arguments. She also flung a dust-sheet over her first husband.
Miss Edwards excellently takes it off. The second husband, John
Marsh, was an advertising copywriter and a PR man. He read

her epic carefully and, among many other things, took out the dashes.

Gone with the Wind was written in a peculiar manner. It is, of course, very long, but epics are supposed to be. (Beckett's epics are short, but no one will confuse Miz Peggy with Beckett.) Many an epic written in the Mid-West has been carried in a steamer-trunk to be freighted to New York publishers: these publishers, in all true films about best-sellers, go about their daily tasks in dinner jackets and critics in tails lecture the authors about the dangers of success. Margaret Mitchell was pre-dinner-jacket and would anyway scarcely have reached up to a cummerbund or braces, but she was keen on etiquette and tutored people in Hollywood on the hurtfulness in the South of a maid being referred to as 'a coloured lady'. The polite thing was to call her 'a coloured maid'. Bessie, the Faithful Bessie of Margaret Mitchell's household, was Ever-Faithful and didn't mind at all about the Ku Klux Klan on account of Miz Peggy being so busy. As to the peculiar method of working on the hated epic, Miss Mitchell wrote the last part first and put it into a manila envelope. Any other part that struck her fancy was also written out of sequence, with a note about a bridge passage being necessary and put into another manila envelope. These envelopes were scattered all over the place: among her hats, in drawers, under the bed, possibly in the fridge. After many, many years there came about the feeling that *Gone with the Wind* had been accomplished, apart from the bridge passages. Her friends in Atlanta were bound to secrecy. A number of them had babies during the writing process, though not she. Baby-having was, in her eyes, much like the act of a car dropping on to the innocent roof of your own, and she resented it.

This dinkie Confederate general grew in militancy as the scattered manila envelopes developed in number. Macmillan, her prospective publishers in New York, exhibited infinite patience as bits and pieces of the manuscript arrived. Long before the manila collection seemed to be complete, they had given her a considerable advance and kept on putting it up of their own volition. Miz Peggy fainted when the proofs came. Best-seller lists were hit. The book won a Pulitzer prize. Sixteen million copies were sold. The book went into every possible language. She made a mint. She covered the walls of the little Mitchell house in peach-and-green striped wallpaper with a couch to match. One doesn't know where her husband or Faithful Bessie sat. Her husband stayed up night after night dealing with foreign rights. He went down to 138 pounds, which is little for an average-sized American, even during the Depression. Why didn't the Mitchells use an agent for the foreign rights? The telephone went from autograph-hunters every three minutes; callers came all the time; Faithful Bessie grew tired, though she remained constant; Miz Peggy had the vapours with the tiresomeness of all this praise. But why didn't they change their telephone number and make themselves ex-directory?

Anne Edwards's book is good. It begins by being skippable when there are too many adjectives and adverbs, but the author of *The Hesitant Heart* is beautifully hesitant to make judgments about her heroine until near the end of the book. It is only then that she starts to say that Miz Peggy became acquisitive and rat-like. There have been wretched stories of her suspiciousness about friends from her days as an Atlantan newspaperwoman, who were trying to help her. Her behaviour to her husband seems to have been altogether abominable.

There are two cliff-hangers to the story. Will the manila envelopes ever be found and pieced together? Will Scarlett O'Hara, named 'Pansy' by Miz Peggy throughout her manuscript, ever be cast for the film? Bette Davis was thought of, to Bette Davis's disgust. Norma Shearer was thought of. Eventually, eventually, Vivien Leigh was chosen by Selznick. She is said by Miss Edwards to have looked extraordinarily like Margaret Mitchell, though not the faintest bit can one discern from the photographs in the book. At the premiere of the film, held in Atlanta, at a branch of Loew's chain decked out with the stately white columns that Selznick thought proper for the film, though they had nothing to do with the Tara described by Margaret Mitchell, Vivien Leigh apparently exclaimed, on hearing 'Dixie', that they were playing the theme-tune composed for the film. There was some trouble over the title of the book. It was to be called 'The Road to Tara'. One of Mrs Mitchell Marsh's invaluable editors found 'Gone with the Wind' buried somewhere in the manila-manacled typescript. It must have been one of the most obstreperous typescripts any publisher has ever had to deal with.

And why was *Gone with the Wind* such a huge success? Miss Edwards suggests that there may be an analogy, in these Depression years, with the hysterical response to Lindbergh. Or has it to do with bringing together a very recently split continent through the sort of romantic saga that is always called feminine, though men readers and critics much respond to it? Or has it to do with its sheer length: when people are starving, does amplitude help, as five-hour dance-drama films aid thin villagers staving off hunger with betel nuts in India? Or is it a help to have a woman writing about men desperately at war? Or is it a help in America that the people of a hundred and thirty years ago embody the characters and ethics of the people of a romanticized Thirties? The questions are interesting and one likes Anne Edwards's book for provoking them, though one still retains disquiet about the stated likeness of Vivien Leigh to a woman in orthopaedic shoes behaving horribly to loyal local friends. Miz Peggy's over-worked second husband, who must often have wanted to have put a dust-sheet over his tired head, as his wife had put it over her first husband's existence and her typewriter, is dismissed by his wife as not being a true Southerner because he didn't come from Atlanta. He came only from Kentucky.

It is often said that wars leave a 'wake of devastation' behind them. *Gone with the Wind* did even before it got started. Miz Peggy was clearly quite wearing. A lot of trouble was taken about her first wedding. Friends and relations were imported from all over. Miz Peggy insisted, probably with some sense of the reality that usually escaped her, that she wanted to carry a bouquet of red roses. It took an army to shove white ones into her hands. And then there was this accident-proneness. Only Miz Peggy could have been concussed by a bottle of whisky waved in the hands of a man pouring himself a drink, a man a good foot taller than her. She seems to have had a dubious sense of humour. One of her jokes was to imitate the pregnancy of her friend Augusta at parties, by wrapping a shawl around herself and rolling a beach ball up and down under it. Her parents and their friends had done their best. The brat had early been taken out in a buggy and told that she was to go to school tomorrow instead of playing hookey and to conquer arithmetic.

This notion of conquering may have done the harm. She seems to have had no notion that Southerners thought of themselves, and still do, as a conquered people, which may well account for their freedom from the Mafia intelligentsia of much of the Eastern and Western cultures of the North. The South remains gentle and mannerly; for all its Ku Klux Klan, blacks are happier in the South and find Manhattan noisy and vicious. Margaret Mitchell heard in her childhood, through her other friends and relations, everything about the Civil War except that the South had lost it. Perhaps that explains a little of the apparent idiocy of the hidden manila envelopes. The ante-bellum chapters were eventually found at the top of the saucepan cupboard. It was as if she were hiding something crucial from herself. But oh, that wake of devastation. Although she had been an adolescent fan-letter writer – to Vincent Benét and to F. Scott Fitzgerald, who was later to be one of the many writers hired and sacked on the script of the film – the admired ones' sage abstention from answering taught her nothing. When *Gone with the Wind* was published, fan letters arrived in sacks which, troubling her not one whit, strained the postman's back. Miz Peggy answered every one of them at a length that apparently reached in total the wordage of the phenomenal novel. This could only have been her decision, but she wore everyone out with it. Instead of getting on with any next piece of work, she complained without cease and eventually fled for privacy to, of all places, a writers' colony.

Alice Thomas Ellis

Lost Cause

A long time ago when I was too young to know better I went beagling on a snowy day and got stuck with a girl whose name, as far as I remember, was Mary Bedstead, and a perfectly stupid hound called Venus. Venus had to be lifted over fences and carried across ditches. Lord knows where the hare and everyone else got to but I don't recall seeing any of them ever again. In the course of time me and Miss Bedstead and Venus staggered back to base, frozen, exhausted and deeply fed up with each other.

Serve us right. I've never had all that much faith in canine sagacity and now two of the silly brutes have got themselves lost up the mountain behind the house. (We're in Wales, not Camden Town.) Some chap took them hunting for foxes and they got separated. The hounds are howling and the chap is bellowing all over the valley and I came here for a spot of peace and quiet. The little girls are distressed at the thought of the poor little lost dogs (what about the poor little harassed foxes?) and have gone out to look for them. If I have to turn out and look for two little lost girls as a consequence of this I shall head straight back to London and the riots. There's a heavy frost outside and a fairly heavy one inside, come to think of it. It could be another world. Only yesterday I was running round Camden Town in sandals and no socks and now I'm huddled over a big fire as close as Shadrach, Meshach and Abednego. I'm not complaining. I made a New Year resolution to stop swearing and complaining, because I was beginning to find myself tedious, and people had started avoiding me. It's an awful old vale of tears but one must grit the teeth and soldier on, I suppose.

I wonder what happened to the guest who set off yesterday to come and stay with us. One of her friends just telephoned and told us that that's what she'd one, but she isn't here. I've looked. Sometimes there are so many people around that one more could pass unnoticed, but not at the moment. Only four of us and all unmistakable, especially Janet who looks like an Abominable Something in about fourteen layers and moon boots. The guest was bringing two Pekineses with her as well and they would certainly not have gone unnoticed – unless they'd whipped up the mountain to look for foxes with the other dopey hounds. Everything is so worrying. Perhaps, I think, dementedly, the guest went up the mountain looking for foxes. It would be out of character, but then life is full of surprises.

Night is beginning to fall and the stars to glitter. The hounds have stopped howling. Is this, I ask myself, because they've eaten the guest? Oh no, surely not. The huntsman has assured the little girls that they are gentle as lambs, affectionate and totally harmless – except, of course, to foxes – and that if they turn up at the house we need feel no fear. And their names are Tanya and Sprocket. As if I cared. The only fear I feel at the moment is that of having to go out in ten below looking for little girls (and the guest) who are looking for hounds who are looking for foxes. I really don't want to have to do that. I'd rather sit by the fire and see pictures in it. No, that's no good. All I can see is mountains and foxes and missing guests. This is a great start to the New Year. Is there any point in having hysterics when there's no one to watch? Janet has taken another departing guest to the station along the icy roads. Will I ever see Janet again? Will she inadvertently run over the guest, who I now picture rushing suddenly out of the hedgerow flapping her arms, pursued by a pack of hounds and some vengeful foxes? I think I'll spend 1987 in a rest home.

The little girls, at least, have just returned so I'll go and beat them to a pulp for frightening me, and then I'll have a stiff vodka, and probably swear a bit.

So much for New Year resolutions. I blame the foxes.

Michael Frayn

from *At Bay in Gear Street*

A FAREWELL TO ARMS

I'm glad the Pope's against war. Because so am I, and so is Horace Morris, and so are quite a number of other people I know.

The Pope and I don't always see eye to eye, but I'm bound to admit that on this one I think he's got hold of the right end of the stick. 'No more war, war never again ...' as he told the assembled delegates at the U.N. 'If you wish to be brothers, let the arms fall from your hands.' It touches a chord. In fact, judging by the headlines and the discussions on television, it seems to have evoked widespread acknowledgement and admiration, and no disagreement at all.

How easy, how tragically easy, would it have been for him to get it all back to front. 'More war, war again and again!' as he might so easily have said. 'Let's have a little more mindless mayhem – let's see the hands fall from your arms!'

All the same, I think it is only fair to point out that the Pope was not the first to declare himself in favour of peace. The previous week very similar views were expressed by Mr Patrick McGoohan, described as Britain's highest-paid television actor, in an interview in *TV Times*.

Mr McGoohan was being interviewed by Iain Sproat (who, the *TV Times* was careful to point out, was educated at Winchester and Oxford, so you can be pretty sure he got it down right). 'We were once talking,' writes Mr Sproat, 'about the totally hypothetical question of what he would do were he Prime Minister. I remember he said nothing for a moment, and then:

' "I would be overwhelmed with fear, but if I were, I would try to get everyone to cease combat just for one minute. Just peace on earth for one minute! It's a fairy tale but you never know. It would feel so good that they might not start again." '

Harold Wilson must be kicking himself. Not once does it seem to have occurred to him to arrange a trial run of peace on earth! That's why they pay Mr McGoohan so much as an actor – to keep him out of politics.

Now I'm not for a moment accusing the Pope of lifting Mr McGoohan's ideas. I don't suppose he even set eyes on a copy of last week's *TV Times*. By some fluke Mr McGoohan missed the headlines – 'MCGOOHAN CALLS FOR PEACE ON EARTH,' 'CEASE COMBAT, URGES HIGHEST-PAID TV ACTOR' – and the Pope collected all the glory for much the same idea. Like Darwin and Wallace discovering evolution. Just one of those coincidences.

'Hasn't this peace business been around before?' asked my friend Horace Morris the other day, as we sat discussing the history of ideas, in the way we often do. 'Weren't there some rather scruffy people you and I knocked around with in our youth who used to walk about the roads every Easter saying roughly, in effect, let the arms fall from your hands?'

'You mean the Aldermaston marchers?'

'That's right. Very statesmanlike of them, one realizes now. Tremendous sense of moral leadership they were showing.'

'Good heavens, Horace, that was a different matter altogether! They were just a bunch of vague, muddle-headed idealists!'

'Not statesmanlike at all?'

'Certainly not. They weren't making a broad appeal to the hearts and minds of mankind – they were trying to get our own Government to disarm! That's politics, Horace. We'd have weakened our strategic posture against Communist intimidation.'

'But haven't the Communists been coming out for peace themselves recently, in a rather broad, statesmanlike way?'

'Broadish, I suppose, Horace. But what the Communists mean by peace is peace in circumstances favourable to the spread of Communist ideas and influence.'

Michael Frayn

'Whereas the Pope means peace in circumstances favourable to the spread of anti-Communist ideas and influence?'

'I should think that's what he means, Horace. He doesn't specify, of course – he's had the sense not to get bogged down in particularities and details. But I don't suppose he means "Let the arms fall from your hands, and let the Communists peacefully take over South-East Asia." '

'I suppose not.'

'For that matter I don't suppose he means "Let the arms fall from your hands, and let the Baluba tribesmen go on peacefully raping nuns." '

'No.'

'There's peace and peace, as I'm sure the Pope would be the first to recognize.'

'What he's telling us is "Let the arms fall from your hands, but go on defending freedom against tyranny and the rule of law against lawlessness"?'

'As it were.'

'By virtue as it were of the tyrants and outlaws responding to this broad supranational appeal too?'

'Exactly, as it were.'

'He sees both sides of the question?'

'I think seeing both sides of the question is his strong point, Horace. For instance, you remember he said he was against birth control?'

'I was a little worried by that, I must admit.'

'Ah, yes, but at the same time, Horace, he came out very strongly against people going hungry.'

'I see what you mean. The broad view? The bipartisan approach?'

'Quite. In fact, he advised people to make new efforts to increase the world's food supply.'

'I thought he'd got hold of a rather good idea there.'

'An extremely practical one, Horace.'

'I see what you mean. Really, short of doing anything it lies in his power to do, like changing his mind about birth control, he's doing everything he can.'

from *At Bay in Gear Street*

MY LIFE AND LOVES

Distinguished civil servants and others, when they realize they are being observed by a journalist, hastily leap up from their arm-chairs and with rather unexpected quiet passion and rather unexpectedly engaging smiles begin to play badminton, collect seventeenth-century Irish egg-whisks, write the standard work on the lesser celandine, reveal a rather unexpected line in wry humour, take a rather unexpectedly serious interest in the campaign to preserve the death-watch beetle, and beget ten rather brilliant children; continuing this dazzling simultaneous exhibition until the journalist leaves, when (I should imagine) they slump heavily back into their arm-chairs rather unexpectedly exhausted.

The behaviour of distinguished actors and actresses when a journalist or handout-writer comes over the horizon is entirely different. They don't start *doing* anything at all. They just start believing in and being intensely moved by and being utterly realistic about. They simply come vibrantly, richly, and passively into contact with life.

Here, for instance, is the throbbing voice of an actress called Yvette Mimieux in a newspaper cutting I have: 'I like snails and hot chocolate and dancing and tangy cheese and soft lead pencils and thick, strong coffee and tangerines and racing cars.'

Imagine the Permanent Secretary at the Ministry of Waste Disposal taking this sort of line. ' "I adore walking in the rain," lisped Mr O.B. Strood, the tough-minded *éminence grise* behind Britain's newest rubbish tip, "and the smell of new bread and comfortably worn dispatch-boxes and thinking and Ministry cars and mid-morning biscuits and chewing my pencil and – oh – and *heaps* of things." ' Be rather unexpected, to say the least.

But it looked perfectly natural when Mr Nicol Williamson, actor, listed *his* loves to Mr Marshall Pugh, journalist, in an interview in the *Daily Mail* last week. Mr Williamson, it appears, loves old wooden houses, Bach, good stew and ale, pubs, belting tennis balls about, and diving into the sea and coming back and scattering his records all over the room.

How he stands on hot chocolate and tangy cheese and soft lead pencils he doesn't say. But he did come out for humility – 'I'm humble in some ways,' he told Mr Pugh, 'much humbler than you think' – and faith. 'Faith bothered him constantly,' reported Mr Pugh. 'It was so bloody personal, such bloody agony.'

Yes! Oh, God, yes! Oh, God, I absolutely bloody agree! The smell of coffee roasting, sunlight falling on hair, the clouds coming down on the mountains – I love them all, too. I may not have mentioned it before, but I'm involved in life up to my bloody eyebrows. Gregorian plain-song, hot, strong cheese and tangy snails – I'm deeply committed to every corny, wonderful, bloody experience in the book. I've never tried diving in the sea and coming back and scattering my records all over the room, but oh God, it sounds marvellous! I'll give it a whirl at the very first opportunity I have.

And there's the snag – opportunity. As Mr Williamson says: 'I want to live intensively, 101 per cent. But how can I do it in this job?'

God, I know the feeling! How can I do it, either, in my job, or you in yours? And if it's not the job stopping us living it's something else. Just as you're about to start living, really 101 per cent living, it's lunch time. Or some damned person rings up. You get inside some lovable pub, and you never have a chance to really experience it, because you have to spend all the time either trying to break into your friends' conversation to ask them what they want to drink, or trying to catch the barmaid's eye.

And the hot chocolate – that turns up just when you feel like the thick, strong coffee, and the thick, strong coffee is wheeled on just about bedtime, when the only thing you want is hot chocolate. Nor is it possible to listen to the Bach properly when you're hunting high and low for something to write with, because all you can find is some damned joky soft lead pencil.

No, if you want to live – *really* live – you've got to get away from life. You've got to find somewhere where you can be completely idle, so that if you want to spend all morning walking in the rain you can, for the simple reason that there's nothing else to do. And if you happen to come across a smell of coffee roasting you can stop and inhale it – and go on inhaling it until you're fed up with it. Then you can sit down in a café somewhere and have a hot chocolate. Have two hot chocolates if you feel like it – there's nothing else to do. Go on guzzling hot chocolate until you're chocolate-coloured in the face. Then you can start walking about in the rain again, trying to get up an appetite for that lunch of stew and ale.

After lunch you could go and look at some wooden houses. Look at them from the front, look at them from the back. Really get an eyeful of them – there's no earthly hurry. Then perhaps you could stroll along and smell the coffee roasting again. Have another hot chocolate. If the weather's cleared up you might go and take a dive in the sea, then go up to your room and chuck the records about. After that you might go out and take another dive, and come back and chuck the records about all over again – you've probably still got about four hours left before dinner.

You could have snails for dinner – there's something to look forward to. If you went in to dinner at eight, and took your time over it, you could probably spin it out till about half-past nine, and then it would be pretty well time to go to bed. You've only got the four hours before dinner to fill in. Could go along and take another look at those wooden houses. Could take another sniff at that coffee roasting. Or take another dive in the ocean. Could do almost anything. Damned hard to find the energy to decide which. You can probably feel that terrible spare sensation coming on already.

No, if you're really going to live – really 101 per cent live – you need some purpose in life. You need to work. Oh, God, think of that bloody marvellous little pub you used to slip out to after a hard day's work! And the Goldberg Variations tinkling quietly away in the background as you worked with the soft lead pencil! Oh God, how bloody wonderful such moments are – in recollection, if you didn't think about them when they happened!

Philip Howard

from *A Word in Time*

> Time is like a river. As soon as a thing is seen it is carried away and another takes its place, and then that other is carried away also.
>
> *Meditations*, iv, *circa* 170, by Marcus Aurelius

Time, like an ever-rolling stream, bears all our words away. *Tout passe, tout casse, tout lasse*, in language as in life. The English of somebody born a generation before us is already beginning to sound dated. That of a century ago needs glosses for anybody who is not a historian of the period. That of five hundred years ago needs a translation, and that of a thousand years ago is another language.

One of the ways that language is continually changing is by indirections and absurdities. Howlers can become 'correct' if enough people persist in making them. This has finally happened to 'prestigious'. Until a century ago it was used only in its etymologically correct meaning, 'practising juggling or leger-demain', related to 'prestidigitation'. Since then, in spite of the protests of pedants, the British have persisted in using it in an 'incorrect' sense to mean 'having or giving prestige', the magic quality of the twentieth century for which we have no other adjective. 'Prestigious' is still a hollower quality than 'distinguished', but the howler has become correct, and if you use 'prestigious' in its old juggling sense of conjurer's tricks, you will be misunderstood. That is a howler that has been enthroned because it fills a gap.

Other howlers arise by simple muddle between two words that sound the same, for example 'appraise' for 'apprise', and 'mitigate against' for 'militate against'. Confusing 'flaunt' with 'flout' was popularized by Noël Coward in a song, and by the former British Prime Minister, Edward Heath. The howler is not established yet, and should be resisted.

'Infer' is widely used to mean 'imply' (and has been in the past by writers as eloquent as Thomas More, Milton, and Walter Scott). This is widely regarded as a howler, and it would be a pity to lose the useful distinction we have evolved between 'infer' and 'imply'. 'Disinterested' is often used to mean 'uninterested' and is widely regarded as a howler. In fact the first recorded uses of 'disinterested', by John Donne and Junius, are to mean 'uninterested' – half a century before 'uninterested' came into English. These are howlers between words that have similar meanings as well as similar sounds, and the boundaries between which will always tend to be fluid and disputed. But where a useful distinction has been evolved between two such related words, it is prodigal and wanton not to observe it. Sometimes a howler wins through by adopting by analogy the wrong preposition from a similar word; though I hope that 'comprised of' and 'inflicted with' can continue to be branded as howlers for a few more years, common though they have become.

We may (and do) deplore many of these changes; but if the tide of *vox populi* has set on a change, in the long trawl not even the strongest swimmer can fight against the tide. Prestigious people, from our best writers to pop singers, have more influence than most in changing the language. But language grows from the bottom up as well as from the top down. Lexicographers and linguists record the grunts and snorts coming up to them from us, established 'howlers' and all. *C'est leur métier*. It is the job of teachers to teach the best contemporary English in its many registers, and to expunge howlers, aware that today's howler may eventually become correct. English is a matter not of morality but of usage.

There is a new howler, which it may already be too late to nip in the bud: there is a creeping confusion between *prevaricate* and *procrastinate*. Here are two recent examples from *The Times*. 'Some fear the Minister will *prevaricate* (without doing anything about computer hackers) until the next election.' And here is the Professor of Law at London University, in an article: 'But still the Government *prevaricates*. It will now await the views of Parliament in the autumn before deciding whether to introduce legislation (about war crimes).' His *prevaricate* made it (disgracefully) into the headline.

The words are both quadrisyllables beginning with 'pr'. But their roots and meanings are quite different. That *cras* in *procrastinate* means tomorrow in Latin; and the word means time-wasting, or putting off until tomorrow. *Prevaricate* means to evade the truth in ways short of lying, to be economical with the truth, and its roots come from walking crookedly. *Varicare* in Latin means to spread the legs apart, to straddle; *varus* is bow-legged. In Latin *praevaricari* meant first to straddle across anything, and then by metaphor in legal jargon for an advocate to act in collusion with his opposite number in order to secure a particular outcome to a trial. Cicero often accuses the other side of *prevarication*: 'He took money from Catiline on condition that he *prevaricated* disgracefully.' *Procrastinate* is the attitude of *mañana*: never do anything today that you can postpone until tomorrow. *Prevaricate* ranges from economy with the truth to falsehood. There is an interesting little incipient division between American and British use of *prevaricate*. In America *prevaricate* has acquired and retains a strong sense of lying, or at least fiddling with the truth. In British English the word has softened and slipped in the other direction, to mean nothing much worse than 'shilly-shally'. This, no doubt, helps to explain the confusion with *procrastinate*. It is a fertile new little source of misunderstanding between American and British English. *Prevaricate* and *procrastinate* are still quite distinct. To muddle them is still a howler, and all good men and women will rally round to maintain the useful distinction.

But if enough professors of law and sub-editors on *The Times* carry on using *prevaricate* where they mean *procrastinate*, the next edition of *The Oxford English Dictionary* will have to record the howler. If Latin were more widely taught, there would be less barbaric (should that be barbarous?) confusion about the roots of our language. Many popular modern howlers, for example, spelling Phillip with two ls, 'miniscule', and pronouncing the word 'dissect' as though it were spelled with a single s and rhymed with bisect, arise only from barbarous (should that be barbaric?) ignorance of our grandmother tongue.

Time makes a monkey of our quotations as well as our syntax and semantics. A quotation is something that somebody once said that seemed to make sense at the time. But times and idiom change. If he were composing today, I do not think that Henry Vaughan, the Welsh mystic poet, could write: 'How brave the prospect of a bright backside!' It was too much for the Rev. H. F. Lyte, anyway: in his edition of Vaughan he amended the last two words to 'traversed plain'. This fundamental erosion of idiom occurs mostly in translation these days, as in the engraved brass plate outside the Mosel riverside hotel at Cochem, which translates: '*Nacht Eingang auf der Rückseite bitte* – Night entry at the backside please.'

I do not suppose that Elizabeth Barrett Browning would put it exactly the way she did in 'Wine of Cyprus':

> *Our Euripides, the human,*
> *With his droppings of warm tears,*
> *And his touches of things common*
> *Till they rose to touch the spheres!*

Time has eroded and custom coarsened some of those words. Would Trollope, if he were writing *The Eustace Diamonds* today, put it: 'As he sat signing letters at the India Board, relieving himself when he was left alone between each batch by standing up with his back to the fireplace, his mind was full of all this.' 'To relieve oneself' has become a common euphemism, and most of us would face the fireplace. Here is another quotation, coarsened by time, from Churchill's *Life of Marlborough*: 'In his last years he had woven Marlborough into the whole texture of his combinations.' And here is H. G. Wells making an anachronism in chapter 14 of *The War of the Worlds*: 'His landlady came to the door, wrapped in dressing-gown and shawl; her husband followed, ejaculating.'

The passage of time and the change of idiom stick out like reefs in books written only a generation ago. The most obvious example of changing idiom rendering quotations offside is the use of 'gay' as a less hostile description of homosexual than

Philip Howard

'queer'. This was first recorded in underworld slang in the Thirties, but since the last war 'gay' has become widely idiomatic in this sense on both sides of the Atlantic. Consequently, a range of famous quotations from Eng. Lit. have become impossible without schoolboy sniggers from the roughs at the back of the class. For example, it is no longer possible for Chaucer's Wife of Bath to ask in her prologue: 'Why is my neighbour's wife so gay?' without some risk of double entendre. The same embarrassment has come upon *Samson Agonistes*:

> But who is this, what thing of sea or land?
> Female of sex it seems,
> That so bedeck'd, ornate and gay,
> Comes this way sailing
> Like a stately ship of Tarsus.

And how about Iago, praising women to Desdemona and Emilia: 'She never lacked gold, and yet went never gay'? In his poem 'The Menagerie', one of William Vaughan Moody's characters advises: 'If nature made you so graceful, don't get gay.' And what are we to make of Yeats's assertion in 'Lapis Lazuli': 'They know that Hamlet and Lear are gay'? Samuel Rogers: 'There's such a charm in melancholy, I would not, if I could, be gay.' Scott in *Guy Mannering*: 'Sophia, as you well know, followed me to India. She was as innocent as gay; but, unfortunately for us both, as gay as innocent.' At Christ Church, Oxford, according to Christopher Hobhouse's *Oxford* (1939): 'The life is easy-going and tolerant; the company is intelligent and gay.'

Poetry in particular treads a perilous tightrope between sublimity and bathos. I know that beauty is in the eye of the beholder, and double entendre in the ears of the Lower Fifth. But there are some words that have become so dodgy because of changing slang that the prudent tightrope-walker avoids them. Take 'pants'. Since about 1840 these have become colloquial for the undergarments that were previously called drawers. This has undermined a series of famous quotations. 'Kubla Khan': 'As if this earth in fast thick pants were breathing.' Shelley in 'Epipsychidion': 'The slow, silent night/Is measured by the pants of their fast sleep.' In *Othello* Cassio prays that Othello might 'make

384

Love's quick pants in Desdemona's arms'. In *Antony and Cleopatra* Antony tells the wounded Scarus to 'leap thou, attire and all,/Through proof of harness to my heart, and there/Ride on the pants triumphing'. Francis Thompson, in 'A Corymbus for Autumn', declares that 'day's dying dragon is panting red pants into the West'. I am trying as hard as I can to be high-minded about this, but I cannot help twitching at those red pants. I am afraid that 'pants', like gay, is a coarsened word that has been ruled out of bounds by the passage of time.

Once you have started spotting double entendres, literature becomes a minefield. *Paradise Lost*: 'And leave a singed bottom all involved with stench and smoke.' *Vanity Fair*: 'Amelia wept confidentially on the housekeeper's shoulder, and relieved herself a good deal.' *Uncle Tom's Cabin*: 'Mrs Shelby stood like one stricken. Finally, turning to her toilet, she rested her face in her hands, and gave a sort of groan.' Literature is as booby-trapped as life.

Alan Bennett

Ten Days That Shook Me

I spent ten days in May in Russia on a visit arranged by the
Great Britain-USSR Society. My colleagues were the novelists
Paul Bailey, Christopher Hope and Timothy Mo (who also
writes for *Boxing News*), the poet Craig Raine (who doesn't) and
the playwright Sue Townsend of *Adrian Mole* fame. I had many
misgivings about the trip, particularly in regard to creature comforts. I wondered, for instance, if the Russians had got round to
mineral water. John Sturrock reassured me. 'Haven't you heard
of Perrierstroika?'

The Writers' Union is a pleasant one-storeyed 19th-century
building set round a leafy courtyard and currently being refurbished against Mr Reagan's visit. He is to have lunch here. We
are never going to have lunch, it seems, as this introductory
session of talks began at ten and it is now 1.30 with no sign of it
ending. We sit down one side of a long green-baize-covered table
with the Soviet writers on the other, the most eye-catching of
them the playwright Mikhail Shatrov, a stocky middle-aged man
with a pallor so striking Sue Townsend insists it owes something
to Max Factor. Shatrov is seemingly contemptuous of these
proceedings; he arrives late, ostentatiously reads a newspaper
during the speeches and from time to time points out items of
interest to his colleagues. Sceptical of the purpose of formal
discussions like these, I find Shatrov's attitude not unsym-
pathetic, particularly when the talk turns to the writer's role in
society. I feel like a not very expert motor mechanic taking part
in a discussion on national transport policy. Presiding over the
meeting is Professor Zassoursky, who holds the chair of journalism at Moscow University. He is an urbane and elegant figure
(in what looks like a Brooks Brothers suit) and witty with it. The

talk among the Soviet writers is all of the coming Party Congress, which they hope will enforce the retirement of the heads of the Musicians' and Writers' Unions, both notorious hardliners. 'But if they resign,' says Zassoursky, 'it could even be worse. After all, they might start writing again.'

The Hotel Ukraina where we are staying looks like the Gotham or the Dakota, those monstrous 19th-century mansions on New York's Central Park West, though this and dozens of buildings like it were built fifty or sixty years later by Stalin. Like the Writers' Union, the Ukraina is being refurbished against The Visit, the refurbishment taking the form of new three-ply cabinets to encase the (old) TV sets. My room has a fridge which lights up nicely, but otherwise just makes the contents (one bottle of mineral water) sweat. An engineer comes and looks at it but is baffled. It is hard to understand, with simple technology such a mystery, why they haven't blown us all up years ago. 'Be fair,' says Sue Townsend. 'I believe they do a very good smelter.' I am disturbed to find Melvyn Bragg working in the hotel as a doorman. He pretends not to recognize me.

To Massenet's *Werther* at the Bolshoi. It is an indifferent production, the scenery and sets almost Music Hall, but the house is packed and Nina and Galina, our guides, say that this is the first time for years they have managed to get a ticket, which makes us all feel worse for not enjoying it. Someone who is enjoying it is Melvyn Bragg, this time in the back row of the chorus. Though food is pretty basic, I find meals the high points of each day, just as they are when filming. One talks about food, thinks about it, and tonight, returning from the opera, we are mortified to find we are too late for supper. Anne Vaughan, our organizer, braves the kitchen and eventually a waitress takes pity on us and gives us some bread and ham and a bit of dog-eared salad which we take upstairs in plastic bags. 'You must be very hungry,' says a man in the lift. 'What country are you coming from?'

Another session at the Writers' Union. Most of the writers we talk to are likeable, decent people and it is this that makes it difficult to raise potentially embarrassing issues like dissidence.

If these were fanatical hardliners it would be easy to ask the hard questions, but they are not. One tells us how she has just translated *Animal Farm* ('Not a good book,' one of us says prissily) and they are so obviously thrilled with what is happening that to inquire, say, about psychiatric punishment seems tactless. What one does not get from them is any sense of what they think of each other. They hear out each other's speeches without comment or dissent and only when Boguslavskaya (Mrs Voznesensky) makes a long self-regarding speech and shortly afterwards sweeps out does one get some hint that they think she is tiresome too.

Breakfast (food again) is self-service and is generally a relatively tranquil meal, but this morning I come down to find we have been invaded by the American Friendship Society ('Lois Ravenna Jr,' says the name tag of the lady opposite). They are a middle-aged to elderly group, ladies whom I would call 'game' (and Barry Humphreys 'spunky'). They know they cannot expect the creature comforts on offer at the Wichita Hilton but they are determined not to complain or be defeated. This sometimes leads them into absurdity. One old lady, not noticing the nearby pile of plates, assumes the plate is just another refinement the Soviet Union has not got round to. No matter. She grits her teeth and piles meat balls on one corner of her tray and porridge onto another, a practice she can only be familiar with from Hollywood prison movies.

Another visit to the Bolshoi, this time for an evening of ballet excerpts. Note the universal presence, even here at the ballet, of small, square old men, their jackets buckling under the weight of medals and ribbons, and looking like the Eastern Front in person. By now I am unsurprised to find Melvyn is in the ballet as well as the opera, and he even takes a curtain call, accompanied as ballet calls are the world over, by a deadly hail of tulips. I have only seen one bit of graffiti in Moscow, a faint felt-tip scrawl on the huge revolving doors of the Ukraina. 'Be Attention. Aids!'

To the Novodevichnaya Cemetery to see the grave of Chekhov. However, today is Saturday, relatives' day, and since we are only tourists and no one, not even Timothy Mo, is related to Chekhov, we are not admitted. Galina, the sterner of our guides, goes into the gateman's office to argue it out. 'I have a delegation of British writers outside.' The man shrugs. 'But these are *writers*.' 'So? I am a reader.' One had not thought deconstruction had reached so far.

After lunch at a Georgian State Restaurant near Pushkin Square we stroll back through the Arbat, a pedestrian precinct crowded with shoppers and sightseers this Saturday afternoon. With its seats and bulbous lamp standards, street pedlars and guitar-players, it could be a precinct anywhere in Western Europe. ('The Russians are like us; they have precincts.') The difference of course is that there is virtually nothing in the shops. There are queues for ice-cream and queues for coffee, but, that apart, no one is selling anything resembling food. I go into a stationer's to buy an exercise book (the word *tetradka* surfacing unbidden from my Russian learned and forgotten 25 years ago). Even in the stationer's there is a queue and a bored shop girl serving a little boy has him trembling on the edge of tears, so I come out. Going into the shop has made me lose the others and hurrying to catch up I pass a middle-aged woman stood at a podium improvised from a cardboard box. It has something written on the front in pencil and on a bench nearby sit a man and a boy whom I take to be her husband and son. She is making an impassioned speech to which no one is listening, the husband looking shame-faced and the boy turning away in embarrassment. Not wanting to contribute to their discomfort, I do not listen to her either or try to read what is written on the box. It is only after I have walked on that I wonder if this is a political protest and think maybe that is what dissidence is like—embarrassing to the general public, shaming for the immediate family, getting a dose of freedom like getting a dose of Jesus.

By overnight train to Orel. It is a bad night and we have to be up at six. Me: 'There are two men playing chess in the next compartment.' Craig Raine: 'One of them isn't Death by any chance?'

None of us has ever heard of Orel and when we come out of the station we realize why. It is Loughborough. We are met by our Intourist guide Marina, a youngish woman, sturdy, solid and with a wide-eyed humourless look I find familiar but hard to place. Of course. What is missing is the wimple. She is a nun. 'Now,' she says briskly, 'we have arrived at our place of destination.' We get into our bus and she seizes the intercom. 'Allow me to compliment you on your choice of season for coming to our city. It is spring and as you see everything is not yet bare still. After your breakfast we will pick up, so to speak, some other writers from the centre of our city and visit the war memorials.' Even on the short journey to the motel one detects the difference in atmosphere between here and Moscow. There we had scarcely seen a slogan and Sue thought that even the pictures of Lenin were not as common as a few years back. Here he is very much in evidence and every factory and public building is still surmounted by calls to action. 'All Power to Soviet Youth.' 'Long Live the Working Class.' Marina drives the point home. 'Let me say something of Orel centre. The city was a witness to many historical events. It has a prolonged form along the river and was one of the 15 most ruined cities by the Fascists. On the right is a monument not to any concrete personality, so to speak, but to the distinction of Orel Steel Rolling Mill which outports to 60 countries in the world.' It is seven o'clock on Sunday morning.

The morning having been devoted to war, the afternoon is set aside for art. 'Here is our museum of Orel writers,' announces Marina as our bus draws up. 'Now we are getting out and coming in.' The Orel writers turn out to be Fet, Bunin, Andreev, Novikov and (somewhere out in the country) Turgenev. What they all have in common, having been born in Orel, is that they got out of it at the earliest opportunity. The museum is full of dark Edwardian furniture. It is like a succession of dentists' waiting-rooms. Soon I am moaning aloud with boredom and I begin to realize what the Queen must feel like.

A tea party to meet the present-day writers of Orel – the ones who haven't managed to get away, that is. My neighbour is a burly playwright who looks more like a butcher. 'Do you like Orel?' I begin vapidly. He shrugs. 'He says it is nice,' Marina explains. 'Less rushing than in Moscow.' 'Were you born here?'

I ask. 'No. He was born in Siberia.' Maybe it is the mention of Siberia that galvanizes Marina, but she decides we have spent long enough on the social chit-chat and ought to get down to business. 'What is love?' she asks firmly. 'That is good question to discuss. Love is, so to speak, many things. Let us discuss that as writers.' Instead we discuss literature and in particular Jerome K. Jerome's *Three Men in the Same Boat*.

We drive 60 kilometres to the east to visit Turgenev's birthplace. Wide-verged roads, thin woods, rolling countryside: the tanks must have had a field day. Marina has the mike again. 'Permit me to say a couple of words about the vegetation of Orel region. There are oak trees, pine trees, birch trees. There are in all many grown-up trees.' Two of the local writers accompanying us take a fancy to Sue Townsend, taking turns to sit next to her, and these manoeuvres generate a sense of hysteria in our party. Lunch is taken at a ranch-style roadhouse in a room hung with chandeliers used for banquets and weddings. We have scarcely started on the food when the toasts begin, the writers popping up one after the other to give long rambling speeches about peace and friendship and the Russian soul. I remember the Russian soul. It was much in evidence 25 years ago when I was on the Joint-Services Russian course at Cambridge; it was always a useful theme to pad out one's weekly essay. None of the writers in Moscow had mentioned it, but here it was in Orel, still alive and kicking. When the lengthy meal is finished, we climb wearily back into the bus, whereupon Oleg, the leader of the Orel writers (and one of the suitors for Ms Townsend), proceeds to harangue us further on the Russian soul. We become more and more hysterical. 'I had been told the English were reserved people,' says Marina. 'But you laugh all the time.' And of course knowing we are behaving disgracefully doesn't help.

When we reach Turgenev's villa Sue Townsend, Craig Raine and I avoid the guided tour and wander by the lake. We then do a perfunctory tour of the house (more dentists' waiting-rooms) and sit by the village pond just outside the gates. The back gardens of some wooden cottages run down to the water and a peasant woman stands on a little jetty washing some buckets. Children play by a lower pond and geese usher their goslings down to the water. It could be a theme park, of course, but it doesn't look to have changed much since the 19th century. It's the sort of scene that youth or love would print on the heart, but with nothing to make one remember, no agent to develop the snapshot, one notes the pond and the peace this warm spring day and that's all.

The coach returns and as we draw near to Orel Sue's admirers become increasingly desperate and try and get her to go for a walk in the woods. One of them (the playwright) coyly opens his briefcase to reveal two bottles of wine. He has his son with him, a shy boy who is about to go into the Army and who speaks a little English. He has to translate his father's ogling remarks. Were the seduction to go according to plan, he would presumably have to stick around until actions began to speak louder than words. In its potential for filial embarrassment it reminds me of a Chekhov short story in which a father and son, sailors on a freighter, draw the winning lots to the cabin spyhole through which they watch a honeymoon couple.

At an Embassy cocktail party back in Moscow I talk to the BBC correspondent Jeremy Harris, who has been at Philby's funeral. He says the first evidence that it was happening was a phone call to a Reuter's colleague to say that Philby's funeral was taking place at the Kurskaya cemetery. 'When?' 'Now,' said the voice, and rang off. They piled into a taxi, got to the cemetery and found it deserted, the only evidence of the coming ceremony an open grave lined with red and black silk. Eventually, a procession threaded its way among the graves with the coffin borne aloft. As it was lowered, they saw that it was open and there was Philby, smiling slightly. The oddest figure there was Philby's son. He must have come straight from the airport, and standing at the graveside he was still carrying his duty-free bag.

Novy Mir had printed bootleg extracts from Sue Townsend's *Diary of Adrian Mole*. Now it is to be officially translated and the translator is to take her out to supper. We go off to a restaurant, where eventually she joins us. The translator has stood her up. Next day he calls to say he had the day confused and thought Tuesday was Thursday. Paul Bailey remarks that this augurs ill for the translation, which will probably read: 'Friday, Got up early and went to Sunday school.'

To Lvov by Aeroflot. It is a two-hour flight and the only refreshment served is a cup of faintly scented mineral water. The stewardess waits while one drinks this (not enough cups), making it seem even more like medicine. Spirits rise as we see another stewardness coming through with a trolley and the passengers falling on the contents. They turn out to be dolls. A second pass through the plane brings little brown bears and plastic carrier bags, and a third the Russian equivalent of Knight's Castile. I imagine if the flight went on long enough we'd be down to Brillo pads and plastic sink tidies. The woman in front of me is nervous of flying. She is sweating a lot and eventually removes her coat. Sitting by the emergency door and not finding anywhere to put her doubtless precious coat, she tries to hang it on the emergency door handle. In an unaccustomed moment of decision, I clasp both arms round her and shout: 'Stop!' She doesn't even look round, just meekly puts the coat across her lap and goes on sweating. On the flight Paul Bailey reads Gibbon, I read Updike, Sue Townsend reads Paul Bailey and Timothy Mo chats to Volodya, our senior representative. He is translating John le Carré and asks Tim for help with some idiomatic phrases. 'What is "Down the hatch"? This is an invitation to drop the liquid, no?' Some of Tim's explanations are as inaccurate as Volodya's guesses. 'At Oxford what is Port Meadow?' Tim describes a rich green pasture where cows stand up to their bellies in the lush grass, a far cry from the patch of scrub bordered by factories and allotments that it really is.

Lvov turns out to be an enchanting place, a 17th- and 18th-century city that is largely intact, with architecture so cosmopolitan one could be anywhere in Northern Europe or even Austria. The city was Polish until 1939, when it came to Russia in the carve-up after the Nazi-Soviet Pact, and is now a centre of Ukrainian nationalism. We are taken to meet the mayor, a large ironic man who gives us coffee in his parlour and tells us of the contacts the city maintains with expatriate Ukrainians, particularly in Canada, where he has just been visiting Winnipeg. I mention that most of the Russians in *An Englishman Abroad* were played by members of the Ukrainian colony near Dundee. 'What a pity,' he says. 'Next time maybe they'll play Ukrainians.'

Lvov is full of churches, Catholic, Orthodox and Uniate, and all of them are packed this Thursday morning because it is Ascension Day. Sue and I go into the cathedral. Although the service is over, women are kneeling, not only in the pews and before the altars, but in the aisles, against pillars, anywhere where there is a spare patch of flagstone (which some of them kiss). We are younger than most of the congregation and a kindly old granny, assuming that it is all mumbo-jumbo to us, starts to explain about the Ascension and Pentecost. She is stopped by a mean-looking old woman who tells me I should not be sitting with my legs crossed in a church. Sue is upset by this attack and starts crying, whereupon the nice granny shoos the old witch away and takes us off behind a pillar in order to continue the lesson.

Such fervour is disturbing. Lvov is still Polish in spirit, which explains part of it, but one realizes there is no easy equation between political liberty and religious freedom, and that faith as blind as this is no more democratic than the regime that would suppress it. It is incidentally very anti-semitic. We ask our guide whether there is a synagogue in the city. There may have been, he says, but he thinks it has been destroyed. Further questions are met with a shrug. Later we discover that during the war Lvov had a large concentration camp on its outskirts.

An afternoon spent in discussions at the local Writers' Union. The most striking person here is a French-speaking Ukrainian woman. She is in her sixties, but chic and smartly-dressed, almost a caricature of a French woman making the most of herself. Her job was to translate approved novels from the French. The approval had its limitations, however, and she was sentenced to ten years in a camp at Magadan. When the official interpreter translates this, she doesn't actually say 'a camp', but 'somewhere far away'. I am not sure if this is because of censorship, voluntary or otherwise, or because it wasn't camp, just a kind of exile. Or maybe it's just that she's naturally embarrased in an atmosphere of cordial discussion to admit there are such places.

There are plenty of cafés in Lvov, more food in the shops than in Moscow, and in the evening the place takes on an Italian atmosphere with the whole town out walking the streets round the main square. On park seats old men play chess, dominoes and a kind of stand-up whist in which the players hurl their cards down on to a low table. Later we go to the opera to see an epic of Ukrainian nationalism, Gulak-Artemosky's *The Ukrainian Cossack beyond the Danube*. It is a simple tale, given once a month by the company and greatly appreciated by the audience, who applaud it way beyond its merits. The orchestra are plainly bored stiff with it, openly reading newspapers and chattering loudly during spoken passages. A pigeon now gets into the roof against the glass. The chorus discuss this while singing and step out of line to look up at the source of the disturbance, as in their unoccupied moments do the leading singers. At the end, bouquets are brought onto the stage and there is the usual hail of tulips and ten minutes of rhythmic applause. Nice to see, though, that Melvyn has caught up with us again, this time giving a somewhat overstated performance as a eunuch in the retinue of the Sultan.

Beer was unobtainable in Moscow except at the hard-currency shop, and before coming to Lvov I bought a dozen or more cans to see me through the trip. However, beer was plentiful in Lvov (though about as alcoholic as dandelion and burdock). So when I board the plane for Moscow I am still carrying a dozen cans of Heineken. It is, I suppose, the closest I shall ever come to being a football hooligan.

Alan Coren

Bohemia

English Bohemianism is a curiously unluscious fruit. It does not belong in the great, mad, steamy glasshouse in which so much of the art of the rest of the world seems to have flourished – or, at least, so much of the pseudo-art. Inside this hothouse, huge lascivious orchids slide sensually up the sweating windows, passion-flowers cross-pollinate in wild heliotrope abandon, lotuses writhe with poppies in the rich warm beds, kumquats ripen, tremble, and plop fatly to the floor – and outside, in a neat, trimly-hoed kitchen garden, English Bohemians sit in cold orderly rows, like carrots.

In our Bohemia, there are no beautifully crazy one-eared artists, no *sans culottes*, no castrated epistolarians, no genuine revolutionaries, no hopheads, no lunatics, not even any alcoholics of note; our seed-beds have never teemed with Rimbauds and Gauguins and Kafkas and d'Annunzios and Dostoievskys; we don't even have a Mailer or a Ginsberg to call our own. Our Bohemia is populated by Civil Servants like Chaucer and Spenser and Milton; by tough-nut professional penmongers like Shakespeare and Dryden and Johnson, who worried as much about underwear and rent as about oxymorons; by corpulent suburban family men like Thackeray and Dickens and Trollope. And whenever an English oddball raises, tentatively, his head, he's a pitifully pale imitation of the real thing – Thom. Gray, sad, thin Cambridge queer, Cowper, mad among his rabbits, Swinburne, a tiny fetishistic gnome as far from Leopold von Sacher-Masoch as water is from blood. The private lives of our great powerhouses of passion, Pope and Swift, were dreary and colourless in the extreme, and Emily Brontë divided her time between *Wuthering Heights* and the Haworth laundry-list. And history, though it may offer our only revolutionary poet the passing tribute of a literary footnote, will probably think of William Morris mainly as the Father of Modern Wallpaper.

There was, however, one brief moment in this socially unostentatious culture of ours when we were touched, albeit gingerly, by the spirit of Bohemia. I am not (how could you *think* a thing like that?) referring, of course, to the Wildean shenanigans at the *fin* of the last *siècle*, which were the product not of an authentic Bohemianism but of the need to dig up a literature and a *modus vivendi* you could wear with spats and a green carnation: that Café Royal crowd was the first Switched-On, With-It Generation England ever had, and the whole megillah should be taken with a pinch of pastis. No, the gang I have in mind are the Lake Poets, who had, for once, all the genuine constituents of real adjustment problems, social malaise, illegitimate offspring, numerous tracts, a hang-out, a vast literature, and, most important of all, a date: 1798. And since at first sight, and for several thereafter, the Lake District, a sopping place of sedge and goat, seems as unlikely a Bohemian ambience as you could shake a quill at, much can be gained by examining the area itself; one can do no better than take the career of its most eminent son, a William Wordsworth, and relate it (as all the local tourist offices do) to every cranny, sheep and sod between Windermere and the Scottish border.

I realize, naturally, that the aforementioned bard left a meticulous record of all that made him what he was, but since all writers are extraordinary liars, poseurs, distorters, and self-deceivers, I have chosen to ignore most of his farragos and interpretations; and for the background to this chapter, I am not indebted to *The Poetical Works Of William Wordsworth* (5 vols, Oxford 1940–49), *Wordsworth: A Re-interpretation* by F. W. Bateson (London 1954), *The Egotistical Sublime* by J. Jones (London 1954), or *Wordsworth and Coleridge* by H. G. Margoliouth (London 1953). In particular, I am not indebted to *Strange Seas of Thought: Studies in Wordsworth's Philosophy of Man and Nature* by N. P. Stallknecht (North Carolina 1945). However, I gather from friends in the trade that no work of serious scholarship is complete without a list of references and sources three times the size of the thing itself, so for devotees of this sort of *narrischkeit*, a fuller bibliography will be found sewn inside the lining of my old green hacking-jacket.

Cockermouth, Cumberland, was the spot where, on April 7, 1770, William Wordsworth first drew breath, and the location goes a long way towards explaining his characteristic lugubriousness. In the Old Hall, now derelict and seeping, Mary Queen of Scots was received after her defeat at Langside in 1568; her gloom was plumbless, and her host, Henry Fletcher, gave her thirteen ells of crimson velvet for a new dress. This could hardly have compensated for having her army trodden into the mud, but it ranks as one of history's nicer gestures to Mary. Nearby stands Harry Hotspur's house, contracts for which had just been exchanged when the new proprietor was butchered at Shrewsbury, in 1403, and within spitting distance can be found a few lumps of twelfth-century castle: this was captured in 1313 by Robert the Bruce, and spent the rest of the century under constant attack and bombardment by any Scots infantrymen who happened to be in the neighbourhood. During the Wars of the Roses, it was first Yorkist, then Lancastrian, and the catalogue of woe was finally brought to an end during the Civil War, when it was demolished by the Roundheads. A mile or so away, at Moorland Close, is the 1764 birthplace of Fletcher Christian, leader of the *Bounty* mutineers, and the 1766 birthplace of John Dalton, the physicist whose nefarious theories led ultimately to the destruction of Hiroshima.

Given this agglomerated misery, it isn't difficult to see how young Wordsworth could become aware, very early, of the general rottenness of intelligent bipeds, by comparison with whom the local trees, thorns, and general flora assume a commendable innocence. One imagines John Wordsworth taking his little offshoot on trots through the topography, pointing out the various scenes of butchery and nastiness, totting up the huge casualty list, and pondering aloud on the question of how long it would take that diabolical infant prodigy John Dalton to come up with a hydrogen bomb. It's little wonder that William decided early on who his friends were, and began associating with daffodils. Not that the idea of Nature possessing a mean streak escaped him, either; the news that Fletcher Christian got his come-uppance for interfering with the rights of breadfruit was undeniably traumatic for young Wm. – thereafter, as the *Prelude* indicates, he couldn't break a twig or step on a toadstool without feeling that the crime would be expunged in blood.

He went on to Hawkshead Grammar School, where little seems to have happened to him, except that he befriended a lad called John Tyson, who immediately died, aged twelve, to be later commemorated in 'There was a boy, / Ye knew him well, ye cliffs and islands of Winander . . .' This drove Wordsworth even further towards the mountains and shrubbery, who were obviously bound to enjoy a longer life-span and weren't going to peg out just when William was getting to know them. This was now his period of greatest involvement with Nature, a time spent sculling about the lakes with which the area is infested and grubbing about in the undergrowth, one ear cocked for the song of earwig and slug, the other for That Still Spirit Shed From Evening Air. It rained most of the time. And, as the years rolled by and William grew to pubescence, talking the whiles to roots and knolls, he became more and more aware of humanity in general as a collection of blots and errors. One could rely on the crocus; every year it re-emerged from the turf, developed into its tiny, private perfection, and then quietly pegged out. And other mates of the poet, like Skiddaw and Scafell and Easedale Tarn, changed very little from year to year. But as the maturing bard pottered around Cumbria, he bumped inevitably into some of the area's human population, later immortalized and now available in paperback, who served only to convince him that after the fifth day, the Almighty's unerring talent for creating perfection deserted him: the life of Wordsworth the Teenager teemed with mad old women, decayed sailormen, idiot children, dispossessed cottars, impoverished leech-gatherers, bereaved lovers, unscrupulous potters, orphans, mutes, destitutes, and chronic bronchitics. Why the Lake District should have seethed with such sad misfits and sufferers to the point where Wordsworth never met anyone else is a question I gladly leave to medical historians or any similar forager with the necessary time on his hands. But I would just like to point out to all those scholars who have wondered why Wordsworth should have been a believer in metempsychosis (that dubiously scientific process whereby souls pass on from one corporeal form to another as the subsequent mortal coils get shuffled off) that he quite clearly needed the hope it offered: souls inhabiting the forms of Lake District inhabitants were so unfortunately lumbered, that only the belief in their ultimate transmogrification into a hollyhock or woodlouse sustained Wordsworth's faith in God's pervading goodness. There is, indeed, much evidence to show that the poet would have given his eye-teeth to have been a clump of heather.

In 1787, he went up to Cambridge. Everyone drank port and spoke Latin, and the nearest Cumberland beggar was three hundred miles to the NW. Wordsworth was desolate, left the university, utterly unnoticed, and took ship for the Continent. It was here that he burgeoned and ripened under the cucumber-glass of Italian culture and Gallic revolution, suddenly exposed to all that the Lake District was not: Bohemianism took root in the Cumbrian corpuscles, and in the general uproar following the coup of 1789, Wordsworth sang in the streets, went about with his shirt unbuttoned, and seduced the daughter of a French surgeon. Again, scholars have been baffled by the whole Annette Vallon business: why the mystery, the concealment of Words-worth's bastard son, the failure to return with its father to England? What the scholars have in textual fidelity, they lack in imagination; even without dwelling on the unwholesome possi-bility that Wordsworth's boudoir techniques, picked up at sec-ondhand from observations of Esthwaite sheep, must have left much to be desired, we can make a fair guess at Annette's response to the poet's suggestion that she accompany him back to the fells to meet Mad Margaret, Peter Bell, Old Matthew, and the rest of the gang. At all events, Wordsworth came home alone, and unable to face the quiet of the Lakes, took Dorothy down to Somerset, which by now had got a reputation for having Coleridge on the premises. The two met up. Coleridge had already collected a Lake Poet, Robert Southey, and together they had concocted a form of early communism which they called Pantisocracy, so that by the time Wordsworth fixed his wagon to their star, the nub of Bohemianism had been unmistakably shaped: of these two ur-Marxists, Southey had already distinguished himself for his opposition to flogging, Coleridge was smoking pot and seeing visions, and the pair of them had been writing like things possessed. With Wordsworth in tow, the poetic output stepped up enormously, and in 1798, he and Coleridge hit the market with their *Lyrical Ballads*, and everyone took off for the Lake District. The years that followed were ambrosial for Wordsworth: at last he could stop mooning about and involving himself with the problems of the educationally sub-normal citizens of Westmorland and Cumberland, and throw himself into the serious business of Bohemianism. Night after night the fells echoed to revelry and pentameters as the wild poets of Cumbria entertained thinkers and versifiers from all over the civilized world. Scott came, and Lamb, and Hazlitt, and de Quincey, until the nights of riot and boozing and composition surpassed anything the literary world had seen since William Shagsper, Kit Marlowe, Francis Bacon, the Earl of Oxford and Robert Greene had all stabbed one another in the Mermaid Tavern, leaving the responsibility for Elizabethan drama entirely in the hands of a Mr W. H. Grobeley, the inn's landlord, who subsequently wrote it to avoid suspicion falling on his hostelry. No visit to Dove Cottage, Grasmere, is complete without examining the outhouse where Hazlitt's father, a Unitarian minister of strong liberal views, attempted to put his hand up Dorothy Wordsworth's skirt, and at Greta Hall, Keswick, can be seen the faded, bloody marks following a fight over the rent-book by its two most illustrious tenants, Coleridge and Southey.

But ultimately, as it will, Bohemianism died. Coleridge left in 1809, went south, and died of opium poisoning. Southey became Poet Laureate in 1813, and took to wearing hats and drinking lukewarm herb tea. In the same year, Wordsworth became the Distributor of Stamps for the County of Westmorland at £400 per annum, and as befitted a civil servant, moved to Rydal Mount, turned his back on liberalism, and finally petered out in 1850, leaving his cottage to de Quincey, who hadn't touched a drop for the past thirty years.

Today, there are few reminders of those high and far-off times: the occasional grocer with the ineradicable Hazlitt family nose, or the Coleridge lip; fading graffiti on some derelict farmhouse wall, retailing bizarre local legends in the language and forms set down in the famous *Preface* of 1798; the empty gin-bottles that have bobbed on Ullswater and Bassenthwaite for the past century and a half; a crumbling gazebo on the outskirts of Keswick, built by Southey and from which he would pounce on passing milkmaids. Naturally, there are far more memorials to the more respectable aspects of the Bohemians' life and work, and during the summer, the roads of the two counties are filled with coachloads of people from Bromley and Philadelphia being driven to Gowbarrow Park to look at the descendants of the original daffodils.

The traditions, too, are dead. Not only is the local population conspicuously sane, sober, ungrieving, unstarving and totally unlike the *dramatis personae* of Wordsworth's records, the visitors are similarly unpoetic and unBohemian. They throng the Lake District between April and October in great tweed crowds; they wear sensible shoes, and corduroy knee-breeches, headscarves and duffle-coats, balaclavas and plastic macs; they carry stolid-looking walking-sticks, and rucksacks, and notebooks for pressing bog asphodel and saxifrage in, and Aer Lingus bags containing tomato sandwiches and flasks of Bovril; they have rosy cheeks, and hearty, uncomplicated laughs, and sturdy calf-muscles; they eat ham teas, and hold sing-songs in Youth Hostels, and go to bed at nine o'clock to listen to the wind in the eaves. Or else they come in Ford Cortinas and Bedford Dormobiles, with primus stoves and Calor Gas and tents from Gamages, to take their children boating on Windermere. And every year, they pay homage at the verdant shrine of someone whom they vaguely remember as being a poet, or something, simply because the guide book has led them to his grave, and because all tombs demand equal reverence. So they stand, heads bowed briefly, in St Oswald's churchyard, Grasmere.

Never for one moment realizing that Wordsworth himself would have thrown up at the sight of them.

Alan Coren

Thanks for the Memory

> The President has agreed to make available notes he made
> during the White House discussions on the arms sale to Iran.
> The notes are those the President takes to help him write his
> memoirs. At the end of the day, he writes down his impressions
> of the day's events, the people he has met and what he thought
> of them, and the decisions that were taken.
>   The committee investigating the Iran affair believes the
> notes will make clear the President's position.
>
> The Times

MONDAY EVENING

Dear Diary,
Today was a real hard day.

It started off where I ate a little house. I did not know I had
ate a little house until I found a little elf in my spoon. First off,
I thought it was a roach, but when I looked on the back of the
pack it said this was my lucky day because each Grape Nuts
pack contained a little elf and a little house, and what you did
was you put the little elf in the little house and then you would
have a little house with a little elf in, and you could add it to
your collection. When I found the little elf in my spoon I tipped
all the Grape Nuts on to the table but there was no little house.

I guess I will have to go into Bethesda Naval and have the
little house taken out. Otherwise my collection will look dumb,
just a little elf standing next to a little witch and a little dragon
and a little goblin and not in his little house.

George Shultz came in right after breakfast.

Here is the conversation:
'*Good morning, Mr President.*'
'*I ate the little house, George.*'
'*Good. I think we should go up to the meeting now.*'

The meeting was a tough meeting. Here are my notes:

As you look at the back of Caspar Weinberger's envelope, Iran is on the right and is joined to Iraq on the left. They are written down IraN and IraQ so we all know exactly who's who, because they are both of them followers of Islam, a camel-driver, but George says don't worry, anybody could get confused, and I should look at the photographs of an IraQi and an IraNi in my update file.

Here is the conversation:
Me: '*They both look kind of Jewish, George.*'
Weinberger: '*What did the President say, George?*'
Shultz: '*He said they both look kind of Jewish.*'
Weinberger: '*Okay. Just checking.*'

The discussion opened up right after that, and I formed the impression that IraQ and IraN are different kinds of Islams and are fighting a war due to this, and the object is to get right to the other side of Weinberger's envelope. I also formed the impression, at 11.20 approximately Eastern Standard Time, that I had got the mango Danish.

Here is the conversation:
Shultz: '– or, alternatively, laundered through Tel Aviv?*'
Me: '*Who ordered the mango Danish?*'
Meese: '*What?*'
Me: '*This seems to be a mango Danish. I ordered a blueberry muffin.*'
Weinberger: '*I have your muffin, Mr President.*'
Me: '*Then you get the mango Danish, am I right?*'
Weinberger: '*I was the pretzel.*'
Shultz: '*I have the pretzel. I ordered the cinnamon toast.*'
Meese: '*I have the cinnamon toast. I ordered the mango Danish.*'
Me: '*Great! Now, just to kind of re-cap, IraQ is the flakies with the long black shirts, right?*'

In the afternoon session, Shultz brought up some kind of thing we signed one time about a worldwide embargo against arms sales to IraN, due to where they took US hostages. Weinberger said that we ought to look at this in the light of the fact that it was now the Lebanon that had the US hostages. I said maybe we ought to bomb it again. They all looked at me.

Here is the conversation:

Weinberger: 'We never bombed the Lebanon, Mr President.'

Me: 'Horse feathers! Gimme a map. Okay, what's that under my pinkie?'

Shultz: 'Tripoli, Mr President.'

Me: 'Hardy-ha-ha! Tell me we didn't bomb the hell out of Tripoli!'

Shultz: 'You are pointing at Tripoli, Lebanon, Mr President. We bombed Tripoli, Libya.'

Weinberger: 'If I can return to the matter of the Hawk sales to . . .'

I went out to the john. I think the little house is wedged somewhere. It gave me time to think. So we hit the wrong Tripoli. We bombed the Tripoli that didn't have our hostages and we didn't bomb the Tripoli that did. Don't tell me it's an easy mistake, Diary, some of those Navy pilots are pulling down a hundred thousand plus.

Still, I guess it's lucky we didn't take out Tripoli, Iowa.

TUESDAY EVENING

Dear Diary,

I missed the rest of yesterday's afternoon session, but I guess you know that. I hope you enjoyed *The Flintstones*. What I don't understand is, when they go to the drive-in on their dinosaur, how come the movie they see is in colour? I remember when colour came in, it was 1935. This is just like the Tripoli screw-up. Details count.

George Shultz came in right after breakfast.

Here is the conversation:

'Good morning, Mr President.'

'Look, George, I got another little house out of the new Grape Nuts pack. I now have two little elfs. Should I have one little elf inside and one outside, or what?'

Alan Coren

'I think we should go up to the meeting now.'

The meeting was even tougher than yesterday. Here are my notes:

This is the story so far, as I understand it. We are at war with IraN because of the hostages they took and so we are not going to give them any arms or let anybody else give them any arms, except that we are going to give them arms because we bombed the wrong Lebanon and so we are at peace with IraN for maybe a couple of weeks, but we will have to go to war with them again as soon as they have used our arms to bomb the right Lebanon and get US hostages back, but any arms they have not used we are going to have to get back, in case we have to use them to bomb IraN if they start taking US hostages.

Also, nobody must find out, because the Soviets are supplying arms to IraN which we have condemned on the grounds that this is destabilizing the area and, as a neutral, we cannot allow IraN to fall into the Soviet orbit because that would mean it fell out of the US orbit and we have to be friendly to IraN because we are at war with it. Also, the Soviets are shipping arms to IraQ. I guess this must be because IraQ is holding Soviet hostages, but Shultz just looks at the ceiling when I ask this, clearly it is something he does not want minuted at this moment in time, it is a damned sensitive area.

I went out right after the summary on account of Edwin Meese got the wrong waffle and Weinberger found mayo on his BLT and Shultz said what the kitchen needed was authority at the highest level and nobody could do it better than me so why didn't I go straighten them out? I am a sucker for flattery, Diary, it's the way I'm made, I guess. Hollywood can do that to you. I got back kind of late due to where they had *The Price is Right* on in the kitchen. A guy, just an ordinary guy from Topeka, Kansas, guessed the price of a new hi-fi system right to the damned cent! Where do we get such men?

When I got back, Shultz was talking about sending arms to Israel.

Here is the conversation:

Me: 'Great play, George! Israel will zap Lebanon and get the US

hostages, so we don't have to sell arms to Iran and screw up relations with anybody, right?'
George: 'No, Israel will sell the arms to Iran.'
Me: 'I thought they were enemies.'
George: 'They are.'
Me: 'How's the waffle, Ed?'
Meese: 'Terrific, Mr President.'

I looked out the window for a while. Weinberger was saying how the guy they were going to use as a go-between for Colonel Oliver North was Adnan Khashoggi. He is a Saudi-Arabian, so I guess that as a sworn enemy of both Israel and Iran, he is in an ideal position to help them.

After a couple of hours, I realized I did not know who this Colonel Oliver North was.

Here is the conversation:
Weinberger: 'He is the Marine officer who headed up the investigation into the Lebanon bombing. He led the hunt for those responsible.'
Me: 'Did he get the guys who hit the wrong Tripoli?'
Weinberger: 'Not that Lebanon bombing, Mr President. This was the Lebanon bombing in 1983 when the Lebanese killed 241 US Marines.'
Me: 'Holy Moly! You mean the Lebanese got the wrong Tripoli, too? Isn't it about time they changed the name before anybody else gets killed? How about Walnut Creek? I always thought Walnut Creek was a great name for a town. It sounds like a good, clean town, a good town to live in, a good place to raise your kids. I grew up in a town like that. It was called Dixon, Illinois. Nobody ever bombed Dixon, Illinois.'
Weinberger: 'That was a really terrific bacon-lettuce-and-tomato, Mr President. Nobody could have swung it in that kitchen like you swung it. I don't suppose you could, I mean I hate to ask, but, you know, talking makes me kind of hungry, and . . .'
Me: 'Say no more, old buddy. While I'm up, who needs more coffee?'

But here's the crazy thing, Diary. When I got back, the room was empty. I guess they moved to another room for security purposes. It was a smart thing to do, I never did find out where they went, which just goes to show how secure it was. I have a great team there!

George came by tonight to say he's fixed it for me to go into Bethesda Naval tomorrow to have the little house removed. He says it's worth ten poll points, minimum, and be sure and wave from my window right after. Maybe hold up the little house.

I asked him about that other thing, with the **Q** and the **N** and all that, and he said not to worry, it would all be taken care of.

Auberon Waugh

Mothers and Daughters

'She was silent within my embrace and I stroked her hair, there was a tangle at the back, in one of the flaxen fronds that fell and parted around the nine-year-old hollow apricot neck.'

So Polly Devlin sets the scene for a 'moment of truth' with her nine-year-old daughter, to be shared with two million or so readers of the *Sunday Times* as they sit around burping and farting after their Sunday breakfasts. Next in the series of 'Conversations with my daughters' is promised for this week. If nothing more dramatic crops up, I hope to discuss the series week by week, as it appears, but she has certainly given us plenty to think about for the present.

The drama begins when, during a row with her mother, the daughter picks up a postcard on which she has previously written 'I love you', crumples it up and throws it in the wastepaper basket. Daughter Devlin then leaves the room, Mother Devlin rescues postcard from wastepaper basket like some lawyer collecting evidence. Re-enter Daughter Devlin:

' "I don't love you," she said, "any more. What will happen?" '
' "Nothing will happen," I said. '
' "What will you do?" '
' "I'll be sad for a while," I said. Was that the right answer? "But it will be all right. We'll love each other again. I'll rescue it." '

Was that the right answer? Mother Devlin reveals that her natural reaction had been to scream at the girl, kick her and hit her. Would that have been better, she asks.

It seems to me she has several problems to face. The first concerns her daughter's hair. Flax is not something of which I have much experience, but I imagine it to be a coarse, fibrous substance of yellowish grey colour when untreated. If it covers her daughter's head in fronds, or leafy branches, tangled at the back, I should recommend a powerful shampoo. The very least Mother Devlin might do is to set the girl a good example by brushing her own hair thoroughly. As it appears in the *Sunday Times* photograph it might provide a friendly shelter for half a dozen sparrows, a colony of bats and even some flying foxes, but it is scarcely a good example to any daughter with hair problems.

The hollow apricot neck sounds more serious. I do not know whether Mrs Devlin is suggesting that her daughter's neck has the colour or the texture of an apricot, but in either case I would suggest that it is a matter for the family doctor, if not a specialist. All necks, I suppose, are hollow to the extent that they contain a trachea and an oesophagus, and there need be nothing to worry us there, but if her daughter's neck seems somehow hollower than most, she might be well advised to consult her doctor once again, if only for reassurance. It is not the sort of thing which comes right after an aspirin or two, or some syrup of figs.

On the great postcard question, my own reaction would have been one of mild annoyance at the waste of a postcard. One should try to discourage children from scribbling on every available surface, even if they write twee little messages like 'I love you'. Perhaps the *Sunday Times* provides postcards free to its female employees for this purpose, but even so the finances of Times Newspapers are not so strong that they can afford to throw away these important documents. What will the *Look!* pages use for their Christmas number? Even so, I feel that to scream, kick *and* hit the girl would have been an over-reaction. A short lecture on the perils of waste would surely have been enough. But Mother Devlin was not going to let the matter rest there. She decided to take the opportunity for a long lecture on child relationships and reproduction, for later publication in the *Sunday Times*:

' "If your love isn't very strong, or is very new, or you can't trust the person you love, or trust their love, which is much the same, then you can *really* hurt or be hurt – you can do a lot of damage. But the love between a mother and a daughter is old and very deep, even though you're young. Because remember before we knew each other to look at, we knew each other: you were inside my body – nothing could be closer than that." '

No doubt this advice was well-intended. Mother Devlin sincerely hoped to bring them closer together by reminding her daughter that she, the daughter, was once in Mummy's tummy. She expected, and by her own account received, an affectionate and grateful reaction along the lines of, 'Gosh, thanks, mum. Now I understand why we are such good friends.' Perhaps modern children genuinely react in this way to such reminders, but I should have thought it was the ultimate snub or put-down for a child to be reminded of where it comes from, far worse than being asked to stand up when grown-ups come into the room, or even than being told that children should be seen and not heard.

It is also, or so I should have thought, the ultimate self-indulgence for a mother to be constantly reminding her offspring that they were once foetuses, inside her reproductive system. The truth is that once children are born they have a character and identity of their own. Modern mothers having once given birth must simply learn to belt up. The nightmares which children used to suffer from being told that a long red-legged scissor man would cut off their thumbs if they sucked them must pale into insignificance beside this constant injunction to get back into their mother's womb. I can well believe that Mrs Devlin's daughter is odious as well as stroppy, that her cute little ways and leafy branches of matted, fibrous hair hide a calculating brain, but this is no way to put her in her place.

Nor do I think it is a very good idea for journalists, when short of copy, to take up acres of newsprint with discussion of their children. Both Sir William Rees-Mogg and Captain Simon Raven have been criticized for this in their time, but at least they refrained from harping on the biological aspect of their relationship. They did not feel it added to their parental authority to remind their lads that they were both in their times, one of 75 million or so spermatozoa swimming around which happened to have won the race – a sort of glorified *Sunday Times* Fun Run – to the ovaries of their dear mothers. One may marvel, as a parent, that any child of one's own can ever win any sort of

Auberon Waugh

race, but that is food for private thought, part of the wonder of creation. It would be extraordinarily offensive to tell one's children that they were once carried around in one's testicles and must therefore realize how close they are to one emotionally.

My own anxieties about the Devlin household do not end with the children. After the two of them have – by Mother Devlin's own account – bored each other stiff in this moment of truth, we learn that Daughter Devlin 'trotted out to the garden, accompanied by a large mewling cat and terribly overweight dachshund'.

This information raises so many questions that we must leave them for another week. Broadly, they are: 1) why did Daughter Devlin trot? 2) why did the cat mewl? and 3) why was the dachshund overweight? This last question may require immediate action. Is Mother Devlin not aware that it is extremely cruel to allow dogs to become overweight? As founder of the Dog Lovers' Party of Great Britain, I think I may have to draw this to the attention of the appropriate authorities. Nor do cats mewl, when going out into the garden, unless they are in pain. When we add to this the evidence which we have already discussed about the condition of Daughter Devlin's hair and neck, I think it may well be time the Devlin household received a few visitors.

Clive James

A Blizzard of Tiny Kisses

Princess Daisy by Judith Krantz (Sidgwick and Jackson, 1980)

To be a really lousy writer takes energy. The average novelist remains unread not because he is bad but because he is flat. On the evidence of *Princess Daisy*, Judith Krantz deserves her high place in the best-seller lists. This is the second time she has been up there. The first time was for a book called *Scruples*, which I will probably never get around to reading. But I don't resent the time I have put into reading *Princess Daisy*. As a work of art it has the same status as a long conversation between two not very bright drunks, but as best-sellers go it argues for a reassuringly robust connection between fiction and the reading public. If cheap dreams get no worse than this, there will not be much for the cultural analyst to complain about. *Princess Daisy* is a terrible book only in the sense that it is almost totally inept. Frightening it isn't.

In fact, it wouldn't even be particularly boring if only Mrs Krantz could quell her artistic urge. 'Above all,' said Conrad, 'to make you see.' Mrs Krantz strains every nerve to make you see. She pops her valves in the unrelenting effort to bring it all alive. Unfortunately she has the opposite of a pictorial talent. The more detail she piles on, the less clear things become. Take the meeting of Stash and Francesca. Mrs Krantz defines Prince Alexander Vassilivitch Valensky, alias Stash, as 'the great war hero and incomparable polo-player'. Stash is Daisy's father. Francesca Vernon, the film star, is her mother. Francesca possesses 'a combination of tranquillity and pure sensuality in the composition of the essential triangle of eyes and mouth'. Not just essential but well-nigh indispensable, one would have thought. Or perhaps that's what she means.

This, however, is to quibble, because before Stash and Francesca can generate Daisy they first have to meet, and theirs is a meeting of transfigurative force, as of Apollo catching up with Daphne. The scene is Deauville, 1952. Francesca the film star, she of the pure sensuality, is a reluctant spectator at a polo game – reluctant, that is, until she claps eyes on Stash. Here is a description of her eyes, together with the remaining component of the essential triangle, namely her mouth. 'Her black eyes were long and widely spaced, her mouth, even in repose, was made meaningful by the grace of its shape: the gentle arc of her upper lip dipped in the centre to meet the lovely pillow of her lower lip in a line that had the power of an embrace.'

And this is Stash, the great war hero and incomparable polo-player: 'Valensky had the physical presence of a great athlete who has punished his body without pity throughout his life and the watchful, fighting eyes of a natural predator. His glance was bold and his thick brows were many shades darker than his blonde hair, cropped short and as coarse as the coat of a hastily brushed dog ... His nose, broken many times, gave him the air of a roughneck ... Not only did Valensky never employ unnecessary force on the bit and reins but he had been born, as some men are, with an instinct for establishing a communication between himself and his pony which made it seem as if the animal was merely an extension of his mind, rather than a beast with a will of its own.'

Dog-haired, horse-brained and with a bashed conk, Stash is too much for Francesca's equilibrium. Her hat flies off.

'Oh no!' she exclaimed in dismay, but as she spoke, Stash Valensky leaned down from his pony and scooped her up in one arm. Holding her easily, across his chest, he urged his mount after the wayward hat. It had come to rest two hundred yards away, and Valensky, leaving Francesca mounted, jumped down from his saddle, picked the hat up by its ribbons and carefully replaced it on her head. The stands rang with laughter and applause.

Francesca heard nothing of the noise the spectators made. Time, as she knew it, had stopped. By instinct, she remained silent and waiting, passive against Stash's soaking-wet polo shirt. She could smell his sweat and it confounded her with desire. Her mouth filled with saliva. She wanted to sink her teeth into his tan neck, to bite him until she could taste his blood, to lick up the rivulets of sweat which ran down to his open collar. She wanted him to fall to the ground with her in his arms, just as he was, flushed, steaming, still breathing heavily from the game, and grind himself into her.

But this is the first of many points at which Mrs Krantz's minus capability for evocation leaves you puzzled. How did Stash get the hat back on Francesca's head? Did he remount, or is he just very tall? If he did remount, couldn't that have been speci-fied? Mrs Krantz gives you all the details you don't need to form a mental picture, while carefully withholding those you do. Half the trick of pictorial writing is to give only the indispensable points and let the reader's imagination do the rest. Writers who not only give the indispensable points but supply all the concrete details as well can leave you feeling bored with their brilliance – Wyndham Lewis is an outstanding example. But a writer who supplies the concrete details and leaves out the indispensable points can only exhaust you. Mrs Krantz is right to pride herself on the accuracy of her research into every department of the high life. What she says is rarely inaccurate, as far as I can tell. It is, however, almost invariably irrelevant.

Anyway, the book starts with a picture of Daisy ('Her dark eyes, not quite black, but the colour of the innermost heart of a giant purple pansy, caught the late afternoon light and held it fast . . .') and then goes on to describe the meeting of her parents. It then goes on to tell you a lot about what her parents got up to before they met. Then it goes on to tell you about *their* parents. The book is continually going backwards instead of forwards, a canny insurance against the reader's impulse to skip. At one stage I tried skipping a chapter and missed out on about a century. From the upper West Side of New York I was suddenly in the Russian Revolution. That's where Stash gets his fiery temperament from – Russia.

'At Chez Mahu they found that they were able only to talk of unimportant things. Stash tried to explain polo to Francesca but she scarcely listened, mesmerized as she was with the abrupt movements of his tanned hands on which light blonde hair grew, the hands of a great male animal.' A bison? Typically, Mrs Krantz has failed to be specific at the exact moment when specificity would be a virtue. Perhaps Stash is like a horse not just in brain but in body. This would account for his tendency to view Francesca as a creature of equine provenance. 'Francesca listened to Valensky's low voice, which had traces of an English accent, a brutal man's voice which seemed to vibrate with an underlying tenderness, as if he were talking to a newborn foal . . .'

There is a lot more about Stash and Francesca before the reader can get to Daisy. Indeed, the writer herself might never have got to Daisy if she (i.e. Mrs Krantz) had not first wiped out Stash and Francesca. But before they can be killed, Mrs Krantz must expend about a hundred and fifty pages on various desperate attempts to bring them alive. In World War Two the incomparable polo-player becomes the great war hero. Those keen to see Stash crash, however, are doomed to disappointment, since before Stash can win medals in his Hurricane we must hear about his first love affair. Stash is 14 years old and the Marquise Claire de Champery is a sex-pot of a certain age. 'She felt the congestion of blood rushing between her primly pressed together thighs, proof positive that she had been right to provoke the boy.' Stash, meanwhile, shows his customary tendency to metamorphose into an indeterminate lifeform. 'He took her hand and put it on his penis. The hot sticky organ was already beginning to rise and fill. It moved under her touch like an animal.' A field mouse? A boa constrictor?

Receiving the benefit of Stash's extensive sexual education, Francesca conceives twins. One of the twins turns out to be Daisy and the other her retarded sister, Danielle. But first Stash has to get to the clinic. 'As soon as the doctor telephoned, Stash raced to the clinic at 95 miles an hour.' Miserly as always with the essentials, Mrs Krantz trusts the reader to supply the information that Stash is attaining this speed by some form of motorized transport.

Stash rejects Danielle, Francesca flees with Danielle and Daisy. Stash consoles himself with his collection of jet aircraft.

Mrs Krantz has done a lot of research in this area but it is transparently research, which is not the same thing as knowledge. Calling a Junkers 88 a Junker 88 might be a misprint, but her rhapsody about Stash's prize purchase of 1953 is a dead giveaway. 'He tracked down and bought the most recent model available of the Lockheed XP-80, known as the Shooting Star, a jet which for many years could outmanoeuvre and outperform almost every other aircraft in the world.' USAF fighter aircraft carried 'X' numbers only before being accepted for service. By 1953 the Shooting Star was known as the F-80, had been in service for years, and was practically the slowest thing of its type in the sky. But Mrs Krantz is too fascinated by that 'X' to let it go. She deserves marks, however, for her detemination to catch up on the arcane nomenclature of boys' toys.

Stash finally buys a farm during a flying display in 1967. An old Spitfire packs up on him. 'The undercarriage of the 27–year-old plane stuck and the landing gear could not be released.' Undercarriage and landing gear are the same thing – her vocabularies have collided over the Atlantic. Also an airworthy 27–year-old Spitfire in 1967 would have been a very rare bird indeed: no wonder the undercarriage got in the road of the landing gear. But Mrs Krantz goes some way towards capturing the excitement of machines and should not be mocked for her efforts. Francesca, incidentally, dies in a car crash, with the make of car unspecified.

One trusts that Mrs Krantz's documentation of less particularly masculine activities is as meticulous as it is undoubtedly exhaustive, although even in such straightforward matters as food and drink she can sometimes be caught making the elementary mistake of piling on the fatal few details too many. Before Stash gets killed he takes Daisy to lunch every Sunday at the Connaught. After he gets killed he is forced to give up this practice, although there is no real reason why he should not have continued, since he is no more animated before his prang than after. Mrs Krantz has researched the Connaught so heavily that she must have made herself part of the furniture. It is duly noted that the menu has a brown and gold border. It is unduly noted that the menu has the date printed at the bottom. Admittedly such a thing would not happen at the nearest branch of the

Golden Egg, but it is not necessarily the mark of a great restaurant. Mrs Krantz would probably hate to hear it said, but she gives the impression of having been included late amongst the exclusiveness she so admires. There is nothing wrong with gusto, but when easy familiarity is what you are trying to convey, gush is to be avoided.

Full of grand meals served and consumed at chapter length, *Princess Daisy* reads like *Buddenbrooks* without the talent. Food is important to Mrs Krantz: so important that her characters keep turning into it, when they are not turning into animals. Daisy has a half-brother called Ram, who rapes her, arouses her sexually, beats her up, rapes her again, and does his best to wreck her life because she rejects his love. His passion is understandable, when you consider Daisy's high nutritional value. 'He gave up the struggle and devoured her lips with his own, kissing her as if he were dying of thirst and her mouth were a moist fruit.' A mango? Daisy fears Ram but goes for what he dishes out. 'Deep within her something sounded, as if the string of a great cello had been plucked, a note of remote, mysterious but unmistakable warning.' Boing.

Daisy heeds the warning and lights out for the USA, where she becomes a producer of television commercials in order to pay Danielle's hospital bills. She pals up with a patrician girl called Kiki, whose breasts quiver in indignation – the first breasts to have done that for a long, long time. At such moments one is reminded of Mrs Krantz's true literary ancestry, which stretches all the way back to Elinor Glyn, E.M. Hull and Gertrude Atherton. She is wasting a lot of her time and too much of ours trying to be John O'Hara. At the slightest surge of congested blood between her primly pressed together thighs, all Mrs Krantz's carefully garnered social detail gives way to eyes like twin dark stars, mouths like moist fruit and breasts quivering with indignation.

There is also the warm curve of Daisy's neck where the jaw joins the throat. Inheriting this topographical feature from her mother, Daisy carries it around throughout the novel waiting for the right man to kiss it *tutto tremante*. Ram will definitely not do. A disconsolate rapist, he searches hopelessly among the eligible young English ladies – Jane Bonham-Carter and Sabrina Guinness are both considered – before choosing the almost inconceivably well-connected Sarah Fane. Having violated Sarah in his by now standard manner, Ram is left with nothing to do except blow Daisy's secret and commit suicide. As Ram bites the dust, the world learns that the famous Princess Daisy, star of a multi-million-dollar perfume promotion, has a retarded sister. Will this put the kibosh on the promotion, not to mention Daisy's love for the man in charge, the wheeler-dealer head of Supracorp, Pat Shannon ('larky bandit', 'freebooter' etc)?

Daisy's libido, dimmed at first by Ram's rape, has already been reawakened by the director of her commercials, a ruthless but prodigiously creative character referred to as North. Yet North finally lacks what it takes to reach the warm curve of Daisy's neck. Success in that area is reserved for Shannon. He it is who undoes all the damage and fully arouses her hot blood. 'It seemed a long time before Shannon began to imprint a blizzard of tiny kisses at the point where Daisy's jaw joined her throat, that particularly warm curve, spendthrift with beauty, that he had not allowed himself to realize had haunted him for weeks. Daisy felt fragile and warm to Shannon, as if he'd trapped a young unicorn [horses again – C.J.], some strange, mythological creature. Her hair was the most intense source of light in the room, since it reflected the moonlight creeping through the windows, and by its light he saw her eyes, open, rapt and glowing; twin dark stars.'

Shannon might think he's got hold of some kind of horse, but as far as Daisy's concerned she's a species of cetacean. 'It was she who guided his hands down the length of her body, she who touched him wherever she could reach, as playfully as a dolphin, until he realized that her fragility was strength, and that she wanted him without reserve.'

Daisy is so moved by this belated but shatteringly complete experience that she can be forgiven for what she does next. 'Afterward, as they lay together, half asleep, but unwilling to drift apart into unconsciousness, Daisy farted, in a tiny series of absolutely irrepressible little pops that seemed to her to go on for a minute.' It takes bad art to teach us how good art gets done. Knowing that the dithyrambs have gone on long enough, Mrs Krantz has tried to undercut them with something earthy. Her tone goes wrong, but her intention is worthy of respect. It is like one of those clumsy attempts at naturalism in a late-medieval painting – less pathetic than portentous, since it adumbrates the great age to come. Mrs Krantz will never be much of an artist but she has more than a touch of the artist's ambition.

Princess Daisy is not be to despised. Nor should it be deplored for its concern with aristocracy, glamour, status, success and things like that. On the evidence of her prose, Mrs Krantz has not enough humour to write tongue-in-cheek, but other people are perfectly capable of reading that way. People don't get their morality from their reading matter: they bring their morality to it. The assumption that ordinary people's lives could be controlled and limited by what entertained them was always too condescending to be anything but fatuous.

Mrs Krantz, having dined at Mark's Club, insists that it is exclusive. There would not have been much point to her dining there if she did not think that. A bigger snob than she might point out that the best reason for not dining at Mark's Club is the chance of finding Mrs Krantz there. It takes only common sense, though, to tell you that on those terms exclusiveness is not just chimerical but plain tedious. You would keep better company eating Kentucky Fried Chicken in a launderette. But if some of this book's readers find themselves day-dreaming of the high life, let us be grateful that Mrs Krantz exists to help give their vague aspirations a local habitation and a name. They would dream anyway, and without Mrs Krantz they would dream unaided.

To pour abuse on a book like this makes no more sense than to kick a powder-puff. *Princess Daisy* is not even reprehensible for the three million dollars its author was paid for it in advance. It would probably have made most of the money back without a dime spent on publicity. The only bad thing is the effect on Mrs Krantz's personality. Until lately she was a nice Jewish lady harbouring the usual bourgeois fancies about the aristocracy. But now she gives interviews extolling her own hard head. 'Like so many of us,' she told the *Daily Mail* on 28 April, 'I happen to believe that being young, beautiful and rich is more desirable than being old, ugly and destitute.' Mrs Krantz is 50 years old, but to judge from the photograph on the back of the book she is engaged in a series of hard-fought delaying actions against time. This, I believe, is one dream that intelligent people ought not to connive at, since the inevitable result of any attempt to prolong youth is a graceless old age.

Germaine Greer

from *The Female Eunuch*

Perhaps it is no longer true that every young girl dreams of being in love. Perhaps the pop revolution which has replaced sentiment with lust by forcibly incorporating the sexual ethos of black urban blues into the culture created by the young for themselves has had a far-reaching effect on sexual *mores*. Perhaps young girls have allowed an actual sexual battle to replace the moony fantasies that I certainly fell for in my teenage years. Nevertheless, it is only a perhaps. Dr Peter Mann's researches at the University of Sheffield show that twenty-five to forty-five-year old women are avid readers of romantic fiction, especially housewives and secretarial workers. Some buy as many as eighty books a year. The market is bigger than ever before. *Romance still lives!* cried the *Woman's Weekly*, 'famed for its fiction', as recently as August 1969.

For all their new freedoms, the majority of 'young people of today' still dream the same dreams, find life as adventurous and appreciate the best values as have the generations before them.

... Kathy, on the lawn that evening, might have been modelling an illustration for a Victorian love story. Her white dress, of some filmy material, was high at the throat and went down to her black satin slippers. She had a black velvet ribbon round her small waist and wore an old gold chain with a locket, and her black hair was parted in the middle ... 'She's going to her first ball,' her mother said to me ... 'She's wildly excited.'

... For every sad daughter whiffing in marijuana in some darkened discotheque, there are thousands like Kathy, 'wildly excited' in their first formal dance frock.

This apparently is romance. The stress placed by the male author of this piece on the dress which is appropriate to romance is typical of the emphasis which characterizes such lore. The dance is the high mass in which Kathy will appear in her glory, to be wooed and adored. Her young man will be bewitched, stumbling after her in his drab evening dress, pressing her cool hand, circling her tiny waist and whirling her helpless in his arms about the floor. He will compliment her on her beauty, her dancing, thank her for an unforgettable evening.

Debutantes still come out every year, in their virginal white, curtseying to the Queen, the Mayor, the Bishop, or whomever, pacing their formal patterns with downcast eyes. The boys ask politely for dances while the girls accept prettily, or try to find pretexts for refusing in the hope that someone nicer will ask. Their beaux ought to have given them flowers. But every girl is hoping that something more exciting, more romantic than the expected sequence of the social event will happen. Perhaps some terrifyingly handsome man will press a little closer than the others and smell the perfume of her hair. Perhaps after supper, when they stroll upon the terrace, he will catch his breath, dazzled by the splendour of her limitless eyes. Her heart will pound, and her cheeks mantle with delicious blushes. He will say wonderful things, be strangely tender and intense. She may be swept into his masterful arms. Nothing more sexual than a kiss, no vulgar groping embraces, only strong arms about her protecting her from the coarseness of the world, and warm lips on hers, sending extraordinary stimuli through her whole body.

In the romantic world, kisses do not come before love, unless they are offered by wicked men who delude innocent girls for a time, for they will soon be rescued by the omnipotent true lover. The first kiss ideally signals rapture, exchange of hearts, and imminent marriage. Otherwise it is a kiss that *lies*. All very crude and nonsensical, and yet it is the staple myth of hundreds of comics called 'Sweethearts', 'Romantic Secrets' and so forth. The state induced by the kiss is actually self-induced, of course, for few lips are so gifted with electric and psychedelic possibilities. Many a young man trying to make out with his girl has been surprised at her raptness and elation, only to find himself lumbered with an unwanted intense relationship which is compulsorily sexless.

When it happens it will be wonderful, unforgettable, beautiful. It will be like Mimi and Rodolfo singing perfect arias at their first meeting. Perhaps they will not fall in love all at once but feel a tenderness growing until one day POW! that amazing kiss. The follow-through would have to be the constant manifestation of tenderness, esteem, flattery and susceptibility by the man together with chivalry and gallantry in all situations. The hero of romance knows how to treat women. Flowers, little gifts, love letters, maybe poems to her eyes and hair, candlelit meals on moonlit terraces and muted strings. Nothing hasty, physical. Some heavy breathing. Searing lips pressed against the thin stuff of her bodice. Endearments muttered into her luxuriant hair. 'Little things mean a lot.' Her favourite chocolates, his pet names for her, remembering her birthday, anniversaries, silly games. And then the foolish things that remind him of her, her perfume, her scarf, her frilly underthings and absurd lace hankies, kittens in her lap. Mystery, magic, champagne, ceremony, tenderness, excitement, adoration, reverence – women never have enough of it. Most men know nothing about this female fantasy world because they are not exposed to this kind of literature and the commerce of romanticism. The kind of man who studies this kind of behaviour and becomes a ladies' man whether for lust or love or cupidity is generally feared and disliked by other men as a gigolo or even a queer. Male beauticians and hairdressers study the foibles of their customers and deliberately flirt with them, paying them compliments that they thirst for, hinting that they deserve better than the squalid domestic destiny that they bear.

If *Sweethearts* and the other publications of the same kind with their hallucinated love imagery are American, it is unfortunately true that they find a wide distribution in England. There are also trash weeklies called *Mirabelle*, *Valentine*, *Romeo* and, biggest of all, *Jackie* selling upwards of a million copies a week to girls between ten and sixteen years of age, which set forth the British ideals of romance. The girls are leggier and trendier, with tiny skirts, wild hair and sooty eyes; mostly they avoid the corniness of the psychedelic kiss. The men are wickedly handsome on the lines of the Regency Buck, more or less dapper and cool, given to gazing granite-jawed into the glimmering eyes of melting females. The extraordinary aspect is the prominence given to fetish objects. Romance appears to hinge on records, books, knick-knacks, and, in one case which appears to the detached observer to be almost surreal, a park bench. Kate and Harry are sweethearts. They sit on a bench in the park and exchange dialogue thus:

'Oh, Kate, I love you more than anything on earth.'
'And I love you more than anything in the whole universe, darling.'

The bench becomes enormously important in their relationship and when the council decides to move it Kate dashes to Harry's office in the Town Hall with a demand that they sit in, on it. Harry does so until his boss, the borough surveyor, tells him he'll lose his job if he holds out any longer. He gives in, leaving Kate to defend her bench alone. She takes it as an indication of the shallowness of his love for her. But one of the people involved in the moving of the bench, obviously a lover because of his granite jaw and Byronic hair, takes his place beside her. 'We'll save this bench for you, for the past and all the lovers to come.' The last frame shows our heroine peering dewily at him through tear-dimmed eyes, her baby pouting lips a hair's breadth from his rugged prognathous contours. 'But you'll lose your job for nothing. Do ... do you really think we can beat them?' says her balloon. 'I know we can beat them,' his balloon rejoins. 'People can do anything if they try hard enough and love well enough. Let's try ...' *The end*, to say the least.

The lover in romance is a man of masterful ways, clearly superior to his beloved in at least one respect, usually in several, being older or of higher social rank and attainment or more intelligent and *au fait*. He is authoritative but deeply concerned for his lady whom he protects and guides in a way that is patently paternal. He can be stern and withdrawn or even forbidding but the heroines of romance melt him by sheer force of modesty and beauty and the bewitching power of their clothes. He has more than a hint of danger in his past conquests, or a secret suffering or a disdain for women. The banked fires of passion burn just below the surface, muted by his tenderness and omnipotent understanding of the heroine's emotional needs. The original for such characters is in fact romantic in the historical sense for perhaps the very first of them are Rochester, Heathcliff, Mr Darcy and Lord Byron. However, the sense of Austen and Brontë is eclipsed by the sensibility of Lady Caroline Lamb. Exploiting the sexual success of the Byronic hero in an unusually conscious way Georgette Heyer created the archetype of the plastic age, Lord Worth, the Regency Buck. He is a fine example of a stereotype which most heroes of romantic fiction resemble more or less, whether they are dashing young men with an undergraduate sense of humour who congratulate the vivacious heroine on her pluck (the most egalitarian in conception) in the adventure stories of the thirties, or King Cophetua and the beggar maid.

He was the epitome of a man of fashion. His beaver hat was set over black locks carefully brushed into a semblance of disorder; his cravat of starched muslin supported his chin in a series of beautiful folds, his driving coat of drab cloth bore no less than fifteen capes, and a double row of silver buttons. Miss Taverner had to own him a very handsome creature, but found no difficulty in detesting the whole cast of his countenance. He had a look of self-consequence; his eyes, ironically surveying her from under world-weary lids, were the hardest she had ever seen, and betrayed no emotion but boredom. His nose was too straight for her taste. His mouth was very well-formed, firm, but thin-lipped. She thought he sneered ...

Worse than all was his languor. He was uninterested, both in having dexterously averted an accident, and in the gig's plight. His driving had been magnificent; there must be unexpected strength in those elegantly gloved hands holding the reins in such seeming carelessness but why in the name of God, why must he put on such an air of dandified affectation?

Nothing such a creature would do could ever be *corny*. With such *world-weary*! With the patrician features and aristocratic contempt which first opened the doors of polite society to Childe Harold, and the titillating threat of *unexpected strength*! Principally, we might notice, he exists through his immaculate dressing – Beau Brummell is one of his friends – but when he confronts this spectacle –

from *The Female Eunuch*

She had rather have had black hair; she thought the fairness of her gold curls insipid. Happily, her brows and lashes were dark, and her eyes which were startlingly blue (in the manner of a wax doll, she once scornfully told her brother) had a directness and fire which gave a great deal of character to her face. At first glance one might write her down a mere Dresden china miss, but a second glance would inevitably discover the intelligence in her eyes, and the decided air of resolution in the curve of her mouth.

Of course her intelligence and resolution remain happily confined to her eyes and the curve of her mouth but they provide the excuse for her naughty behaviour towards Lord Worth, who turns out to be that most titillating of all titillating relations, her young guardian, by an ingeniously contrived mistake. He, confronting her in this charming dress – 'a plain round gown of French cambric, frilled around the neck with scolloped lace; and a close mantle of twilled sarsenet. A poke bonnet of basket willow with a striped velvet ribbon ...' – and most compromisingly placed shaking a pebble out of her sandal, and so having to hide her stockinged foot in her skirts, sweeps her up into his arms and hurls her into his curricle (for at this point neither of them knows their relationship) where he 'took the sandal from her resistless grasp, and calmly held it ready to fit on to her foot'. Then to provoke her charming indignation still further he kisses her. At such a rate of conquest the novel would be merely twenty pages long, if it were not that as her guardian Worth is too much of a man of principle to pay his addresses to her. She becomes, with his help, given sternly and diffidently, the belle of the season, wooed by all but loving none (but him). She has eighty thousand pounds a year, which is the motive for one sort of suitor; lustful desire for her is the motive of the rest, the most remarkable being the Prince of Wales, whose advances are so repugnant that she faints dead away to be brought around and carried home by her masterful father–lover, who alone loves her without greed or self-interest (being fabulously wealthy), steadfastly and strong. He protects her all the time, even though most of the time she is unaware of it, until her majority when, after a moment of looking down into her face, he sweeps her into his arms. Georgette Heyer has a streak of discretion, or

427

perhaps prudery, which prevents her from exploiting the sexual climaxes in the writing: Barbara Cartland, on the other hand, overwrites the imagery of embracements and thereby reveals much more of the essential romantic preoccupations. In *The Wings of Love* she divides the love interest in two with Lord Ravenscar, the forty-year-old lecher who covets tiny Amanda's lovely body and forces his hideous attentions on it . . .

His hold on her tightened; his lips fastened to hers were like a vice [*sic*]. She felt his passion rising within him like an evil flame; and then suddenly he lifted her in his arms.

'Amanda!' he said hoarsely, 'Damme! Why should we wait?' He was carrying her to a large sofa in the corner of the room; and as she struggled, fighting with every ounce of her strength, she knew how small and ineffectual she was and that her resistance was merely exciting him.

'Amanda! Amanda!'

His thick lips were on her eyes, her cheeks, her throat. She felt him lay her down on the sofa, while she fought fruitlessly to regain her feet, knowing as she did so that she was quite powerless. She heard the fichu of her gown tearing beneath his hands.

The utterly ineffectual heroine is the most important part of the story, ineffectual against ravishment (for how could such a delicate thing kick a peer of the realm in his rising passion?) and against more agreeable forms of sexual conquest, at the hands of the other male, the hero who will protect her from his own animal passions and the crimes and follies of the world.

She turned towards the door and then suddenly Peter Harvey had dropped on one knee beside her. She looked at him wonderingly as he lifted the hem of her white muslin gown and touched his lips with it. 'Amanda,' he said, 'that is how a man, any man, should approach you. No one – least of all Ravenscar – is worthy to do more than to kiss the hem of your gown. Will you remember that?'

That's the kind of man you marry. On his knees chewing her muddy hem and still her moral tutor. Miss Cartland's taste for titillation as far exceeds Heyer's as Heyer's researches into historical colour exceed her own. By a series of preposterous contrivances the lovers meet in a brothel bedroom where he is engaged in rescuing her. Amanda confesses her love in a more decorous setting.

'Amanda, you are making it unbearable for me,' Peter said, and his voice sounded as if it was strangled.

'You do not want me,' she said.

'One day I will make you apologize for that,' he said. 'Just as one day I will kiss you until you cry for mercy. Until that day comes – and pray God it will come soon – take care of yourself, my little beloved.'

He took both her hands and raised them to his lips. Instead of kissing the back of them he turned them over. She felt him kissing the palms with a reverence, and, at the same time, a hungry passion that made her thrill until her whole body trembled with a sudden ecstasy.

They have not actually kissed yet because Peter has said, 'If your lips touched mine I should not be answerable for the consequences.' Indeed when handkissing results in orgasm it is possible that an actual kiss might bring on epilepsy. She is at the altar repeating the vows which will bind her to Ravenscar for life when her lover unmasks him as a traitor, duels with him, and takes his place at her side.

She felt her love rise up in her like a flame. She felt her whole body tremble with the *excitement and the ecstasy of the thrill* that swept over her, because she knew that in a few seconds she would be his wife and belong to him forever.

Both these books I bought for three and sixpence in a supermarket, but it could not claim to have been a random choice, because I remembered these names, Heyer and Cartland, from my fantasy-ridden teens. Indeed I met Miss Cartland in a cascade of aquamarines at a university debate where the topic was 'Be good sweet maid and let who will be clever', Miss Cartland of course taking the affirmative, as if it were possible to be good without being clever! Nowadays she seems to have set up as a sentimental counsellor and purveyor of honey-based aphrodisiacs and may point to her daughter's success in happily marrying into the peerage. If women's liberation movements are to accomplish anything at all, they will have to cope with phenomena like the million dollar Cartland industry. The third book bought on that same day was bought on spec. It was called

The Loving Heart, and described as 'another great romantic story of the Australian outback'. All the well-tried paraphernalia of romance were there. In inventing Grant Jarvis, Lucy Walker availed herself of the feudal paternalism of the sheep-station set-up. Not only is her hero wealthy, he directly rules a society of loyal retainers, white and relatively infantile, as well as black and totally infantile.

In order to bring the elements of her story unto the juxtaposition that will provide the maximum in sentimental thrills, Lucy Walker devises a situation so intricate and unlikely that it would take as long to summarize as it did to invent. All we need to know is that Elizabeth Heaton is posing as Grant Jarvis's fiancée to protect him from designing women who desire him for motives of alliance and ambition. They are fast, energetic and gorgeous, but she has an English complexion and purity, as well as a trick of imitating the queen in carrying out her functions as lady of the worse-than-feudal manor. Her modesty is so excessive that she suffers acutely when, on her first night on the station, the resolution of a crisis involves her in sleeping in her slip on the ground beside the fire, with Grant's body shielding her on the cold side. When Grant visits her bedroom in broad daylight, despite the fact that she is not alone she cannot 'for the life of her' prevent 'the tell-tale blush that crept up her cheeks'. She is thankful that 'the breakfast tray lay across her knees . . . some kind of symbolic shield'. Physically Grant is well-constructed as the father-phallus, 'extremely handsome', 'with cold grey-blue eyes', which coupled with his straight mouth and firm jaw 'gave an impression of hardness . . . and indifference'. All her efforts in the book are expended to earn his approval, and in her quiet moments when not teaching the children, or washing the Union Jack (truly!), she falls to contemplation of his hard masculine beauty, and to masochistic reverie.

Yet as she looked at Grant, leaning on that balustrade, staring out over the plain, with that fine white scar showing on his arm, she felt he was, for all his wealth and power, a lonely man. Whether he was isolated by his personal tragedy or by his great wealth Elizabeth did not know. If he required her to stay on she would not raise difficulties. She had a strange compulsive inclination to serve him.

All romantic novels have a preoccupation with clothes. Every sexual advance is made with clothing as an attractive barrier; the foot fetish displayed in Miss Walker's descriptions is an optional extra. The book has been through four impressions in the Fontana edition, and the authoress has written eleven others at least. The climax of the titillation comes when Grant Jarvis joins the ship in which Elizabeth is travelling home to London at Colombo.

She knew he was real because the tweed of his coat hurt her nose, and she could feel the great power of his arms as he crushed her to him ...
The incredible had happened. Someone in the world had crossed continents and flown oceans to get *her* ... Elizabeth Heaton, typist ...
He bent his head and his lips met her lips. For a long moment Elizabeth had the taste of heaven on her mouth.

This is the hero that women have chosen for themselves. The traits invented for him have been invented by women cherishing the chains of their bondage. It is a male commonplace that women love rotters but in fact women are hypnotized by the successful man who appears to master his fate; they long to give their responsibility for themselves into the keeping of one who can administer it in their best interests. Such creatures do not exist, but very young women in the astigmatism of sexual fantasy are apt to recognize them where they do not exist. Opening car doors, manoeuvring headwaiters, choosing gifts, and earning money, are often valued as romantic attainments: in search of romance many women would gladly sacrifice their own moral judgement of their champion. Many a housewife thrills to the story of Charmaine Biggs, and in telling her story to the dailies the train-robber's wife or her ghost has known just which aspects of a relatively sordid and confused life to delineate and emphasize. Biggs's size, physical strength and daring are reiterated, along with his impudence in courtrooms and remand centres, his cavalier attitude to money and his prowess in bed. Even an adultery has been taken in stride.

Although romance is essentially vicarious the potency of the fantasy distorts actual behaviour. The strength of the belief that a man should be stronger and older than his woman can hardly be exaggerated. I cannot claim to be fully emancipated from the dream that some enormous man, say six foot six, heavily shouldered and so forth to match, will crush me to his tweeds, look down into my eyes and leave the taste of heaven or the scorch of his passion on my waiting lips. For three weeks I was married to him. The impression that women dress to please men must be understood as meaning that women dress to create an impression which corresponds they think to the devastation wrought on Peter Harvey by Amanda in white muslin. Ballroom dancing is an extraordinary capitulation on the part of society to the myth of female submissiveness; the women travel backwards, swept along in a chaste embrace, their faces close to the men's but not actually touching. Such dancing which is only as old as Heyer's Regency Buck may be seen as the expression of middle-class manners, for the aristocratic modes of dancing were formal while the lower orders allowed an independent part to the woman, involving greater or lesser exertion. There is no folk dance or native dance that I have ever heard of in which the man takes over the automotion of the woman. The favourite spectacle of the middle-class female is ballet; all the romantic stereotypes are embodied in it, as the female, although her solo exhibitions demand great power and discipline, *leaps* but *appears to be lifted* like a leaf or a pile of swansdown. Even at the merely social level successful ballroom dancing involves the same contradiction. The woman must exercise physical control so that she appears to be guided weightless about the floor.

Miles Kington

A High-class Tipple, Make No Mistake

'And oh, what a confection of delights you find in a glass of this Brouilly! A daisy-like floweriness coddled in the almondy scents of a Bakewell tart assaults you at a sniff. There's a rubberiness, yes, as you would expect, but high-class rubber, make no mistake. Take a swig (for, despite the price, this remains essentially a swigging wine), and in roar the cherry fruits. There's a touch of cream, a stab of pepper ... even a faint edge of cheese ... It's a serious example of a marvellously unserious wine.'

I have been carrying around this heady, vivacious cutting since I first read it in *The Mail on Sunday* magazine. Bright and puppy-dog keen then, it has become more and more dog-eared and creased, which shows how often I have referred to it, sometimes dipping into it, sometimes devouring it with my eyes – for I think it remains above all a piece to be devoured.

Yet it only appeared under Jill Goolden's name on 3 March 1991. How well it has matured already! And what a redolent example of the wine-writer's craft it is!

Those cheeky little exclamation marks, for instance, the flirtatious 'And oh, what a confection', the chatty little 'yes' and 'make no mistake' – these do not lead us to expect anything but a lightweight wine-writer, do they? And yet suddenly in roar the flavoursome words such as 'confection', 'almondy' and 'coddled' to make us realize that here we have a big and serious talent.

Vocabulary, yes, but you expect that. This is high-class vocabulary, make no mistake. Not only that – it is creative high-class vocabulary, because the writer is joyously trying to suggest that daisies have a smell, whereas we all know that they do not, and that this non-existent smell is coddled in the almondy scent of a Bakewell tart. And the exciting sounds of cherry fruits as they roar in – without ever having exactly heard a cherry, one knows what she is getting at, doesn't one?

Of course one does. And so it was that I found myself in the purlieu of a wine shop yesterday, finally feeling up to buying a bottle of this Olympian Brouilly. Alas, the oft-read cutting had by now fallen to dust, so I had to resort to my own memory of the exquisite experience.

'A bottle of Brouilly, please,' I said.

'What sort of Brouilly?'

Here was a poser. I tried to recollect exactly what the writer had said, but the aftertaste of the article was already vanishing.

'It's like a three-course meal, I think,' I said.

'What kind of three-course meal?'

'What? Oh, well, there was cheese, and cream and pepper . . . Crudités to start with. And an almondy Bakewell tart, and cherry fruits.'

'OK. What was the main course?'

This stumped me.

'I know this sounds silly, but the word "condom" keeps coming to mind.'

The wine man goggled.

'Hold it a moment,' I said, recollection coming back. 'Rubber, that was the clue. High-class rubber.'

'Ah,' he said. 'Sounds like rump steak cooked English style to me. You know, you ask for it rare and it comes back overcooked but elastic.'

'Right. So, have you got a Brouilly like that?'

'Not precisely,' he admitted. 'But I tell you what. We've got a classy little Morgon that is not unlike a classic British breakfast. There's a feathery fungoid softness, yes, like mushrooms swaddled in tomatoes, but there's a touch of lamb and mint sausage, a dig in the back from a rasher of crispy bacon – and what's that suddenly roaring in? Could it be a squadron of low-flying melba toast? No, it's eggs! Scramble, everybody!'

'Mmm,' I said. 'I'm not really sure . . .'

'Or what about this Australian Cabernet Sauvignon? Uncann-
ily reminiscent of a barbie for 48 people, this swashbuckling
little number not only pushes a plate of kangaroo steak into
your hand but calls you Barry and introduces you to a lovely
bunch of people, all with crinkled foreheads and a touch of skin
cancer . . .'

I finally settled for a bottle of Bulgarian red.

I took it home just in time for the three-course meal my wife
had cooked for us. And what a meal! How can I describe it? It
was not unlike a half dozen bottles of very high-class Provençal
rosé . . .

(Continued some other time, perhaps.)

Miles Kington

The Life and Times of the Famous One

Yesterday I joined Mrs Thatcher's so far unavailing search for a co-writer who could help her write her life story. At enormous expense I asked *The Independent* computer to try its hand at writing parts of her life story in the styles of several different authors. No agents or publishers have telephoned to sign it up, so it is obviously time to try again.

Well, it seems that the computer has tired of the Westland story, which I asked it to deal with yesterday, and would quite like to have a bash at the Cecil Parkinson episode. It seemed only fair to ask it to try first to produce a Barbara Cartland version.

'How could you, Cecil? How could you?'

I beat my head against my pillow and let the tears soak into the comforting cotton. But let me start at the beginning.

My name is Maggie, and I had come to London to earn my fortune. There, after various adventures, I had become leader of my country, the first woman ever to do so. But I was still young and not unattractive, and my life was all still in front of me.

After all, what is it to be leader of your country if you do not have a man you can rely on at your side, a man with clear vision, good skin and a fine chin?

And then one day I met the man who I knew at once would be that man. His name was Willie, and I knew that with his help I could stride bravely and firmly through the rest of my life.

I soon realized I was wrong. After that, I met the man I knew would be that man. He was called Pym. Or Biffen. Or Prior. I do not remember their names now. And I was wrong every time.

Then I met Cecil. This time I knew I was right. But how wrong a girl can be to think she is right!

'Oh, Cecil, how could you do this to me?'

This is getting nowhere. Is there not some other female author superior to Barbara Cartland in stature whom we might try? Yes, of course. Enid Blyton!

The Famous One was on holiday again, with her dog Denis. No wonder she woke up at five in the morning, wrote up her notebooks, filled in her log, read the newspaper, then went downstairs to see if anyone else was around. Denis wagged his tail in greeting.

'Gosh, Denis,' she cried. 'It's such a lovely morning! Let's go out and have an adventure!'

Let me introduce you to the member of the Famous One. She was a girl called Maggie, who was tremendously plucky and always getting into scrapes and getting out of them again, because she was very good at organizing people to help her. On one previous holiday she had found some Spanish-speaking villains occupying some islands they didn't own (see *The Famous One Goes to the Falklands*) and had got them out. On another holiday she had found some valuable treasure belonging to the family and sold it all to help pay for things (see *The Famous One Privatizes Everything*).

'I wonder what adventure we will have this time, Denis!' she said, as she cycled along the lanes, Denis bringing up the rear. Just then, her eye was caught by the sight of some villainous men whispering behind a hedge. She got off her bike and crept over to listen to them.

'What's the plan, Arthur?' said one.

'Easy,' said their ringleader called Arthur. 'We refuse to dig any more coal up unless they give us lots more money and make us promises.'

'My goodness,' thought the Famous One, and she cycled away to warn someone. Luckily, she bumped into a friendly policeman and told him what she had heard.

'Money and promises, eh?' said the bobby. 'We'll see about that. I'll go and get my men and we'll wade in and stop them doing any such thing. As for you, young lady, thank you. You've probably saved the country.'

'We'll have another adventure after lunch, Denis,' said the Famous One. 'In fact, let's not even stop for lunch. Come on!'

Well, not much about Cecil Parkinson there. I think the computer is confused. Perhaps that is because I showed it an advance copy of the latest interview with Mrs Thatcher. And maybe that is why it volunteered this short version of Mrs Thatcher's life by Samuel Beckett, off its own bat.

The lights gradually come up to reveal a woman standing alone in the middle of the stage, almost completely hidden by copies of Vanity Fair, *which are piled up to her neck.*

Woman: Nothing. Nowhere. Gone. All. Gone. *A phone rings somewhere offstage.*

Hello, Ronald? Hello, George? Hello, François? Hello, Mikhail? *The phone stops ringing.*

No one. Nobody. Gone. Lost. *The lights gradually go down again until we are in darkness.*

I can see there is more to this life story lark than I had realized. Some other time, perhaps.

Fiona Pitt-Kethley

from *Journeys to the Underworld*

There was a fly in the bottom of my *cappuccino* in the little bar at the station.

Palermo probably has the nicest first-class waiting room in Italy. My peep through the door impressed me. (I was too honourable to go in.) I always travel second – I can't see the fun of paying extra to travel with a lot of nasty old businessmen and have an antimacassar behind my head.

The bookshops outside sold the usual Italian mixture of trash reading, plus textbooks and poetry. I have to believe that the average Italian is far more literate than the equivalent British person. I couldn't see W. H. Smith selling things like Chaucer in the original to commuters. Yet Dante goes like hot cakes in Italy. There was an intriguing title amongst the educational stuff – *Vademecum del Single Boy.*

I posted my cards in the postbox in the station. Like those outside it had a little sticker USA IL CAP. For a moment I thought that some mischievous Prot had stuck contraceptive ads all round the city in the night. Probably, though, it just means use your boring old postcode. The Italians have one for every city. They are usually made up of the first two letters of the place name, or else the first and last.

I was vaguely tempted to buy some Sibyl Caramels from the bar, as they claimed to have my future written in them, but decided the fly had been enough of an omen.

At half past eight I boarded the slow train to Marsala. It was four hours of little local stops in extremely dirty carriages. The train had come overnight from the north of the mainland and was full of the remains of people's breakfasts, lunches, suppers and breakfasts.

Outside everything looked very clean. There seems to be a peculiar clarity about the air in Sicily that lets you see for a long way. I found I could pick out the individual trees and bushes on hills as the train went by. It was far on in summer. The land looked parched, but the vines and prickly pears were still doing well. Most of the stops along the way seemed to be in the middle of nowhere. At the larger stations a little boy got on and walked the length of the train with a bucket full of iced drinks and a satchel of sandwiches. These boys are a feature of the railway network. They do a sort of nasal howl of all the things they've got on offer: '*Birra, Coke, Fanta, acqua, panini* . . .'

After some salty wastes the train arrived at Marsala, which looked like a one-platform station for a one-horse town. I was wearing black, which is what I usually do for dirty trains. It was stiflingly hot, so I went into the buffet for a sort of lemon-ice drink, a *granita*. This made me feel a lot worse, because the coldness of the ice went straight to my eyeballs. The locals were viewing me with extreme suspicion by now. A soldier came up and asked whose funeral I'd come for. I told him I just liked wearing black, which killed that conversation.

I now had the job of asking if there was a cheap hotel nearby. Nobody wanted to tell me. The barman eventually gestured vaguely across the railway lines and said there was one to the right. I started off, still lugging my suitcase. An old man with one green tooth left in the lower set followed me. He didn't have much hair, just a lot of bristles sprinkled indiscriminately like iron filings over face and head. He told me that I'd never find the hotel on my own, but that he'd help me if I had lunch with him first. I refused this kind offer and darted across the lines, thinking I'd find the place on my own even if it killed me.

I stopped a few people on the road and asked. Eventually a woman told me where to go. Her accent was clearer, so I assumed she'd just been unfortunate enough to marry one of the locals. Her children helped me with my bag and I gave the little boy something as he worked at the hotel. Naturally she'd directed me to the dearer of the two possibles because of this. Still, it was only one night, so I was able to get my value in showers, clothes-washing and toilet-paper.

When I'd showered and changed out of my funeral gear, I hit the streets armed with a sixty-year-old guide book which had no map, but detailed all the roads. Unfortunately, most of the street names had changed.

A few turns away from the hotel I was confronted with what must be the most hideous fountain in Italy. It has a bronze sculpture of a kicking donkey, three barrels and a naked woman whose tits spurt. Maybe if I tossed a coin in the water I would never have to come back to Marsala.

Fountain designers are a sadistic breed. They never put a drinking tap or a lavatory near their creations. Yet, invariably, when you hear a fountain, you need to pee or drink, or both.

The *Christian Club Chemise* shop operates near this fountain. It is as dowdy as it sounds and also horribly expensive. The whole town seems very prosperous – probably because of the wine industry. There's an air of eccentricity about the shops – a Persian carpet importer's opposite the station and a café with stuffed sea birds further into town.

By this stage in my walkabout, I had been hailed by several kerb-crawlers saying: '*Dove vai?*' (Where are you going?) They offered me various destinations. It was only afternoon and the full heat of the day, yet already they were making life difficult. In most other towns in Italy they only do this at night. After a while, I realized that absolutely every car was stopping. Every man in Marsala seemed to be a kerb-crawler.

Most of the men in these cars seemed to be in twos. Now and again, one would get out, grab me roughly by the shoulders and start demanding reasons why I wouldn't go with them. '*Perchè no?*' I find it quite extraordinary that any man should want to know why a woman he's never met before doesn't want to get into a car to be fucked by him and his friend a long way from home.

It was Sunday and absolutely nothing was open, not even the churches. All I could do was shake the clutching hands off angrily, cut across roads and double back, trying to get out of the path of each new would-be pick-up. From time to time I answered the *Dove Vais* with translations of Garbo's famous statement – 'I want to be alone!'

The few men who didn't say '*Dove vai?*' or '*Va a passaggio?*' (Going for a ride?) just hissed – a sort of long drawn-out *pss* ... Across the town I came on a pedestrian precinct. At least only the hissers could follow me there. On the left I passed the cathedral. According to my guide book this one is dedicated to St Thomas of Canterbury. A ship containing his relics was wrecked off the coast of Marsala and the pious locals took advantage.

At last my guide book was beginning to prove useful. The names of the roads tallied. At the end of Via XI Maggio I could see the Porta Nuova. The buildings here were older and nicer but crumbled by time. On my left there were two museums tucked away through an arch. They looked very thoroughly closed. There was grass in the courtyard between them and the shell of a rusted car. On the left a flight of steps led to the *Pinacoteca*, on the right to the Museo Garibaldi. Just round the corner, a man was advertising electroencephalographs on his side wall. That sounded a lot nastier than Basil Apples of Naples.

I went through the Porta Nuova and turned right into the Giardino Cavalotti. I was glad to get into the shade. The gardens were dark and full of tropical plants and trees. There was a notice by the entrance saying that the area had been officially certified disinfected and pesticided. Nature had left a telling note at the foot of the post – a cast snakeskin. Perhaps its former owner was lurking nearby.

There were large palm trees and oleander bushes everywhere. Near the entrance there was a sinister banyan tree – growing up and down to meet itself. Water bubbled from a metal post almost hidden in the ground at its feet. Behind the vast grey trunk a man was hissing at me.

Everything in that park seemed to hiss. The hot wind crackled in the sun-scorched leaves at the top of the few deciduous trees in the park. It was like sibilant speech. I found myself trying to make out some whispered language. I walked to the end where a dried-up fountain rambled in a series of Baroque steps or levels up to a belvedere. There is a Spanish feel to this part of the architecture. It must have been handsome when the water was flowing. Now the whole thing smells putrid.

I was glad to get back into the fresh air again. The human snake had followed me all round the park. I knew I was near the place where the Sibyl's Grotto is supposed to be. I asked a newspaper seller for the Chiesetta di San Giovanni and was directed to a small chapel in the middle of a piece of waste ground. I passed a larger building on the way – a big impressive Neoclassical 1930s cinema – the Cine Impero. Its splendours were deserted and all the windows had been smashed.

I walked round the chapel and found the doors were shut. There were no notices of services, but the same could be said for a lot of more important churches in Italy. I think the Italians like to make you ask for things. It's probably one of their main entertainments, listening to the horrors of English Italian.

I wondered if I was in the wrong place until I saw the name of the little church carved faintly on one of the doors. The land there is open to the scorching west wind which blows straight from Africa. Every weed is blasted. The dust and the flowers have turned an even grey. I could just about recognize the petrified remains of dog's mercury, fat hen and spearmint in the dark sand at my feet. I saw the same effect in my garden, more than a year later, after the hurricane of October 1987. Then, the only plant that stayed fresh and green and seemed to enjoy it all was my rosemary bush. Perhaps they should plant rosemary in every place where a harsh salt-laden wind blows.

I followed a faint track away from the chapel. I could half imagine I saw the stumps of pillars from a vanished portico, but when I looked closely the stony remains seemed much more like concrete. This path led me to the beginning of the Via della Sirene. The next road to this – the only other romantically-named one in the town – was the Via Sibilla. I walked along this, looking for clues of some kind. I passed block after block of modern flats and a sort of table-football club full of desiccated old men. A starving black cat with one yellow eye ran snarling across my path.

I cut back to the seafront and was harassed by *Dove Vais* promising ever more distant destinations. One even offered a

Fiona Pitt-Kethley

boat ride. This part of the port doesn't look as if it's changed much since the Romans fought the Carthaginians. I would have liked to walk out on one of the moles and see the town from the sea, but as soon as I started I was followed. It seemed to be the sort of town where you can't be left alone to do anything at any time of day. You'd think the buggers would go to sleep and leave the hot afternoon to mad dogs and Englishwomen.

The shore had the same burning smell as the towns of the Phlegrean Fields. Maybe that sort of air goes with sibylline spots. Either that, or someone had made a bonfire of the weeds. The shoreline was scorched beside the black sand. The water laps close, just a few feet drop down from the main road. Part of the port has large oblong granite blocks like the ones outside Naples. The water is teeming with algae and the greener types of seaweed. It is a clear dark blue though which makes it cleaner-looking than a seaweedy bit of British sea. If it has occupants, at least you ought to be able to see them coming. I fancied swimming, but again couldn't. I felt too much of a target for the passers-by.

I made one more trip out that day, in the evening. As I'd expected, the *Dove Vais* were even more active. The kerb-crawlers were interspersed with huge lorries full of grapes making for a local market. There was a caramel smell in the air – some vital stage in the local wine-making, I should imagine. By this time I was beginning to have paranoid fantasies. I kept remembering an old horror film I'd seen where the only stranger in town had to be sacrificed to ensure a good vintage in some old French château. I dismissed this idea as ridiculous. After all, in the film, the victim had at least been given a good time first. Besides, most of the local wine industry is run by the English – Ingham, Woodhouse and Whitaker – according to my little red guide book. The English don't do things like that.

Was the town immersed in a sort of harvest riot, I wondered, or were the men always rabid? In the old Dionysian routs it was men who got torn to bits, not women. Mind you, in those days, women stuck together. That September evening I seemed to be the only woman on Marsala's streets. I don't say I blame the others for staying in. On the other hand, I'm inclined to believe women should go out most in places like that, in order to stake an equal claim to the freedom of the road and the night. If men can persuade us that we are only safe when we are with them, that ups their value. Women have to humour them to get small privileges. The most unattractive, vicious man is thus given more worth and more chance of a partner by being seen as a useful protector. Damn the lot of them, I say. I'll force them to accept that a woman can walk alone and doesn't *need* any of them.

I realized after a while that one of the *Dove Vais* kept coming back. I suppose he hoped that I might think he was the best of a bad lot when I'd turned down a couple of hundred others. I didn't. He was a lout with a clapped-out car, or a clapped-out lout with a car, I hardly remember which. I got seriously annoyed by the way he kept almost running me down, then trapping me in an angle between his car and the wall. I was also infuriated by his persistence in getting out and offering his dubious charms to me. I was so cross that I decided to yell at him the worst possible thing you can say to an Italian male. I was taught this by a carpenter in exchange for similar English expressions during an extremely boring week I once spent on Elba. By now, the fat-thighed lout had followed me to the forecourt of my hotel. I got a few yards ahead and bawled '*Va fa 'n culo!*' at him with a suitable gesture of repudiation. My would-be *inamorato* looked so hurt that I began to find the situation amusing. (Swearing at men is fun – they nearly always get that look – English and Italian alike.) I find it slightly surprising, though, that this particular phrase affronts Italians so much, considering that it only means *go and do it up the arse*. Doing it that way may be illegal in England, but it's something some Italians are supposed to like. The one in front of me muttered a few things that I couldn't quite catch and probably wouldn't have understood. I think he finished with wishing me the same before he went off. I was rather proud of myself. My accent had sounded quite plausible. It's always better when I shout. It's asking for things politely in shops makes me sound very English.

I went upstairs and showered. While I was under the water, the phone rang. I had a sudden fear that the hotel might have given that jerk my room number. Perhaps he had Mafia connections. Maybe he was ringing to tell me he was on his way to do it up my arse. I took a long time answering. When I did it was only room service asking if I needed a drink. I did, but I didn't.

Marsala in the morning seemed a shade more genial. In the hotel foyer I bought a card of the Medusa mosaic pavement which is used almost as a logo on the local tourist brochures. Much as they advertise that pavement, the fact is that it can't be seen, because it lies under the Cine Impero, which has been closed for decades.

A little way down the road I bought a bunch of grapes for my breakfast. They tasted very winy and the black juice ran under my nails. As Marsala is a clean town I only dropped my pips down the gutter gratings. I can't yet face the Italian trick of swallowing them.

The clerk in the Bank of Sicily seemed suspicious of my passport and travellers' cheques. He queried every English word in the passport, then photocopied it all to be on the safe side. I noticed that the bank had the wrong date on the wall – the right day of the week, but the wrong date. That takes talent. Still, at least they didn't throw my money at me like they do in Naples.

I went back to the cathedral and the museums hoping to find something open. The cathedral was, but my enthusiasm for Baroque sculptures, particularly those of Gagini, is limited. I didn't know how I was going to find out about the Sibyl's Grotto. My out-of-date guide said that the key for it was to be obtained from the Biblioteca next door to number 2, Via XI Maggio. Museums and libraries don't usually move, but this one had. There was nothing there now except the *Photo-Jolly* shop. This was filled with pictures of brides. One of them was obviously pregnant. She must have taken a lift from one of the *Dove Vais*.

It's a pity the men in Marsala seem to be such pricks. Some of the girls there are very pretty and a lot better dressed than the women of Naples. The only thing I can say for Marsalan men is that they are definitely less prone to resting their hands on their cocks than the average Neapolitan.

I tried some of the streets further away from the sea, looking for some other kind of museum with a knowledgeable curator who could help me. There were interesting buildings tucked away here with Moorish touches and funny little unexplained details – a stone cross and wings above a Medieval gate. I popped into the decrepit St Anne's. They were about to hold some important local funeral – probably the one the soldier thought I had come to town for. Outside, beneath a huge cross covered in electric lightbulbs, a fat girl stood waiting with YES in diamanté on her tee-shirt dress. The cross had slipped sideways and a plug and flex dangled, swinging slightly in the breeze.

The man who had sold me grapes boasted that it never rained in Marsala. I wished I could have brought them a good English shower to wash the *Dove Vais* off the streets. Perhaps Queen Elizabeth should visit – she always seems to bring rain.

I bought a pair of leather and wood sandals for the equivalent of a pound on my way to the station. They were every bit as uncomfortable as what I had on, but at least they hurt in different places.

I was met by a tall gipsy with a baby on the station platform. I thought she was about to beg, but she only wanted to know if I was a stranger and if I was married. When she found I wasn't married, she asked where my parents were. She shook her head in sympathy and disbelief when I said they were in England. I didn't bother to say my father was dead – that would have made me sound even more alone.

As I sat waiting I was joined by a deaf and dumb man. I thought he seemed fairly pleasant – he kept smiling – until he started to go into an awful mime about doing a shit, when he recognized a crony of his. Although he couldn't speak, he could easily manage farting noises. I wasn't going to relinquish my half of the seat, though, just because he was mad. Behind us, I could hear something nasty going on – a murder perhaps – six ticket inspectors were quarrelling in the ticket office.

The train was packed with students, most of whom got out at little stops early on. When I reached Palermo I went straight to the tourist office for a list of cheap hotels. There seemed to be plenty of them. The first few were full up. I climbed flight after flight of stairs with my case and was turned away. I stood on one fourth floor, hopelessly pushing the lift button, only to be told by the proprietor that some fool had left the door open below and that's why it didn't work. That fool was me. At last I found a place down near the docks. The room had blue walls framed in panels and a mock crystal lightshade. The ripples of light were meant to look like the sea. The owner was very proud of this.

I ate out that night. I have been told that Palermo is a very unsafe place, but I didn't find it so. I only had one kerb-crawler after me – you could get that anywhere – and a few *Ciao Bellas*, which are quite good for the ego.

Biographical Notes

KINGSLEY AMIS (b. 1922) Born in London. Poet, novelist and occasional essayist, whose non-fiction is often conceived in a spirit as wry and comic as that of his best-known works.

BEACHCOMBER One of the most highly regarded of English humorists, J. B. Morton (1893–1975) took over the 'Beachcomber' column in the *Daily Express* from his friend D. B. Wyndham Lewis in 1924, and continued in this position for the next fifty-one years. An inspired, and inspiriting, comic writer.

MAX BEERBOHM (1872–1956) Born in London. Essayist, parodist, caricaturist and aesthete. His only novel, *Zuleika Dobson* (1911), is an extravaganza, and it was followed a year later by *A Christmas Garland* (literary parodies). In 'Then and Now' – a late piece – he imitates the manner of an aged *grande dame*. Famous for his whimsicality and aplomb.

ALAN BENNETT (b. 1934) Yorkshire dramatist, author and actor, who came to prominence with *Beyond the Fringe* (1960), and has gone on receiving acclaim for his dry and satirical approach ever since. Found a natural home for his occasional pieces in the *London Review of Books*.

P. Y. BETTS (b. 1909) Born in London. Author of a novel, *French Polish*, and contributor to a number of periodicals, including *Punch*. Worked as a farm labourer during the Second World War and then moved to a farm in Wales, where she has lived ever since. *People Who Say Goodbye* was described by Graham Greene as 'the most amusing book of childhood memories I can remember reading'.

ELIZABETH BOWEN (1899–1973) Born in Dublin. Anglo-Irish novelist, short-story writer, essayist and reviewer. Author of many complex and stylish works, with a considerable talent for social comedy, whether in fiction or non-fiction.

BRIGID BROPHY (b. 1929) Author of six urbane and distinctive novels. May be placed among the most cogent and illuminating critics and reviewers of the last thirty years.

JAMES CAMERON (1911–85) Distinguished journalist, foreign correspondent, *Guardian* columnist and astute social critic.

PATRICK CAMPBELL (1913–80) 3rd Baron Glenavy. Joined the *Irish Times* in the 1930s, and went on to become assistant editor of *Lilliput*, *Sunday Times* columnist and television personality. An irrepressible teller of humorous stories.

ANTHONY CARSON Pseudonym of Peter Brooke. Author of some autobiographical pieces disguised as travel writing, including *A Rose by Any Other Name* (1960) and *Carson Was Here* (1962). Contributor to the *New Statesman* and *Punch*, and eccentric humorist.

CLAUD COCKBURN (1904–81) Born in China. *Times* correspondent (1929); diplomatic correspondent for the *Daily Worker*; novelist, journalist and author of three volumes of autobiography. Had an acute eye for the absurdities of popular fiction, as his study *Bestseller* (1972) shows.

CYRIL CONNOLLY (1903–74) Essayist and critic. Editor of *Horizon* (1940–49); author of *Enemies of Promise* (1938) and *The Unquiet Grave* (1944).

ALAN COREN (b. 1938) Assistant editor, and then became editor of *Punch* (1977); radio and television broadcaster and newspaper columnist. Humorist *par excellence*, and editor of *The Penguin Book of Modern Humour*.

E. M. DELAFIELD Pseudonym of Edmée Elizabeth Monica de la Pasture (1891–1943). First novel *Zella Sees Herself* published in 1917; achieved fame with her 'Provincial Lady' diaries, which were issued in instalments in *Time & Tide* from 1929 on, before being published in book form. Her straightforward journalism, no less than the diaries, is informed by an appetite for amiable mockery.

MARY DUNN (1901–1958) Humorist, contributor to *Punch* and author of the highly successful *Lady Addle Remembers* (1936), in which the typical high-society memoir was subjected to exorbitant ridicule. *The Memoirs of Mipsie* (1945) was an equally hilarious sequel to the first collection of spoof reminiscences.

GERALD DURRELL (b. 1925) Brother of the novelist. Naturalist, founder of the Jersey Zoo, writer and occasional humorist, as in his auto-biographical *My Family and Other Animals*.

LAWRENCE DURRELL (1912–90) Novelist and poet. Made a brief excursion into the field of humour with a couple of books containing sketches of the diplomatic life, *Esprit de Corps* (1957) and *Stiff Upper Lip* (1958).

ALICE THOMAS ELLIS Pseudonym of Anna Haycraft (b. 1933). Engaging and idiosyncratic novelist, and *Spectator* columnist.

PETER FLEMING (1907–71) Novelist, journalist and *Spectator* columnist, but best known as a travel writer and author of such works as *Brazilian Adventure* (1933) and *News From Tartary* (1936).

E. M. FORSTER (1879–1970) Regarded as one of the most distinguished novelists of the twentieth century, though he wrote no more fiction after *A Passage to India* in 1924. His subsequent career as a critic, political commentator and advocate of civil liberties kept him at the forefront of literary activity in Britain.

MICHAEL FRAYN (b. 1933) Novelist, playwright and highly regarded *Observer* columnist during the 1960s.

PENELOPE GILLIATT (b. 1932) Novelist, short-story writer, scriptwriter and critic. Author of six collections of stories, many of which had first appeared in the *New Yorker*. Stylist and wit.

GRAHAM GREENE (1904–91) Distinguished novelist, short-story writer and occasional essayist, born in Berkhamsted, Hertfordshire. His collection *The Lost Childhood and Other Essays* was published in 1951.

GERMAINE GREER (b. 1939) Critic, journalist and broadcaster. Born in Melbourne. Contributor to the *Listener*, *Sunday Times*, *Spectator*, *Oz* and *Rolling Stone*. Best known for her influential feminist study of 1971, *The Female Eunuch*.

A. P. HERBERT (1891–1971) Novelist, humorist, barrister-at-law and campaigner for reform of the divorce laws, he was a regular *Punch* contributor, and one of the most entertaining comic writers of the mid-century.

PHILIP HOWARD (b. 1933) One of the guardians of the English language, and very funny about the changes which keep overtaking it. He is literary editor of *The Times*.

CLIVE JAMES (b. 1939) Born in Sydney. Novelist, mock-epic poet, critic and television performer.

Biographical Notes

HUGH KINGSMILL (1889–1949) Born Hugh Kingsmill Lunn. Biographer, literary critic, anthologist, parodist and novelist.

MILES KINGTON (b. 1941) Journalist, humorist and indefatigable entertainer. Contributor to many newspapers and periodicals, including *The Times*, *Punch* and the *Independent*.

LORD KINROSS (1904–76) Author and journalist. Worked on editorial staff of various newspapers. Best known for humorous writings such as *The Century of the Common Peer* (1954).

MARGHANITA LASKI (1915–88) Novelist, critic and broadcaster. Worked as a nurse, dairy farmer and in intelligence during the Second World War. Wrote for *The Times* and *The Times Literary Supplement* until her death in 1988, and chaired Arts Council and other committees. Author of *Love on the Super-tax* (1944) and *Mrs Ewing, Mrs Molesworth and Mrs Hodgson Burnett* (1950).

C. A. LEJEUNE (1897–1973) Born in Manchester. Broadcaster, television scriptwriter and film critic for the *Observer* (1928–60). Her diverting film reviews were collected under the title *Chestnuts in Her Lap*.

BERNARD LEVIN (b. 1928) Celebrated author, journalist and broadcaster. Wrote brilliant parliamentary commentaries for the *Spectator* under the pen-name of 'Taper'.

D. B. WYNDHAM LEWIS (1891–1969) Humorist, journalist, biographer and one of the two compilers of the celebrated anthology of bad verse, *The Stuffed Owl*. His hilarious account of the novel *Irene Iddesleigh* by Amanda McKittrick Ros ('the world's worst novelist') drew an over-the-top response from the outraged author (unfortunately too verbose and daft to stand reprinting).

SERENA LIVINGSTONE-STANLEY Pseudonym of Beckett W. Lindsay. *Through Darkest Pondelayo* is a very funny send-up of the intrepid woman traveller.

ROBERT LYND (1879–1949) Born in Belfast. A distinguished man of letters and long-time contributor to the *New Statesman and Nation*; his essays were issued in thirty volumes between 1908 and 1945. Very popular in his day, he passed into obscurity after his death in 1949. However, his value as a social commentator is now beginning to be acknowledged.

JULIAN MACLAREN-ROSS (1913–64) Author of a good many stories affording enticing glimpses into army life and the slightly seedy London of the early post-war years. The prose piece 'Good Lord, Jeeves' shows him to be an effective parodist too. Best known for his *Memoirs of the Forties*, which was unfinished at the time of his death.

LOUIS MACNEICE (1907–63) Born in Belfast. He is just beginning to receive due recognition as one of the major poets of the twentieth century, after having been eclipsed by W. H. Auden (and even by C. Day Lewis and Stephen Spender). Educated at Marlborough and Oxford, he worked for the BBC for many years. Also wrote occasional prose, including one or two sardonic side-glances at public occasions, such as 'Under the Sugar Loaf'. A witty and astute commentator.

ARTHUR MARSHALL (1910–89) Born in London. One of the most distinctive humorists of the twentieth century. Well known for his 'Nurse Dugdale' radio series, for his affectionate mockery of school-girls' stories (in particular the works of Angela Brazil) and, in his later years, as a television personality.

JOHN MORTIMER (b. 1923) Distinguished novelist, barrister and play-wright, perhaps best known for his television series *Rumpole of the Bailey*. Author of a stylish and humorous volume of autobiography, *Clinging to the Wreckage* (1982).

MALCOLM MUGGERIDGE (1903–90) Author, journalist and social critic. Associated with the *Manchester Guardian* before going on to be editor of *Punch* (1954–7). Achieved fame as a cantankerous Englishman. Wry and humorous, especially in his volume of social history, *The Thirties* (1940).

HAROLD NICOLSON (1886–1968) Biographer, novelist, diplomat and husband of Vita Sackville-West. *Spectator* columnist.

FLANN O'BRIEN One of the pseudonyms of Brian O'Nolan (1911–66), who was also famous as an *Irish Times* columnist under the name of Myles na gCopaleen, and an unerring satirist and wit. Born in Strabane, Co. Tyrone, but a long-term resident of Dublin, where he contributed greatly to the gaiety of life.

GEORGE ORWELL Pseudonym of Eric Blair (1903–50). Novelist, satirist, social commentator and essayist. His exasperated appraisal of popular boys' papers offended the usually amiable author of the Grey-friars stories, Frank Richards; however, there is no doubt that Orwell's essay 'Boys' Weeklies' is exceptionally witty and perceptive.

Biographical Notes

FIONA PITT-KETHLEY (b. 1954) *Enfant terrible* of English letters, poet, unabashed libertine and disenchanted travel writer.

V.S. PRITCHETT (b. 1900) Best known as a masterly short-story writer, he has also received considerable acclaim for his reminiscences and criticism. A collection of his essays and reviews, *In My Good Books*, was published in 1942.

ROBERT ROBINSON (b. 1927) Perhaps best known as a television and radio broadcaster, he has also achieved celebrity as a journalist, film critic and author of many humorous pieces.

ALAN ROSS (b. 1922) Poet, critic and travel writer. Associated with John Lehmann's *New Writing*, the *Listener* and the *New Statesman* during the 1940s. Edits the *London Magazine*.

JAMES STEPHENS (1882–1950) Irish author of *The Crock of Gold* (1912), and acclaimed not only for his fiction, but as a poet, essayist, dramatist, critic and reviewer. Friend and associate of Yeats, Joyce and other leading figures in the Irish Literary Revival; he lived in London from 1925 until his death.

A.J.P. TAYLOR (1906–90) Distinguished historian, perhaps best known for his *Origins of the Second World War* (1961). Also a journalist and television personality. Contributed, at intervals, a lively and idiosyncratic diary to the *London Review of Books* until a year or two before his death.

DYLAN THOMAS (1914–53) Born in Swansea. Poet, prose writer, dramatist and scriptwriter. Famous for the richness (some would say overrichness) and evocativeness of his poetry; also produced stories, articles and radio broadcasts of great verve and charm. Died while on a poetry-reading tour of the USA.

HONOR TRACY (d. 1989) Journalist, novelist and woman of letters. Spent two years in Dublin, during which time she was associated with the *Bell*. *Sunday Times* columnist.

AUBERON WAUGH (b. 1939) One-time novelist, editor of the *Literary Review* and outstanding (and outspoken) newspaper columnist and reviewer.

EVELYN WAUGH (1903–66) Celebrated novelist and satirist who extended the range of English comic writing with such novels as *Scoop*, *Put Out More Flags* and *The Ordeal of Gilbert Pinfold*. His non-fiction is often as funny as his fiction; in 'Awake My Soul! It is a Lord' we find him giving full expression to the comic tetchiness for which he became well known.

DENTON WELCH (1915–48) Best known for his autobiography *Maiden Voyage* (1943), written after he had suffered the bicycle accident that eventually caused his early death. Can be very funny, as we see in his account of a visit to the painter Sickert.

REBECCA WEST Pseudonym of Cicily Fairfield (1892–1983). An early feminist and contributor to the *Freewoman* from the age of eighteen, she went on to become a highly acclaimed novelist, critic, social commentator and woman of letters. Her early journalism in many ways shows her at her most attractive – forceful, funny, audacious and opinionated.

P. G. WODEHOUSE (1881–1975) Probably the most famous English comic writer of the century, and no less polished an entertainer when he takes a rest from Jeeves, Lord Emsworth and the rest to try his hand at a scintillating piece of non-fiction. His essay on the type of thriller that flourished in the 1920s and 1930s is a model of urbanity and frivolity.

Acknowledgements

Thanks are due to the copyright holders of the following stories for permission to reprint them in this volume:

Kingsley Amis: to Jonathan Clowes Ltd, London, on behalf of Kingsley Amis for 'Age-old Ceremony at Mumbles' from *What Became of Jane Austen?* (Jonathan Cape, 1970), copyright 1956 © 1970 by Kingsley Amis

Max Beerbohm: to Sir Rupert Hart-Davis for 'Then and Now' by Vera Lady Elderton from *A Peep into the Past & Other Prose Pieces*, ed. Rupert Hart-Davis (Heinemann, 1972), copyright © Mrs Eva Reichmann

Alan Bennett: to Peters Fraser & Dunlop Ltd for 'Ten Days That Shook Me' from the *London Review of Books* (15 September 1988)

P. Y. Betts: to Souvenir Press Ltd for an extract from *People Who Say Goodbye* (Souvenir Press, 1989)

Elizabeth Bowen: to Curtis Brown Ltd, London, Literary Executors of the late Elizabeth Bowen, for 'On Not Rising to the Occasion' (first published in the *Listener*, 1956)

Brigid Brophy: to the author for 'Henry Miller' (first published in *London Magazine*, June 1963), copyright © Brigid Brophy

James Cameron: to Nicholas Thompson on behalf of the Estate of James Cameron for 'Bertie's Booster' (5 August 1980) from *Cameron in the Guardian, 1974–1984* (Grafton Books, 1987)

Patrick Campbell: to Pavilion Books for 'A Boy's Best Bodyguard' and 'Doing the Cobblers' Trot' from *The Campbell Companion*, ed. Mick O'Connor (Pavilion Books, 1987)

Anthony Carson: to David Higham Associates Ltd for 'A Hot Bath at Rotorua', 'Lecture to the Troops' and 'The Wardrobe' from *A Rose by Any Other Name* (Methuen, 1960)

Claud Cockburn: to Macmillan Ltd, London, for 'Vagabond but Gentleman Too' from *Bestseller* (Sidgwick & Jackson, 1972)

Cyril Connolly: to Rogers, Coleridge & White Ltd for 'Where Engels Fears to Tread' from *Press Gang*, ed. Leonard Russell (Hutchinson, 1937)

Alan Coren: to Robson Books Ltd for 'Thanks for the Memory' from *Bin Ends* (Robson Books, 1987) and 'Bohemia' from *All Except the Bastard* (Robson Books, 1969)

E. M. Delafield: to Peters Fraser & Dunlop Ltd for 'Femina's Supplement' from *Press Gang*, ed. Leonard Russell (Hutchinson, 1937)

Gerald Durrell: to Harper Collins Publishers Ltd for extracts from *My Family and Other Animals* (Rupert Hart-Davis, 1956)

Lawrence Durrell: to Curtis Brown Ltd on behalf of the Estate of Lawrence Durrell for 'Case History' from *Esprit de Corps: Sketches from Diplomatic Life* (Faber & Faber, 1957), copyright © Lawrence Durrell, 1957

Alice Thomas Ellis: to Gerald Duckworth & Co., Ltd for 'Lost Cause' from *Home Life Three* (Duckworth, 1988)

Peter Fleming: to Kate Grimond for 'Death and Mrs Dale' from *My Aunt's Rhinoceros* (Rupert Hart-Davis, 1956)

E. M. Forster: to Hodder & Stoughton Ltd for 'Mrs Grundy at the Parkers'' from *Abinger Harvest* (Edward Arnold Publishers, 1936)

Michael Frayn: to Elaine Greene Ltd for 'A Farewell to Arms' and 'My Life and Loves' from *At Bay in Gear Street* (Fontana, 1967)

Penelope Gilliatt: to the author for 'Miz Peggy' from the *London Review of Books* (15 September – 5 October 1983)

Graham Greene: to David Higham Associates Ltd for 'A Hoax on Mr Hulton' from *Collected Essays* (The Bodley Head, 1969), copyright © 1939, 1966, 1969, Verdant SA

Germaine Greer: to Aitken & Stone Ltd for 'Romance' from *The Female Eunuch* (MacGibbon & Kee, 1970)

A. P. Herbert: to A. P. Watt Ltd for 'Topsy and the Fresh Mind' from *Look Back and Laugh* (Methuen, 1960)

Philip Howard: to Sinclair-Stevenson Ltd for 'Time Warps' from *A lord in Time* (Sinclair-Stevenson, 1990)

Acknowledgements

Clive James: to Peters Fraser & Dunlop Ltd for 'A Blizzard of Tiny Kisses' from the *London Review of Books* (5 June – 18 June 1980)

Hugh Kingsmill: to Richard Scott Simon Ltd for 'High Life in Victorian Fiction' from *The Progress of a Biographer* (Methuen, 1949)

Miles Kington: to Rogers, Coleridge & White Ltd for 'A High-class Tipple, Make No Mistake' and 'The Life and Times of the Famous One' (first published in the *Independent*, 1991), copyright © Miles Kington

Lord Kinross: to Peters Fraser & Dunlop Ltd for 'Laughter in the Kitchen' (first published in *Punch*)

Marghanita Laski: to the *Observer* on behalf of *New Statesman & Society* for 'Cheap Clothes for Fat Old Women' from the *New Statesman & Nation* (13 November 1948)

C. A. Lejeune: to Carcanet Press Ltd for 'Toujours Lamour' from *Film Reader* edited by Anthony Lejeune (Carcauet Press Ltd, 1991)

D. B. Wyndham Lewis: to Peters Fraser & Dunlop Ltd for 'Meet Irene' from the *Daily Mail* (17 November 1926)

Robert Lynd: to J. M. Dent & Sons Ltd, Publishers, for 'Noblesse Oblige' from *I Tremble to Think* (Dent, 1936)

Julian Maclaren-Ross: to Alex Maclaren-Ross for 'Good Lord, Jeeves' from *Punch* (20 May 1953), copyright © Alex Maclaren-Ross

Louis MacNeice: to David Higham Associates Ltd for 'Under the Sugar Loaf' from *Selected Prose of Louis MacNeice*, ed. Alan Heuser (Oxford University Press, 1990)

Arthur Marshall: to Sinclair-Stevenson Ltd for 'Christmas Reviews of Books for Girls' from *Girls will be Girls* (Hamish Hamilton Ltd, 1974)

John Mortimer: to Peters Fraser & Dunlop Ltd for extracts from *Clinging to the Wreckage* (Weidenfeld & Nicolson Ltd, 1982)

J. B. Morton: to Peters Fraser & Dunlop Ltd for 'Trousers Over Africa' from *Best of Beachcomber*, ed. Michael Frayn (Heinemann Ltd, 1963)

Malcolm Muggeridge: to David Higham Associates Ltd for extracts from *The Thirties* (Hamish Hamilton, 1940)

Harold Nicolson: to Nigel Nicolson for 'Men's Clothes' from *Small Talk* (Constable & Co., Ltd)

Flann O'Brien: to A. M. Heath & Co., Ltd on behalf of the Estate of the late Flann O'Brien for 'The Trade in Dublin' from the *Bell* (Vol. 1, No. 2, November 1940)

George Orwell: to A. M. Heath & Co., Ltd on behalf of the Estate of the late George Orwell for 'Boys' Weeklies' from *The Collected Essays* (Martin Secker & Warburg Ltd)

Fiona Pitt-Kethley: to Random Century Group for 'Dove Vai?' from *Journeys to the Underworld* (Chatto & Windus, 1988)

V. S. Pritchett: to Peters Fraser & Dunlop Ltd for 'Faits Divers' from *In My Good Books* (Chatto & Windus, 1942)

Robert Robinson: to A. P. Watt Ltd for 'Our Betters' and 'Oh Moses, Moses, You Stubborn, Splendid, Adorable Fool' from *Prescriptions of a Pox Doctor's Clerk* (Weidenfeld & Nicolson, 1990)

Alan Ross: to the author for an extract from *Coastal Lights* (Collins Harvill, 1988)

James Stephens: to The Society of Authors on behalf of the copyright owner, Mrs Iris Wise, for 'Trying to Find the Strand' from *Prose Writings: 1926–37*, ed. Patricia McFate (Gill & Macmillan, 1983; first published in the *London Evening News*, 23 December 1927)

A. J. P. Taylor: to David Higham Associates Ltd for a selection of diaries from the *London Review of Books 1982–1986*

Dylan Thomas: to David Higham Associates Ltd for 'How to Begin a Story' from *Quite Early One Morning* (Dent, 1954)

Auberon Waugh: to Peters Fraser & Dunlop Ltd for 'Mothers and Daughters' from *Another Voice* (Five Thorn Press, 1986)

Evelyn Waugh: to Peters Fraser & Dunlop Ltd for 'Awake My Soul! It is a Lord' and 'The Gentle Art of Being Interviewed' from *Essays, Articles, Reviews of Evelyn Waugh*, ed. Donald Gallagher (Methuen, 1983)

Denton Welch: to David Higham Associates Ltd for 'Sickert at St Peter's' from *A Last Sheaf* (John Lehmann, 1951)

Rebecca West: to Peters Fraser & Dunlop Ltd for 'Spinsters and Art' and 'The Fool and the Wise Man' from *The Young Rebecca: Writings of Rebecca West, 1911–17*, ed. Jane Marcus (Macmillan, 1982)

Acknowledgements

P. G. Wodehouse: to Random Century Group on behalf of the Estate of P. G. Wodehouse for 'Literature and the Arts. 3. Thrillers' from *Louder and Funnier* (Faber & Faber, 1932)

While every effort has been made to find the copyright holders, this has not always been possible, and the publishers will be glad to make good any omissions in future editions.